Yvonne Völkl, Julia Obermayr, Elisabeth Hobisch (eds.)
Pandemic Protagonists

Culture & Theory | Volume 284

Yvonne Völkl is a literary and cultural studies scholar in the field of Romance studies. Her research focuses on 18th-century literature and press, French-Canadian migrant literature and contemporary Corona Fictions.

Julia Obermayr is a cultural studies and media scholar. In 2019 she received the 14th Scientific Award of the Austrian-Canadian Society for her research on female identities in Lesbian Web Series. She specializes in cultural studies, social change, lesbian/LGBT+ studies and diversity, minority identities, and female representations in audiovisual media – currently in Corona Fictions – mainly in Romance speaking Europe and the Americas.

Elisabeth Hobisch is a literary and cultural studies scholar in the field of Romance studies. For her PhD thesis on the epistolary form in the Spanish Spectators, she received the *Award of Excellence 2016* of the Austrian Minister of Science, Investigation and Economy. Her main research interests concern 18th-century moral press in France and Spain, the digital humanities and Corona Fictions.

Yvonne Völkl, Julia Obermayr, Elisabeth Hobisch (eds.)

Pandemic Protagonists

Viral (Re)Actions in Pandemic and Corona Fictions

[transcript]

This volume was peer reviewed and funded by the Austrian Science Fund (FWF): P 34571-G.

Bibliographic information published by the Deutsche Nationalbibliothek
The Deutsche Nationalbibliothek lists this publication in the Deutsche Nationalbibliografie; detailed bibliographic data are available in the Internet at http://dnb.d-nb.de

First published in 2023 by transcript Verlag, Bielefeld
© Yvonne Völkl, Julia Obermayr, Elisabeth Hobisch (eds.)

Cover layout & illustration: Johanna Leitner

https://doi.org/10.14361/9783839466162
Print-ISBN 978-3-8376-6616-8
PDF-ISBN 978-3-8394-6616-2
ISSN of series: 2702-8968
eISSN of series: 2702-8976

Table of Contents

Acknowledgements

We are so very appreciative of this diverse and stimulating collaboration that is now finally coming to fruition – despite all the odds arising from the pandemic challenges of the past few years. Our gratitude goes out to all our contributors' time and effort. Thank you for tackling the complex matter of pandemic protagonists across time, space and media with us!

We especially thank all the authors for their thought-provoking articles as well as the peer reviewers for their precious time and valuable feedback. A special thanks also goes to Albert Göschl, Tommaso Meozzi and Daniel Milkovits for their contribution, time and effort to this volume 'behind the scenes'.

We would also like to thank the Institute of Interactive Systems and Data Science (ISDS) at Graz University of Technology for hosting our interdisciplinary project as well as the Austrian Science Fund (FWF) for the funding of the project *Corona Fictions. On Viral Narratives in Times of Pandemics* (P 34571-G) out of which this volume on *Pandemic Protagonists* results.

Graz, February 2023   Yvonne Völkl, Julia Obermayr, Elisabeth Hobisch

Pandemic Protagonists (Re)Claiming Agency: An Introduction

Yvonne Völkl, Julia Obermayr, Elisabeth Hobisch
(Graz University of Technology)

At the outset of the lockdown measures implemented to various degrees as of March 2020 in many Western countries, the reception and consumption of 'pandemic fictions' such as Albert Camus's *La Peste* (1947) or Wolfgang Peterson's disaster movie *Outbreak* (1995) rose drastically. The strongly emerging need to make sense of communicable diseases, quickly changing societal norms and governmentally decreed restrictions in everyday situations, stirred people towards fictional creations addressing similar experiences in the past. Simultaneously, on the artistic side, we saw a rapid – if not exponential – increase in literary and audiovisual creations responding to the challenges of the Covid-19 pandemic and resulting in the publication of stories, music videos, diaries, web series, films or novels. This new corpus of fictional productions processing the abrupt and mostly unparalleled pandemic life circumstances can be subsumed under the term 'Corona Fictions'. They "pertain to a more generally assumed genre of pandemic narratives and further form part of a global crisis discourse" (Research Group *Pandemic Fictions* 2020, 322). Following the hermeneutic dynamic of a 'pandemic circuit' (fig. 1), these audiovisual and literary cultural productions "not only draw on everyday media and political discourse, but also on previous pandemic fiction, i.e., literary and cultural productions, which rely strongly on the representation and functionalization of pandemics" (ibid., 322f.).

With *Pandemic Protagonists – Viral (Re)Actions in Pandemic and Corona Fictions*, we aim at giving an overview of an array of protagonists from a literary, cultural and media studies perspective. The collection of articles unites analyses from a wide range of audiovisual and literary genres, from (web) series, film and drama to poetry, short fiction and novels. Thereby, the volume puts an emphasis on the rich and varied cultural responses to epidemics and pandemics that span across media, time and space, filtered through diverse cultural perspectives. It offers an interdisciplinary insight into the representation of different types of protagonists acting in or reacting to an epidemic or pandemic outbreak in a fictional world. Simultaneously, on a meta-level, Corona Fictions represent viral reactions by individual producers and producer collectives to the Covid-19 pandemic and its sudden and unprecedented mitigation and containment measures. By reactivating characteristic meta-narratives – e.g., social isolation or anxiety – of pandemic fictions and their characters (cf. Hobisch et al. 2022, 198-204), the producers also function as creators of the new Corona Fictions cultural phenomenon.

In full awareness that the term 'protagonist' can be traced back to antique drama and designates a main character, but is more commonly used in media than in literary studies (cf. Eder et al. 2016, 20ff.),[1] we choose this term to foreground the aspect of agency inherent in its etymological root. The term 'protagonist' – similarly to '(re)act' – has its origin in the proto-Indo-European root 'ag-' meaning "to drive, draw out or forth, move" (Harper 2021), which persisted, e.g., in Greek agon[2] or Latin agere as well as actus[3] and later developed into what we now know as agency. The Greek term protos indicates that a protagonist is the "leading character" (OED 2022) in Greek drama as distinguished from the second (deuteragonist) or third character (tritagonist). The plural use of the term protagonist, however, is very common today (cf. ibid.). Hence, 'pandemic protagonists' are those first or main characters, human or non-human, concrete or abstract that hold the agency to drive forward the main storyline in pandemic and/or Corona

---

1   The term 'character' is more widespread today because "[i]n modern literary theory, the approach that reduced characters to mere functions in the action was put on a new foundation, especially in the plot theories of structuralism and in actant models" (Eder et al. 2016, 20f.). A comprehensive overview of the discussion on characters in fictional worlds across media is provided by Jens Eder, Fotis Jannidis and Ralf Schneider (2016, 3-64) in their eponymous volume or Henriette Heidbrink's article (2016, 67-110) on fictional characters in literary and media studies in the same volume.

2   Agon described "a struggle or debate" in the Greek theatre. "The agon of a Greek comedy was the intense exchange of views between two choruses or characters. Such a debate would sympathize with the 'pro' side, making this sympathetic character the pro-agon-ist, or protagonist. The less sympathetic side, those who obstructed the understandable goals of the protagonist, were 'anti-agon-ists,' or antagonists [italics in orig.]" (Paterson 2011, 10).

3   The Latin verb agere and noun actus refer to the activity and the result of doing something. Latin agere "to set in motion, drive, drive forward," hence "to do, perform"; actus "a doing; a driving, impulse, a setting in motion; a part in a play" (Harper 2021).

Fictions.[4] This aspect of agency – or the lack thereof – is even more important in light of the development of the Covid-19 pandemic, during which many people felt deprived of their ability to act. As we have seen at the beginning of the first lockdowns, which were installed almost simultaneously by national governments worldwide at the beginning of 2020,[5] billions of people – particularly in the Western world – turned to fictional narratives to receive guidance, find meaning in the pandemic crisis and lastly regain their agency.

The contributions to this volume study a large variety of pandemic and Corona Fictions from diverse cultural and linguistic backgrounds, since the Covid-19 pandemic inspired cultural production worldwide. In its entirety, the volume thus offers a transcultural, transnational and multilingual insight into fictional narratives on epidemics and pandemics in human history. Moreover, the contributions examine pandemic and Corona Fictions created in and disseminated across different media – from textual to audiovisual as well as from analog to digital media.[6] Due to their capacity to convey their "knowledge to [their audiences] as experiential knowledge which can be reconstructed step by step, or even more, can be acquired by reliving it" (Ette 2016, 5), pandemic and Corona Fictions provide the public with a first hand account of (previously) experienced or imagined health crises and numerous possibilities of individual and collective (re)actions, represented by a variety of main characters. Given the diverse media influence humans are exposed to today and the fact that the human brain does not process (audio)visual images and words equally (cf. Branigan 1992), the broad selection of contributions to this volume is essential for our interdisciplinary and transmedia focus in the Corona Fictions project (cf. Völkl 2021-2023) as a whole. We intentionally invited diverse theoretical and methodological approaches as well as media-specific understandings of key concepts such as the protagonist – the common thread of this volume.

---

4   Characters can also "be presented without any action, as is the case in portraits, descriptions or sculptures" (Eder et al. 2016, 23).

5   In about 100 countries around the world, partial and full lockdowns were implemented to contain the spread of the coronavirus (cf. Dunford et al. 2020; Mathieu et al. 2020-). They essentially consisted of requiring a country's so-called 'non-essential' workers to stay at home (e.g. artists, restaurant staff or flight personnel) and 'essential' workers (e.g. employees of supermarkets, healthcare workers or teachers) to continue attending their workplaces or to work from their hastily established and often poorly equipped home offices.

6   To gain an insight into the broad variety of media formats and genres within the Corona Fictions corpus, have a look at the Corona Fictions Database (cf. Hobisch et al. 2021-).

The pandemic protagonists are the focus of this volume as the driving forces for the plot. Taken into consideration collectively, they offer an insight into how communities at large act in and react to epidemics and pandemics. For the public, these cultural representations may facilitate a better understanding of epidemics and pandemics than scientific descriptions of communicable diseases:

> Si nous examinons les compositions littéraires[,] nous observons que souvent leurs recensions d'histoires épidémiques transformées en matériau romanesque sont, par certains côtés, disons au moins le côté du vécu, celui du réalisme de la description, plus authentiques, plus détaillées que les textes d'historiens avérés. Cela peut s'expliquer par le fait que le langage scientifique possède des limites, des bornes posées par les préconçus des auteurs.[7] (Gualde 2016, 9)

Pandemic and Corona Fictions are thus narratively creating epidemic or pandemic fictional worlds, which these audiences can experience in the context of their own pandemic experiences, broadening their perspectives and enriching their previous epidemic or pandemic knowledge. Precisely as depicted in the figure of the 'pandemic circuit' (fig. 1), this prior knowledge considerably influences the audiences' perception of the Covid-19 pandemic itself as well as their (re)reception and consumption of pandemic protagonists in pandemic and Corona Fictions.

The arrangement of the articles leads from the representation of individual types of human protagonists, to the representation of protagonists as a collective. The examples examined range from scientists, readers, hysterical men and single mothers to Dallowesque, senior and immune protagonists; and then extend to the depiction of crowds and animals as protagonists. Furthermore, some address more abstract forms of protagonists, such as germs/viruses invisible to the human eye, or explore agency (in combination with narrative identity) and hope (embracing agency as a goal-oriented driving force).

As both, pandemic and Corona Fictions, form part of the general genre of pandemic narratives, the arrangement of the articles alternates between studies investigating fictional narratives before and after the outbreak of the Covid-19

---

7 "If we examine literary compositions, we observe that often their accounts of epidemic stories transformed into novelistic material are, in some ways, let's say at least in the aspect of experience, that of the realism of the description, more authentic, more detailed than the texts of established historians. This can be explained by the fact that scientific language has limitations, bounds set by the authors' preconceptions" (authors' translation).

pandemic, foregrounding the fact that epidemic outbreaks have always existed throughout human history and inspired human imagination. This fact also comes to the fore in the articles studying Corona Fictions published during but imagined (long) before the Covid-19 pandemic, as in the case of the dystopian streaming series *La Valla* and *La Révolution*, Pablo García Casado's novel *La madre del futbolista* or Camille Brunel's novel *Les Métamorphoses*. Studies on cultural productions from the English and Romance-speaking world alternate, thereby underlining the fact that viruses do not respect borders and affect humans and non-humans everywhere.

The *Pandemic Protagonists* volume caters to scholars, students and anyone interested in understanding how fictional epidemic and pandemic oeuvres narrate their worlds and their agents in textual and audiovisual cultural productions. Predominantly written in English, the articles of this volume offer especially non-English storyworlds to an English-speaking academic and non-academic readership.[8]

The volume opens with **Anna Isabell Wörsdörfer**'s "Bloody Investigations. Scientists as Ambiguous Pandemic Protagonists in the Dystopian Streaming Series *La Valla* and *La Révolution*", in which she introduces the virus experts Alma López-Durán and Joseph Guillotin as pandemic protagonists testing and even crossing ethical boundaries in their search for a vaccine against viral contagion and disease. In both dystopian series, blood plays an essential and twofold role: as a source of infection and as an agent for a possible cure. Wörsdörfer conducts her comparative analysis in three steps: a) examining the overarching narratives and motivic analogies of the series' plot structures; b) discussing the culturally influenced semantics of blood, as well as, investigating the blood *leitmotif*'s significance for the serial-narrative discourse structure; and c) concluding by a structuralist-semiotically oriented interpretation (along the definition of heroes according to Hans Wulff) of the two before-mentioned main pandemic protagonists. At the same time, she considers Jurij Lotman's spatial semiotics while also focussing on the virus expert's interaction with zombie-like 'blue blood' beings in *La Révolution* and immune children used as guinea pigs in *La Valla*.

---

8 All articles regardless of their original body text (English, French, Spanish or Italian) feature an abstract in English. Furthermore, to ensure the readability of each article while simultaneously acknowledging the diverse academic and cultural backgrounds of our contributors, all foreign-language quotes were translated into the main language of each individual article and inserted either directly into the body text or provided as a footnote.

Subsequent to this **Martina Stemberger** scrutinizes different reader types in "Corona Palimpsests: Pandemic Protagonists as Readers". In her comparative study, she looks at the occurrence of readers in pandemic and Corona Fictions and on the basis of an extensive multilingual corpus shows that since antiquity palimpsestuality, but also the ability of literature to serve at the same time as a coping or evasion strategy, are main features of epidemic and pandemic writing. Looking at a great variety of reader types appearing in this corpus – from diary writers or professional readers, to naive ones, from hallucinating protagonists to doctors or children as readers –, she demonstrates how many pre-pandemic aesthetic patterns, such as metaleptic and eclectic writings or inter- and metatextuality, have been adapted in recent Corona Fictions and superimpose each other in the manner of a palimpsest in different genres and media. Moreover, she points out that not only the omnipresent readers and readings inside the texts, but also the readers outside the text, play their part in this creatively challenging 'corona literature'. Although she refrains from prematurely drawing definite conclusions about this genre, Stemberger steers our attention towards the innovative potential of the numerous playful, traditional or subversive readings of boundaries concerning genre, media and fiction.

Elisabeth Hobisch dedicates her article "Hysterical Men and Reasoning Women? On Gender Roles and Agency in Corona Fictions" to astereotypical gender representations in Corona Fictions through the lens of hysteria, considered a 'female disease' throughout centuries. She demonstrates how – in Corona Fictions – hysteria often becomes an attribute of male protagonists when dealing with their anxiety in the context of the Covid-19 pandemic, while female protagonists take on a more reasonable attitude towards the spread of the coronavirus and the implemented mitigation and containment measures at the beginning of the outbreak. By presenting three examples of hysterical men from a French feature film, a Spanish mystery novel and a Spanish short narrative, Hobisch examines how these anxious male protagonists regain their agency in an unprecedented and frightening first lockdown. She also offers answers to the question on how these cultural representations of hysterical men reactivate and/or challenge contemporary social norms of masculinity.

In her article "La novela de la pandemia como una modalidad de la novela de la crisis. El caso de *La madre del futbolista* de Pablo García Casado" **Justyna Ziarkowska** relates García Casado's first novel, which was written during the first lockdown, on the one hand, with the dominant topics in the author's former poetic oeuvre (i.e. the social phenomenon of pornography and the power of money) and, on the other hand, with the crisis novel, as described by Jochen Mecke and David Becerra Mayor. The author reconstructs García Casado's literary strategies and the details he used to contextualize his story about the protagonist and single mother Sonia in the contemporary difficulties the Spanish population is facing due to the financial crisis. Ziarkowska then sheds light onto the literary mechanisms used by García Casado to indirectly evoke the additional challenges the Covid-19 pandemic brings about for the protagonist. As a result, the female protagonist serves as a representative of a whole generation of Spaniards for whom, after their optimistic youth in the 1980s, the pandemic and its social and economical consequences are but another crisis on their way into a grim future.

In "Mediated Vulnerabilities: Transforming Virginia Woolf's Characters in Corona Fictions" **Paulina Pająk** explores two Corona Fictions which both point towards Virginia Woolf's works. By transforming their Woolfian protagonists, relocating them in current pandemic times and focusing on their presently relevant vulnerabilities, these transtextual and transmedia protagonists face a different set of challenges. While the 'fictional documentary' *The Waves in Quarantine* (2021) touches upon isolation and gender inequality, the short fiction "Mrs. Dalloway said she would buy the rapid COVID test herself" (2022) ridicules the insufficient containment measures taken by governments and healthcare systems. Despite these differences, however, Pająk concludes that what these Corona Fictions have in common is (re)using/reinventing Woolfian characters in pandemic contexts. By doing so, recent pandemic vulnerabilities cognitively and emotionally become more tangible for diverse audiences due to Woolf's culturally widely known iconic works.

Luana Bermúdez contributes with the article "'¿Te importa?' Entre soledad y olvido: la representación de los ancianos en el teatro español durante la pandemia de COVID-19" to this volume. After a brief overview of the developments in the literary landscape during the first months of the Covid-19 pandemic in Spain, she specifies the difficulties theatre productions had to face due to the social and physical distancing measures. She then selects three Corona Fictions plays by Sebastián Moreno, Jerónimo López Mozo and Raúl Hernández Garrido featuring older adults as protagonists and analyzes the different claustrophobic spaces these stories are set in, as well as, the representation of the characters' interaction or lack of communication in the plays. Moreover, she draws the attention to the authors' strategies for implicitly criticizing the treatment of seniors by the majority discourse during this pandemic.

Another protagonist type comes under scrutiny in **Louis Mühlethaler**'s "Immunity and Community: The Role of Immune Protagonists in Saramago's *Ensaio sobre a Cegueira* (1995) and Roth's *Nemesis* (2010)", in which he seeks to understand how the two fictional immune protagonists in these novels achieve to maintain social cohesion in times of sudden epidemic outbreaks. On the basis of the

Portuguese and US-American case studies, he therefore investigates the relation between immune protagonists and their community affected respectively by blindness and polio. Mühlethaler argues that both immune protagonists are not merely defined by their natural immunity, but rather by their will to resist and to fight for the community for whose survival they deem responsible. He then discusses four main dilemmas the protagonists face concerning resistance, avoiding violence, the conflict between individual and collective well-being, and guilt. Finally, he resumes that in *Nemesis* the philosophical self-blindness is a reaction to symbolic violence by the immune protagonist, who after all his struggles to protect his community turns out to be a carrier of the disease; whereas the afflicted community in *Ensaio sobre a Cegueira* survives thanks to the effort of the female immune protagonist who guides the group towards self-organization and collective resistance against violence.

In "The Crowd as a Pandemic Character: Determinism, Entertainment and Transgression in Literature" **Aureo Lustosa Guerios** examines the literary representation of crowds in the course of cholera outbreaks. Drawing on Italian, French and German examples of cholera literature from the 19th century, he shows how – despite their collective nature – crowds are generally portrayed as a single entity or even as a protagonist. After a short outline of the reasons for and peculiar characteristics of historical cholera riots, the case studies chosen point towards the fact that in literary pandemic fictions cholera is predominantly portrayed as a 'disease of the social body' – an easily communicable disease within a society affecting the community as a whole – in contrast to tuberculosis or cancer, which are generally considered as 'diseases of the individual'. Guerios stresses how across several decades, languages and literary genres, the crowd appears as a topos embodying the responsibility for or source of the outbreak due to its violent or hedonistic transgressions. As crowds seem inevitably connected to epidemic outbreaks, the crowd functions as a visible representation of (during centuries) invisible diseases and, in the end, of an epidemic itself. The persistence of this topos in fictional and non-fictional texts, despite the medical discourse providing evermore enhanced knowledge about communicable diseases, indicates societal tendencies to long for coherent narratives and, thus, to "interpret diseases within moral, cultural or spiritual frames" (p. 174).

Drawing on the interdisciplinary field of Animal Studies, the subsequent two articles look into the subject of human and non-human animals in pandemic and Corona Fictions. In "'C'était quelqu'un de toute façon': les personnages humains et non humains dans le roman animaliste *Les Métamorphoses* de Camille Brunel" **Fleur Hopkins-Loféron** explores the concept of anti-specialism as developed by French author Camille Brunel in his novel *Les Métamorphoses* (2020) from the perspectives of Animal Studies. Written already in the summer of 2019 and finished during the first pandemic lockdown in 2020, the plot of this novel emanates from a global pandemic which transforms all humans into animals. Hopkins-Loféron contextualizes Brunel's literary work within the current debates on ecological consciousness, the animal condition, animalism and ecofeminism. Relating *Les Métamorphoses* with other novels by Brunel, she illustrates how the novelist develops a new perspective on the cohabitation of human animals with non-human animals on earth, radically questioning human dominance and pointing towards ecosophy as a possible solution.

Ana Carolina Torquato and **Aureo Lustosa Guerios** shed light on the functions of animals as protagonists in pandemic fictions in their comparative study entitled "The Role of Animals in Pandemic Narratives: Forewarning Disaster, Causing Outbreaks, Conferring Immunity". Drawing on a wide range of examples from literature, film and other visual arts from Western cultures, they analyze how animals appear simultaneously with pestilence as harbingers of disaster, outbreak triggers and immunity vectors from antiquity to the 21st century. The authors demonstrate that for most of Western history, non-human animals were perceived as foreshadowing disasters and portrayed as victims and co-sufferers alongside human animals. It was not until scientific discoveries and developments in the second half of the 19th century that this cultural perception of animals changed into an epidemiological threat. Finally, Torquato and Guerios do not fail to point out the occasionally emerging fictional examples that show a positive link between animals and the development of immunity in humans.

While literary descriptions of pathogenic organisms and their representations are very rare in pandemic literature (cf. Gualde 2016, 139), filmic representations of epidemics or pandemics repeatedly focus on microscopic organisms as spreaders of disease (cf. Ostherr 2005). This difference can, on the one hand, be attributed to the fact that the discovery of bacteria as a cause for infectious diseases dates back to the late 19th century – as explained in more detail in Torquato and Guerios' article – and consequently new theories of contagion emerged thereafter (e.g. diseases spread by objects such as books, stamps or telephones). Moreover, "the discovery of healthy human carriers and the epidemics they generated – beginning with Typhoid Mary – made those figures increasingly the focus of the danger" (Wald 2008, 75). As an archetype of the carrier, 'Typhoid Mary' and the 'carrier narrative' are used "from the scientific, sociological, and journalistic literature [...] into the present" (ibid., 79). Her story has also often been combined with the narrative of the fallen woman (cf. ibid., 85-94) or the femme fatale (cf. Bronfen 2020, 60-70), both representing independent women as a health threat to society. On the other hand, the difference of microbes as protagonists in literary and filmic representations can be attributed to the heterogeneity of written and audiovisual media. The newly emerging technical possibilities of early cinema turned to germs and viruses as protagonists transmitting a disease. The possibility of "[...] manipulation of the film's speed (producing fast and slow motion) and [...] of the lens (producing enlargements and reductions of the image)" (Ostherr 2005, 54), enabled filmmakers to 'show' organisms invisible to the naked eye. Moreover, "[t]he ability to produce optical 'tricks' through editing was another widely heralded feature of the new[ly developed] medium, as was stop-motion animation" (ibid.).

Such cinematic strategies of narration to make the invisible visible are at the heart of **Claire Demoulin**'s contribution on "Germs as Social Protagonists: (In)visible Enemies and the Fear of Epidemic Invasion in Classical Hollywood Cinema". As the latter is known for its strict censorship policies designed to ensure the portrayal of a morally 'appropriate' society for their audiences, filmmakers developed certain codes to include their content (deemed as inappropriate) such as venereal disease. While examining the biographical film *Dr. Ehrlich's Magic Bullet* (1940) by William Dieterle, the author identifies two key aspects in portraying a germ invasion in the example of syphilis: silence and invisibility. Both cinematic strategies encode their message for the audience within the supposed void due to the audiences' previous knowledge. The invisible germs turn into a visible protagonist, as Demoulin points out the imagery depicting, e.g., the multiplication of bacteria on-screen. Cinematographic representation hereby offers an essential way to additionally capture and/or demonstrate their movement, transforming them into social agents. Finally, she explores how the use of war metaphors in the common 'battle' against epidemiological enemies, used in science and popular culture as early as the late 19th century, continued to be used in subsequent decades against political and ideological enemies.

In literature, viruses take on the role of protagonists (i.e. gain agency) only when forming a symbiosis with humans, such as the human-viral hybrids in Chuck Hogan's *The Blood Artists* (1998). As explained by Priscilla Wald regarding the hybridization phenomenon in this novel: "a virus has no social instinct, but when combined with a human being, it develops conscious agency and becomes a sociopath [...] and a bioterrorist" (Wald 2008, 258). In other words, the human body functions as a host, thereby personifying the virus. Such a personification is also common in visual representations of viruses in comics, in which they equally receive a physical appearance and/or human attributes.[9]

In "Human-Viral Hybrids as Challenge to the Outbreak Narrative and Neo-Liberal Biopolitics" **Małgorzata Sugiera** explores the appearance of human-viral hybrids as protagonists in pandemic and Corona Fictions. She starts off by demonstrating that Priscilla Wald's classic 'outbreak narrative' functions differently in Corona Fictions, as the latter tend to replace the mostly heroic protagonists of pandemic fictions (i.e. scientists and physicians) by traumatized or overwhelmed, hence, helpless ones. Sugiera then turns to two science-fictional pandemic fictions, originating at the turn of the century, to show that a transformation of the classic outbreak narrative protagonists already began at an earlier stage. On the basis of the US-American novel *The Blood Artists* (1998) by Chuck Hogan, and the Canadian *Rifters* trilogy (1999-2005) by Peter Watts, Sugiera depicts the hybridization of two types of protagonists: the epidemiologist-detective and the Patient Zero, who in these novels both turn into 'human-viral hybrids', therefore challenging/questioning the binarities of normality/pathology and life/nonlife in which biopolitics and the neo-liberal capitalism are based.

The last two contributions in this volume use the concepts of agency and hope to explore literary and filmic Corona Fictions. In "Protagonisti in cerca di una nuova *agency*: la pandemia di Covid-19 nella letteratura italiana" **Tommaso Meozzi** scrutinizes three Italian Lockdown Corona Fictions. For his comparative study of the novel *Come il mare in un bicchiere* (2020) by Chiara Gamberale, the anthology *Andrà tutto bene* (2020) – also used as a popular pandemic-related hashtag on social media at the time – and the lockdown diary *Nel contagio* (2020) by Paolo Giordano, he follows Mustafa Emirbayer and Ann Mische's sociological concept of agency, which foregrounds the importance of narrative identity. Meozzi's main concern is to identify the different strategies of the protagonists in (re)acting to the new experience of confinement. In particular, he is interested in understanding how the main characters maintain a coherent narrative in times of limited self-determination, when a repetitive lockdown routine particularly complicates this endeavour. His study, among others, reveals the common need to create comprehensible temporal structures in terms of content and form, as well as a predilection for the autobiographical genre and references to dystopia in the context of the Lockdown Corona Fictions.

---

9 See, for example, the project 'World of Viruses Covid-19', which aims at creating "engaging, scientifically accurate, and high quality [sic] comic stories" for educational purposes (https://worldofviruses.unl.edu/).

Finally, in "Corona Fictions Agents: Cinematic Representations of Hopeful Pandemic Protagonists in Early Corona Fictions" **Julia Obermayr** examines the concept of hope as a goal-oriented process – following Rick Snyder's 'model of hope' – in the two early audiovisual Corona Fictions comedies from France and Spain *8 Rue de L'Humanité* (2021) and *¡Ni te me acerques!* (2020). In both films regaining agency plays an essential role for the protagonists, as it functions as a driving force for their transformational stories from fear/anxiety to hope, as well as, for the hopeful overall theme cinematically narrated throughout the films investigated. Focusing on the mechanisms of evoking the audiences' emotional engagement with filmic protagonists and the advantages of the comedy genre to uplift the mood in socially challenging times, Obermayr further analyzes the cinematic representations of two exemplary pandemic protagonists on their journey towards hope, and therefore transforming into Corona Fictions agents.

The 14 articles of this book underline the diversity of pandemic protagonists, from 'bloody investigations' to 'hope', not solely due to falling in either the category of pandemic fictions or Corona Fictions but more so due to a diverse range of interdisciplinary theoretical approaches by our contributors and a consciously very multimodal corpus including written, visual, audiovisual and performance fiction. Regardless of national, cultural or linguistic borders – and in this sense mimicking the nature of pandemics – pandemic protagonists range from representations as humans, animals, depictions of disease to more philosophical concepts needed in times of crises. What they all have in common, however, is their unwavering representation of the Other inspired by unfamiliar social conditions in a (story)world constantly (re)creating itself. The pandemic protagonists' power lies in reclaiming and consequently regaining their agency, in shifting from viral reactions towards viral actions. Pandemic and Corona Fictions both demonstrate how narratives shape our perception of the world and, thus, may provoke a figurative kind of contagion by spreading ideas such as hope to take on the challenges of epidemics and pandemics in the future.

BIBLIOGRAPHY

Branigan, Edward (1992) *Narrative and Comprehension of Film*, London/New York, Routledge.

Bronfen, Elisabeth (2020) *Angesteckt. Zeitgemässes über Pandemie und Kultur*, Basel, Echtzeit Verlag.

Dunford, Daniel et al. (2020) "Coronavirus: The World in Lockdown in Maps and Charts", *BBC News*, 2020-04-07, https://www.bbc.com/news/world-52103747, 2023-01-11.

Eder, Jens/Jannidis, Fotis/Schneider, Ralf (2016) "Characters in Fictional Worlds. An Introduction", Jens Eder/Fotis Jannidis/Ralf Schneider (eds.) *Characters in Fictional Worlds: Understanding Imaginary Beings in Literature, Film, and Other Media*, Berlin, De Gruyter, 3-64.

Ette, Ottmar (2016) *TransArea: A Literary History of Globalization*, Berlin, De Gruyter.

Gualde, Norbert (2016) *Les épidémies racontées par la littérature*, Paris, L'Harmattan.

Harper, Douglas (2021) "Etymology of *ag-", *Online Etymology Dictionary*, 2021-03-19, https://www.etymonline.com/word/*ag-, 2022-12-13.

Heidbrink, Henriette (2016) "Fictional Characters in Literary and Media Studies. A Survey of the Research", Jens Eder/Fotis Jannidis/Ralf Schneider (eds.) *Characters in Fictional Worlds. Understanding Imaginary Beings in Literature, Film, and Other Media*, Berlin, De Gruyter, 67-110.

Hobisch, Elisabeth/Völkl, Yvonne/Obermayr, Julia (2021-) "Corona Fictions Database", *Zotero Group Library*, https://www.zotero.org/groups/4814225/corona_fictions_database/library, 2023-01-23.

Hobisch, Elisabeth/Völkl, Yvonne/Obermayr, Julia (2022) "Narrar la pandemia. Una introducción a formas, temas y metanarrativas de las Corona Fictions", Ana Gallego Cuiñas/José Antonio Pérez Tapias (eds.) *Pensamiento, Pandemia y Big Data. El impacto sociocultural del coronavirus en el espacio iberoamericano*, Berlin, De Gruyter, 191-211. DOI: 10.1515/9783110693928-013.

Mathieu, Edouard/Ritchie, Hannah/Rodés-Guirao, Lucas/Appel, Cameron/Giattino, Charlie/Hasell, Joe/Macdonald, Bobbie/Dattani, Saloni/Beltekian, Diana/Ortiz-Ospina, Esteban/Roser, Max (2020-) "Policy Responses to the Coronavirus Pandemic", https://ourworldindata.org/policy-responses-covid, 2023-01-27.

OED (2022) "protagonist, n.", *Oxford English Dictionary Online*, Oxford University Press, 2022-09, www.oed.com/view/Entry/153105, 2022-12-03.

Ostherr, Kirsten (2005) *Cinematic Prophylaxis. Globalization and Contagion in the Discourse of World Health*, Durham, Duke University Press.

Paterson, Doug (2011) "Putting the 'Pro' in Protagonist: Paulo Freire's Contribution to Our Understanding of Forum Theatre", *Counterpoints* 416, 9-20.

Research Group *Pandemic Fictions* (2020)* "From Pandemic to Corona Fictions: Narratives in Times of Crises", *PhiN-Beiheft* 24, 321-344, http://web.fu-ber

lin.de/phin/beiheft24/b24t21.pdf, 2023-01-11. [*Yvonne Völkl/Albert Göschl /Elisabeth Hobisch/Julia Obermayr].

Völkl, Yvonne (2021-2023) *Corona Fictions. On Viral Narratives in Times of Pandemics*, FWF-Project [P 34571-G], https://www.tugraz.at/projekte/cofi/ home, 2022-11-29.

Wald, Priscilla (2008) *Contagious: Cultures, Carriers, and the Outbreak Narrative*, Durham, NC, Duke University Press.

FIGURES

Figure 1: 'Pandemic Circuit'

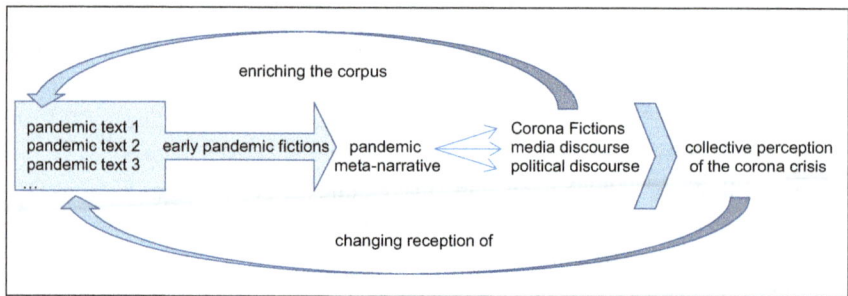

Source: Research Group *Pandemic Fictions* 2020, 324.

Bloody Investigations.
Scientists as Ambiguous Pandemic
Protagonists in the Dystopian Streaming
Series *La Valla* and *La Révolution*

Anna Isabell Wörsdörfer (University of Münster)

In loving memory of M.W.

Abstract
By focusing on the French alternate history drama *La Révolution* and the Spanish futuristic dystopia *La Valla* (both 2020), this article confronts two divergent representations of the virus expert as pandemic protagonist: the virtuously acting practical physician (Joseph Guillotin) and the epidemiological researcher crossing ethical boundaries (Alma López-Durán). It is important to consider the specialist's object of investigation, i.e., blood, as a fundamental element: as a source of infection as well as a potential agent for a cure during the outbreak, blood represents a serial key element and a narrative *leitmotif* in both pandemic fictions. Among the three analytical aspects of striking heroic or nuanced unscrupulous character description, the protagonist's spatial-semantic localization and interaction with groups of further epidemic agents – infected aristocrats in the French series, immune children in the Spanish series –, this study systematically and contrastively examines the positioning of the respective medical main character within the series' specific value system (also taking into account the different aesthetics representing the viral thread). On the basis of this narratological inventory, it can moreover be demonstrated that these dystopian fictions, despite their amimetic nature, negotiate critical issues of the current pandemic.

PANDEMIC PROTAGONISTS GOING VIRAL
ON NETFLIX – AN INTRODUCTION

Scientists, especially virologists, infectious immunologists, human physicians, and microbiologists, are not only in demand in our new Covid-19 reality when it comes to communication about the virus – its structure, transmissibility and containment – but they also play a leading role in pandemic and Corona Fictions films and series as actively involved key characters in effectively combating the viral threat. Indeed, in addition to literary outbreak fictions, audiovisual outbreak fictions in particular are experiencing an extraordinary boom during the Covid-19 pandemic as artistic-cathartic forms of coping (cf. Bronfen 2020, 14 and 134). This can be seen both in the increased demand[1] for older and more recent pandemic fictions 'classics' of the last decades – for example, Wolfgang Petersen's *Outbreak* (1995) and Steven Soderbergh's *Contagion* (2011) – as well as in the multitude of new pandemic and Corona Fictions' creations since 2019/2020. In particular, streaming platforms such as Netflix and Amazon Prime which are profiting from the pandemic and physical distancing, are targeting epidemic or pandemic disaster[2] series and films, such as *The Rain* (2018-2020) and *Songbird* (2020). This tendency includes the two drama series focused in this study, *La Révolution* (France 2020) and *La Valla* (Spain 2020). Production of these series started before the pandemic: filming for *La Valla* took place from February 2019, and for *La Révolution* from July 2019. This circumstance shows that the demand for epidemic productions existed even before the Covid-19 pandemic. However, the topicality of the subject has probably intensified interest in them.[3]

---

1   A series of statistics on the impact of the Covid-19 pandemic on streaming behaviour in Germany and worldwide is provided by the website *Statista.com* (cf. Rabe 2022a). One statistic there shows that Netflix subscriber numbers reached their highest level ever in the fourth quarter of 2021 with 221 840 000 international payers; in the meantime, the numbers are declining slightly again (after lockdowns and physical distancing restrictions were lifted) (ibid. 2022b).

2   As fictions that stage profound impacts of disasters on the affected societies (national health emergency, environmental degradation, collapse of the political system, etc.), the aforementioned series fit the concept of disaster genre. Nevertheless, a precise distinction between emergency, disaster and catastrophe (cf. Montano 2020) should be made when categorizing these fictions.

3   Netflix keeps viewership figures a closely guarded secret. But the fact that in the case of *La Valla*, Netflix becomes the third diffusion medium after the Spanish streaming provider Atresplayer Premium and the public broadcaster Antena 3, suggests Netflix's

Both series implement the formulaic plot and stereotypical tropes of the outbreak narrative (cf. Wald 2008, 2; Schweitzer 2018, 40) into a dystopian setting. In the French format an alternate history stages the events in the historical past of 1787, whereas the Spanish production represents a near future dystopia of the post-apocalyptic year 2045. In these European series, the virus expert – more precisely: the general practitioner Joseph Guillotin (Amir El Kacem) in *La Révolution* and the epidemiologist Alma López-Durán (Eleonora Wexler) in *La Valla* – represents a central character. Even if both roles (of the opposite sex) are diametrically opposed from a moral point of view, they reflect the broad typology of the scientist as a pandemic protagonist in fictional outbreak stories. Fundamental to the characterization of the medical main characters is their respective relation to blood, the serial fulcrum of the viral narrative of both streaming productions, which, in its ambivalence as infectious carrier substance and basis of a possible vaccine, according to the guiding thesis of this paper, decisively shapes the panoramic ambiguity of the researcher in these two epidemic fictions. In other words, with regard to the narrative construction of characters, it depends on whether the vital fluid, the specialist's object of investigation, is conceived in the series as 'good blood' or 'bad blood' (Knust/Groß 2010, 7) and in what way the virus expert relates to it.

The following comparative analysis of *La Révolution* and *La Valla* is divided into three parts: First, both outbreak series are examined for overarching narrative and motivic analogies of their plot structures with regard to their divergent dystopian subgenres. This will be followed by a discussion of the always culturally shaped, ambivalent semantics of blood, illustrated by examples from the two series. The seriality of this *leitmotif* is also examined in its significance for the serial-narrative discourse structure. Finally, a detailed structuralist-semiotically oriented interpretation of the two fictional medical specialists Joseph Guillotin and Alma López-Durán will follow in three steps. In a first step, the two pandemic protagonists will be analyzed according to Hans Wulff's definition of heroes and with regard to the respective value system of the series universe. Secondly, this classification will be deepened by a consideration of the spatial-semantic location of both protagonists, taking into account Jurij Lotman's spatial semiotics. Thirdly, a close look at the interaction structures between the researching main characters and further central groups of people in the epidemic, namely the infected literal

---

expectation of high demand during the lockdown. However, for the broadcast on Antena 3 from September to December 2020, Gregory (2021, 166) testifies to a mediocre audience rating.

'blue bloods', i.e., the aristocrats mutated into zombie-like beings in Joseph's case, and the immune children, Alma's experimental subjects, ends the examination.

DYSTOPIAN SERIES GENRES AND VIRAL AESTHETICS

In both the francophone and hispanophone worlds, the Covid-19 pandemic has spawned several thematic series productions (with regional peculiarities of content and form), of which *Épidémie* (TVA, Canada 2020) and *En Thérapie* (Arte, France 2021-2022), *Diarios de la cuarentena* (RTVE, Spain 2020), and *Raúl con Soledad* (Movistar Plus+, Peru since 2020) are just a few of the numerous titles. The major difference between these and the two series examined here is that *La Révolution* and *La Valla* are dystopian fictions (classified under the overarching science fiction genre) in which an amimetic serial world forms the spatiotemporal background.[4] As a transmedia genre producing literary, cinematic/televisual, and hybrid works (cf. Jenkins 2003) and despite some isolated precursors, dystopia builds on the horror scenarios of the 20th century (fascism, world wars and the Nazi regime) and the turn of the millennium (terrorism, scarcity of resources, overpopulation, climate change) by representing these scenarios and their consequences in fictions of a post-apocalyptic and/or posthuman world (cf. Voigts 2015, 2; Stein 2016, 47; cf. particularly Claeys 2017). Regardless of this science-fictional effect of alienation, several references that critically reflect our social reality are clearly discernible – especially with regard to the two series discussed.

The Netflix series *La Révolution*, released on October 16, 2020 with eight episodes, belongs to the subgenre of alternate history, whose basic characteristic is the altered repetition of history, in this case of the conflictual events leading to the French Revolution in the county of Montargis (about 120 km south of Paris).[5] The

---

4   On the tradition of fantastic and science fiction series in French and Spanish TV, see Evrard 2020, Sánchez Trigos et al. 2015, and Cascajosa Virino 2018. Furthermore, it remains to be said that the SF genre is dominated by anglophone productions, see Favard/Machinal 2022.

5   As a literary genre, alternate history is to be distinguished from counterfactual history (Gallagher 2018) as a subject of historical scholarship. The founding text of the otherwise Anglo-American-dominated genre is Louis-Napoléon Geoffroy-Château's *Napoléon et la conquête du monde, 1812 à 1832. Histoire de la monarchie universelle* (1836) – *Napoléon apocryphe* in short – which, like *La Révolution*, also deals with the historical events of 1789 (cf. further Roberts 2019). The genre explanations have already been published in somewhat modified form in Wörsdörfer 2022, 185f.

so-called nexus story, which is based on a genetic model of history, i.e., which places cause and effect at the center, focuses on that moment in the French past from which the fictional events take a different path to the actual historical course of events with which we are familiar (cf. Hellekson 2013, 2 and 5): the game changing appearance of an existence-transforming virus with which King Louis XVI pursues the 'big plan' of a truly blue-blooded, posthuman noble race. If the plot of the French series, due to the revolt of the common people against the aristocrats, can therefore also be assigned to the subcategory of battle story (cf. ibid., 7), it also corresponds to the special form of secret history (cf. Morgan/Palmer-Patel 2019, 20), insofar as it – linking the 'what if'-question to a conspiracy theory,[6] as in Dan Brown's *The Da Vinci Code* (2003) – follows the nexus point event with a supposed cover-up, with the result that it is the goal of the serial narrative to reveal the 'true' story.

The (up to now)[7] 13-episode series *La Valla*, first broadcasted on the VoD provider Atresplayer Premium (weekly from January 19, 2020) and then publicly on Antena 3 (weekly from September 10, 2020) and finally on Netflix (weekly from September 11, 2020), sets its plot in the opposite temporal direction, namely in the future of the year 2045 following the outbreak of World War III and a nuclear catastrophe. Unlike other futuristic series, however, the fictional world is not determined by robotic-machine and biomedical future technologies, such as cloning (cf. Graumann 2013; Tiehen 2016); rather, after the collapse, it has undergone a social regression into a form of state authoritarianism, the concrete manifestations of which are reminiscent of both the Nazi era and the phase of the era of *franquismo* (cf. Gregori 2021, 167 and 175-179; Léger 2022).[8] In this series, too,

---

6   The possibility is real that by using the motif of secret intrigue, *La Révolution* could have promoted conspiracy theories and fake news in the reception context of the Corona pandemic. Here, an explanatory handling of fictionality by the series makers would have been desirable.

7   In contrast to the French series *La Révolution*, which was not continued after one season despite initial plans (and therefore comes to an abrupt, open end), there is the Netflix announcement of a renewal for a second season for *La Valla*.

8   In his address to the nation, the Minister of Health, Luis Covarrubias (Abel Folk), Alma's husband, quotes the national writer Federico García Lorca, who was killed at the beginning of the Spanish Civil War: "Federico García Lorca once wrote: 'There are things hidden in walls that, if they suddenly came out into the street and shouted, would fill the world'" (cf. XII El discurso [37:55-38:11 min.]) ("Federico García Lorca escribió: 'Hay cosas encerradas dentro de los muros que si salieran de pronto a la calle y

a conspiracy at the highest political level plays a role, so that the macrostructural narrative and motivic parallels to *La Révolution* already become quite evident.

As different as the two dystopian series may be in their temporal setting, they possess a fundamental commonality in their either very clear or only implied reference to national crisis-like states of emergency. The fictional *Ancien Régime* on the eve of the French Revolution and the Franco dictatorship following the Spanish Civil War, which in *La Valla* is the model for the new social structure of the series world, are equally characterized by an arbitrary leadership style of the powerful and authoritarian state structures: In *La Révolution*, for example, Donatien (Julien Frison), the new Count of Montargis, after his posthuman transformation spreads fear and terror among the population of the county, and describes its task as follows: "People need to remember what their fate is: to submit, to obey… and to feed us" (VIII. La révolte [08:51-09:21 min.]).[9] Besides, the ruthless captain of the guard, Pérouse (Dimitri Storoge), embodies the police apparatus marked by the use of violence. His counterpart in *La Valla* is the newly appointed *comandante* of state security, Coronel Enrique Jiménez (Manu Fullola), who not only allows but actively supports the most brutal interrogations of prisoners (III. Los niños perdidos [26:02-26:26 min. and 28:19-30:16 min.]). In the Spanish series, moreover, drones, informers (the groundskeeper Begoña), and vast numbers of soldiers for the constant surveillance of the population of New Spain are omnipresent from the beginning.

In terms of the elaboration of the outbreak narrative underlying both epidemic fictions, *La Révolution* and *La Valla* each follow one of the two variants distinguished by Bronfen (2020, 140): while the French series, by presenting the nobles as infected with a mysterious virus that turns the blood blue, equates the epidemic with a political infection, the Spanish series frames the outbreak of the noravirus as a struggle on two fronts: against the deadly spread and against the corrupt structures within the state leadership (most notably the unscrupulous president and parts of the medical department). In dealing with the virus as an overarching motif, a specific design is conspicuous in each case with regard to the series' aesthetics: as in other pandemic productions about the undead (cf. ibid., 78), *La Révolution* gives a concrete face to the threat in the form of the posthuman aristocrats –; these aristocratic monsters visualize the horror, whereas in *La Valla* the virus remains almost invisible as one of several serious problems of its post-apocalyptic society

---

critaran, llenarían el mundo'"). In addition to the historical references, there is an intramedial allusion to the dystopian Hulu's series *The Handmaid's Tale* (since 2017).

9　All translations are the author's and followed by the original in the footnote. "Le peuple doit se rappeler à quoi il est destiné: se soumettre, obéir… et nous nourrir".

in the first half of the series:[10] After individual sufferers appear in secondary strands at the midpoint of the season, for example a dying woman who has recently given birth in episode 5 [13:39-14:46 min.] and an infected person in a queue in episode 7 [6:56-7:04 min.], it is not until episode 10 that a viral chain reaction leads to an ever-widening outbreak in the home of the Minister of Health and his wife Alma. This circumstance visualizes the serial moment of the virus narrative, which in both epidemic streaming series follows less a dramatic structure – inscribed in other pandemic fictions (cf. Research Group *Pandemic Fictions* 2020) – but rather, in keeping with the genre, a serial principle that is closely linked to the motif of blood.

AMBIGUITY AND SERIALITY OF BLOOD

In all civilizations, human blood has a socio-culturally shaped meaning that goes beyond its biological value as a vital substance; the semantics of blood are socio-cultural constructions that may well be contradictory to one another and move between the poles of life preservation and life endangerment, but equally metaphorically, for example, in the realms of personality constitution, (group) solidarity and (moral) contamination (cf. Levina 2015, 8; Knust/Groß 2010, 7f.). In *La Valla*, blood – more precisely, the blood of 'special children' that provides a sufficiently strong immune response to the noravirus for a vaccine – is of central interest. Accordingly, it is regarded as the sole elixir of survival, helping to reassure the continued existence of mankind. However, the fact that the test subjects are defenceless children gives the experiments performed on them without safety precautions (cf. IX. Recuerda quién eres [04:42-05:14 and 45:38-46:18 min.]) a dubious image from an ethical point of view, bringing forth a tension in the viewers' minds between the potential sacrificing of a few to the healing of many. The structure of meaning of blood in *La Révolution* is different: here, blood applies to posthuman aristocrats – in analogy to other monster narratives (cf. Marigny 2003, 190-192 and 196-202) – as a source of nourishment and, within the 'bloodthirsty' series aesthetic, above all to the visual hyperbolization of violence, for example when the bloodied face of Donatien's sister Marie (Philippine Martinot) is seen in long close-up immediately after her transformation and the bite of her first victim

---

10 The viral spread is initially only discussed in the sound channel of the president's televised speech; in the image channel, the threat remains relatively unspecific during the disinfection of the new arrivals and the isolated exposure of a sick person (cf. I. Otro mundo [01:03-03:17 min. and 21:40-22:22 min.]).

(cf. VI. L'alliance [38:04-38:14 min.]). Joseph Guillotin's resistance against the 'bloodsuckers' accordingly proves to be a justified fight against evil in *La Révolution*.

In general, blood is a polysemantic basic motif of the plot in the French series examined. For the class-conscious noble family of Montargis, the continuation of the bloodline is of essential importance. However, the unstable condition of Donatien (cf. II. Le revenant [06:04-06:23 min.]), who suffers from gangrene, which means that he had contaminated blood in his organism before his transformation, is a symbol of the decay of this aristocratic dynasty. Consequently, the degenerated scion Donatien represents the last 'withered branch' of a traditional and prestigious family tree. The succession of blood, in terms of a biological family genealogy, is subsequently substituted by the posthuman Donatien through the monstrous transmission of his now blue blood, with which he creates an entire army of aristocratic zombie creatures. Moreover, the serial transmission of the infected blood on the content level corresponds very clearly with the seriality of the streaming production on the discourse level, which is in line with the genre (cf. Wünsch 2010, 194-200, cf. fundamentally Eco 1990): the narration of the viral infection via the blood follows a serial growth, which is implemented in *La Révolution* by means of the exponentially increasing number of infected: if in the first episode there is only one carrier of the virus in the county with the old count, in episodes 2 to 4 another one is added with Donatien's transformation. In the sixth episode, he transforms four people (in addition to Marie, three close friends) and in the seventh episode, a total of 12 representatives of the provincial nobility into his equals (cf. Wörsdörfer 2022, 188). The task of the scientist, who is now focused, is in a first step to follow these blood traces.

THE SCIENTIST AS PANDEMIC PROTAGONIST

Of Noble Goals and a Black Soul:
(Un-)Heroic Characterisations of the Virus Expert

The ambiguity of the character of the virus expert, which is now to be analyzed by using the two dystopian streaming series as examples, becomes particularly evident by taking Hans Wulff's definition of the hero into account. According to Wulff, the hero is, on the one hand, a value-neutral text-functional figure and, on the other hand, an ideological figure that is subject to the discourse of values as well as characterized, among other things, by actionality, liminality and transgression of boundaries (cf. Wulff 2002). While Joseph from *La Révolution* and Alma from *La Valla* correspond equally to the first determination of the hero, which coincides with the function of the protagonist, these two characters position themselves on different sides of the heroic with regard to the second evaluative determination.

Both characters undoubtedly have an unchallenged pioneering role in the (bio-)medical field: Alma is, according to her own statement, the best virologist in the country, whose ground-breaking research will change the world (cf. XI. La soledad de dos [26:14 min.] and VII. Un asunto de familia [31:11 min.]); Joseph has already distinguished himself by means of self-experimentation through the successful discovery of a smallpox vaccine (cf. I. Les origines [20:25-20:50 min.]).[11] As a professionally rational representative of the Enlightenment[12] and a man of action – central characteristic of the hero – his scientific work is not based on pure book study (e.g. in the seclusion of the abandoned Lazarus Church), but decisively on experimental research on the medical object (cf. Wörsdörfer 2022, 187): he and his assistant Katell (Isabel Aimé González-Sola) make the decisive discovery for the mode of action of the mysterious virus during the dissection of an experimentally infected rat. Medially, the cognitive process is made visible through the close-up shot of a magnified microscope view (cf. II. Le revenant [34:34-34:39 min.]) – a shot that represents one of the outbreak tropes (cf. Schweitzer 2018, 50-54). Joseph reapplies the experimental method within his historical context when he (unsuccessfully) tests the blood of the Brotherhood's members for possible immunity using vials, pipettes and small bowls in a serial

---

11 The smallpox reference is based on the fact that the historical Joseph-Ignace Guillotin, on whom the main character in the series is modelled, was an ardent supporter of smallpox vaccination (cf. Korn 1891, 28f.). Otherwise, we can speak of a highly fictionalized exaggeration of the Guillotin figure in comparison to the historical model, as Korn and others portray it (cf. also Pigaillem 2004). In French history, the guillotine, this apparatus of mass killing used since 1792, is named after Guillotin – a fact from which the historical doctor has suffered much. If *La Révolution* had been extended for a second season, the guillotine might have become an effective killing instrument in the struggle of the revolutionaries headed by Joseph against the aristocratic zombies.

12 Joseph increasingly comes into contact with the 18th century revolutionary narrative: in a confidential conversation with his assistant Katell, she uses arguments for popular resistance to the rulers in free reference to *Qu'est-ce que le Tiers Etat?*, the influential 1789-pamphlet by Emmanuel Joseph Sieyès (cf. II Le revenant [35:52-36:23 min.]). While one group of the insurgents relies on armed force and thus stands for the radical part of the revolutionaries, Joseph, representative of the moderate position, speaks out for non-violence.

experiment (cf. VII. Le dilemme [30:18-31:42 min.]). Similarly, in *La Valla*, as director of the CIM (*Centro de Investigaciones Médicas*), Alma proves herself to be an active agent, responsible for the use of the most modern technology by her research team in the laboratory experiments on the children.

As virus experts, both aim to generate a vaccine against viral contagion and disease, but the approaches they take are of a very different nature: while Alma is willing to use any means to obtain the medical key, Joseph respects the limits of what is ethically acceptable. Here, the gender aspect is also of some interest: As a career-oriented female scientist, Alma is portrayed in a relatively negative light, whereas Joseph is idealized as a man taking matters into his own hands in an analogous fight against a viral threat. Nevertheless, he too commits a (heroic) transgression in his search for the cause of death of the first victim by secretly dissecting a corpse (cf. I. Les origines [32:19-33:23 min.]). Yet, he pleads for a humane-peaceful approach – for example, while rescuing some prisoners – in the process of deciphering the mystery. Whereas Joseph selflessly sacrifices himself for the weakest – his first appearance is in the treatment of children in an orphanage (cf. I. Les origines [17:23-18:42 min.]) –, Alma turns out to be an entirely unheroic, calculating careerist who uses children who have exceptional biological conditions as experimental subjects, thereby overstepping all bounds of ethical and good scientific work. If her research partner has moral doubts about pushing the treatment of the children to the extreme, she coldly replies: "These kids were out on the street, they were miserable, and if they can't take the dose, there's a much better place for them. [...] heaven [...]. They're already in hell" (I. Otro Mundo [57:58-58:18 min.]).[13]

She is also condescending and inhumane in the relations she has with her servants, referring to her importance as a virus expert: "I am valuable. Very valuable. My children as well. You're not. You're worth nothing" (cf. IV. El roce de la piel [24:30-24:40 min.]).[14] Thus, 'Alma' turns out to be a telling name that refers to the dark soul of the unscrupulous scientist who, moreover, is mostly dressed in black in accordance with the series aesthetic.[15] Apart from this and in terms of her

---

13 "Estos niños están en la calle, son desgraciados, y si no aguantan la dosis, hay un sitio mucho mejor para ellos: el cielo, Tomás. Ellos ya están en el infierno".

14 "Yo soy valiosa. Muy valiosa. Mis hijos también. Tú no. No vales nada".

15 Gregori (2021, 179) also draws the historical parallel to Evita, María Eva Duarte de Perón, involving Alma's political ambitions at the end of the season, which is reinforced by casting the Argentine actress Eleonora Wexler in the role. As in many pandemic fictions, evil comes from outside (cf. Schweitzer 2018, 44-47). In *La Révolution*, e.g., the virus also comes from abroad, here from the New World.

overall character, her extramarital affair with *comandante* Jiménez, one of the series' villains, positions her on the amoral side, although her self-sacrificing and determined actions on behalf of her infected son Iván (Nicolás Illoro) appear, at least to some extent, to make her seem more human. In this the more traditional aspects of the female personality – the social care of her family and her maternal protection – cast Alma in a more positive light. This is further evidence of the gender-specific portrayal of the virus expert. Like numerous women in outbreak narratives (cf. Bronfen 2020, 47-71), Alma is an ambivalent figure who literally walks over dead bodies as she pursues her ambitious research objectives, while also promising salvation. Unlike Joseph, the idealized male saviour, in *La Révolution*, she cannot be described as heroic, since she shares far too many characteristics of a villain. Joseph, by contrast, grows more and more into the role of the virtuous hero, even building up his fellow fighters against the epidemic and also the noble monsters in a rousing speech before the big showdown (cf. VII. Le dilemme [35:24-36:30 min.]). In the role of the advancing leader, Joseph's unqualified heroism is revealed.

In Front of and Behind the Border: The Protagonist's Spatial-Semantic Locations

The different positioning of the virus expert in *La Révolution* and *La Valla* can also be confirmed by referring to the spatial semantics of the cultural semiotician Jurij Lotman. According to Lotman, the fictional world is constructed in particular through spatial relations to which semantic fields are assigned, whereby the plot unfolds eventfully whenever a character crosses the boundary between spaces (cf. Lotman 2006). In the Spanish series, the meaningful bifurcation of space is already implied in the title: 'la valla' – the border fence[16] divides the fictional Madrid of the year 2045 into two different sectors: sector 1, the small, ideal enclave where the powerful and rich of the country live in luxury and with an intact nature; and sector 2, which is marked by the apocalyptic events of nuclear war and environmental destruction and the accompanying deprivation and misery.[17] In *La Révolution*, a similar demarcation is not made explicit, but is nevertheless firmly integrated. The juxtaposition of the opulent night-time festivities at the Montargis

---

16 Gregori (2021, 170) interprets this wall as reminiscent of the border fences of Melilla and Ceuta, which separate Spain, a paradise for migrants from the African continent.

17 The division into two sectors is a standard trope of dystopian fiction, as also evidenced by *The Hunger Games* (2012). The existing class issues are spatially emphasized.

chateau and the sheer poverty on the streets and especially in the town's orphanage is particularly contrasting (I. Les origines [05:28-06:13 and 17:20-18:27 min.]).

The exclusive sector 1, where Alma and her family live in a luxurious mansion, is like a gated community (cf. further Tschilschke 2018) due to the border protection system that runs through the middle of Madrid. The rigorous access controls, which include the verification of personal data and obligatory disinfection (I. Otro mundo [47:33-48:40 min.]), are strictly supervised by soldiers. The two worlds of post-apocalyptic Madrid are juxtaposed in terms of colour aesthetics: if the space of the ordinary population presents itself in shades of gray and brown, behind the border a light-flooded nature dominated by green unfolds; above the tree-lined manicured lawns of the villas, birdsong can be heard in the sound channel (cf. Otro mundo [49:00 min.]).[18] As the wife of the Minister of Health and a leading researcher, Alma is on this side of the protective fence; within this little paradise, time seems to stand still: lavish dinner parties are the order of the day here (while everything is lacking in sector 2), where the poor – the majority of the population – are condescendingly discussed (cf. II. Mi hermana Sara [32:26-33:42 min.]). Alma herself behaves disrespectfully toward her servants, e.g., when throwing a cold cup of tea at the feet of the maid Manuela (Yaima Ramos) (cf. III. Los niños perdidos [13:26-13:37 min.]). With her location in the morally negatively semanticized space defined by abuse of power and arrogance, Alma is clearly anchored as a villainous character. She commits a borderline violation in Lotman's sense whenever she abuses the innocent children from sector 2 in her research facility for her experiments.

While Alma is located on the sunny side of the bipartite space, Joseph in *La Révolution* is located in the spatial and semantic field of misery and poverty. By intending to uncover the murder of the young peasant woman – and subsequently the disappearance of numerous others posted on the town missing persons board (cf. II. Le revenant [23:00-23:25 min.]) –, thereby exonerating an innocent prisoner, he moves on the side of moral virtue. Following up with his investigation, he initially enters a phase of liminality in the Lazarus ruins in the forest, from which he returns to the world, equipped with extensive additional knowledge about the origin and effects of the virus, in order to cross the border into the space of the zombie-like aristocrats. The shot of the insurgents' procession toward Versailles, preceded by a sequence illustrating the sumptuous halls in the Palace of

---

18 In addition to the spatial contrast between sectors 1 and 2, *La Valla* also presents a temporal contrast: The dam outside the capital, densely forested 25 years ago, has given way to a wasteland in the fictional present, as a dissolve shows: Water and plants have disappeared (cf. VIII. El hijo de nadie [03:13-03:19 min.]).

Versailles, which represent the spatial background of Donatien's meeting with the monstrous Louis XVI, also opens with a long close-up of Joseph, to whom the camera returns again and again (VIII. La révolte [39:08-39:57 min.]). Joseph and Alma stand on different sides of the semantically charged two-world structure, both crossing borders in the other direction, marking them within the ambiguous spectrum of the virus expert in the value system of the series as either a good (Joseph) or an evil (Alma) pandemic protagonist.

Of Monsters and Angels:
Interactions with the Mighty and the Innocent

The interaction of the scientist characters with other groups of the outbreak narrative shows the diametrically opposed determination of the two experts. In this context, the blood metaphor is again of relevance. Joseph resists in both medical and direct-body combat the blue-blood contaminated nobles who literally bleed the people dry. Within this group of pandemic protagonists, blood takes on the meaning of disease and death: whoever comes into contact with it perishes as a human being. In contrast, Alma interacts with the pandemic group of children who are immune to the noravirus and whose blood, due to its particular composition, promises healing and continuity. In *La Valla*, blood is thus the source of life and – through the development of a vaccine – the basis of solidarity for the cohesion of society.

In *La Révolution*, the constellation of characters between Joseph and his posthuman opponents is determined by the monstrosity of the latter. The aristocrat is not figuratively but literally a blue-blooded bloodsucker who poses a danger to his subordinates (cf. further Wörsdörfer 2022, 181-183). In contrast to literary and media tradition, the aristocrat is not associated with the elitist vampire, but with a zombie horde, whose bloodthirsty actions depict the anarchic conditions at the time of the French Revolution (cf. Hoquet 2014). The shots in the final episode 8, in which the infected nobles crouch over the corpses of the fallen and eat their flesh in the dirty city streets immediately after the barricade fight, can be described as iconic (cf. Wörsdörfer 2022, 190; VIII. La révolte [30:05-30:14 min.]). In contrast to the aristocrats' monstrous-animalistic libidinal behaviour stands Joseph's selfless-humanitarian self-sacrifice in the preceding sequences of the bloody battle fought with extreme brutality: it is the common man Joseph who, as a physician, cares for the wounded in the field at the greatest risk to his own life (VIII. La révolte [26:33-26:58 min.]). Joseph thus assumes the role of the good resistance and monster fighter, as the pandemic protagonist in the series system of drawing rigorously black-and-white characters.

In *La Valla*, Alma confronts the crowd of child probands as a group of pandemic protagonists. After the research breakthrough in CIM – and again and again from then on – she stylizes the 'special children' as her angels (cf. III. Los niños perdidos [37:28 min.]). During a visit to these boys and girls, she ostensibly mimes the familiar guardian, but what begins as a caring fairy tale lesson ends with the children being anesthetized by the yogurt provided and prepared for blood transfusion in the service of experimental purposes (cf. Los niños perdidos [38:04-40:49 min.]). For Alma, their value lies not in their ideal being, but in their material potential. The innocence of the defenseless children contrasts with Alma's calculation and manipulativeness, which she displays, for example, when she impresses upon little Marta (Laura Quirós), before returning to her father, that she is fine and that no one has done any harm to her (cf. V. Los inocentes [04:33-04:38 min.]). By taking the stance in her high-risk research that sacrificing a few for the salvation of many is an acceptable trade-off, Alma reveals herself, in juxtaposition with her 'little angels', to be the diabolical string-puller of an infernal plan. This virus expert, whose interaction partners are the weakest and most vulnerable people in society, is – unlike Joseph, who heroically fights monsters – a conscienceless and unscrupulous pandemic protagonist.

CONCLUSION

This study has analyzed the broad spectrum of the role of the virus expert in audiovisual pandemic fictions: In *La Révolution*, Joseph Guillotin is a heroic investigator of the virus's origins who fights for the cause of the tormented people and stands fearlessly on their side against the monstrous blue bloods. In *La Valla*, Alma López-Durán herself fills the role of the (complexly designed) villain, who spatially stands on the side of the exploitative elite and fights for the noble goal of eliminating the virus by carrying out high-risk experiments on defenseless children, thus transgressing ethical boundaries. While neither of these two streaming series provide a realistic depiction of the world as such, due to their dystopian science-fictional setting, their motivic and narrative constants nevertheless appear also to be valid for our present-day Covid-19 reality and, in the form of indirect serial commentary, sometimes offer orientation in the pandemic crisis period.

Regarding the role of the virus expert in epidemic/pandemic times, a critical questioning of scientific research thus takes place with different approaches for response. *La Valla* clearly problematizes a concept of science without limits, in which incalculable risks are to be feared for the individual. In contrast, *La Révolution* creates a firm belief in the good, selfless, self-sacrificing physician who places his skills at the service of the community. Both series denounce the possible abuse of power by ruling elites, especially in chaotic times, with Joseph and Alma on different sides. In general, both Netflix series – and this should be critically noted in conclusion – fuel conspiracy myths, as they also circulate in our pandemic present, in which the virus expert takes an ambiguous position within the outbreak narrative – a position which, overall, does not inspire confidence.

BIBLIOGRAPHY

Corpus Analyzed

Écija, Daniel (dir.) (2020) *La Valla*, Spain, Artesmedia/Good Mood Productions.
Molas Aurélien (dir.) (2020) *La Révolution*, France, John Doe Production.

Works Cited

Ascenzo, Bruno (dir.) (2020-) *Raúl con Soledad*, Peru, Tondero Films.
Bronfen, Elisabeth (2020) *Angesteckt. Zeitgemäßes über Pandemie und Kultur*, Basel, Echtzeit Verlag.
Brown, Dan (2003) *The Da Vinci Code*, New York, NY, Random House.
Cascajosa Virino, Concepción (2018) "Televisión 2000–2015", Teresa López-Pellisa (ed.) *Historia de la ciencia ficción en la cultura española*, Madrid/Frankfurt am Main, Iberoamericana/Vervuert, 357-379.
Claeys, Gregory (2017) *Dystopia: A Natural History. A Study of Modern Despotism, Its Antecedents, and Its Literary Diffractions*, Oxford, Oxford University Press.
Eco, Umberto (1990) "Serialität im Universum der Kunst und der Massenmedien", Umberto Eco, *Im Labyrinth der Vernunft. Texte über Kunst und Zeichen*, Leipzig, Reclam, 301-324.
Evrard, Audrey (2020) "Topographies fantastiques dans la fiction télévisée francophone: *Les Revenants* (Canal +, 2012; 2015) et *Zone blanche* (France 2, 2017-2019)", *TV Series* 18, s.p.
Favard, Florent/Machinal, Hélène (2022) "Les séries de science-fiction au croisement d'un genre fictionnel et d'une forme narrative audiovisuelle", *ReS Futurae. Revue d'études sur la science-fiction* 19 [en ligne], s.p. DOI: 10.4000/resf.11137.
Fernández Armero, Álvaro/Marqués, David (dirs.) (2020) *Diarios de la cuarentena*, Spain, Morena Films.

Gallagher, Catherine (2018) *Telling It Like It Wasn't. The Counterfactual Imagination in History and Fiction*, Chicago, IL, University of Chicago Press.

Graumann, Sigrid (2013) "Genetische Gerechtigkeit? Zukunftsvisionen und die Beurteilung neuer biomedizinischer Technologien", Viviana Chilese/Heinz-Peter Preusser (eds.) *Technik in Dystopien*, Heidelberg, Winter, 195-208.

Gregori, Alfons (2021) "Posapocalipsis, historia y espacio en la serie *La valla*", David Roas/Flavio García/Marisa Martins Gama-Khalil (eds.) *Ficções pós-apocalípticas nas vertentes do fantástico*, Uberlândia, Editora da Universidade Federal de Uberlândia, 163-183.

Hellekson, Karen (2013) *The Alternate History: Refiguring Historical Time*, Ashland, OR, Kent State University Press.

Hoquet, Thierry (2014) "Cyborg, Mutant, Robot, etc. Essai de typologie des presque-humains", Elaine Després/Hélène Machinal (eds.) *PostHumains*, Rennes, Presses universitaires de Rennes, 99-118.

Jenkins, Henry (2003) "Transmedia Storytelling: Moving Characters from Books to Films to Video Games Can Make Them Stronger and More Compelling", *MIT Technology Review*, 2003-01-15, https://www.technologyreview.com/2003/01/15/234540/transmedia-storytelling/, 2023-01-13.

Kainz, Kenneth/Arthy, Natasha (dirs.) (2018-2020) *The Rain*, Denmark, Miso Film.

Knust, Christina/Groß, Dominik (2010) "Blut. Die Kraft des ganz besonderen Saftes in Medizin, Literatur, Geschichte und Kultur. Eine thematische Einführung", Christina Knust/Dominik Groß (eds.) *Blut. Die Kraft des ganz besonderen Saftes in Medizin, Literatur, Geschichte und Kultur*, Kassel, Kassel University Press, 7-13.

Korn, Georg (1891) *Joseph-Ignace Guillotin (1738-1814). Ein Beitrag zur Geschichte der Medizin und des ärztlichen Standes*, Berlin, Schade.

Lanouette Turgeon, Yan (dir.) (2020) *Épidémie*, Canada, Sphere Media.

Léger, Jérémy (2022) "*La Valla, L'Autre (VF)*", *Cahiers d'histoire. Revue d'histoire critique* [en ligne] 153, 210-214. DOI: 10.4000/chrhc.18979.

Levina, Marina (2015) *Pandemics and the Media*, New York/Frankfurt am Main, Peter Lang.

Lotman, Jurij (2006 [1970]) "Künstlerischer Raum, Sujet und Figur", Jörg Dünne/Stephan Günzel (eds.) *Raumtheorie. Grundlagentexte aus Philosophie und Kulturwissenschaften*. Frankfurt am Main, Suhrkamp, 529-545.

Marigny, Jean (2003) *Le vampire dans la littérature du XXe siècle*, Paris, Honoré Champion Éditeur.

Mason, Adam (dir.) (2020) *Songbird*, USA, Invisible Narratives/Platinum Dunes/Endeavor Content/ICM Partners/Catchlight Studios.

Miller, Bruce (dir.) (2017-) *The Handmaid's Tale*, USA, Daniel Wilson Productions, Inc./Littlefield Company/White Oak Pictures/Toluca Pictures/MGM Television.

Montano, Samantha (2020) "Not All Disasters Are Disasters: Pandemic Categorization and Its Consequences", *items – Insights from the Social Sciences*, Social Science Research Council, 2020-09-10, https://items.ssrc.org/covid-19-and-the-social-sciences/disaster-studies/not-all-disasters-are-disasters-pandemic-categorization-and-its-consequences, 2023-01-13.

Morgan, Glyn/Palmer-Patel, Charul (2019) "Introduction", Glyn Morgan/Palmer-Patel, Charul (eds.) *Sideways in Time. Critical Essays on Alternate History Fiction*, Liverpool, Liverpool University Press, 11-28.

Petersen, Wolfgang (dir.) (1995) *Outbreak*, USA, Punch Productions.

Pigaillem, Henri (2004) *Le docteur Guillotin. Bienfaiteur de l'humanité*, Paris, Pygmalion.

Rabe, L. (2022a) "Wie wirkt sich das Coronavirus auf die Nutzung digitaler Medien aus?", *Statista*, 2022-06-24, https://de.statista.com/themen/6289/auswirkungen-des-coronavirus-covid-19-auf-digitale-medien/#dossierContents__outerWrapper, 2022-08-19.

Rabe, L. (2022b) "Anzahl der zahlenden Streaming-Abonnenten von Netflix weltweit vom 3. Quartal 2011 bis zum 3. Quartal 2022", *Statista*, 2022-10-19, https://de.statista.com/statistik/daten/studie/196642/umfrage/abonnenten-von-netflix-quartalszahlen/, 2022-11-18.

Research Group *Pandemic Fictions* (2020) "From Pandemic to Corona Fictions: Narratives in Times of Crises", *PhiN-Beiheft* 24, 321-344, http://web.fu-berlin.de/phin/beiheft24/b24t21.pdf, 2022-09-18.

Roberts, Adam (2019) "Napoleon as Dynamite. Geoffroy's *Napoléon Apocryphe* and Science Fiction as Alternate History", Glyn Morgan/Charul Palmer-Patel (eds.) *Sideways in Time. Critical Essays on Alternate History Fiction*, Liverpool, Liverpool University Press, 31-45.

Ross, Gary (dir.) (2012) *The Hunger Games*, USA, Lionsgate/Color Force.

Sánchez Trigos, Rubén/Mondelo González, Edisa/Peláez Paz, Andrés (2015) "Un nuevo modelo de series fantásticas en la ficción televisiva", Belén Puebla Martínez/Nuria Navarro Sierra/Elena Carrillo Pascual (eds.) *Ficcionando en el siglo XXI. La ficción televisiva en España*, Madrid, Icono 14 Editorial, 277-308.

Schweitzer, Dahlia (2018) *Going Viral. Zombies, Viruses, and the End of the World*, New Brunswick, NJ, Rutgers University Press.

Sieyès, Emmanuel Joseph (1931 [1789]) *Qu'est-ce que le tiers état?*, publié par Kurt Glaser, avec les annotations de Georgette Schüler, Leipzig, Quelle & Meyer.

Soderbergh, Steven (dir.) (2011) *Contagion*, USA/UAE, Participant Media/Imagenation Abu Dhabi/Double Feature Films.

Stein, Karen F. (2016) "Post-Apocalypse, Post-Human: Some Recent Dystopias", Louisa MacKay Demerjian (ed.) *The Age of Dystopia: One Genre, Our Fears and Our Future*, Cambridge, Cambridge Scholars Publishing, 47-58.

Tiehen, Jeanne (2016) "Dystopian Drama: Imagining Science without Limitations", Louisa MacKay Demerjian (ed.), *The Age of Dystopia: One Genre, Our Fears and Our Future*, Cambridge, Cambridge Scholars Publishing, 59-72.

Toledano, Éric/Nakache, Olivier (dirs.) (2021-2022) *En Thérapie*, France, Les Films du Poisson/Arte/Federation Entertainment/Ten Films.

Tschilschke, Christian von (2018) "Betreten verboten! Gated Communities in der Literatur und im Film Lateinamerikas", Walburga Hülk/Stephanie Schwerter (eds.) *Mauern, Grenzen, Zonen. Geteilte Städte in Literatur und Film*, Heidelberg, Winter, 109-124.

Voigts, Eckart (2015) "Introduction: The Dystopian Imagination – An Overview", Eckart Voigts/Alessandra Boller (eds.) *Dystopia, Science Fiction, Post-Apocalypse. Classics – New Tendencies – Model Interpretations*, Trier, WVT, 1-11.

Wald, Priscilla (2008) *Contagious: Cultures, Carriers, and the Outbreak Narrative* Durham, NC, Duke University Press.

Wörsdörfer, Anna Isabell (2022) "What If? Epidemic Discourse and Serial Narration in the Alternate History Series *La Révolution* (2020)", *French Cultural Studies* 33/2, 179-195. DOI: 10.1177/09571558211063334.

Wulff, Hans J. (2002) "Held und Antiheld, Prot- und Antagonist: Zur Kommunikations- und Texttheorie eines komplizierten Begriffsfeldes", Hans Krah/Claus-Micheal Ort (eds.) *Weltentwürfe in Literatur und Medien. Phantastische Wirklichkeiten – realistische Imaginationen. Festschrift für Marianne Wünsch*, Kiel, Ludwig, 431-448.

Wünsch, Michaela (2010) "Serialität und Wiederholung in filmischen Medien", Christine Blättler (ed.) *Kunst der Serie. Die Serie in den Künsten*, München, Fink, 191-203.

Corona Palimpsests: Pandemic Protagonists as Readers

Martina Stemberger (University of Vienna)

Abstract
Readers and readings are omnipresent not only in the controversial genre of 'corona diaries', but also in corona fiction; drawing on a rich literary and cinematographic epi-/pandemic tradition, early corona literature rapidly took a striking meta-turn. Based on a large comparative corpus, this paper examines its palimpsestic dynamics through the prism of reader protagonists: the analysis of reader characters and reading contexts provides valuable insights into the ways this recent literary production revisits and adapts pre-existing aesthetic and ideological patterns in a new social and media context, integrating a multitude of intertextual and intermedial references. Staging multiple acts of reading, metaleptically blurring the boundaries between reality and fiction, this corpus poses a creative challenge to us as readers – never quite – 'outside the text'; at the same time, it offers a polyvalent model of (un-)making meaning, of possibly mending, with the aid of literature, a crisis-shaken world.

INTRO: READING AGAINST THE PLAGUE

"Lisez", recommends Emmanuel Macron in his much-commented confinement speech on March 16, 2020, encouraging his fellow citizens to seek comfort in "a sure value: reading" (Gary 2020).[1] Indeed, at least from a socially and globally rather privileged point of view, the Covid-19 pandemic also appears as a literary

---

1   All terms and phrases enclosed in double quotation marks are literal quotations, translated into English where appropriate; all translations are the author's, unless indicated otherwise.

event: during the first lockdown, the French not only read more than ever (cf. Le Breton 2020); in considerable numbers, they ventured into creative territory, one out of ten admitting to some literary endeavour in the said period (cf. Gary 2020). In France and beyond, editors and agents confirm "a big spike in submissions" triggered by the pandemic (Juliet Mushens in Vincent 2020), low-threshold digital formats favouring an explosion of "user-created media content" (Foss 2020). "Lezen tegen de pest?" (Baetens 2020): in a frenzy of both writing and "reading against the plague", literature, thus, proves itself once more as a reservoir of effective crisis coping strategies.

In his *Bibliothèque de survie*, Frédéric Beigbeder (2021, 66) pays homage to fiction as an antidote to solitude. Defying isolation, fiction also provides a "frame of reference" (Ma 2018, 29) for dealing with an often imagined "kind of disaster" (Yu 2020) turned reality: rejected as "extremely unrealistic" in 2005, Peter May's thriller *Lockdown* is hastily published in spring 2020 (Elassar 2020). If filmic "pandemic practice" improves crisis resilience (Scrivner et al. 2021), the same might be supposed for literature-based exercise – an insight that writers have since long been familiar with: apart from his *non-superstitiousness* and affinity to "solitary life", the hero of George R. Stewart's *Earth Abides* (1949) lists being "a reader" as a key survival trait in a virus-devastated world (Stewart 2015, 38f.). Some decades later, one of the protagonists in Emily St. John Mandel's *Station Eleven* (2014) owes his "disaster preparedness" to action movies (Mandel 2015, 21).

But no less than films like Wolfgang Petersen's *Outbreak* (1995) and Steven Soderbergh's *Contagion* (2011) or Ndemic Creations' video game *Plague Inc.* (2012), equally valued as a means of "engag[ing] the public on serious public health topics" (Khan 2013), literature still constitutes a precious source of pandemic knowledge; in this context too, reading allows access to a new repertoire of "qualified gestures" (Macé 2011, 57). All you need to know in times of pandemics, for François-Henri Désérable, is already "dans les livres" (*TC* 46-50)[2] – and not just in the most obvious ones: for good reason, Beigbeder's survival canon includes, besides 'confinement classics' such as Xavier de Maistre's *Voyage autour de ma chambre* (*A Journey around My Room*), Fyodor Dostoevsky's *Zapiski iz podpol'ja* (*Notes from Underground*) and Thomas Mann's *Der Zauberberg* (*The Magic Mountain*), suggestions for antipodic, i.e. thematically opposed reading, from Colette's *Le Pur et l'Impur* to Despentes's *Vernon Subutex*. Jacques Drillon proposes a round of applause not only for top confinement candidate

---

2   *TC* = Coll. (2020) *Tracts de crise. Un virus et des hommes. 18 mars / 11 mai 2020*, Paris, Gallimard.

Marcel Proust, but also his other faithful companions Alexandre Dumas and Charles Baudelaire (cf. *TC* 519); amateur readers, in their turn "saved by books", spotlight *À la recherche du temps perdu* or, for instance, the writings of Simone de Beauvoir (Kronlund 2020b).

From March 2020, a new critical subgenre flourishes: between "Your Quarantine Reader" (Khatib et al. 2020) and the finest literary selection in times of "Coronavirus: de Sophocle à Stephen King [...]" (Houot 2020), international media rival in the digitally accelerated renegotiation of an old-new epi-/pandemic canon. "Boccaccio, Defoe, García Márquez, the usual suspects" (Carlos Fonseca, *ST* 384)[3] are eagerly rediscovered; Boccaccio's "livre multimédia" (Nathalie Koble in Benetti 2020), notably, inspires a substantial corpus of print and digital neo-Decamerons or 'Coronamerons' (cf. Stemberger 2021, 56-61). In addition, lesser-known works from national corpora are promoted, such as Filip De Pillecyn's 1951 plague novella *Rochus* (cf. Janssens 2020) or Curzio Malaparte's *La pelle* (1949), initially "La peste", renamed because of Camus (cf. Zampieri 2020). "Camus versus Garcia Marquez": from this "match littéraire" staged by *L'Express* (Payot 2020), the former emerges victorious, too. An "instant bestseller" (Rose 2020) in its time, *La Peste* rebecomes "a global sensation" (Earle 2020), provoking some iconoclastic pushback: "Je n'aime pas Camus", declares Emmanuel de Waresquiel (Dupont 2020), while Mario Vargas Llosa labels *La Peste* a "mediocre book" (*ST* 33).

And yet: "Il faut relire *La peste*" (Malka 2020); performatively claiming a common cultural heritage, Sugy (2020) explains "Pourquoi nous relisons *La Peste* de Camus".[4] Gallimard's *Tracts de crise*, intended as another "*Décaméron* pour le Coronavirus" (Régis Debray, *TC* 557), emphasize the literary community factor, combining a collective of contemporary writers with 14th century poet Guillaume de Machaut and Camus. The example of *La Peste*, presented as "the Bible of these tormented times" (Philippe 2020), paradigmatically illustrates the ambiguities between a classic's actualization and its recuperation: without being illegitimate, readings of Camus's novel as "a guidebook for Covid-19" (Rickard 2021) frequently seem somewhat simplistic, just as the keen association of the current pandemic's key actors – Wuhan whistleblower Li Wenliang or U.S. Chief Medical Advisor Anthony Fauci (cf. Robert Zaretsky in Illing 2020) – with Camus's iconic Dr. Rieux. However, between Covid-19, climate change and BLM,

---

3   *ST* = Stavans, Ilan (ed.) (2020) *And We Came outside and Saw the Stars Again. Writers from around the World on the COVID-19 Pandemic*, Brooklyn, NY, Restless Books. [E-Edition]

4   "We must reread *The Plague*"… "Why we reread Camus's *The Plague*".

Camus's novel, still a strong "texte politique" (Compagnon 2021), also incites more thorough (e.g. new gender and postcolonial) reinterpretations. Overall, corona readings of *La Peste* testify to literature's doubly cathartic function: "Sometimes we turn to novels to make sense of our world, and sometimes to escape it. Yet in hard times, we often ask them to do both at once: to make sense of our world, all the better to escape it" (Earle 2020). Despite its vivid depictions of illness, suffering and death, Camus's "'optimistic tragedy'" finally brings the reader "good news", celebrating the "triumph of solidarity" in the face of absurdity (Erofeev 2002, 291, 308).

Although a particularly striking example, *La Peste* is far from being the only literary 'survival tool' widely reactivated in the context of Covid-19. Corona literature (or, briefly, 'corona-lit') displays – and reflects on a meta-level – a rich panorama of (anti-)pandemic readings; in the following, crucial reader types and reading patterns are analyzed on the basis of a large comparative corpus of exemplary texts, starting with the controversial genre of the 'corona diary'.

GENRE, CLASS AND GENDER TROUBLE: READERS AND READINGS IN CORONA DIARISM

In times of Covid-19, literature is also addressed in terms of social privilege. In France, Leïla Slimani's and Marie Darrieussecq's *journaux de confinement* triggered a heated – and eminently gendered – controversy (cf. Stemberger 2021, 42-44); amongst a wave of parodies and pastiches, Lemaître (2020) stresses that the genre's only *raison d'être* consists in its capacity "to seize the social", a challenge taken up by Nesrine Slaoui's and Cécile Coulon's respective "anti-journal de confinement" (cf. Stemberger 2021, 44) or *France Culture*'s "Journal de non-confinement" (Kronlund 2020a), featuring the pandemic experience of exposed workers whose most pressing concern, as one easily imagines, is not exactly a new in-depth reading of Boccaccio and Camus. At the same time, the literary field's expansion accentuates the "cultural gap" (Serrell 2020) between established authors and the creative precariat, represented by "*picaro*"[5] Diane Ducret (2020).

Even so, all around the world, authors in lockdown – literary aristocrats and picaros alike – tend, rather unsurprisingly, to write about (the difficulties of) reading and writing. "I've always coped with anxiety and the unknown by reading", admits Grace Talusan, prey to a coping mechanism spiraling out of control: "[…] I've read and read until I feel sharp stabs behind my eyes" (*ST* 395). Confined in

---

5   All italics in quotations are in the original.

her mother's apartment, Arshia Sattar revisits her adolescent readings of Orwell, Kafka, Huxley or Zamyatin, whose "paranoid dystopias" have now "become the gross and brutal reality of my time" (*ST* 371). In the twinkling of a pen, writers' block in lockdown turns into a corona topos: Arthur Dreyfus meditates on a sudden "impossibilité d'écrire" (*TC* 66-71), while Nancy Huston analyzes her "*paralysie scripturale*" (*TC* 228). "How to write is not so simple", confirms Javier Sinay, hypnotized by the "biothriller, told in fragments" by social media: "I haven't even been able to read more than four pages of a book since all of this began […]" (*ST* 60). For Carlos Fonseca, reading other writers' diaries grows into an obsession; temporarily "incapable of writing", the author metamorphoses into a 'diary thief' (*ST* 374f.).

Most corona diaries are also reading chronicles: published first serially online, Fang Fang's inaugural *Wuhan Diary* (2020) makes not only considerable space for other, less prominent voices, involving an active readership; it offers as well a portrait of the writer as an eager and eclectic reader. Fang Fang comments on news about the epidemic, messages from net friends and fiends (cf. ibid., 119f.), but also on classical Chinese poetry, Heidegger's philosophy, a Taiwanese martial arts novel or an Appalachian Trail hiking diary (cf. ibid., 264-267). True to literature's cathartic potential, she announces her return to fiction and the forthcoming payment of "manuscript debts" (ibid., 231); what about putting the "true whistle-blower" of Wuhan in a novel (ibid., 329)?

"Écrirai-je encore un roman? Rien n'est moins sûr", notes Éric Chevillard (*L'Autofictif*, 2021-06-21).[6] With all due respect for a "contexte funeste" (Chevillard 2021, 7), his parodic confinement diary *Sine die* relies on humour as a "force de résistance" (ibid., 124): dismantling the genre's pathos and paradoxical conformism, he self-ironically depicts the dilemma of an author who, in pace with an army of ambitious colleagues, sets out to write about the pandemic. In the midst of a Paris haunted by nose-blowing bats and "hordes of rabid pangolins" (ibid., 11f.), the narrator squats in de Maistre's fauteuil, while "domestic spider" Lachésis (ibid., 99), a suspicious insect named Gregor (cf. ibid., 56) and other two- or more-legged intertextual specters make mischief: "*Ô toison, moutonnant jusque sur l'encolure!*", scoffs Baudelaire's ghost (ibid., 96);[7] in desperate need of a hair-dresser's attention, his distant descendant regrets that, apart from the flesh being sad, "tous les livres" are read. Fortunately, literature does not end with Mallarmé,

---

6   "Will I write another novel? Nothing is less certain".

7   "O fleecy hair, falling in curls to the shoulders!" ("La Chevelure", trans. William Aggeler: https://fleursdumal.org/poem/203, 2022-08-26).

after all, "[n]ous avons maintenant Éric-Emmanuel Schmitt [...]" (ibid., 19f.).[8] Authorial animosities aside, literature, in times of confinement and reconfinement, still holds a promise of "grands espaces" (ibid., 7), beyond the new subgenre of the *Corona-Travel-Diary* (Görk 2020).

PANDEMIC PALIMPSESTS: CONTEXTUALIZING CORONA-LIT

Playfully problematizing literature's status between social relevance and artistic autonomy, Chevillard's idiosyncratic meta-diary points to some key features of early corona literature: drawing on a rich literary and cinematographic tradition, the latter rapidly takes a striking meta-turn. This penchant is, of course, not radically new: since ancient Greece, epi-/pandemic writing has been unfolding in profuse palimpsestuality. Camus's chronicler looks back on a long history of epidemics, including "la peste de Constantinople" (2020, 51) documented by Procopius of Caesarea who, as does Lucretius, recycles Thucydides's *History of the Peloponnesian War*. With his epigraph from Defoe's preface to the third volume of *Robinson Crusoe*, Camus also hints to the author's *Journal of the Plague Year* (1722), whose narrator "H. F." employs an appreciable part of a "dismal time" in "reading books" and "writing down my memorandums of what occurred to me every day [...]" (Defoe 1995, ebook). Mary Shelley has her eponymous *Last Man* (1826) read "the accounts of Boccaccio, De Foe, and Browne" (Shelley 2006, ebook); in "2100, last year of the world", Lionel Verney departs from Rome with merely "a few books; the principal are Homer and Shakespeare", but in a life now devoid of humans, "the libraries of the world are thrown open to me [...]" (ibid.). Shelley's paradigm-setting dystopic novel marks epi-/pandemic literature up to our days; symbolically enough, in Mandel's *Station Eleven*, another murderous "prophet" dies with his personal palimpsest in his pocket, a copy of the New Testament scribbled over to the point of illegibility (2015, 303).

However, against the backdrop of this rich heritage, corona-lit still stands out by its dense, complex intertextuality (often nested and squared), partly conditioned by a certain 'discomfort in literature': the first corona works already convey a sense of anticipatory weariness, of 'too soon' and 'too much'. Somewhat

---

8   As an epitome of commercially successful and aesthetically somewhat disputable literary production, Schmitt, a popular Franco-Belgian writer and film director, is one of Chevillard's notorious *bêtes noires*; he is also one of the main targets – and sources – of Chevillard's parodic *Défense de Prosper Brouillon* (2017).

paradoxically, writers and critics castigate the excesses of a "chatty" pandemic (Le Goff 2021, 11f.), further inflating a quickly growing corpus; herself author of an early corona novel (*Iznanka* ["Inside Out"], 2020), Inga Kuznetsova is nevertheless reticent about this new "trend" (Tolstov 2020). In reaction to a pronounced "anxiety of influence" (Bloom 1973), oriented at once towards the past, contemporary competitors and a future corona canon, many writers opt for 'going meta' right from the start; this is where reader protagonists come into play, as diegetic 'carriers' of epi-/pandemic inter- and metatextuality and, as such, a crucial aesthetic device.

BLURRING BOUNDARIES: READER PROTAGONISTS AND THE CONFIGURATION OF A TRANSGENERIC GENRE

Virus infection can be considered as a process of "transcription" (Krämer 2008, 138); in some corona texts, SARS-CoV-2 is indeed represented as a scriptural agent and/or metaphorical reader, as in Kuznetsova's *Iznanka* or Charles Yu's story "Systems", narrated in a collective viral voice (cf. Stemberger 2021, 97-102). But mostly, more conventionally conceived human readers appear, alongside with doctors, researchers, etc., as key protagonists; among these reader characters, the analysis of our corona-lit corpus reveals several recurrent prototypes.

Professional readers – such as writers, critics or teachers – are a rather obvious choice, plausibilizing, on a diegetic level, a wide range of references and a ludically didactic role. Academic writers preferably portray academic readers: thus, in a university-based Canadian online collection of *Récits infectés* (Brassard 2020), Artaud specialist Simon Harel ("Antonin, la Covid et moi") exploits his expertise for parodic purposes, anchoring his reflections on "Le Théâtre et la Peste" (1933) and preparing his plot's surrealist turn. Via another erudite reader, Thea Dorn transforms a controversial essay into "a kind of corona novel" in epistolary form (Bartels 2021), using her rebellious protagonist as a mouthpiece against German pandemic policy. For all its ambivalence, *Trost. Briefe an Max* ("Consolation. Letters to Max", 2021) constitutes an exemplary reading exercise: corresponding with her former philosophy professor, Dorn's heroine involves the recipient in her "adventure" of reading books that demand "to be conquered": "Texte wie Festungen, in die kein Weg hineinzuführen scheint" (ibid., 56);[9] carving her path across philosophy, dictionaries and fiction, Johanna comments on a multiplicity

---

9 "Texts like fortresses into which no path seems to lead".

of readings, from Plato and Seneca via Gryphius, Goethe and Heine, Zola and Canetti to Beauvoir.

But naive reader characters, unbound by academic conventions, have their advantages, too. While the heroine of Frédérique Lamoureux's "Fragments de quarantaine" readily identifies with Hans Castorp as a confinement fellow (cf. Brassard 2020), Alberto Vázquez-Figueroa's protagonist does not mince his words about Mann's classics, *Der Zauberberg* ("Tanta muerte y tanto intelectual tuberculoso […]") and *Der Tod in Venedig* (*Death in Venice*) with its "viejo pedófilo" (2020b, 26).[10] *Cien años después* (*One Hundred Years Later*) and *La vacuna* ("The Vaccine") illustrate even popular corona-lit's meta-dimension: amidst a "Dantesque spectacle" (ibid., 83), reading provides a "refugio" (2020a, 14) and a means of evasion; anyway, as self-declared globetrotter Samuel finally admits, he owes most of his "historias" to his library (ibid., 85). In an autoreferential loop, Vázquez has his characters discuss "un libro sobre la epidemia" that someone must be writing (2020b, 7); meanwhile, artist Víctor tackles a *Don Quixote* corona comic (cf. ibid., 27).

By choosing, for his narrative entitled *Corona*, an unpretentious but assiduous reader, Martin Meyer (2020) avoids all ambivalence issues associated with writer and/or academic protagonists: most conveniently, his Matteo, being "no professor and no critic" (ibid., 186), but just a modest elderly bookseller, can calmly delight in "the great classics' genius" (ibid., 41). Having "read in a writer that the latter had read another writer […]" (ibid., 25), he takes the reader on another palimpsestic, if rather conventional parcours, from the Bible via Boccaccio, Defoe, Jeremias Gotthelf and Mann to *La Peste*, one of his "favorite books" (ibid., 186); recycling his own research, Camus biographer Meyer (*Albert Camus. Die Freiheit leben*, 2013) has his hero refute the idea of an epidemic's "higher morality" and claim the necessity of defining one's "attitude" (2020, 190-194).

Instead of a single protagonist, Ivan Ivanji's novel *Corona in Buchenwald* (2021), self-ironic Decameron *en abyme*, presents a polyphony of simple and sophisticated storytellers and readers: the author's alter ego, writer Alexander Mihályi-Mihajlović alias Sascha, and a polyglot philology professor interact with non-literary narrators, including an ex-boxer and a Jehovah's Witness, naive exegete of the New Testament (cf. Stemberger 2021, 61-64).

Children, as readers (or adult readers' audience), play a non-negligible role: in Alejandro Zambra's "Screen Time", a writer couple, confronted, by the "shitty virus", with the "futility of each and every word", seeks solace in their son's

---

10 "So much death and so many tuberculous intellectuals […]"… "old pedophile".

children's books (*DP* 131f.).[11] Chiara Gamberale's corona "quaderno" (2020, 8) reflects not only the narrator's adult readings – such as the "immortal correspondence" between Sigmund Freud and Arthur Schnitzler or the letters exchanged between Rainer Maria Rilke and Marina Tsvetaeva (ibid., 19, 41) –, but also her three-year-old daughter Vita's fairy tale repertoire (cf. ibid., 22f.).

By conjuring up multiple readers and reading acts, early corona literature thus integrates an eclectic variety of intertexts: our corpus's protagonists turn to ancient and modern classics of epi-/pandemic fiction, dystopian novels and travel literature, to philosophy and poetry, to others' diaries and correspondences, to dictionaries and scientific discourse – and, occasionally, an even larger panoply of concrete and metaphorical texts.

CROSSED (MIS-)READINGS:
SYLVIE GERMAIN'S *BRÈVES DE SOLITUDE*

"Chaque être crie en silence pour être lu autrement. Qui peut se flatter qu'il lira juste?":[12] quoting en exergue Simone Weil, Sylvie Germain, in *Brèves de solitude* (2021), illustrates her characters' disarray in the face of the pandemic by a puzzle of crossed (mis-)readings. Just before lockdown, a group of strangers gathers in a small urban park, all of them challenged by some kind of text and entangled in a web of mutual misunderstandings: an elderly lady remembers her dead husband, named, by his immigrant father, in honour of Émile Littré, before struggling once more with her crossword magazine (cf. ibid., 16-21); immersed in his paperback edition of John's Apocalypse, a would-be novelist, who has left to a former companion his incomplete set of *À la recherche du temps perdu*, treads water with his project of a Bible rewrite (cf. ibid., 24-29, 133). An androgynous punk and perfumery student strives to comprehend an arduous essay, feeling like Alice falling down the rabbit-hole (cf. ibid., 51); a homeless black man, the narration's marginal pivot, pretends to read, in an effort to keep up appearances, an equestrian magazine (cf. ibid., 22). Another old woman, fighting dementia, feels like "un verbe en voie de désagrégation" (ibid., 72);[13] her foreign nurse, with her own dark back-story

---

11 *DP* = The New York Times Magazine (ed.) (2020) *The Decameron Project. 29 New Stories from the Pandemic*, New York, NY, Scribner.

12 "Every being cries out in silence to be read differently. Who can flatter themselves that they will read right?"

13 … "a verb in the process of disaggregation".

and scar-covered body, is haunted by a frightening as well as fascinating child-hood tale (cf. ibid., 116-118).

Ingeniously, Germain uses very young and very old, physically and/or men-tally impaired characters to convey general confusion; the difficulty of seizing the invisible danger is spun throughout the text. Co-protagonist Serge loses his mother to senility and a solitary death; at her incineration, he involuntarily channels her addled mind, "Coronavalgus! [...] Coronabrutus! Coronavénus! [...] Coronagi-bus! [...] Coronarébus! [...] Coronacrésus! [...] Coronacrocus! Coronanégus! [...] Coronasinus! [...] Coronaphallus! [...] Coronafocus! Coronanimbus! [...] Coronarhésus! [...] Coronafœtus! Coronahumus!", briefly, a whole "lamentable Coronaopus" wildly interfering with literary and musical reminiscences from bet-ter times (ibid., 177). And yet, literature is still able to restore some coherence to a fragmented world: a former art teacher metamorphoses into "Monsieur Merlin" for his little lockdown neighbor, telling her stories, including *Nils Holgersson's Wonderful Journey through Sweden*, whereas an anxious adolescent, on the other adjacent balcony, prefers to discuss George Orwell's *Animal Farm* (ibid., 107-111).

In terms of theory, it is particularly striking to observe the emergence of co-rona-lit as a not only markedly inter- and metatextual, but also transversal, even transgeneric genre with strong metaleptic affinity; reader protagonists play a cru-cial role in blurring the boundaries between reality and fiction, another key feature of recent pandemic texts.

HALLUCINATING RIEUX: ERIK EISING'S *TAGEBUCH DER SANFTEN QUARANTÄNE*

Thus, Erik Eising's *Tagebuch der sanften Quarantäne* ("Diary of Gentle Quaran-tine", 2021) disrupts an instantly clichéd form. While the narrator, in his report about the first weeks of the pandemic, does not forget "those who do not have the comfort of just writing behind their windowpanes" (ibid., 79), his own confine-ment revolves around a bookcase full of classical and contemporary "dusty friends" (ibid., 7). In the company of Proust, Mann, Artaud and (of course) Camus, Eising's protagonist sets out for a literary journey; even if "reading about it" is sometimes "simply not enough" ("Nein, davon zu lesen genügt einfach nicht [...]"; ibid., 61), it provides depth and distance from a crisis still "too close" (ibid., 72). Tweets from "real dystopia" (ibid., 78) mingle with the story of the Great Plague of Marseille (cf. ibid., 36); *La Peste* helps contextualize Macron's war rhetoric and the German government's "first war metaphors" (ibid., 13). Camus leads once more back to Defoe's *Journal*, but also to *Robinson Crusoe* and Lutz Seiler's *Kruso* (2014).

In his pandemic mini-theatre, Eising summons familiar literary ghosts: in a strangely transformed cellar, his protagonist is awaited by none other than Seiler's "Herr Bendler" and Camus's "Herr Doktor Rieux" (ibid., 35-37). Drawing the reader in a metaleptic swirl, Rieux comments on his host's "Coronologie"; Bendler would rather spend the lockdown with Boccaccio's "seven pretty Florentine ladies", but alas, "we have to take what comes" (ibid., 71). The underground trio launches into a discussion about "copying and recopying", about real and imaginary epidemics present and past: Rieux recalls "a similar case in Oran", "worse actually", since "the plague and coronavirus" are after all "two completely different things" (ibid., 35-38). Afflicted by a suspicious cough, Camus's plague survivor nevertheless succumbs to Covid-19: "Zum Abschied ein letztes Schulterklopfen, doch er war schon ganz kalt" (ibid., 73).[14]

CAMUS "AT FIRST DEGREE"?
ALEXANDRE NAJJAR'S *LA COURONNE DU DIABLE*

With *La Couronne du diable* (2020), dedicated to all corona victims, Alexandre Najjar claims in his turn the heritage of Camus's "obstinacy of testimony" (2021, 13) and the writer's "responsibility" (Montpetit 2020). The paratext, announcing alternatively a 'novel' and a collection of 'corona stories', testifies to a certain generic hybridity; tying in with an established "drama-inspired pandemic metanarrative" (Research Group *Pandemic Fictions* 2020, 328) and, more specifically, the theatrical structure of *La Peste*, Najjar emphasizes the importance of giving voice to the witnesses by staging "l'acte premier de la tragédie" (2021, 152). His polyphonic narrative takes the reader on an express trip around a pandemic-stricken world, intertwining fiction and facts (e.g. the fate of Li Wenliang, quarantined cruiser Diamond Princess, actor Luca Franzese's Facebook video about his sister's Covid-19 death, the conflict about sanitary rules in the Maronite church).

La Couronne du diable epitomizes the strategic use of reader protagonists in early corona fiction. For his Paris chapter, Najjar chooses a literature teacher on lockdown: charged with a double intra- and extradiegetic didactic mission, the narrator proposes a "remake" of La Fontaine's plague fable and a re-reading of *La Peste* "au premier degré" (2021, 48-51); as Eising's protagonist, she analyzes

---

14 "As a farewell, a last pat on the back, but he was already quite cold".

Macron's speech through the prism of Camus's "pestes et guerres" (2020a, 49). An Italian film student adds a new array of references between Soderbergh, Visconti and Mann: "Je ne voudrais pas mourir comme Aschenbach" (Najjar 2021, 82).[15] Beyond explicit intertextuality, Najjar rewrites crucial traits of Camus's text. While his French teacher adopts the chronicler's role, his Italian narrator, following Rambert, incarnates an exemplary evolution towards reflected solidarity; fleeing from "Milan, ville fantôme", he has already made it across the border, when a telephone call from his exhausted mother, chief nurse in a regional hospital, persuades him to return: "Ma décision est prise: je ne peux pas, je ne veux plus m'enfuir" (ibid., 85-87).[16] The Lebanese episode showcases another critical reader (among other texts, of Sartre's *Le Diable et le bon Dieu*) and Camusian *revenant*: protesting against the governing "'mafiature'" and religious misinterpretations of the pandemic, Najjar's enlightened "père jésuite" appears as a contemporary anti-Paneloux (ibid., 91-95). The final U.S. chapter presents a paradigmatic bad reader, failing, as a health journalist, due to his affinity to "*conspiracy theories*" (ibid., 133); a Madrid-based "médecin par vocation et éditeur par passion", modeled after the author's real Spanish publisher, establishes the link between science and literary engagement (ibid., 119).

DOCTORS AS READERS: LAWRENCE WRIGHT, WIM DANIËLS & CO.

The medical doctor or researcher as reader is indeed a key figure in recent pandemic fiction. Written before the current crisis and published in April 2020, Lawrence Wright's *The End of October* centers around a brilliant epidemiologist who is also an enthusiastic reader: when Henry Parsons discovers, on the e-reader left behind by his predecessor aboard submarine Georgia, "a long list of classics", he gratefully dives into *War and Peace* at the point where his since deceased colleague broke off, his minuscule underwater refuge opening onto vast imaginary spaces and a vision of "Pierre on the battlefield in his swallowtail coat" (2020a, 265). The battle against a "modern plague" (ibid., 116) will be lost; for all his fidelity to genre clichés, Wright refuses a happy end. On a meta-level, the protagonist's portrait mirrors the novel's making: starting with his epigraphs from Defoe and Camus, Wright pays tribute to literary tradition, specifying, though, that his supposed "prophecy" is "the fruit of research" (2020b). With *The Plague Year.*

---

15 "I would not want to die like Aschenbach".

16 "My decision is made: I cannot, I do not want anymore to run away".

America in the Time of Covid (2021), he reverts to journalism; the dynamic inter-action between pandemic facts and fiction is, however, evident enough.

In a post-corona world, for Haruki Murakami, literature alone will not suffice, "la science seule non plus" (Nishimura 2020); as a topos of early corona fiction, the alliance between science and literature is often illustrated by a writer/doctor-researcher couple, a pattern present in popular novels, such as Mona Ullrich's *Liebe in Zeiten der Seuche* ("Love in Times of Plague", 2020) or Matti Sund's and Dorit Biel's *Das Corona-Ende* (2020). In the same vein, Wim Daniëls's *Quarantaine* (2020), the first Dutch "coronaroman" (Veen 2020), sets up, in an academic vacation park in rural Dordogne, a medical doctor with a philologist specialized in punctuation marks. Having his protagonists fall ill with a mild form of Covid-19, he creates the perfect setting for an intimate mini-Decameron: this intellectual couple's quarantine essentially consists of conversations, poetry and stories; while Karel's expertise allows for epidemiological digressions, Julia's thesis topic in-vites forays into literary history. Daniëls's crucial intertext is the œuvre of writer-doctor Anton Chekhov, inspiring, from the outset, a playful metaleptic twist: the heroine is introduced as "[d]e dame met het hondje", the "lady with the little dog" (Daniëls 2020, 9); the two Dutch patients enjoy an imaginary trip to Colombo, where Chekhov stops on his way back from Sakhalin (cf. ibid., 88f.). But reading goes beyond escapism and pleasant distraction from "often panicky" pandemic news (ibid., 51); in Daniëls's novel, literature finally unfolds its life-changing force. For Karel, Chekhov's Christmas story "Vosklicatel'nyj znak" ("The Excla-mation Mark") marks, in corona March 2020, a turning point; infected not only with SARS-CoV-2, but also with his companion's "punctuation virus", he com-pletes, in fast motion, his *éducation sentimentale*: "[…] dan, ja dan…!!!" (ibid., 119f.).

READING CHEKHOV IN CORONA TIMES: GARY SHTEYNGART'S *OUR COUNTRY FRIENDS*

"I reread all my Chekhov […]", reveals Gary Shteyngart in an interview (Cum-mins 2022) about his corona novel *Our Country Friends* (2021). Against the back-drop of "a scary time" (Shteyngart 2022, 49), he proceeds to another parodic re-staging of Boccaccio, gathering a heterogeneous assembly on an upstate New York country estate – among them several writers, a psychiatrist and a narcissistic actor, flaunting "his love of the Greek classics" (ibid., 111) and his disdain for his fellow lodgers' work: "Do you know […] what all of your scripts lack?" (ibid., 95). Savouring their suffering in comfortable conditions – "Most of literature is about privileged people being unhappy. *Anna Karenina* much?" (ibid., 162) –, Shteyngart's pandemic refugees, "surrounded by typewriters" (ibid., 244) or "rows of books imprisoning them" (ibid., 118), bring early corona fiction's literary as well as sanitary anxiety to full bloom. A young writer with a working-class background resents "missing more references than usual": "White ignorant folk like me, she thought, we're the immigrants today" (ibid., 56); an essay about her "childhood obsession with *Gone with the Wind*" (ibid., 196) gets her into serious trouble in times of BLM. Meanwhile, the decades-old friendship between two once inseparable "city-college Scheherazades" (ibid., 137) is nearly shattered when it turns out that host Sasha Senderovsky, years ago, purposely discouraged his guest from publishing an excellent novel – whose manuscript he now tries "to entomb [...] inside a groundhog's hole" (ibid., 127).

In a sophisticated spatio-textual construction, the "Petersburg Bungalow", full of original and translated classics ("Is one of these books *Crime and Punishment*?"), forms, within Senderovsky's estate, a second-degree literary microcosm, crystallizing issues of reading, writing and authority (Shteyngart 2022, 52). Subtly, the library irradiates its surroundings, the characters thinking more and more "[i]n accordance with the rules of Russian novels" (ibid., 139). Once more, metaleptic confusion, a frequent device in corona fiction, reflects the chaos of a world resembling "Genesis in reverse" (ibid., 267): "Was all this really happening: masks and tyrants, aerosol sprays and gun-toting clowns?" (ibid., 287).

Chekhov, key intertext among an eclectic corpus ranging from Homer to Joan Didion, comes to new life when misjudged novelist Vinod, knowing "exactly where Vanya sulked amid the colorful mass of bookshelves" (Shteyngart 2022, 117), retrieves a copy in the said Russian bungalow. As Daniëls's Karel, Shteyngart's protagonist considers his life in Chekhovian terms: "[...] he had to think like a character in a Chekhov play [...]" (ibid., 120); but, on the other hand, "[w]hat if he were not a Chekhovian character [...]? What if he –" (ibid., 175). Seemingly "summoned by a madman out of Gogol or Cervantes" (ibid., 119), the estate easily adapts to his "*Uncle Vanya*-influenced imagination" (ibid., 121); reading Chekhov on his "Brazilian area rug", Vinod takes off in a whirl of textiles and texts: "'*A country house on a terrace. In front of it a garden.* [...] *It is three o'clock in the afternoon of a cloudy day.*' It was so, precisely" (ibid., 122). As the famous actor carries in the fatal virus, the reader on his rug slides into a long agony, *A Hero of Our Time* falling "out of his grasp" (ibid., 259). Listlessly, he assists to a last *Uncle Vanya* representation, hypocritically staged in his honour; while the other characters obediently assume their Chekhovian roles, the clouds, this time, "would not cooperate" (ibid., 291-293).

Having once performed as the eponymous orchard in "a very avant-garde version […] in Berlin" (ibid., 117), the actor anticipates another Chekhov play embedded in Shteyngart's plot: out of money and correspondingly casted, for *Djadja Vanja*, as "impoverished landowner" Telegin (ibid., 292f.), Senderovsky, with his leitmotivic tree troubles, is on the verge of losing his beloved estate but – like the protagonists in *The Cherry Orchard* – unable-unwilling to do something about it. Steering towards an ambiguous half-happy ending, however, his 'country friends' manage to save the estate; at this point, Chekhov fan Vinod (whose name, coincidentally or not, starts and ends with the original *Višnëvyj sad*) will already have died out of – or into – the text.

PROCOPIUS, POETRY AND POLITICS:
VINCENT MESSAGE'S *LES ANNÉES SANS SOLEIL*

Published after the first wave of corona-lit, Vincent Message's *Les Années sans soleil* ("The Sunless Years", 2022) calls for a cautious historical approach: although the context (confinement, overburdened hospitals, etc.) is clear, the author avoids naming the disease, giving his text – an elaborate meditation on literature between business, engagement and *l'art pour l'art* – a wider scope. His narrator, an avid reader and moderately successful writer who earns his living as a bookshop assistant, concentrates multiple facets of literary life: he comments on the challenges of the book market, especially in pandemic times, on the misfortune of writers whose new works – like his own – (dis-)appear during lockdown (cf. ibid., 116), but also, more generally, on the logic of the literary field; a self-ironic representative of France's "précariat intellectuel" (ibid., 194), transferring, after his bookstore's closure, to bicycle delivery service, he is perfectly aware of his own lack of auctorial posture and "capital narratif" (ibid., 117).

For obvious reasons, Message's Elias, at the difference of Meyer's Matteo, feels some ambivalence towards the classics and still more towards contemporary colleagues, the most successful ones being "en général" not the most deserving (ibid., 47). A permanent reminder of "the incredible multitude of existing books", the bookshop's heterotopia both fascinates and paralyzes him (ibid., 70f.); at home as well, negotiating space between literature and family matters, Elias fights to create some blanks among masses of books: "[…] les interstices se fermaient, tout ce monde se serrait sur les étagères jusqu'à ne plus pouvoir bouger [...]" (ibid., 25f.).[17]

Much of Message's plot consists of us readers watching the protagonist read: in the midst of "the great confinement" (ibid., 169), Elias, like Eising's narrator, retires into his basement; as Gamberale (cf. 2020, 51f.), he secretly admits what he would not confess even "under torture", namely, the fact that he appreciates "certain aspects of this catastrophic period" (Message 2022, 90). Paradoxically only at first glance, reading about even worse historical catastrophes allows 'breathing better' in corona times (cf. ibid., 129); searching online for information about the worst moments in human history, Elias comes across the Justinianic Plague. "Rien que dans la capitale, il meurt dix mille personnes par jour [...]" (ibid., 85):[18] paraphrasing the same passage as Camus's Rieux (cf. 2020a, 51), he launches into a much more detailed commentary of Procopius, explicating the novel's title and epigraph.

Thus recontextualized, Procopius's report about climate change in the middle of the 6th century and associated "wars, pestilences or other deadly plagues" (Message 2022, 9) reads almost like a contemporary work (cf. ibid., 173); not a particularly innovative writer, but rather a fine copyist on the tracks of Herodotus and Thucydides, the Byzantine historian also refers to the issue of originality – and the advantages of arriving "so late in the history of humanity" (ibid., 107-109): just as Elias's crammed bookshelves, "the wall of centuries" (ibid., 241) keeps, thanks to new scientific knowledge, moving and opening up. With his predecessor's help, the protagonist frames his observations on this or that "anomaly that Procopius would surely have noted [...]" (ibid., 207); participating in protests against police violence, he identifies with Procopius's "chef des Goths", battling against "l'Empire" and "cette paix romaine" that, throughout the ages, suits and supports only the status quo (ibid., 221).

Procopius's *Histories* are not the only intertext spilling over into diegetic reality. In company with "ce vieil ami sur qui je pouvais compter, le vieux poète maboul, mon Friedrich Hölderlin" (ibid., 227),[19] the narrator ruminates on the still vital question of poets' role "in meagre times": *"Wozu Dichter in dürftiger Zeit?"* (ibid., 140). Doubly confined, after his clash with authorities, in his Toulouse apartment, telephone and Internet temporarily cut, Elias Torres relates all the more with Hölderlin in his tower; under adverse circumstances, reading saves

---

17 "[...] the gaps were closing, everything was squeezed on the shelves until nothing could move any more [...]".

18 "In the capital alone, ten thousand people die every day [...]".

19 ... "this old friend I could count on, the crazy old poet, my Friedrich Hölderlin".

Hölderlin's human *"conversation"* (ibid., 170) or Camus's "dialogue", "la communication universelle des hommes entre eux" (2017, 670). "Friedrich" cheerfully joins him in the form of a poetry-loving wagtail, triggering a new metaleptic turn: chasing the bird's feline murderer across the quarter's rooftops, Elias mimics another epidemic classic's hero; quite symbolically, Message's meta-hussar lands right in the library of his old poet friend who, after gifting him his Procopius edition (and leaving behind a transcultural reincarnation of Giono's Pauline), has just died from unnamed Covid-19 (Message 2022, 228-236).

Even if Message mentions Camus only *en passant*, camouflaging an all-too manifest intertext, his protagonist, as a multiple reenactor, finally follows in the printsteps of *La Peste* and *L'Homme révolté*. "Je me révolte, donc nous sommes" (Camus 2020b, 38): almost accidentally, Elias becomes a politically engaged writer, switching, in a viral post, from a conflicted 'I' to a solidary *"nous"* (Message 2022, 218f.). Involving also the reader, the narrator metamorphoses into "une voix qui a votre voix dans votre tête. Un visage incertain qui se reflète dans le miroir" (ibid., 191);[20] his remarks about his manner of sneaking secretly, but "tout entier" in his work (ibid., 118) hint to a transdiegetic game of hide-and-seek: endowed with a fictive œuvre of his own, he sets about writing a novel entitled *Les Années sans soleil*. At the end of Message's self-begetting text (cf. Kellman 1980), the protagonist will have found an at least provisional answer to the problem of being a poet in new 'meagre times': abandoning his project of a historical novel, he decides, after an intertextual detour that was not one after all, to tell not only "mon histoire à moi", but also "notre histoire à nous" (Message 2022, 254).

TENTATIVE CONCLUSION: TOWARDS A POETICS OF CORONA FICTIONS

With regard to a still ongoing pandemic, any definitive conclusions about Corona Fictions as a new literary genre would inevitably be premature. Nevertheless, an approach through the prism of reader protagonists provides valuable insights into the palimpsestic dynamics of an evolving genre, into the ways in which early corona-lit, recycling a multitude of intertextual and intermedial references, revisits and adapts pre-existing aesthetic and ideological patterns in a new social and media context. As shown above, readers and readings are indeed omnipresent not only in the controversial genre of corona diaries, but also in corona fiction; in our comparative corpus, we encounter professional as well as amateur, erudite as well

---

20   ... "a voice that has your voice in your head. An uncertain face reflected in the mirror".

as naive, docile as well as rebellious reader characters of different backgrounds, genders and ages, all of them associated with specific reading choices, experiences and strategies. Staging multiple acts of reading, metaleptically blurring – and, thus, paradoxically, re-precising – the boundaries between reality and fiction, this corpus poses a creative challenge to us as readers – never quite – 'outside the text'; at the same time, it offers a polyvalent model of (un-)making meaning, of possibly mending, with the aid of literature, a crisis-shaken world.

BIBLIOGRAPHY

Corpus Analyzed

Beigbeder, Frédéric (2021) *Bibliothèque de survie*, Paris, Éd. de l'Observatoire.

Brassard, Léonore (ed.) (2020) *Récits infectés*, Montréal, https://recitsinfectes. com, 2022-08-26.

Camus, Albert (2017) *À Combat. Éditoriaux et articles, 1944-1947*, Paris, Gallimard.

Camus, Albert (2020a [1947]) *La Peste*, Paris, Gallimard.

Camus, Albert (2020b [1951]) *L'Homme révolté*, Paris, Gallimard.

Chevillard, Éric (2007-) *L'Autofictif* [Blog], http://autofictif.blogspot.com, 2022-08-26.

Chevillard, Éric (2021) *Sine die. Chronique du confinement, 19 mars-12 mai 2020*, Bordeaux, L'Arbre vengeur.

Coll. (2020) *Tracts de crise. Un virus et des hommes. 18 mars / 11 mai 2020*, Paris, Gallimard. [*TC*]

Daniëls, Wim (2020) *Quarantaine*, Amsterdam, Thomas Rap.

Defoe, Daniel (1995 [1722]) *A Journal of the Plague Year*, https://www.guten berg.org/files/376/376-h/376-h.htm, 2022-08-26.

Dorn, Thea (2021) *Trost. Briefe an Max*, München, Penguin.

Eising, Erik (2021) *Tagebuch der sanften Quarantäne*, Norderstedt, BoD. [E-Edition]

Fang, Fang (2020) *Wuhan Diary. Tagebuch aus einer gesperrten Stadt*, Hamburg, Hoffmann und Campe.

Gamberale, Chiara (2020) *Come il mare in un bicchiere*, Milano, Feltrinelli. [E-Edition]

Germain, Sylvie (2021) *Brèves de solitude*, Paris, Albin Michel.

Görk, Manfred (2020) *Lockdown in New Zealand. Corona-Travel-Diary*, Norderstedt, BoD. [E-Edition]

Ivanji, Ivan (2021) *Corona in Buchenwald*, Wien, Picus.

Kuznecova [Kuznetsova], Inga (2020) *Iznanka*, Moskva, AST.

Ma, Ling (2018) *Severance*, New York, NY, Picador/Farrar, Straus and Giroux. [E-Edition]

Macron, Emmanuel (2020) "Adresse aux Français, 16 mars 2020", *Élysée*, 2020-03-16, https://www.elysee.fr/emmanuel-macron/2020/03/16/adresse-aux-fran cais-covid19, 2022-08-26.

Mandel, Emily St. John (2015 [2014]) *Station Eleven*, London, Picador.

Message, Vincent (2022) *Les Années sans soleil*, Paris, Seuil.

Meyer, Martin (2020) *Corona*, Zürich/Berlin, Kein & Aber.

Najjar, Alexandre (2021 [2020]) *La Couronne du diable*, Paris, Plon.

Shelley, Mary (2006 [1826]) *The Last Man*, https://www.gutenberg.org/files/18247/18247-h/18247-h.htm, 2022-08-26.

Shteyngart, Gary (2022 [2021]) *Our Country Friends*, London, Allen & Unwin. [E-Edition]

Stavans, Ilan (ed.) (2020) *And We Came outside and Saw the Stars Again. Writers from around the World on the COVID-19 Pandemic*, Brooklyn, NY, Restless Books. [E-Edition] [*ST*]

Stewart, George R. (2015 [1949]) *Earth Abides*, London, Gateway. [E-Edition]

Sund, Matti/Biel, Dorit (2020) *Das Corona-Ende*, Berlin, Steffen.

The New York Times Magazine (ed.) (2020) *The Decameron Project. 29 New Stories from the Pandemic*, New York, NY, Scribner. [*DP*]

Ullrich, Mona (2020) *Liebe in Zeiten der Seuche. Gefühle, Zweifel, Corona*, Weinheim, Achter.

Vázquez-Figueroa, Alberto (2020a) *Cien años después*, Madrid, Kolima. [E-Edition]

Vázquez-Figueroa, Alberto (2020b) *La vacuna*, Madrid, Kolima. [E-Edition]

Wright, Lawrence (2020a) *The End of October*, New York, NY, Alfred A. Knopf. [E-Edition]

Wright, Lawrence (2021) *The Plague Year. America in the Time of Covid*, New York, NY, Alfred A. Knopf.

Works Cited

Baetens, Jan (2020) "Lezen tegen de pest?", *Coronameron. A Diary of the Covid Year*, 2020-05-19, https://www.arts.kuleuven.be/literatuurwetenschap/corona meron/la-peste/lezentegendepest, 2022-08-26.

Bartels, Gerrit (2021) "Thea Dorns Corona-Buch. Auf bedenklicher Freiheitsmission", *Der Tagesspiegel*, 2021-03-15, https://www.tagesspiegel.de/kultur/

thea-dorns-corona-buch-auf-bedenklicher-freiheitsmission/27004364.html, 2022-08-26.

Benetti, Pierre (2021) "'Décamérez!', un an après" [Interview with Nathalie Koble], *En attendant Nadeau*, 2021-03-17, https://www.en-attendant-nadeau. fr/2021/03/17/decamerez-entretien-koble, 2022-08-26.

Bloom, Harold (1973) *The Anxiety of Influence. A Theory of Poetry*, New York, NY, Oxford University Press.

Compagnon, Antoine (2021) "'Nous ne commettons pas de contresens en lisant *La Peste* comme une allégorie de notre condition'", *La Croix*, 2021-05-14, https://www.la-croix.com/Debats/Nous-commettons-pas-contresens-lisant-Pes te-comme-allegorie-notre-condition-2021-05-14-1201155764, 2022-08-26.

Cummins, Anthony (2022) "Gary Shteyngart: 'We're Entering a Time of Permanent Crisis'", *The Guardian*, 2022-01-29, https://www.theguardian.com/ books/2022/jan/29/gary-shteyngart-were-entering-a-time-of-permanent-crisis, 2022-08-26.

Ducret, Diane (2020) "'Journal du confinement': la vie un peu trop rose de Leïla Slimani", *Marianne*, 2020-03-19, https://www.marianne.net/agora/humeurs/ journal-du-confinement-la-vie-un-peu-trop-rose-de-leila-slimani, 2022-08-26.

Dupont, Laureline (2020) "Emmanuel de Waresquiel: 'Je n'aime pas Camus. En plus, je trouve qu'il écrit mal'", *L'Express*, 2020-05-13, https://www.lexpress. fr/culture/livre/emmanuel-de-waresquiel-je-n-aime-pas-camus-en-plus-je-trou ve-qu-il-ecrit-mal_2125860.html, 2022-08-26.

Earle, Samuel (2020) "How Albert Camus's *The Plague* Became the Defining Book of the Coronavirus Crisis", *The New Statesman*, 2020-05-27, https:// www.newstatesman.com/long-reads/2020/05/the-plague-albert-camus-corona virus-resurgence, 2022-08-26.

Elassar, Alaa (2020) "A Pandemic Thriller, Once Rejected by Publishers for Being Unrealistic, Is Now Getting a Wide Release", *CNN*, 2020-04-04, https://edi tion.cnn.com/2020/04/04/us/peter-may-lockdown-coronavirus-book-trnd/in dex.html, 2022-08-26.

Erofeev, Viktor (2002 [1972]) "Mysli o Kamju", *Labirint Dva. Ostaetsja odno: proizvol*, Moskva, Éksmo-Press/Zebra E, 278-310.

Foss, Katherine A. (2020) "How the 1918 Pandemic Got Meme-ified in Jokes, Songs and Poems", *Smithsonian Magazine*, 2020-07-31, https://www.smith sonianmag.com/history/memes-1918-pandemic-180975452, 2022-08-26.

Gary, Nicolas (2020) "Sondage: les Français ont lu 2,5 livres durant le confine-ment", *ActuaLitté*, 2020-05-11, https://actualitte.com/article/7653/enquetes/ sondage-les-francais-ont-lu-2-5-livres-durant-le-confinement, 2022-08-26.

Houot, Laurence (2020) "Coronavirus: de Sophocle à Stephen King, quinze livres inspirés par des épidémies à lire ou à relire", *France Info*, 2020-03-05, https://www.francetvinfo.fr/culture/livres/roman/covid-19-de-sophocle-a-ste phen-king-quinze-livres-inspires-par-des-epidemies-a-lire-ou-a-relire_3853 615.html, 2022-08-26.

Illing, Sean (2020) "What Camus's *The Plague* Can Teach Us about the Covid-19 Pandemic" [Interview with Robert Zaretsky], *Vox*, 2020-07-22, https://www. vox.com/future-perfect-podcast/2020/7/22/21328295/albert-camus-the-plague-covid-19-robert-zaretsky, 2022-08-26.

Janssens, Bart (2020) "Filip De Pill[e]cyn, *Rochus* (1951)", *Coronameron. A Diary of the Covid Year*, 2020-05-19, https://www.arts.kuleuven.be/literatuur wetenschap/coronameron/la-peste/filipdepillcynrochu, 2022-08-26.

Kellman, Steven G. (1980) *The Self-Begetting Novel*, New York, NY, Columbia University Press.

Khan, Ali S. (2013) "Plague Inc.", *CDC. Public Health Matters Blog*, 2013-04-16, https://blogs.cdc.gov/publichealthmatters/2013/04/plague-inc, 2022-08-26.

Khatib, Joumana/León, Concepción de/Tarng, Tammy/Alter, Alexandra (2020) "Your Quarantine Reader", *The New York Times*, 2020-03-12, https://www.ny times.com/2020/03/12/books/coronavirus-reading.html, 2022-08-26.

Krämer, Sybille (2008) *Medium, Bote, Übertragung. Kleine Metaphysik der Medialität*, Frankfurt am Main, Suhrkamp.

Kronlund, Sonia (2020a) "Journal de non-confinement: une caissière et un livreur", *France Culture*, 2020-04-10, https://www.franceculture.fr/emis sions/les-pieds-sur-terre/journal-de-non-confinement-une-caissiere-et-un-livreur, 2022-08-26.

Kronlund, Sonia (2020b) "Confinement: sauvées par les livres", *France Culture*, 2020-12-16, https://www.franceculture.fr/emissions/les-pieds-sur-terre/confi nement-sauvees-par-les-livres, 2022-08-26.

Le Breton, Marine (2020) "Pendant le coronavirus, la lecture comme antidote aux angoisses", *HuffPost*, 2020-08-22, https://www.huffingtonpost.fr/life/article/ pendant-le-coronavirus-la-lecture-comme-antidote-aux-angoisses_169037. html, 2022-08-26.

Le Goff, Jean-Pierre (2021) *La Société malade*, Paris, Stock. [E-Edition]

Lemaître, Félix (2020) "Lettre aux écrivains bourgeois qui nous refourguent leur journal du confinement", *Brain Magazine*, 2020-03-19, https://www.brain-magazine.fr/article/brainorama/60184-Lettre-aux-ecrivains-bourgeois-qui-vou draient-nous-refourguer-leur-journal-de-confinement, 2022-08-26.

Macé, Marielle (2011) *Façons de lire, manières d'être*, Paris, Gallimard.

Malka, Salomon (2020) "'Nous sommes tous un peu des personnages de Camus'", *FigaroVox*, 2020-03-20, https://www.lefigaro.fr/vox/culture/nous-sommes-tous-un-peu-des-personnages-de-camus-20200320, 2022-08-26.

Montpetit, Caroline (2020) "*La couronne du diable*: Coronavirus – acte I", *Le Devoir*, 2020-05-28, https://www.ledevoir.com/lire/579711/livre-coronavirus-acte-i, 2022-08-26.

Ndemic Creations (2012) *Plague Inc.*, USA, https://www.ndemiccreations.com/en/22-plague-inc.

Nishimura, Karyn (2020) "Dans le monde d'après le coronavirus 'la littérature seule ne suffira pas, la science seule non plus', confie l'écrivain Haruki Murakami", *France Info*, 2020-12-21, https://www.francetvinfo.fr/culture/livres/roman/dans-le-monde-d-apres-le-coronavirus-la-litterature-seule-ne-suffira-pas-la-science-seule-non-plus-confie-l-ecrivain-haruki-murakami_4228505.html, 2022-08-26.

Payot, Marianne (2020) "Camus versus Garcia Marquez: le choix des écrivains", *L'Express*, 2020-05-24, https://www.lexpress.fr/culture/livre/camus-versus-garcia-marquez-le-choix-des-ecrivains_2126120.html, 2022-08-26.

Petersen, Wolfgang (dir.) (1995) *Outbreak*, USA, Warner Bros./Punch Productions/Kopelson Entertainment.

Philippe, Elisabeth (2020) "Albert Camus avait vraiment tout prédit, étape par étape", *Le Nouvel Observateur*, 2020-03-26, https://www.nouvelobs.com/bibliobs/20200326.OBS26640/coronavirus-albert-camus-avait-vraiment-tout-predit-etape-par-etape.html, 2022-08-26.

Research Group *Pandemic Fictions* (2020) "From Pandemic to Corona Fictions: Narratives in Times of Crises", *PhiN-Beiheft* 24, 321-344, http://web.fu-berlin.de/phin/beiheft24/b24t21.pdf, 2022-08-26.

Rickard, Robert (2021) "Camus's *The Plague*: A Guidebook for Covid-19?", *RSA*, 2021-08-04, https://www.thersa.org/comment/2021/08/camuss-the-plague, 2022-08-26.

Rose, Jacqueline (2020) "Pointing the Finger: Jacqueline Rose on *The Plague*", *London Review of Books* 42/9, 2020-05-07, https://www.lrb.co.uk/the-paper/v42/n09/jacqueline-rose/pointing-the-finger, 2022-08-26.

Scrivner, Coltan/Johnson, John A./Kjeldgaard-Christiansen, Jens/Clasen, Mathias (2021) "Pandemic Practice: Horror Fans and Morbidly Curious Individuals Are More Psychologically Resilient during the COVID-19 Pandemic", *Personality and Individual Differences* 168, s.p. DOI: 10.1016/j.paid.2020.110397.

Serrell, Mathilde (2020) "Journaux de confinement, la lutte des classes", *France Culture*, 2020-03-20, https://www.franceculture.fr/litterature/latheorie-jour naux-de-confinement-la-lutte-des-classes, 2022-08-26.

Soderbergh, Steven (dir.) (2011) *Contagion*, USA/UAE, Warner Bros./Participant Media/Imagenation Abu Dhabi/Double Feature Films/Regency Enterprises.

Stemberger, Martina (2021) *Corona im Kontext. Zur Literaturgeschichte der Pandemie*, Tübingen, Narr Francke Attempto.

Sugy, Paul (2020) "Pourquoi nous relisons *La Peste* de Camus", *FigaroVox*, 2020-03-17, https://www.lefigaro.fr/vox/culture/pourquoi-nous-relisons-la-peste-de-camus-20200317, 2022-08-26.

Tolstov, Vladislav (2020) "Avtor romana o koronaviruse Inga Kuznecova: 'Pandemija ne izmenila moego čuvstva skorotečnosti žizni'", *Peterburgskij dnevnik*, 2020-11-09, https://spbdnevnik.ru/news/2020-11-09/avtor-romana-o-koro naviruse-inga-kuznetsova-pandemiya-ne-izmenila-moego-chuvstva-skorotech nosti-zhizni, 2022-08-26.

Veen, Evelien van (2020) "Wim Daniëls: 'Ik schrijf voor mijn moeder, ook al is ze al lang dood'", *De Volkskrant*, 2020-05-14, https://www.volkskrant.nl/ mensen/wim-daniels-ik-schrijf-voor-mijn-moeder-ook-al-is-ze-al-lang-dood~ bea56633, 2022-08-26.

Vincent, Alice (2020) "Will We Ever Be Ready for the Covid-19 Novel?", *Penguin*, 2020-07-06, https://www.penguin.co.uk/articles/2020/july/covid-fiction-pandemic-corona-literature.html, 2022-08-26.

Wright, Lawrence (2020b) "Lawrence Wright's New Pandemic Novel Wasn't Supposed to Be Prophetic", *The New York Times*, 2020-03-12, https://www. nytimes.com/2020/03/12/books/review/lawrence-wright-end-of-october-pan demic-novel-essay.html, 2022-08-26.

Yu, Charles (2020) "The Pre-pandemic Universe Was the Fiction", *The Atlantic*, 2020-04-15, https://www.theatlantic.com/culture/archive/2020/04/charles-yu-science-fiction-reality-life-pandemic/609985, 2022-08-26.

Zampieri, Chiara (2020) "*La pelle* di Curzio Malaparte (1949)", *Coronameron. A Diary of the Covid Year*, 2020-05-19, https://www.arts.kuleuven.be/literatuur wetenschap/coronameron/la-peste/lapelledicurziomalaparte, 2022-08-26.

Hysterical Men and Reasoning Women? On Gender Roles and Agency in Corona Fictions[1]

Elisabeth Hobisch (Graz University of Technology)

Abstract
In human beings, a common reaction to an external threat, crisis or death is fear. Although fear is a primary feeling of human beings, its expression and handling are well defined by cultural norms according to social categories such as gender. Albeit the analysis of social sciences showing that at the beginning of the Covid-19 pandemic women were more affected by anxiety and fear (cf. Singer et al. 2021, 64f.), many cultural productions classified as Corona Fictions (cf. Research Group *Pandemic Fictions* 2020, 322f.) feature male protagonists reacting in a hysterical way to the situation. How are these fictitious hysterical men represented? How do male protagonists deal with their anxiety? In which ways do they (re-)gain agency in this extraordinary situation? How do these hysterical men challenge the social norms of masculinity?

INTRODUCTION

In human beings, a common reaction to an external threat, crisis or death is fear. Although fear is a primary feeling of human beings,[2] its expression and handling

---

1   This research was funded by the Austrian Science Fund (FWF): P 34571-G; Project team: Elisabeth Hobisch, Julia Obermayr and Yvonne Völkl.

2   According to Robert Plutchik (1980, 14-16), contrary to the popular understanding of fear as an emotion, it is one of the primary feelings in human beings and animals and,

are well defined by cultural norms, therefore varying considerably according to the cultural context.

The Covid-19 pandemic – from the perspective of the global north representing a crisis of an unexpected or extraordinary scale in the 21st century – struck most people unprepared and suddenly confronted many with their own vulnerability and mortality (cf. Pérez Tapias 2022). In combination with the political reactions to it, including drastic measures to mitigate or contain the spread of the virus, this caused a sudden rise in anxiety and the feeling of insecurity (cf. Singer et al. 2021, 60-71). Albeit the analysis of social sciences showed that women were more affected by anxiety and fear at the beginning of the Covid-19 pandemic (cf. ibid., 64f.) (or alternatively they may have been more likely to admit these feelings), many cultural productions classified as Corona Fictions (cf. Research Group *Pandemic Fictions* 2020, 322f.) feature male protagonists reacting in a hysterical way to the situation. How are these fictitious hysterical men represented? How do male protagonists deal with their anxiety? In which ways do they (re-)gain agency in this extraordinary situation? How do these hysterical men reactivate or challenge the social norms of masculinity?

After outlining the relation between gender, social norms and the contemporary importance of hysteria, this article will elaborate briefly on the concepts of agency and anxiety in Corona Fictions. Based on this conceptual frame, three representations of hysterical men in Corona Fictions will be described with a literary, media and gender studies perspective.

GENDER, SOCIAL NORMS AND HYSTERIA

The binary, complementary and hierarchical understanding of gender has been common ground in Western societies since the 18th century. From the naturalist argumentation of an organic difference between women and men (cf. Laqueur 1990) the theory of their different characters, strengths and weaknesses according to biological gender affiliation was developed (cf. Hausen 1976; Honegger 2011, 104f.; Gronemann 2013, 43). The social norms resulting from this view of human beings determined binary gender roles, clearly defining gender-specific possibilities and obligations within a society (cf. Honegger 2011, 104). From the start, the emotions were an essential part of this binary, complementary and hierarchical gender model and its systematic. Due to the presumed dominance of emotions in

as a response to a cognition process, an essential part of his conceptualization of emotions in a broader scientific context.

their character, women were considered less capable of reasoning (cf. Micale 2008, 102; Zehetner 2012, 150); from this 'fact' many restrictions for female education, professional perspectives and self-determination were deduced (cf. Honegger 2011, 102-105). Of course, the discourse disseminating the binary gender model also influenced the understanding of virtues and vices and established clear rules for socially acceptable behaviour for men and women (cf. Gronemann 2013; Völkl 2022). For example, men were ridiculed when expressing fear and women admonished for any excessive emotional expression (cf. Völkl 2022, 299f. and 313). Consequently, the socially accepted ways of expressing emotions, such as fear, vary according to gender and are strongly determined by social norms of behaviour also in the world today.

In a similar way, social norms in combination with the medical discourse and the current scientific view of the human body define the border between legitimate forms of expression or behaviour and pathologies, especially in psychiatry (cf. Zehetner 2012, 148f.). For the feminist literary and cultural studies of recent decades, hysteria is a prime example of the disadvantages suffered by women in a society shaped by the binary, complementary and hierarchical understanding of gender.[3] The male scientific medical discourse defines what is normal and sane and also what is to be considered as a disorder. At the same time, men examine and analyze women judging if the symptoms indicate a certain disease,[4] often without being conscious of their gendered view of their patients. In order to have their complaints legitimized as a socially acknowledged disease,[5] women have to consult doctors who a are mainly men, educated with a deeply rooted medical male gaze, who are to examine, describe and interpret their symptoms. At the same time, due to the societal frame and the restrictions in higher education over a long time, it was impossible for women to get access to the scientific elite (cf. Micale 2008, 100f.), which would have theoretically enabled them to enrich the medical discourse on women with a genuinely female perspective (cf. Zehetner 2012, 150).

---

3   Cf. for example Shorter 1994; Showalter 1997, 52-54; Micale 2008; Zehetner 2012.

4   In this case I chose to only refer to male doctors and female patients, because during the main epoque of medical interest in hysteria, the 19th and early 20th century, it was impossible for women to become doctors, but the main portion of patients being diagnosed with hysteria were female (cf. Showalter 1997, 33; Micale 2008, 5f.).

5   It is important to underline that 'disease' means a culturally constructed and medically classified combination of symptoms, which is socially legitimized and entails a diagnosis as well as a therapy, whereas the term 'illness' refers to the personal experience of suffering (cf. Theriot 1993, 3; Zehetner 2012, 119).

With regard to hysteria, numerous feminist analyses and critical studies have shown that since antiquity it stands out as a disease that was diagnosed by male doctors in female patients.[6] Although downplaying the social inequalities and the lack of possibilities for women to develop personal interests and have a fulfilling life this diagnosis gave the female patients a form of expressing – in a socially accepted way, in the form of a disease – their suffering within this unequal society (cf. Zehetner 2012, 148f.). Therefore, as soon as a suffering patient receives a diagnosis and is able to denominate his/her 'illness' as a recognized 'disease', the indefinite suffering is also converted into a socially accepted form of expression of the body or the mind, which equals some sort of agency.[7] Hence, due to the inequality of power in this hierarchical system, the risk of a creation of diseases by iatrogenesis[8] and of a simple silencing of women, who are unable or unwilling to act according to their social role, by pathologizing their behaviour as (mental) diseases is not to be underestimated (cf. Showalter 1997, 8; Zehetner 2012, 153).

All these circumstances lead to the definition of hysteria as an exclusively female disease, which turned out to be very persistent and was a valid diagnosis for women patients over a long period of time.[9] For centuries, it was also understood,

---

6 Cf. Porter 1993; Micale 2008, 5f.; Shorter 1994.

7 As Showalter (1997, 50f.) shows, frequently the aim of hysteria treatments in women involved a reduction of their agency even more, for example with the "Weir Mitchel rest cure" prohibiting mental activities, reading and social life in combination with bed rest and a high-fat diet.

8 Meaning induced by the doctor, the medical system or a medical treatment (cf. Zehetner 2012, 119). As the frequently mentioned example of the mutual influence of Jean-Martin Charcot and "his" hysterics at the end of 19th century teaches us, the iatrogenous creation of diseases can also be to a certain degree beneficial for both parties. As mentioned above, on the one hand, it can provide the patients with a legitimization for their suffering. On the other hand, the doctor Charcot funded his medical celebrity on his "observations" and some of the hysterical women in the hospital Salpetière, originally of the working-class, became as famous as actresses at the time. In the historical context, of course, the benefit is much more considerable for the (male) doctor than for the (female) patients (cf. Showalter 1997, 34f.; Zehetner 2012, 132f. and 154).

9 In his study on hysterical men, Mark S. Micale (2008, 6) draws the attention to the predilection of men to analyze women: "Since ancient times, physicians, philosophers, and natural scientists closely observed and extravagantly theorized female weakness, emotionality, and madness. What this long procession of male experts signally failed to see, to acknowledge, and to ponder was the existence of masculine nervous and mental illness among all social classes and in diverse guises".

that if men were diagnosed as hysterical, their manhood was directly put into question (cf. Micale 2008, 278; Zehetner 2012, 151 note 13). Hence, doctors used to diagnose men as affected by nervous disorders instead – and even when they showed clear symptoms of hysteria – diagnosing them with diseases such as the railway spine syndrome, neurasthenia or shell shock, according to the current medical fashion of their time.[10]

Elaine Showalter proves by her historical analysis that hysteria is not an anachronical phenomenon of the past.[11] The symptoms vary according to the socio-cultural context and historical period, but up until the 20th century people developed – from an organic-medical perspective inexplicable – symptoms associated with hysteria, due to stress and the overburdening by society or their life circumstances. The variety of historically modified male counterparts of hysteria, as well as the different forms hysteria takes, according to Showalter (1997), in the 20th century, clearly indicate the relevance of psychosomatic disorders through until today (cf. Zehetner 2012, 122-128). Whereas in psychoanalysis individual traumata and life circumstances are frequently considered to be responsible for the development of hysteria (ibid., 157), phenomena like the shell shock or Gulf War Syndrome show that potentially traumatizing collective experiences are also likely to provoke psychosomatic symptoms (cf. Showalter 1997, 75f.) – in precisely the same way as the Covid-19 pandemic we are experiencing right now.

AGENCY AND ANXIETY

Gender roles and the social norms related to them define the society members' frames of agency, according to their status, age, gender, race, etc. In the sense of the "viral (re)actions" referred to in the title of this volume, I understand agency as a multidimensional concept, on a diegetic and a meta-diegetic level. First, on the diegetic level, agency is a narratological feature, that enables the development of a fictional plot and, therefore, the definition of a character within a fictional creation as the protagonist. Only if a character or abstract concept drives the plot forward and enables the emotional identification of the public,[12] it can be

---

10 Cf. for example Showalter 1997, 62-77 or Zehetner 2012, 151.

11 Showalter (1997,115-207) analyzes for example the Chronique Fatigue Syndrome, Recovered Memory and Satanic Ritual Abuse as some types of hysterical epidemics.

12 As Eder (2008, 507) points out, the perspective in film is closely linked to the emotional engagement of the audience. He emphasizes, nevertheless, that emotional engagement

considered a protagonist.[13] Secondly, on a meta-diegetic level, the reactions of creators and public to the psychological strains caused by the outbreak of the Covid-19 pandemic – and the drastic measures taken by political authorities to confront it – are to be understood as another type of agency. Although they are fictional narratives, the creation and consumption of pandemic and Corona Fictions alike proved to be beneficial for the personal resilience of creators and consumers in real life (cf. Völkl 2023). The third type of agency constitutes a link between the diegetic and meta-diegetic level of agency, as it focusses on the potential of the fictional representation of strategies and decisions to deal with the pandemic for the audience. According to Ette (2016, 5), for the public the knowledge represented in the fictional realm is accessible as experiential knowledge. Hence, the agency appearing in Corona Fictions on a diegetic level – for the personal and the social realm – contributes to broaden the consumers' perspective on their own agency on an extra-diegetic level. For this contribution, the term agency mainly refers to the third understanding of agency as a transferable knowledge from diegesis to "real life".

According to the established gender role of heterosexual men, they should always be tough and reasonable, refraining from emotional self-expression (cf. Micale 2008, 54f.); but how could they fulfil this role in the middle of a global pandemic? Anxiety is a basic human reaction to this extraordinary situation, but, whereas women have learned possibilities of expressing their anxiety in socially acceptable ways, there are neither role models nor patterns of agency for men. Classic male virtues such as physical strength and activity (cf. Honegger 2011, 104) do not help against an invisible virus, which is transmitted via aerosols. As a consequence of this outbreak, many people have been forced to stay at home losing not only their social life, but also their economic subsistence (cf. Singer et al. 2021, 62f. and 90), a very stressful experience. Hence, the frames imposed on men by social norms not only lack patterns of agency to confront the threat of the pandemic, neither do they provide agency for handling the overwhelming anxiety. Because of this tension, men become hysterical. I understand hysteria in the

---

does not necessarily mean sympathy with the character, but that this can also refer to antipathy or a lack of feelings.

13 According to the understanding of the Corona Fictions as a transmedia genre characterized by meta-narratives (cf. Research Group *Pandemic Fictions* 2020), it is also legitimate to understand an abstract concept or recurring stereotypical figure identified as important in several independent Corona Fictions as a protagonist in the sense of a main character in the whole genre decisive for the transmedia storytelling (Jenkins 2007) of Corona Fictions.

context of the Covid-19 pandemic, in the way Showalter (1997, 9) defined it "as a cultural symptom of anxiety and stress. The conflicts that produce hysterical symptoms are genuine and universal [...]". Consequently, the hysterical men in Corona Fictions do not show hysteria according to one specific medical definition. Nevertheless, keeping in mind the variety of symptoms attributed to hysteria in the course of its history (cf. Micale 2008, xiv) and the fact that the term also has a popular understanding, it seems appropriate to use it. Furthermore, many of the social mechanisms enabling the development of this specific disease and its understanding are still present in the society of 21st century and, as will be shown, drastically limit the possibilities of agency for pandemic protagonists.

In the following, we will see that the three protagonists analyzed in this article develop their own ways of dealing with their hysteria and, therefore, choose different ways of regaining agency. These three examples of hysterical men are drawn from two hispanophone (both from Spain) and one francophone (a French Belgian co-production) cultural production in different media and different genres: Roberto Domínguez Moro's (2020) novel *El confinado. Un thriller que supera la ficción*, Jaime Rodríguez Z.'s (2020) first-person account "El miedo en tiempos del coronavirus. Crónica sin aire desde un hospital en Madrid", and Dany Boon's (2021) feature film *8 Rue de l'Humanité*, also broadcast under the English title *Stuck Together*.[14]

AGENCY BY STRICTLY FOLLOWING THE RULES

The first example of hysterical men is Martin, one protagonist of the French Netflix original Corona Fictions comedy *8 Rue de l'Humanité* (2021) by Dany Boon.[15] The plot is about a residential building in Paris situated in number 8 Humanity Street, where at the beginning of the first lockdown in France the neighbours, who represent a wealth of very different people, find themselves caught with one

---

14 The choice of these three Corona Fictions as the corpus for this contribution is mainly due to the prominent role the male hysterics take in the respective plots. The decision to consider different media and different genres is, on the one hand, due to the frequent presence of the hysterical man in Corona Fictions across different media and, on the other, to the interdisciplinary nature of the research project on Corona Fictions (cf. Völkl 2021-2023).

15 For a detailed analysis of this film, see the contribution of Julia Obermayr in this volume; for its representation of social cohesion and resilience in film, see Obermayr/Völkl 2022.

another in the limited space of their apartment building and as the official title of the English version indicates, they are *Stuck together*. Due to this exceptional situation, the protagonists, who did not know each other previously, must negotiate and organize their cohabitation. Martin is a family father who takes the threat of the pandemic very seriously and, out of the fear of contagion, begins to meticulously follow all hygiene and behavioural rules, tyrannizing his family and neighbours by establishing ridiculous health protection measures within the building.[16]

He obliges his wife Claire and daughter Louna to disinfect themselves after returning to the living room from the daily clapping for the healthcare workers on the balcony (cf. Boon 2021 [00:02:48-00:03:25 min.]). When Martin has to walk the dog, he puts on cleaning gloves, a jumpsuit and a diving mask, closes all gaps with scotch tape and then faints because of the lack of oxygen, before he can even get out of the house (cf. Boon 2021 [00:39:14-00:40:18 min.]). Due to his excessive anxiety, he spreads distrust and fear in his family and throughout the building. For example, when his wife Claire tries to calm their daughter's fears of falling ill and dying, he undermines her attempts by arguing: "Ça commence par un petit rhume, une grippette. Puis après, ça descend sur les poumons, ça t'attrape, ça te serre, tu peux plus respirer. Et tu meurs étouffé [sic]!" (Boon 2021 [00:04:23-00:04:39 min.]).[17]

He judges others because of their careless acts and denounces their supposed infraction of rules. For example, Martin and other residents of the building consider Leila, a doctor who leaves the building daily at unusual times, as an offender and call the police. When, one evening, the officers arrive at the building, it turns out that Leila is a doctor working at the local hospital in a Covid unit. To minimize the risk of spreading the virus, she has tried to keep her distance and avoided the contact with her family and neighbours (cf. Boon 2021 [01:33:40-01:34:51 min.]).

In general film descriptions, the protagonist Martin is often denominated as a 'hypochondriac', but his attitude is, in fact, more than that. He is not only perceiving symptoms in himself and attributing them to a specific disease, but he is more generally afraid of contagion and distrusts his family and neighbours. Although the *Diagnostic and Statistical Manual of Mental Disorders* (DSM-5) redefined the

---

16 As an example, he pours vinegar onto his doormat to avoid the virus from entering his apartment on the shoes of family members. The smell of the vinegar is annoying for his neighbours, but he reacts very impolitely to their complaints (cf. Boon 2021 [00:21:48-00:21:59 min.]).

17 "It starts with a cold. A light flue, then it gets in[to] the lungs, and it clings to you. It squeezes you and you can't breathe anymore. And you suffocate to death!" (English translation according to *Stuck Together*).

disease 'hypochondriasis' as two different diseases a decade ago, namely 'somatic symptom disorder' and 'illness anxiety disorder', the term 'hypochondria' is still widely used in everyday language. The new definition of illness anxiety disorder[18] fits very well to Martin's behaviour, but due to this disorder being a somatic disorder, it is nevertheless appropriate to interpret Martin as a man becoming hysterical because of a 'pandemic shock'.[19]

In the film, Martin is afraid, causes conflicts and disruption and behaves in an unconventional way, but he does not really verbalize his fear. He attracts the attention of his fictitious cohabitants as well as of the audience only by means of his behaviour.

Although Martin is suffering in his situation, is struggling, afraid and frustrated, the audience cannot sympathize with, but laughs at him instead. In this comedy's constellation of protagonists, Martin has the role of the comic relief. He experiences several slapstick-like situations[20] and seems to be ridiculously overreacting; especially in contrast with his wife Claire, who works as a lawyer and is struggling to keep up with the household duties, her daughter's distance learning and her work life (via video conferences). She represents a very calm, reasoning and practical attitude towards the pandemic, therefore reinforcing the comic and ridiculous impression her husband Martin gives to the audience. With this reasonable behaviour – according to conventional gender roles unusual for a woman –

---

18 According to one of the doctors involved in the redefinition process, "[p]atients with illness anxiety disorder may or may not have a medical condition but have heightened bodily sensations, are intensely anxious about the possibility of an undiagnosed illness, or devote excessive time and energy to health concerns, often obsessively researching them. [...] Illness anxiety disorder can cause considerable distress and life disruption, even at moderate levels" (N.N. 2013).

19 The term "shock pandémico [pandemic shock]" to designate the unexpected confrontation of inhabitants of the global north with their vulnerability and mortality in the Covid-19 pandemic was coined by Pérez Tapias (2022, 24).

20 For example, when walking the dog, he wears the diving mask and gloves, loses the dog and, when he is controlled by the police, refuses to take of his diving mask to be identified with his documentation. After some discussion he agrees to take off the mask, but first, wants to control the policemen's body temperature and takes out his digital thermometer. The policemen confusing it with a taser, wrestle Martin down and hold him on the floor (cf. Boon 2021 [00:41:47-00:43:38 min.]).

her character highlights the fact that Martin's behaviour and the way he expresses his anxiety are not acceptable for a man, but are ridiculous.[21]

Becoming hysterical is for Martin one way of reacting to the feeling of loss of control caused by the pandemic. Trying to thoroughly avoid contagion and following meticulously official rules, are his ways of retaining control and regaining agency in the middle of the pandemic fear. At the end of the film, the character suffers a case of poetic justice, as he becomes the victim of the mad professor Gabriel, who tests his experimental vaccines on the inhabitants of the building. Martin can luckily escape from the professor's experiments and when he becomes conscious of the risk, he is cured of his hysteria and returns to a "normal" social interaction with his cohabitants.

Martin shows the audience one possible reaction to the pandemic outbreak. At the same time, the film's dramaturgy advises the public that this is not a suitable, socially accepted way for a man to react to such a stressful situation; meaning that instead of challenging the social gender roles, this hysterical man is contributing to a reaffirmation of them.

AGENCY BY AN OUTBURST OF VIOLENCE

The Corona Fictions novel *El confinado. Un thriller que supera la ficción*[22] (2020) was published within the first months of the pandemic by the Spanish author Roberto Domínguez Moro and, as many other textual productions at that time (cf. Stemberger 2021, 11f.), appeared as a freely accessible online-book.[23] The novel is designed as a diary, has 22 chapters, of which only some have titles indicating the date. 19 of the chapters are narrated by the protagonist Juan himself over nine days and the chapters 20-22 at the end of the novel contain excerpts of a police report and interviews with Ana, Juan's ex-girlfriend, and Pilar, Juan's sister.

Once again, an apartment building is the stage in which this plot is set. By contrast to *8 Rue de l'Humanité*, however, the apartments in this residential

---

21 Claire even literally expresses the attitude the audience should take towards Martin's behaviour, when she says he exaggerates (Boon 2021 [00:04:15-00:04:20 min.]) and calls him dumb (Boon 2021 [00:40:17-00:40:21 min.]).

22 "The Inmate. A Thriller That Surpasses Fiction" (author's translation).

23 The book is structured by chapters but has no page indications. References to the text are thus by chapter, but not by page numbers.

building in Madrid are nearly all empty.[24] The protagonist Juan, a thirty-something man living alone, describes the first days of the first lockdown in Spain. In long sections of the novel, the perspective of Juan alone is provided in the form of a first-person narrative. The conceptual design of the novel plays with this limited perspective of the diary, as the protagonist with whom the readers have soon developed sympathy, gradually turns out to be an unreliable narrator.

On the one hand, as a reader one identifies with Juan and his daily worries.[25] On the other hand, it is noticeable that he engages very intensively in certain behaviours. His extreme cleanliness is remarkable and narratologically emphasized by the perspective of other fictional characters. More precisely, Juan remembers that in the past his mother was proud of her exemplary son and Ana called him a "maniático de la limpieza" (Domínguez Moro 2020, ch. 6).[26] Since the outbreak of the pandemic, he uses to wash his hands compulsively, even if he has not left the house[27] and tracks the published numbers of coronavirus cases very closely.[28] Additionally, he keeps a close eye on his body temperature and excrements, even protocolling them (cf. Domínguez Moro 2020, ch. 6). Juan's accuracy stands out, but in the exceptional situation of the pandemic, for the reader his anxiety and strange behaviour initially seem understandable.

When the lockdown is declared in Spain, only an elderly couple of foreign tourists lives in the building in addition to Juan and his neighbour Julia. At the beginning of the novel, Juan meets the couple at the building entrance, assumes

---

24 As it is explained in the text, most of the flats in the building are normally let to tourists, who only stay for some days or weeks, which is why they are nearly all empty during the pandemic and there is no relationship between the neighbours (cf. Domínguez Moro 2020, ch. 1).

25 In middle of a pandemic, it seems understandable to try to get out of the house by going for a walk with a pretext (cf. Domínguez Moro 2020, ch. 13), to initiate contact with his attractive neighbour via the balcony (cf. Domínguez Moro 2020, ch. 16) and to have the typical online conversations with the worried family (cf. Domínguez Moro 2020, ch. 8, ch. 15, and ch. 17).

26 "Cleaning maniac" (author's translation).

27 The intense hand washing rituals Juan describes indicate that there is a gradual development taking place in his personality. Whereas in chapter 2 he follows the instruction popularized at the beginning of the pandemic, to wash hands during the time it takes to sing "Happy Birthday" twice, in chapter 3 he already decides to sing it three times, just to be sure.

28 During the pandemic, the term 'doomscrolling' gained popularity referring to an excessive media consumption of negative news concerning the pandemic (cf. N.N. 2022).

that they are Italian and slowly develops an obsession about them. Juan is torn between worrying for their health and wanting to help them (cf. Domínguez Moro 2020, ch. 11) and fear of these Italians as "importers" of the virus to Spain as the first confirmed European cases of Covid-19 were detected in Italy. Juan makes several attempts to establish contact with the elderly couple next door, always cautiously keeping his physical distance. First, he tries to talk to them directly, but by covering himself with improvised protective equipment, he ends up frightening them away.

> He construido el mejor equipo aislante que he podido. Unos pantalones de chándal que me quedan un poco ajustados, unos calcetines altos por fuera, para que la goma sujete bien. Las zapatillas de andar por casa, enrolladas en film transparente, que no toquen el suelo. En la parte de arriba, una camiseta de manga larga que voy a echar a lavar a noventa grados en cuanto termine, una de las mascarillas que conseguí en la farmacia, unas gafas de sol que pienso desinfectar después y unos guantes desechables sobre otros guantes de hace tres o cuatro inviernos sujetos con cinta de embalar alrededor de las muñecas.[29] (Domínguez Moro 2020, ch. 6)

The way Juan meticulously covers his body with several layers of protective clothes in this scene, is strongly reminiscent of the many graphic representations of hysterical men in audio-visual Corona Fictions, covering themselves with improvised protective devices, such as cleaning gloves, jackets and diving masks.[30] Additionally, Juan is closely monitoring the sounds he can perceive from the flat next door, with special attention to cough as a symptom of the coronavirus (cf. Domínguez Moro 2020, ch. 3). After some days, Juan realizes that there is no life sign of the elderly couple next door anymore and, after trying one last time to contact them together with his neighbour Julia (cf. ibid., ch. 16), does not mention them anymore.

---

29 "I've built the best insulating equipment I could. Tracksuit bottoms that are a snug fit, high socks on the outside, so that the rubber holds well. The slippers, rolled up in cling film, so they don't touch the ground. On top, a long-sleeved T-shirt that I'm going to wash at ninety degrees as soon as I finish, one of the masks I got at the pharmacy, some sunglasses that I'm going to disinfect later and some disposable gloves over other gloves from three or four winters ago, fastened with packing tape around my wrists" (author's translation).

30 Cf. for example Boon 2021 [00:39:14-00:40:18 min.], Villanuevamente 2020, 1x03 [00:00:29-00:00:53 min.], and mathieucyr 2020 [00:00:36-00:00:38 and 00:00:46-00:00:58 min.].

Simultaneously, he is engaging step by step in some sort of romance with Julia. They have previously lived next to each other for years without ever having really noticed one another or knowing each other's names, but in the middle of the pandemic they share their isolation. One evening, when Juan invites Julia for dinner, she tells him how much she misses human contact and starts kissing him; Juan at that moment thinks of contagion and the saliva drops as a source of infection, but he overcomes his fear and sleeps with her:

> Se ríe, y con su sonrisa se me olvidan el virus, el confinamiento, las medidas de seguridad y hasta mi nombre completo. Me besa, nos besamos. El beso tiene algo de torpe, de primera vez y también algo de prohibido. No deberíamos tocarnos tanto. La principal vía de contagio son las gotas de saliva de alguien infectado. Ya no digo el torrente que nos intercambiamos Julia y yo en cada beso con lengua.[31] (Domínguez Moro 2020, ch. 17)

As a reader, one feels Juan sliding more and more into hysteria and paranoia. Since this is a gradual development described from Juan's perspective, it is very difficult to draw a line between what could be considered normal behaviour, corresponding to social norms, and from which point on, it is to be considered hysterical. In some moments, identification dominates, in others, the alienating effect does. This fuels the uncertainty and adds to the suspense of this Corona Fictions novel.

Nevertheless, the reader's perception and judgement of the protagonist are also influenced by the comments of Juan's ex-girlfriend and his mother on his cleanliness, which Juan remembers throughout his account. Moreover, Juan's hysterical perspective of the pandemic is also contrasted with Julia's calm and pragmatic perception of the situation, when she, for example, explicitly calls him "paranoid".[32]

---

31 "She laughs, and with her smile I forget the virus, the confinement, the security measures and even my full name. She kisses me, we kiss. There's something awkward about the kiss, something strange, something first time, and also something forbidden. We shouldn't touch each other so much. The main way of contagion is the saliva droplets of someone infected. Not to mention the torrent that Julia and I exchange in every tongue kiss" (author's translation).

32 When calling at the neighbours' door to ask if they need help, due to his fear of contagion, Juan keeps Julia from simply touching the doorbell. Then she comments on his behaviour saying: "Vamos, no seas paranoico. [Come on, don't be paranoid]" (Domínguez Moro 2020, ch. 16; author's translation).

At the end of the novel, the readers learn that the unease Juan's behaviour provokes during the reading is justified. In the final chapters composed by police interviews and reports, it turns out that after their passionate night together, Juan drugged Julia and locked her without cell phone, internet or key in his flat. Additionally, the police report reveals that he is the stalker of his ex-girlfriend Ana and brutally killed his elderly neighbour – leaving his wife in shock, of which the elderly lady also died– and he also killed Julia's dog disposing of the bodies partly in his freezer, partly in dustbins in the neighbourhood. The readers also find out that Juan suffered from some undefined mental problems in the past, which were intensified by the pandemic and the lockdown.

Juan shows similar behavioural traits to those of Martin: He tries to seek information in the media, to follow the rules and to survey his body functions, but this agency, as Martin applies it, is not enough for him. His hysteria rises to the extreme in which he takes drastic actions and becomes a killer. The protagonist Juan reproduces the established gender roles in a very negative way and, when lacking alternative patterns of agency, relies on physical violence. This narrative results in a very interesting and intriguing novel, but in fact it is a warning example and presents the worst way in which men deal with tension and fear – the harming of others.[33]

AGENCY BY TRANSFERRING EMOTIONS

The narrative "El miedo en tiempos del coronavirus. Crónica sin aire desde un hospital en Madrid"[34] by Jaime Rodríguez Z. is a first-person account of a man falling ill during the pandemic and waiting in a hospital's hall until being treated.[35] The narrative is told retrospectively and achronologically – jumping repeatedly

---

33 As the UN Women report shows, the lockdowns as a result of the pandemic around the world caused a rise in domestic violence against girls and women: "Widespread stay-at-home orders to curb the spread of COVID-19 potentially locked women down with their abusers, creating dangerous conditions for violence against women, often with tragic consequences. [...] UN Women research has found that violence against women and girls has intensified since the outbreak of COVID-19" (UN Women 2021, 3).

34 "Fear in Times of Coronavirus. Chronicle without Air from a Hospital in Madrid" (author's translation).

35 As this narrative is not structured by chapters or page numbers, the citations will refer to the specific parts of the text using the paragraphs of the online version of the text (indicated by 'par.').

between past and present events. As the title indicates, it has the form of a chronicle, but also shows characteristics of an internal monologue. Moreover, it remains unclear whether it is an autobiographical or autofictional narrative. This narrative about a hysterical man was published in March 2020 in the online magazine *VICE* and it thus constitutes an example at the margins of the Corona Fictions' definition, in terms of its degree of fictionalization. Nevertheless, I decided to include it in the corpus of Corona Fictions and in this analysis, because it has a clear literary concern, it is one of the rare cases of narratives in Corona Fictions about a person actually falling ill[36] and it reflects the conflict of male social gender roles and personal feelings in an extraordinarily concise way.

At the beginning of the Covid-19 pandemic in Spain, the narrator, a man apparently originally from Peru and living in Madrid falls ill. After some days at home with fever, coughing and pain in the limbs, he begins to have difficulties breathing and his family decides to call an ambulance. He is taken to the hall of a hospital in Madrid, where he has to spend 32 hours waiting for treatment. It turns out that he has Covid-19 and has also developed pneumonia. During the waiting time already, he reflects on his own behaviour and on how the mechanisms of social gender roles and images of masculinity influence the way in which he deals with his own illness.

Although the protagonist is theoretically aware of how the social gender roles represented in media[37] influence the behaviour and the image men create of themselves and others,[38] he cannot avoid reactivating these patterns of agency in his extreme situation. During his internal monologue, he keeps assuring himself that he is not afraid, but also repeatedly verbalizes his inner conflict. "Tengo cuarenta y seis años y la sensación es extenuante. El dolor intenso. La falta de sueño

36 Unlike the narratives classified as pandemic fictions, in the Corona Fictions we have analyzed until now, the development of the disease, the sick body and the symptoms of illness have had only very little presence (cf. Hobisch et al. 2022, 206).

37 He mentions for example Achilles and Tyler Durden as examples forming the social idea of masculinity and the character played by John Hurt in Michael Radford's film *Nineteen Eighty-Four* (1984) as an outstanding example of a coward and traitor (cf. Rodríguez Z. 2020, par. 3 and 16).

38 He mentions that he was preparing a workshop on the construction of masculinity in literature (cf. Rodríguez Z. 2020, par. 3).

empieza a volverme loco. Me dispara la ansiedad. Pero no tengo miedo" (Rodríguez Z. 2020, par. 15).[39]

He feels extreme anxiety and is afraid of dying, but his hysteria makes him rely on a traditional pattern of male agency, which, in his case, is denying his fear and acting in an extremely altruist way by taking care of others. The protagonist, who remains unnamed, starts observing the other patients waiting in the hall, who are mainly seniors, and looks for someone who might be needing his help. In order to stimulate his own feeling of control and optimism, he thinks of all the elderly, fragile bodies surrounding him and of places with less possibilities of good quality public medical care, such as the United States or Peru (cf. Rodríguez Z. 2020, par. 7f.). He talks to his family (apparently two female family members) on the phone and lies to them, assuring them that he is fine, despite actually being anxious and feeling very ill. He finds he is unable to avoid acting in this way and is astonished by the power of the social gender roles: "¿Por qué soy capaz de mentir a las personas que quiero? ¿Qué hay en mi cerebro que es más fuerte que la confianza, que la lealtad, que la verdad?" (Rodríguez Z. 2020, par. 5).[40]

Of course, the internalized social gender roles, also apply to other patients and the judgement the protagonist impulsively makes of them. For example, he feels disgusted by a man who overtly expresses his hysteria and does not, as he himself does, cover this over with learned masculine agency.

> Entra un tío gigante en una silla empujada por una enfermera. Debe medir 1.90 y pesar 100 kilos. Llora y gime sin parar. Es la primera persona que veo llorar. No puedo evitarlo, no siento compasión alguna, sino un profundo rechazo por esta persona. Soy incapaz de experimentar lo que llamamos empatía. Ante su dolor, su padecimiento y su forma de expresarlo. Me repele. Me doy cuenta de que lo considero un traidor y un cobarde.[41] (Rodríguez Z. 2020, par. 11)

---

39 "I am forty-six years old and the feeling is exhausting. The pain is intense. The lack of sleep is starting to drive me crazy. It triggers my anxiety. But I am not afraid" (author's translation).

40 "Why am I capable of lying to the people I love? What is it in my brain that is stronger than trust, than loyalty, than truth?" (author's translation).

41 "In comes a giant guy in a wheelchair pushed by a nurse. He must be 1.90 m tall and weigh 100 kilos. He's crying and moaning non-stop. He is the first person I have seen crying here. I can't help it, I don't feel any compassion, but a deep rejection for this person. I am incapable of experiencing what we call empathy. Faced with his pain, his suffering and the way he expresses it. I am repulsed. I realize that I consider him a traitor and a coward" (author's translation).

After 32 hours in the hall, the protagonist is admitted to a hospital bed and a room where he is treated for his bilateral pneumonia. He shares his hospital room with another man, he finds to be in a worse physical condition than he is himself, which is why he feels entitled to take care of him and to assist him in his daily needs. So, again, instead of admitting his own suffering, weakness and fear, he transfers his caring to his roommate.

> Pongo en Jose todas las debilidades que no me permito. Estoy enfermo de la cabeza. Pienso en mi curso sobre la construcción de la masculinidad, pienso en Tyler Durden como la proyección de lo que el narrador quiere ser. Pelear así, follar así. Yo hago lo mismo, pero a la inversa. Soy los pulmones manchados de Jose. Soy la fiebre de Jose. Soy el miedo de Jose.[42] (Rodríguez Z. 2020, par. 17)

At the end of his narration, the protagonist is overwhelmed by all the emotions he had denied and covered up by traditional patterns of male agency. When he is recovered and comes back home, his suppressed anxiety results in the development of strong hysterical symptoms. He suffers of nightmares of suffocation and panic attacks, which induce further critical reflections on masculinity.[43]

Although he is not able to act alternatively in the middle of the traumatizing situation, this anonymous protagonist is the only hysterical man who is conscious of the power social gender roles have on his own behaviour. He admits that his social role determines and limits his frame of agency. He does not harm others by his way of dealing with anxiety, but, in the end, the supressed emotions cause hysterical symptoms, harming himself and his life quality. At least in a retrospective view, he is able to perceive and verbalize the tension between his feelings and

---

42 "I put on Jose all the weaknesses that I don't allow myself. I am sick in the head. I think of my course on the construction of masculinity, I think of Tyler Durden as the projection of what the narrator wants to be. Fight like this, fuck like this. I do the same, but in reverse. I am Jose's stained lungs. I am Jose's fever. I am Jose's fear" (author's translation).

43 The symptoms described by the protagonist clearly indicate what is currently called post traumatic stress disorder (PTSD) (cf. for example Ford 2009, 3, 12-18). Yet, Ford (2009, 14) refers to the historical relation of PTSD with diagnoses such as railway spine and war neurosis. These historical diagnoses were, in turn, frequently mentioned as male counterparts of hysteria (cf. for example Zehetner 2012, 151), and Showalter (1997, 75f.) explicitly describes PTSD as one of the forms of contemporary male hysteria, in the broad sense of the term, as psychosomatic symptoms provoked by stress and overburdening (cf. Showalter 1997, 9).

the gender role and to reflect critically on the need to learn alternatives (cf. Rodríguez Z. 2020, par. 5, 21).

CONCLUSION

In this final part, I would like to summarize the results concerning the questions of (1) the representation of hysterical men in Corona Fictions, (2) their dealing with anxiety issues, and (3) their attainment of agency. The remaining question, (4) how these hysterical men reactivate or challenge the social norms of masculinity, will be answered thereafter.

(1) The three hysterical men analyzed in this article are represented very differently, although their characterization shares some common traits. All three take up a lot of space in the respective Corona Fictions, but due to the medium, are also represented differently. The two textual narrations (first-person accounts) are dominated by the perspectives of the hysterical men themselves; even though Martin gets a lot of screen time in the film, he is not the only protagonist and the dominant narrative perspective is that of Basil, the son of the building owner.

The noteworthy common trait in their representation is that all three protagonists are characterized in contrast with a reasoning woman. Furthermore, comments by other fictional characters underline the fact that the protagonists' behaviour does not meet the social norms and guide the perception of the audience in this direction.

(2) When it comes to dealing with anxiety, Martin is perceived through his behaviour as frightened, ridiculous and an exaggerator. He seeks orientation by information and sticks to rules. Juan, who is also fearful and extremely accurate, embodies a development from anxiety to hysteria, hence, challenging the readers' judgement. The anonymous third protagonist canalizes his anxiety into a very altruist behaviour, transferring the emotions he does not want to confront to others, constantly verbalizing his conflict. Hence, these exemplary Corona Fictions make clear that, however they express it, in all protagonists the source of hysteria is the same: the tension of anxiety without socially acceptable agency to handle it.

(3) These men, however, have chosen different ways of dealing with their hysteria and regaining agency. Martin sticks to the rules, Juan kills and the anonymous third protagonist transfers his fears to others. Whereas he and Martin are able to critically reflect on their behaviour, Juan sticks to his view of the pandemic and is unable to question his acts, even if confronted with alterative perspectives.

(4) In the context of social gender roles, calling men hysterical still seems to be revolutionary in 21st century. Nevertheless, from a gender studies perspective,

the representation of hysterical men in Corona Fictions is not at all revolutionary, but extremely conventional. My initial expectation for this contribution was that the broad representation of male hysteria would challenge established gender roles, but this is not the case. The Corona Fictions analyzed in this article provide models for men of how NOT to deal with the pandemic, of how NOT to treat others and remind men of NOT showing anxiety. So, instead of providing alternative gender specific agency that could be transferred to the real life of the audience, all three Corona Fictions analyzed here – with the exception in the third example of at least reflecting on the need of alternatives – reproduce and reinforce the established social gender roles.

Moreover, from a historical point of view, it is remarkable that in these fictional representations all three men succeed in finding ways of agency. Their hysteria, exactly like the hysteria of countless female patients in history (cf. Showalter 1997), has its roots in the lack of agency provided by social norms to people due to their gender affiliation. But, whereas the diagnosis of hysteria in female patients during centuries reduced their agency even further or lead to being locked up in psychiatric clinics, all three hysterical men described in this article find a way of their own for dealing with their hysteria and, in the end, regain agency.

BIBLIOGRAPHY

Corpus Analyzed

Boon, Dany (dir.) (2021) *8 Rue de l'Humanité* [engl. *Stuck Together*], France, Netflix.

Domínguez Moro, Roberto (2020) *El confinado. Un thriller que supera la ficción*, Madrid, Maeva Ediciones.

mathieucyr (2020) "Le CoronaVirus – Mat Cyr & Jérémy Demay", https://youtu.be/6QhZqoA0DdU, 2023-01-03.

Rodríguez Z., Jaime (2020) "El miedo en tiempos del coronavirus. Crónica sin aire desde un hospital en Madrid", *VICE online*, 2020-03-29, https://www.vice.com/es/article/8843x5/el-miedo-en-tiempos-del-coronavirus, 2022-11-24.

Villanuevamente (2020) "El amor en los tiempos del corona 1x03 – El viaje a Senegal. [WebserieConfinados]", https://youtu.be/lUd3JPo4Cw0, 2022-11-23.

Works Cited

Eder, Jens (2008) *Die Figur im Film. Grundlagen der Figurenanalyse*, Marburg, Schüren Verlag.

Ette, Ottmar (2016) *TransArea: A Literary History of Globalization*, trans. by Mark W. Person, Berlin, De Gruyter. DOI: 10.1515/9783110480177.

Ford, Julian D. (2009) *Posttraumatic Stress Disorder. Scientific and Professional Dimensions*, Amsterdam, Elsevier.

Gronemann, Claudia (2013) *Polyphone Aufklärung. Zur Textualität und Performativität der spanischen Geschlechterdebatten im 18. Jahrhundert*, Frankfurt am Main, Vervuert. DOI: 10.31819/9783954872312.

Hausen, Karin (1976) "Die Polarisierung der Geschlechtercharaktere. Eine Spiegelung der Dissoziation von Erwerbs- und Familienleben", Werner Conze (ed.) *Sozialgeschichte der Familie in der Neuzeit Europas*, Stuttgart, Klett-Cotta, 363-393.

Hobisch, Elisabeth/Völkl, Yvonne/Obermayr, Julia (2022) "Narrar la pandemia. Una introducción a formas, temas y metanarrativas de las Corona Fictions", Ana Gallego Cuiñas/José Antonio Pérez Tapias (eds.) *Pensamiento, Pandemia y Big Data: El impacto sociocultural del coronavirus en el espacio iberoamericano*, Berlin, De Gruyter, 191-211. DOI: 10.1515/9783110693928-013.

Honegger, Claudia (2011) "Die kognitiven Prinzipien der neuen Wissenschaften vom Menschen und die Genese einer weiblichen Sonderanthropologie in Frankreich", Theresa Wobbe et al. (eds.) *Die gesellschaftliche Verortung des Geschlechts. Diskurse der Differenz in der deutschen und französischen Soziologie um 1900*, Frankfurt am Main, Campus, 93-113.

Jenkins, Henry (2007) "Transmedia Storytelling 101", *Pop Junctions: Reflections on Entertainment, Pop Culture, Activism, Media Literacy, Fandom and More*, 2007-03-21, http://henryjenkins.org/blog/2007/03/transmedia_storytelling_101.html, 2022-05-03.

Laqueur, Thomas (2003 [1990]) *Making Sex. Body and Gender from the Greeks to Freud*, Cambridge, Harvard University Press.

Micale, Mark S. (2008) *Hysterical Men: The Hidden History of Male Nervous Illness*, Cambridge, MA, and London, England, Harvard University Press. DOI: 10.4159/9780674040984.

N.N. (2013) "DSM-5 Redefines Hypochondriasis" *Mayo Clinic, Medical Professionals Psychiatry and Psychology*, 2013-11-15, https://www.mayoclinic.org/medical-professionals/psychiatry-psychology/news/dsm-5-redefines-hypochondriasis/mac-20429763, 2022-11-21.

N.N. (2022) "On 'Doomsurfing' and 'Doomscrolling'. Can You Think of a Better Way to Spend Your Time?", *Merriam Webster Dictionary*, https://www.merriam-webster.com/words-at-play/doomsurfing-doomscrolling-words-were-watching, 2022-11-30.

Obermayr, Julia/Völkl, Yvonne (2022) "Corona Fictions as Cultural Indicators of Social Cohesion and Resilience in the Wake of the Covid-19 Pandemic", *Momentum Quarterly* 11/2, 129-142. DOI: 10.15203/momentumquarterly.vol11.no1.p129-142.

Pérez Tapias, José Antonio (2022) "Finitud y vulnerabilidad. Humanos bajo *shock* pandémico", Ana Gallego Cuiñas/José Antonio Pérez Tapias (eds.) *Pensamiento, Pandemia y Big Data. El impacto sociocultural del coronavirus en el espacio iberoamericano*, Berlin, De Gruyter, 23-39. DOI: 10.1515/9783110693928-003.

Plutchik, Robert (1980) "A General Pychoevolutionary Theory of Emotion", Robert Plutchik/Henry Kellerman (eds.) *Emotion. Theory, Research, and Experience*, New York, NY, Academic, 3-33.

Porter, Roy (1993) "The Body and the Mind, the Doctor and the Patient: Negotiating Hysteria", Sander Gilman et al. (eds.) *Hysteria beyond Freud*, Berkeley, CA, University of California Press, 225-266. DOI: 10.1525/9780520309937-004.

Radford, Michael (dir.) (1984) *Nineteen Eighty-Four*, UK, Virgin Films/Umbrella-Rosenblum Films/Atlantic Entertainment Group.

Research Group *Pandemic Fictions* (2020) "From Pandemic to Corona Fictions: Narratives in Times of Crises", *PhiN-Beiheft* 24, 321-344, http://web.fu-berlin.de/phin/beiheft24/b24t21.pdf, 2022-11-29.

Shorter, Edward (1994) *Moderne Leiden. Zur Geschichte der psychosomatischen Krankheiten*. Reinbek bei Hamburg, Rowohlt.

Showalter, Elaine (1997) *Hystories: Hysterical Epidemics and Modern Culture*, New York, NY, Columbia University Press.

Singer, Tania/Koop, Sarah/Godara, Malvika (2021) "The CovSocial Project: How Did Berliners Feel and React during the COVID-19 Pandemic in 2020/21? Changes in Aspects of Mental Health, Resilience and Social Cohesion", *The CovSocial Project*, Berlin, Max Planck Society, https://www.covsocial.de/wp-content/uploads/2021/11/CovSocial_EN_WEB.pdf, 2022-11-18.

Stemberger, Martina (2021) *Corona im Kontext: Zur Literaturgeschichte der Pandemie*, Tübingen, Narr Francke Attempto.

Theriot, Nancy M. (1993) "Women's Voices in Nineteenth-Century Medical Discourse: A Step toward Deconstructing Science", *Signs. Journal of Women in Culture and Society* 19/1, 1-31.

UN Women (2021), *Measuring the Shadow Pandemic. Violence against Women during COVID-19*, s.l., United Nations Women, https://data.unwomen.org/sites/default/files/documents/Publications/Measuring-shadow-pandemic.pdf, 2022-11-24.

Völkl, Yvonne (2021-2023) *Corona Fictions. On Viral Narratives in Times of Pandemics*, FWF-Project [P 34571-G], Project team members: Yvonne Völkl, Julia Obermayr, Elisabeth Hobisch, Tommaso Meozzi, https://www.tugraz.at/projekte/cofi/home, 2022-11-29.

Völkl, Yvonne (2022) *Spectatoriale Geschlechterkonstruktionen. Geschlechtsspezifische Wissens- und Welterzeugung in den französisch- und spanischsprachigen Moralischen Wochenschriften des 18. Jahrhunderts*, Bielefeld, transcript. DOI: 10.14361/9783839461037.

Völkl, Yvonne (2023) "The Pandemic Crisis through the Lens of Corona Fictions. Insights from the Lockdown Diary", Richard Hölzl/Andrew Gross/Silke Schicktanz (eds.) *Narrating Pandemics: Transdisciplinary Approaches to Representations of Communicable Disease*, Toronto, ONT, University of Toronto Press [forthcoming].

Zehetner, Bettina (2012) *Krankheit und Geschlecht. Feministische Philosophie und psychosoziale Beratung*, Wien/Berlin, Turia + Kant.

La novela de la pandemia como una modalidad de la novela de la crisis. El caso de *La madre del futbolista* de Pablo García Casado

Justyna Ziarkowska (Universidad de Wrocław)

Abstract

The aim of this article is to demonstrate, on the basis of Pablo García Casado's *La madre del futbolista* (2022), that the pandemic novel can establish a modality of the crisis novel. First, we present the characteristics of the crisis novel proposed, among others, by Jochen Mecke and David Becerra Mayor, such as the reduction of the plot, the concentration on the description of everyday life, the decline of the protagonist and the focus on the victim of the economic situation in order to analyze how they are manifested in García Casado's novel. Later, we observe in detail the social phenomenon that has stood out during the pandemic confinement in Spain, that is, a large increase in the consumption of pornography and its reflection in the novel analyzed. The novel's protagonist's work as an adult film actress adheres to the rules of the free market system.

LA MADRE DEL FUTBOLISTA DE PABLO GARCÍA CASADO

El poeta cordobés, Pablo García Casado, desde 1997 autor de seis poemarios, reconocido, premiado y traducido, aprovechó el propio confinamiento para escribir *La madre del futbolista* (2022), su primera novela. A este género nuevo ha trasladado sus anteriores protagonistas poéticos: la actriz del cine porno que habitaba *La cámara te quiere* (2019) y el *Dinero* que protagonizaba el tomo homónimo de 2007. Pablo García Casado como novelista escenifica lo mismo como Pablo

García Casado como poeta, es decir, el instante en el que su protagonista cae en la cuenta de que ha fracasado, el momento de su hundimiento. Aquí la tensión consiste en cómo, durante el confinamiento, la madre, que es actriz porno *online*, puede, frente a su hijo adolescente, mantener en secreto su profesión. García Casado no recurre al canon de las ficciones pandémicas que incluye obras de Boccaccio, Camus o Saramago. Ni siguiera alude a las novelas pandémicas de lengua española como *El amor en los tiempos de cólera* de García Márquez o *Las virtudes del pájaro solitario* de Juan Goytisolo. Él recurre, más bien, a la literatura de la crisis económica incluidos sus propios libros poéticos.

Como en la mayoría de las narraciones de la crisis, también Pablo García Casado relaciona en su novela la historia individual de Sonia con la historia colectiva que se extiende entre dos grandes acontecimientos: la crisis económica de 2008 y la pandemia de 2020. La obra muestra que las consecuencias de la pandemia constituyen un paso más en el mismo fenómeno de la desestabilización del conjunto de valores sociales resultante de la crisis financiera; no cambian el rumbo sino, al revés, aceleran o profundizan la puesta en cuestión del sistema político y económico surgida alrededor de 2008. Por lo tanto podemos llamar la novela de la pandemia una modalidad de la novela de la crisis. La trama arranca el día 12 de marzo de 2020, un día después de que la Organización Mundial de la Salud declarara la pandemia global del coronavirus y pidiera que todos los países adaptaran medidas de distanciamiento social. Dos días después, el gobierno español anunció el confinamiento de toda la población. La protagonista de la novela, Sonia, una mujer divorciada, se hace cargo por petición de su exmarido, Pedro, del hijo de ambos, Samuel, de quince años. Aunque la acción principal transcurre durante varias semanas de la primavera de 2020, conocemos toda la biografía de la pareja, que se vuelve paradigmática para una generación nacida a caballo entre la década de los 70 y los 80. Sonia y Pedro son coetáneos de la Constitución de 1978 y víctimas del sistema político que surgió de ella.[1] Pasaron sus primeros treinta años en una época de obligatorio y patológico optimismo en la que los ciudadanos españoles creían –en palabras de Muñoz Molina– pisar por la tierra firme e imaginaban que "el futuro se parecería al presente y las cosas seguirían mejorando de manera gradual, o si acaso progresarían algo más despacio" (Muñoz Molina 2014, 9). A esta generación la crisis económica les cayó encima cuando tenían los treinta años recién cumplidos (son ellos los participantes principales del movimiento del 15-M) y diez años más tarde volvieron a ser directamente afectados por la pandemia.

---

1   Sobre los intelectuales orgánicos del régimen del 78 y su confrontación con los participantes del 15-M escribe David Becerra Mayor (2021) en su libro *Después del acontecimiento. El retorno de lo político en la literatura española tras el 15-M.*

Sonia y Pedro provienen de pueblos pequeños y de familias humildes. Pedro quedó huérfano de padre cuando era adolescente y tuvo que hacerse cargo de su hermano menor a costa de la carrera deportiva con la que soñaba. El intransigente padre de Sonia no aceptó su decisión de vivir en la ciudad por su propia cuenta lo cual le hizo romper todas las relaciones con su familia. Son dos jóvenes sin formación y sin poder contar con ningún apoyo de su entorno. Encuentran trabajo en las empresas de un poderoso matrimonio formado por Julián Sotomayor y Lucía Martínez da Costa, dueños de constructoras, negocios de energía solar, de tiendas, hoteles y restaurantes. Pedro, un hombre tosco, duro, seco es capaz de gran esfuerzo y de una incondicional y feroz lealtad hacia su jefe, por lo que se vuelve su secretario personal. Involucrado en varias transacciones ilegales de los Sotomayor, Pedro pasa por todos los altibajos de su carrera financiera. Antes de la crisis vive en un apartamento nuevo en la playa de Manilva, tiene coche lujoso y viste ropa elegante; con el tiempo, después de que en diciembre de 2009 el inversor, buscado por Interpol, se refugiara en México, debe cambiar de casa, de coche y de estilo de vida. Sonia quiere ser libre e independiente: terminado el bachillerato y sin posibilidades para los estudios universitarios, encuentra empleo en una panadería de Sevilla. Sin embargo, después de la boda con Pedro, acepta pasivamente la generosa propuesta de su marido y de los Sotomayor de dejar el trabajo y cuidar la casa. Renuncia a sus aspiraciones por ser autosuficiente a cambio del sueño de construir su propio espacio, a costa de la ilusión de alcanzar su propia casa, para formar su propio hogar. Sonia, como muchos de los españoles a principio de este milenio, vive una vida ilusoria, vive en una especie de jaula de oro gozando de una prosperidad fingida y de una seguridad ficticia. La metáfora barroca del simulacro ha sido invocada varias veces en la narrativa de la crisis: por ejemplo Muñoz Molina en su conocido ensayo habla de España como el país de "los espejismos y de los retablos de maravillas" (Muñoz Molina 2014, 156). Sonia despierta del sueño o se da cuenta del predominio de la apariencia sobre la realidad cuando observa cómo Manilva, que en verano parece un alegre paisaje de grúas, se transforma en otoño en un paisaje de locales con persianas cerradas y de la gente con dificultades para sobrevivir. La Manilva de verano es un mundo al revés, una experiencia de fiesta dentro de la rutina real. Las tensiones y las inquietudes económicas que sufre Julián Sotomayor se traducen en la creciente frialdad de Pedro y finalmente en el divorcio del matrimonio. Sonia se traslada con su hijo a un piso alquilado e intenta, en el umbral de la crisis económica, encontrar trabajo como madre soltera. A Mari, su amiga, la dueña extravagante del videoclub de Manilva, le dice: "En apenas un año había pasado de ser cliente de un videoclub a trabajar para la dueña. «Creía que lo tenía todo y ahora ya ves»" (García Casado 2022, 81). Le resulta imposible encontrar un empleo fijo: trabaja por períodos cortos como empleada en un supermercado, camarera en un restaurante, señora de limpieza en la hacienda de Mari. Obligada a ahorrar en todo, varias veces pasa hambre. Le obsesiona la idea de que no pueda garantizar la comida a su hijo.

> Podía pedirle a Pedro un dinero, al fin y al cabo, ella estaba asumiendo al chico, y el chico comía. Vaya si comía. […]. En la nevera quedaban dos filetes de pechuga de la noche anterior. "Ahora te aso los filetes y te pongo una ensalada. Alíñatela tú, que no quiero pasarme con la sal y el aceite". Todavía con el pelo mojado, sacó de mala gana la sartén y con una gota de aceite asó vuelta y vuelta los dos filetes y los puso en el plato. "¿Tú no comes nada?", preguntó Samuel. "No, ya he picado algo por el camino. No tengo hambre". Quiso preguntar Samuel dónde había *picado* algo si todos los bares estaban cerrados, si incluso, como decía el telediario, había controles para la gente que caminaba por la calle [cursiva del original]. (García Casado 2022, 163-164)

Samuel es el único punto que orienta a Sonia en la vida. Precisamente su gran amor hacia su hijo le hace mantenerse en pie y buscar soluciones: la única que ve es la de ser actriz en el cine para adultos y, luego, ofrecer servicios pornográficos *online*. Ante su hijo finge ser promotora de ventas y cuando el hijo vuelve de la casa de su padre esconde el ordenador en el armario y esparce por la casa folletos. Hay que subrayar aquí que, entre muchas otras cosas, *La madre del futbolista* es también la historia de una madre que hace todo por su hijo. Se trata de un modelo de maternidad que acepta todo el sacrificio y hasta la anulación de su personalidad a fin de garantizar la felicidad a su hijo. Samuel a lo largo de toda la novela permanece impenetrable, mustio, no muestra emociones, rechaza gestos de cariño, pronuncia sólo los monosílabos. Sólo dirá un par de frases que, precisamente, cerrarán la novela.

LA MADRE DEL FUTBOLISTA COMO UNA NOVELA DE LA CRISIS ECONÓMICA

La madre del futbolista, obviamente, se inscribe en el género de la novela de la crisis económica: el hundimiento de 2008 no constituye su telón de fondo, sino que la trama no puede prescindir de él. La obra cumple casi todas las características genéricas de la novela de la crisis propuestas por Jochen Mecke (2017, 199-229). Primero, las novelas de la crisis en vez de contar eventos y argumentos espectaculares, describen lo cotidiano, se centran en los detalles mínimos e insignificantes de la vida diaria. En el caso de la novela de García Casado se cuentan acciones rutinarias: cómo servir la pechuga de pollo para la cena, ducharse, la necesidad de cambiarse de ropa. Los acontecimientos históricos solo se aluden. La reducción de la trama y la concentración de la atención en la cotidianeidad las podemos también relacionar con varias teorías de crisis. Reinhard Koselleck o Bauman y Boldoni demuestran que la crisis en la época moderna abarca simultáneamente varias áreas de la vida social e influye en ellas de forma inesperada y radical así como consiste –en palabras de Bourdieu (2008, 225-231)– en una sincronización de múltiples disfunciones del sistema social. Éstas provocan la suspensión del funcionamiento automatizado, rutinas diarias y procesos habituales. Tal interrupción que, a lo largo, permite cuestionar el sistema, en un primer momento desorienta a los protagonistas, quienes pueden controlar solamente lo más cotidiano. El trajín diario testimonia asimismo –es la tesis de la pensadora polaca, Jolanta Brach-Czaina (2018, 67-96)– nuestro arraigo en lo cotidiano, posibilita marcar territorio propio y, sobre todo, subraya nuestra autoría y nuestra fuerza motriz. Los protagonistas de las novelas de la crisis, limitados a lo cotidiano, luchan contra su total impotencia frente al sistema. A su vez Jochen Mecke (2017, 208-209) lo une con otra característica del género afirmando que la reducción del argumento de la novela corresponde con la concepción de los personajes, que siempre son incapaces de actuar, carecen de ambiciones, les falta el ánimo. La falta de una acción veloz se debe a que los protagonistas han perdido el sentido que pudiera orientarles en la vida. Los personajes de *La madre del futbolista* también son pasivos y dependen de los demás: Pedro de su amo, Sonia de su marido. Obedecen las reglas del sistema. Ninguno de los dos sabe reaccionar adecuadamente ante lo que les pasa. No pueden encontrar otro camino fuera del designado por el mercado.

El siguiente rasgo que une *La madre del futbolista* con las demás novelas de la crisis es la descripción del descenso de los protagonistas desde una situación de relativa comodidad hacia un estado de escasez. Sin embargo, García Casado no divide la vida de sus protagonistas en una época feliz de antes de la crisis y un período desdichado posterior a 2008. Es decir, aquí no hallaremos una nostalgia de los tiempos anteriores a la caída de Lehman Brothers, responsable según David Becerra Mayor de una parte de las novelas de la crisis (cf. Becerra Mayor 2018, 45-62). Todo lo contrario, nos damos cuenta del rumbo peligroso por el que había optado la economía española desde hacía varias décadas. Quizá la vida de Sonia habría que dividirla en tres etapas de acuerdo con el modelo de Koselleck: la estabilidad, la estabilidad imaginada y la culminación de la crisis (cf. Schmuck 2017, 172). Aunque en la mayoría de las novelas de este género suele haber una oposición entre varios grupos sociales, entre los beneficiados y las víctimas del sistema capitalista, aquí, al final de la obra de García Casado las fronteras entre los poderosos y los débiles quedan diluidas: desde los exitosos Sotomayor hasta Sonia pasando por Pedro y el matrimonio de Mari y Josh, todos resultan perdedores. La crisis –utilizando el lenguaje epidemiológico– ha aplanado la curva del triunfo. En *La sociedad del descenso* Oliver Nachtwey recuerda el concepto de "efecto ascensor" acuñado por Ulrich Beck para el colectivo desarrollo individual de los hijos de familias de clase obrera en Alemania. En el mismo ascensor subían los ciudadanos de varios niveles sociales. Para el análisis de las décadas sucesivas Nachtwey propone la metáfora de la escalera mecánica en la que unos ya han subido y otros están bajando (cf. Nachtwey 2017, 27-30, 79-81). Aquí, sin embargo, volvemos a la imagen del ascensor, pero en el que bajan colectivamente representantes de varios niveles sociales. En *La madre del futbolista*, como en las demás novelas de la crisis, la acción está focalizada en el personaje más perjudicado por el hundimiento. A través de la perspectiva subjetiva de la protagonista Sonia, que aparece ya en el título del libro, conocemos a quien ha pagado enormes costes personales primero por la crisis, luego por la pandemia. Se trata de conocer la historia desde la perspectiva del sujeto explotado. La novela de la crisis busca también una respuesta al responsable de la desdicha del personaje. Está claro que, aunque la caída de Sonia ha sido engendrada por su severo padre, la actitud egoísta de los Sotomayor, la postura de su marido, su propia obediencia y sueños ingenuos, es ella la víctima de la construcción del mercado laboral inestable, del sistema político, social y económico de los que no es culpable en el mínimo grado. La novela de la crisis –lo advierte David Becerra Mayor– pone en duda la ideología dominante, pero no propone nuevas modalidades, no pertenece a ningún "árbol genealógico" (Becerra Mayor 2021, 48-50). Se vuelve obvio el desmoronamiento de las estructuras políticas y económicas actuales, pero no hay esperanza para que surja una solución positiva. Sonia, desorientada en sus valores, no tiene ninguna confianza en un posible cambio.

LA MODALIDAD PANDÉMICA EN *LA MADRE DEL FUTBOLISTA*

Según los autores del artículo "From Pandemic to Corona Fictions: Narratives in Times of Crises" (Research Group *Pandemic Fictions* 2020, 327f.), la novela de la crisis pandémica sigue la estructura del drama clásico propuesta por Gustav Freytag: la exposición (aquí p.ej. el incremento de la tasa de mortalidad en China), la acción ascendente (el incremento de infecciones), el clímax (el inicio de la cuarentena), la acción descendente (la esperanza y el miedo por una segunda oleada) y la resolución (la vacunación). La obra de García Casado se inscribe en este modelo parcialmente. Aunque la tensión del relato está causada por el anuncio del confinamiento por parte del gobierno español, ésta no va a crecer a la par del aumento de las infecciones sino en función de la disminución del poder adquisitivo de la protagonista, su inseguridad y su miedo. La catástrofe final, el clímax, aunque está provocada directamente por el cierre social y la prohibición de los contactos, tiene su origen en la situación económica de Sonia. La ficción pandémica se resuelve con la vacunación o el fin del aislamiento. Una vez más en García Casado el final de la historia coincide con el anuncio por parte del gobierno de que se van a levantar las restricciones, pero ello no soluciona el problema principal. El virus que se propaga rápido queda comparado con los vídeos de Sonia que con la rapidez viral llegan a todo el mundo. El virus lo mata a Josh mientras que los vídeos pornográficos de Sonia revelan los secretos y las mentiras de la madre. Su calamidad, en comparación con la pandemia, tiene una duración más larga y una solución mucho más difícil ya que requiere un cambio de modelo global, del sistema entero de creencias. Todos los protagonistas de García Casado están totalmente solos y abandonados en sus esfuerzos por vivir dignamente. El confinamiento pandémico sólo acelera y agrava los procesos causados por la construcción socio-política. Susan Sontag (1996, 80) analizando las metáforas del sida advertía que por afectar a Occidente esta enfermedad no se la trataba como un fenómeno "natural", una parte del ciclo, un aspecto más de la naturaleza, sino como una calamidad cargada de significado histórico que trastoca la sociedad. Podemos trasladar esta observación a las novelas de la crisis donde las calamidades sufridas por las víctimas del sistema capitalista son observadas por los miembros privilegiados de la sociedad como si se tratara de un mero desastre natural. La supuesta "naturalidad" del sistema socio-político hizo formular a Federic Jameson o Slavoj Žižek la conocida frase que es más fácil imaginarse el fin del mundo que el fin del capitalismo (cf. Lynteris 2020, 136).

En el caso concreto de *La madre del futbolista* de Pablo García Casado los rasgos de la modalidad pandémica de la novela de la crisis serían la exploración de la explotación humana llevada al extremo y la reducción total del hombre a su materialidad. En otras palabras, en la modalidad pandémica de la novela de la crisis se intensifican y se agravan los elementos y las situaciones de la vulnerabilidad social surgidos a partir de 2008 y causados por un sistema social y económico injusto. En una entrevista García Casado afirmó que la crisis de 2008 "fue la crisis moral más grande desde 1898" (Cedillo 2022, s.p.). Efectivamente, la crisis ha destruido el sueño colectivo dejando a una sociedad desengañada y desconfiada, consciente de la fragilidad de su situación existencial, de su impotencia frente a la economía de mercado, de la existencia constante del peligro incontrolable. Nadie puede estar seguro de su salud, de su puesto de trabajo, de su posición social. Es la llamada sociedad del riesgo, amenazada de que las catástrofes y los estados excepcionales, o sea, las crisis se vuelvan norma. El nuevo estado de excepción, la pandemia del COVID-19, ha traído –nos acordamos de las metáforas de la crisis observadas por Muñoz Molina como "aterrizaje", "desaceleración", "ralentización"– una parada total y literal. La nueva catástrofe ha subido el volumen de la misma ansiedad relacionada con la situación económica, añadiendo a ello el pánico vinculado con la salud y, además, el confinamiento drástico y obligatorio que ponía al descubierto las relaciones familiares de la gente. El encierro severo de varias semanas hace imposible esquivar los problemas, las infidelidades y las mentiras. La pandemia desnuda los verdaderos sentimientos y, en el caso de Sonia, las verdaderas ocupaciones. La sociedad pandémica vista a través de los ojos del narrador de *La madre del futbolista* es no solamente desengañada y desconfiada, pero también insensibilizada frente a la crueldad y el sufrimiento. En las escenas finales del libro varios internautas observan, graban y difunden en la red el sexo entre Sonia y Josh, enfermo, muriéndose de covid.

LA MUJER EN EL MERCADO CAPITALISTA COMO PROTAGONISTA PANDÉMICA

En su libro, Pablo García Casado da la voz a Sonia, una mujer, madre soltera y actriz del cine porno. Así convierte en protagonista una voz que muy pocas veces se puede oír en las obras literarias como si el fenómeno de la pornografía no existiera. La pandemia ha provocado la ansiedad por la paralización de la economía, por la posible repetición de los cortes presupuestarios de hace una década, por la salud, por la necesidad de permanecer encerrados que, como muestran numerosas estadísticas (cf. Lorente-Acosta 2020, 139-145), provocó el aumento de la violencia de género y el incremento del maltrato de los más débiles: los niños y las personas mayores. Estos mismos temores han provocado también el gran incremento del consumo de pornografía. Según un informe publicado por una web de pornografía, PornHub, analizado por varios periodistas (cf. Atienza 2021, s.p.), España está entre los países que más acceden a esta web y durante el confinamiento llegó a ser líder en las visualizaciones de la pornografía con un crecimiento de más del 61% por encima de la media diaria habitual. Esta creciente demanda es resultado de la estrategia del individuo para reducir el estrés, pero también puede estar unida con el miedo epidemiológico ante una relación directa con otra persona, con el confinamiento y el trabajo desde casa.

Desde que entró en la industria pornográfica, Sonia ha sido maltratada varias veces por los hombres, conociendo el dolor, el sufrimiento, la humillación y hasta la violación. A través de sus perfiles en los medios de comunicación sociales y la webcam de contenido pornográfico conoció en qué consiste el libre comercio, la competitividad y la globalización. Compitiendo con las actrices de cine porno rusas, se vuelve dependiente de sus observadores en Internet.

> Día a día iba cayendo en el *ranking*, su foto estaba cada vez más abajo en la pantalla […]. Las peticiones de los usuarios eran de lo más extravagantes, así que sólo atendían las más sencillas, las que ya tenían habladas, "pronto tendremos más sorpresas", decía Sonia [cursiva del original]. (García Casado 2020, 170-171)

Ya lo observaron Barba y Montes (2007, 163) en su conocido ensayo y subrayaron que las nuevas tecnologías hacen que el consumidor del sexo comercial se transforme en productor, que se vuelva sujeto activo de la producción porno. Vicente Verdú en su ensayo *El estilo del mundo. La vida en el capitalismo de ficción* dice que la pornografía *online*, al alcance de cualquier ciudadano, ya en el año 2003 se ha convertido en el primer producto de éxito dentro del comercio electrónico y que el 68% del comercio electrónico de ese momento es de contenido pornográfico (cf. Verdú 2003, 171). En la novela de García Casado vemos que toda producción de cine para adultos y más aún en los nuevos medios tecnológicos lleva consigo la indiferencia de los observadores respecto a las trabajadoras del sexo comercial, su permiso a la crueldad, la disminución del valor del cuerpo y las emociones femeninas. Hablamos del cuerpo femenino porque la inmensa mayoría de los que demandan el cine para adultos son los hombres y la inmensa mayoría de las que lo ofertan son las mujeres. Y no podemos perder de vista que el cuerpo de la mujer convertido en objeto de consumo o en una mercancía se debe a la dominación masculina; que el cuerpo femenino entendido solo como fuente del goce de un sujeto exterior y explotador que está fantaseando sobre su apropiación es resultado de esta dominación:

> La dominación masculina convierte a las mujeres en objetos simbólicos cuyo ser es un ser percibido y tiene el efecto de colocarlas en un estado permanente de inseguridad corporal o, mejor dicho, de dependencia simbólica. Existen fundamentalmente por y para la mirada de los demás, es decir, en cuanto que objetos acogedores, atractivos, disponibles. (Bourdieu 2000, 86-87)

En muchos casos no conocemos quienes dirigen esta mirada alienada, cosificante y fetichista sobre el cuerpo de Sonia, pero a veces el narrador nos los deja ver:

"Espera un minuto, que el niño está llorando". *JorgeT86* se levantó, se acercó a la cuna y cogió al bebé entre sus brazos para consolarlo. La cámara seguía conectada y los minutos corrían, pero a él parecía no importarle. Sonia no sabía qué hacer, la situación era, como menos, ridícula. […] Ahora se fijaba más que nunca en las casas. En la decoración, en los cuadros, en las plantas. En las zapatillas de paño gastadas que asombraban junto a la puerta. A veces se escuchaba a las esposas llamar a la ducha a algún niño, preguntar si había bajado la basura. Alguno incluso utilizaba los mismos auriculares *gamer* que Samuel. Todos en chándal, sin afeitar, todos con cara de no haber dormido. Tratando de sonreír. Y queriendo hablar, más que nunca hablar. "Esto nos hará mejores", había escuchado en la radio, pero no era verdad, eran las mismas ratas sin salir de la ratonera [cursiva del original]. (García Casado 2022, 169)

La mirada exterior, pornográfica, alienadora del cuerpo femenino vuelve a ser metáfora de la alienación de todos los individuos confinados en la pandemia que no saben comunicarse y que a través de las pantallas no se enteran de los sentimientos de los otros. La tecnología distancia físicamente, pero también provoca distanciamiento en la comunicación, en la empatía, en el compromiso con la solidaridad social. Observamos cómo la crueldad de la pandemia, con muertes anunciadas a cada momento en la televisión,[2] es directamente proporcional a las formas de gozo provenientes de la explotación de la mujer y al aislamiento de la gente mediante su desensibilización frente al sufrimiento de los otros, pues cuando hablamos de la pornografía, hablamos de miseria, dolor, miedo y vergüenza. Para Sonia la prostitución es una de las pocas opciones para conseguir dinero y las consecuencias devastadoras de la pobreza se manifiestan en su nivel individual, pero también a nivel social. Así volvemos a *La cámara te quiere* y *Dinero*.

---

2   El Centro de Coordinación de Alertas y Emergencias Sanitarias informaba que hasta mediados de junio de 2020 se han registrado en España cerca de 250 000 de personas contagiadas y más de 27 000 fallecidos.

BIBLIOGRAFÍA

Bibliografía primaria

García Casado, Pablo (2022) *La madre del futbolista*, Madrid, Visor Libros.

Bibliografía secundaria

Atienza, Jara (2021) "Pornhub, en cifras: cómo se ha convertido en la web más valiosa y visitada de Internet", *Forbes*, 2021-12-10, https://forbes.es/empre sas/124369/pornhub-en-cifras-como-se-ha-convertido-en-la-web-mas-valiosa -y-visitada-de-internet/, 2022-10-01.

Barba, Andrés/Montes, Javier Barba (2007) *La ceremonia del porno*, Barcelona, Anagrama.

Bauman, Zygmunt/Boldoni, Carlo (2016) *Estado de crisis*, Barcelona, Paidós.

Becerra Mayor, David (2018) "El relato de la pérdida y las representaciones del fin de la clase media en las novelas de la crisis", Jaume Peris (ed.) *Cultura e imaginación política*, Ciudad de México/Paris, RILMA 2/ADEHL, 45-62.

Becerra Mayor, David (2021) *Después del acontecimiento. El retorno de lo político en la literatura española tras el 15-M*, Barcelona, Bellaterra.

Boccaccio, Giovanni (2019 [~ 1349-1353]) *El Decamerón*, Madrid, Albor Libros.

Bourdieu, Pierre (2000) *La dominación masculina*, Barcelona, Anagrama.

Bourdieu, Pierre (2008) *Homo academicus*, Buenos Aires, Siglo XXI Editores.

Brach-Czaina, Jolanta (2018) *Szczeliny istnienia*, Warszawa, Dowody na istnienie.

Camus, Albert (1990) *La peste*, Barcelona, Edhasa.

Cedillo, Jaime (2022) "Una historia de fútbol y porno: el debut en la novela del poeta Pablo García Casado. Entrevista", *El Cultural* (*El Español*), 2022-09-03, https://www.elespanol.com/el-cultural/letras/20220903/historia-futbol-porno-novela-pablo-garcia-casado/700180347_0.html, 2022-10-01.

García Casado, Pablo (2007) *Dinero*, Barcelona, DVD Ediciones.

García Casado, Pablo (2019) *La cámara te quiere*, Madrid, Visor Libros.

Goytisolo, Juan (2007) *Las virtudes del pájaro solitario*, Barcelona, Galaxia Gutenberg.

Koselleck, Reinhard (2007) *Crítica y crisis: un estudio sobre la patogénesis del mundo burgués*, Madrid, Trotta.

Lorente-Acosta, Miguel (2020) "Violencia de género en tiempos de pandemia y confinamiento", *Revista Española de Medicina Legal* 46/3, 139-145. DOI: 10.1016/j.reml.2020.05.005.

Lynteris, Christos (2020) *Human Extinction and the Pandemic Imaginary*, London/New York, Routledge.

Mecke, Jochen (2017) "La crisis está siendo un éxito… estético: discursos literarios de la crisis y las éticas de la estética", Jochen Mecke/Ralf Junkerjürgen/ Hubert Pöppel (eds.) *Discursos de la crisis: respuestas de la cultura española ante nuevos desafíos*, Madrid, Vervuert, 199-229.

Muñoz Molina, Antonio (2014) *Todo lo que era sólido*, Barcelona, Seix Barral.

Nachtwey, Oliver (2017) *La sociedad del descenso precariedad y desigualdad en la era posdemocrática*, Barcelona, Paidós.

Research Group *Pandemic Fictions* (2020) "From Pandemic to Corona Fictions: Narratives in Times of Crises", *PhiN-Beiheft* 24, 321-344, http://web.fu-berlin.de/phin/beiheft24/b24t21.pdf, 2022-12-12.

Saramago, José (2010) *Ensayo sobre la ceguera*, Barcelona, Alfaguara.

Schmuck, Lydia (2017) "El hundimiento como *Denkbild*. Figuraciones literarias en *Todo lo que era sólido* de Antonio Muñoz Molina", Jochen Mecke/Ralf Junkerjürgen/Hubert Pöppel (eds.) *Discursos de la crisis: respuestas de la cultura española ante nuevos desafíos*, Madrid, Vervuert, 171-183.

Sontag, Susan (1996) *La enfermedad y sus metáforas. El sida y sus metáforas*, Madrid, Taurus.

Verdú, Vicente (2003) *El estilo del mundo. La vida en el capitalismo de ficción*, Barcelona, Anagrama.

Mediated Vulnerabilities: Transforming Virginia Woolf's Characters in Corona Fictions

Paulina Pająk (University of Wrocław, Faculty of Letters)

Abstract

"We are all Mrs. Dalloway now", announced *The New Yorker* (2020), succinctly capturing the pandemic wave of interest in Virginia Woolf's works. Diverse audiences, writers and artists have turned to Woolf's writings on illness, survival and death, with a new awareness of their genesis in the aftermath of not only WWI but also of the global influenza pandemic of 1918-19 (cf. Outka 2019).

This article examines Corona Fictions, available in their digital form to the English-speaking global audiences – a special focus is given to transtextual and transmedia protagonists, originating in Woolf's works yet revealing reactions to the recent Covid-19 pandemic. Drawing on current research on the poetics of vulnerability (cf. Ganteau 2015) and postmodern transformations of Woolf's characters (cf. Latham 2021), this article argues that these pandemic works use Woolfian characters across different media to create mediated representations of vulnerabilities exposed by the pandemic.

INTRODUCTION

"We are all Mrs. Dalloway now", announced Evan Kindley in *The New Yorker* (2020), succinctly capturing the pandemic wave of interest in Virginia Woolf's works. Diverse audiences, writers and artists have turned to Woolf's writings on illness, survival and death, with a new awareness of their genesis in the aftermath of not only the First World War but also of the global influenza pandemic of 1918-19 (cf. Outka 2019, 139-141) that might have taken the lives of 100 million people. This article examines Corona Fictions, available in their digital form to the English-speaking global audiences. These works "not only draw on everyday media and political discourse, but also on previous pandemic fiction" (Research Group *Pandemic Fictions* 2020, 322-323), as they recycle Woolf's texts. Contrasting transmedia storytelling with adaptation, Elizabeth Evans emphasizes that "transmedia elements do not involve the telling of the same events on different platforms; they involve the telling of *new* events from the same storyworld [italics in orig.]" (2011, 27). Accordingly, a special focus is given to transtextual and transmedia protagonists, originating in Woolf's works yet revealing current reactions to the Covid-19 pandemic.

The coronavirus pandemic has simultaneously exposed whole communities to mutable, repeated and unpredictable stressors. Responding to new waves of the pandemic, governments have introduced lockdowns, unprecedented public health measures based on social distancing, isolation, home confinement and mass quarantines. Since its outbreak in November 2019, the pandemic has also globally intensified financial stratification, healthcare disparities and gender inequities. To measure and alleviate the psychological impact of the pandemic, social scientists have been adapting the theoretical models of resilience (cf. Masten 2021a; Godara et al. 2022).

Several objections have been raised, however, to the resilience framework. The term 'resilience' itself may be ambiguous, as it has been differently conceptualized as a personality trait, a process, an outcome, a perspective (cf. Godara et al. 2022, 265) in psychological and educational research since the early 1970s, when it was first coined by the psychologist Emmy Werner. In the 2010s, some researchers expressed concerns about the use of reduced resilience theories in neoliberal politics. For instance, the theories of resilience as a personal characteristic/ability may be seen as the "embedding of specifically neoliberal forms of governance" (Joseph 2013, 41), since they put stress on adaptability and responsibility of individual people, rather than on the systems and networks they inhabit. A few researchers even go so far as to equate resilience with the continuity of neoliberal policy itself and argue that it leads to a gradual dismantling of the democratic state (cf. Madariaga 2020, 3f.).

The pandemic models of resilience seem at least partially responsive to this criticism. Currently, resilience is broadly defined in psychology as the "dynamic process" (Godara et al. 2022, 264) or the "dynamic capacity of a complex adaptive system to respond successfully to challenges that threaten the function, survival, or development of the system" (Masten 2021a, 155). Though the focus is on the system, these models acknowledge that resilience may occur on the individual level as well. It then manifests itself as a recuperative ability allowing people to cope with adversities – the effectiveness of their adaptation depends on a number of factors, from their worldviews and resources to the social cohesion of their community (cf. Godara et al. 2022, 270f.). Importantly, this personal resilience is frequently juxtaposed with negatively conceptualized individual vulnerability, or "vulnerabilities in susceptibility to adversity exposure" (Masten 2021b, 4).

Both resilience and vulnerability develop in specific cultural contexts. Hence, among the major strategies for promoting adaptation to the challenges of the pandemic, Ann S. Masten has listed various activities that restore, enhance and support "the power of human adaptive systems", including those that focus on "meaningful cultural practices and celebrations" (2021b, 7). In their recent work on Corona Fictions, Julia Obermayr and Yvonne Völkl (2022, 141) have demonstrated that cultural productions created during the Covid-19 pandemic may not only be used as coping strategies on the individual level, but they may also enhance social cohesion and resilience in audiences.

Similarly, this article argues that Corona Fictions use formal and thematic experiments that respond to challenges brought by the Covid-19 crisis and may foster adaptive ways of coping with pandemic stressors and individual/systemic vulnerabilities on both cognitive and affective levels. In his book *The Ethics and Aesthetics of Vulnerability in Contemporary British Fiction*, Jean-Michel Ganteau delineates the poetics of vulnerability by examining diverse texts that respond to individual, economic, and political forms of vulnerabilities. Combining trauma studies and affect theory, he argues that a vulnerable text "*performs* trauma by imitating the symptoms of the disorder through repetition, rhythmical variation, strict focalisation, and above all recurring spectral visitation [italics in orig.]" (Ganteau 2015, 114f.). In this article, I will analyze the vulnerable protagonists of Corona Fictions, using several categories introduced by Ganteau (2015), from the ghost figure to the staging of characters to the selected markers of characters' vulnerability, including "repetitive language" (95), "internalised alterity" (96), negative affect (103), and their "capacity to fail in achieving [...] agency" (107). Importantly for my discussion, Ganteau's model focuses on the construction of vulnerability in cultural texts.[1]

Drawing on current research on the precarity-continuity dynamics in Woolf's oeuvre (cf. Detloff 2016) and postmodern transformations of Woolf's characters (cf. Latham 2021), I argue that the two selected global Corona Fictions use Woolfian characters across different media to create mediated representations of vulnerabilities exposed by the pandemic. First, this article explores a hybrid combination of theatrical practices and quarantine filming, used by Lisa Peterson in her

---

1   For a discussion of how vulnerability is produced and politicized within neoliberal discourse see Butler et al. (2016).

video-theatre experiment *The Waves in Quarantine* (2021), which transforms the protagonists of Woolf's cross-genre novel *The Waves* into their transmedia equivalents. Then, I analyze parodic strategies applied by Talia Argondezzi and Anna Pook in their short story "Mrs. Dalloway said she would buy the rapid COVID test herself" (2022), using Woolfian characters to reveal systemic vulnerabilities.

THE (PANDEMIC) *WAVES*

In the uncertain spring 2021, the Berkeley Repertory Theatre in California released a daring fictional documentary *The Waves in Quarantine*, co-created by the director and writer Lisa Peterson and the versatile Broadway musical lead Raúl Esparza, who also acted as an associate director for this project. Streamed free on demand at the theatre website, this cycle of six videos – or "movements" as titled by Peterson, who wanted to embrace "the musical nature of the piece" (berkeleyrep 2021 [11:06-11:09 min.]) – was accessed by at least 17 000 global viewers from April 29 till June 30, 2021 (cf. Pfaelzer/Medak n.d.).

In Peterson's own words, this work is "opening the backdoor to the creative process" (berkeleyrep 2021 [12:20-12:26 min.]) by focusing on a team of actors that grapple not only with their own lives in the middle of the pandemic crisis, but also with Woolf's high Modernist novel *The Waves* (1931). However, this work is also transmedially haunted by the 1990 musical adaptation of *The Waves* created by Peterson and the composer David Bucknam for the New York Theatre Workshop – legendary in Broadway, yet not recorded as a whole. In 2018, this spectral musical was re-adapted by Peterson and the composer Adam Gwon for the New York Stage and Film – since *The Waves in Quarantine* reconstructs this process, it is a multi-layered palimpsest echoing with Woolf's works, its two musical adaptations, and spectral visions of their theatrical performances. After the stay-at-home orders were implemented in California in 2020, it also became a transnational and transatlantic project, with the theatrical team scattered across the US, working from California, Arizona, Pennsylvania, New Jersey and New York – and, in the case of the director of photography, even from Sweden. The pandemic left its imprint on the form of the documentary, as the actors were filming their own performances with digital cameras and iPhones.

Peterson has added a telling subtitle to her work, which is indeed "an experiment in 6 movements", combining several layers of metatheatrical and metafictional dimensions – including Woolf's novel. The ground-breaking nature of *The Waves in Quarantine* resonates with Woolf's avant-garde masterpiece: referring to the protean generic nature of *The Waves*, Woolf called it a "playpoem" in her diaries (Woolf 1982, 203). Woolf's hybrid fictional work is divided into nine sections, each opened with italicized vignettes, depicting the course of the sun and its mercurial effects on the coastal landscape. The "novel" simultaneously traces the movements of the sun and the lives of seven characters. While Bernard, Jinny, Louis, Neville, Rhoda, and Susan reveal their own experiences and worldviews in a series of extended monologues, Percival – the seventh character who dies as a young man in India – is silent, though his memory has never ceased to haunt his friends. While the six characters are individualized in the course of *The Waves*, Woolf introduces echoes and repetitions in their monologues, which reveal unexpected similarities. For example, Rhoda and Neville undergo analogous symbolic experiences in their childhood: they are unable to walk past apparently ordinary obstacles, a puddle and an apple tree. While Rhoda grapples with depersonalization: "I came to the puddle. I could not cross it. Identity failed me" (ead. 2011, 49), Neville associates the suicidal death of an elderly man with "the implacable tree with its greaved silver bark" and is "unable to pass by" (ibid., 17). In the following parts of *The Waves*, both characters recall these situations as emotionally charged with an existential fear. Due to these parallels, many critics interpret the novel as a poetic portrayal of group consciousness, or different facets of individual consciousness. Recently, Madelyn Detloff (2016) has proposed that "the oscillation between precarity and continuity" is the main theme of *The Waves*, since this fiction "exposes the self's simultaneous dependency on and isolation from others around it" (Detloff 2016, 53).

Consciously drawing on the ambiguous and oscillatory status of Woolf's characters, Peterson focuses on the process of creating their transmedia versions by actors preparing for their roles. Each transmedia character consists of a recognizable Woolfian inner core and several other layers. Consequently, it may be analyzed within Susana Tosca's (2022) recent model as "a network of floating traits, features, and relations" (213) to reveal which traits are foregrounded or backgrounded (Evans 2022, 222). The zoom conversations of the actors have been recorded, transcribed, scripted and reworked into a film collage (cf. fig. 1), in which – as Esparza explains – "we speak each other's words at certain points" (berkeleyrep 2021 [16:47-16:50 min.]). Christine Froula (2021) notes that the "improvisatory concept [of *The Waves in Quarantine*] arises from an innovative doubling. Living and working in isolation in their far-flung worlds, its six actors move fluidly between playing themselves, playing the six personae of *The Waves*, and playing both at once" (48). Movement 2 "Those We Love" indeed portrays the actors and their corresponding characters as two sides of the same coin. For a brief moment a card appears on the screen: it has the names of Woolf's characters printed on the front: "Jinny & / Louis & / Susan & / Neville & / Rhoda & / Bernard" while the back of the card is covered by the actors' names: "Carmen & / Manu & / Nikki & / Darius & / Alice & / Raúl" (Peterson 2021 Movement 2 [00:21-00:24 min.]).

Yet, this work goes beyond doubling (or even re-doubling) – particularly in the spectral figure of Percival/David. The inner core of this character, Woolf's Percival, has transtextual connections not only with his literary predecessor from Arthurian legends but also with Woolf's brother Thoby Stephen. Peterson has added other layers to Percival's transmedia version: as will be shown, Percival/David shares parallel characteristics with Woolf herself, Raúl/Bernard, and Adam Gwon.

Woolf's absent Percival was based on her brother Thoby who died of typhoid after the Stephens visited Greece in 1906. When Woolf was finishing *The Waves* in summer 1922, she composed in her notebook a poignant farewell to Thoby, possibly a draft epigram for the novel that had not been published (cf. Silver 1983, 235-238). Written on the reverse of Woolf's reading notes, the crossed-out section twice repeats "and, brother, forever now hail and farewell" in Latin, the final line from Gaius Valerius Catullus's *Carmina 101*, in which the poet addresses the "silent ashes" of his brother (2005, 202f.). Given Woolf's distance from the Victorian mourning culture, with its excessive grief displays, funeral extravagances, and pompous commemorative praises, Catullus's elegy offers an alternative model of valediction, rooted in the stoic and secular vision of existence. It also provides a closure to the writer's relationship with her brother based on intellectual cooperation and rivalry: it was Thoby who introduced the girl Virginia to Greek culture, discussed with her Shakespeare's plays and Latin poetry.

Correspondingly in *The Waves in Quarantine*, the deceased composer and lyricist David Bucknam recurs as "David" in his music, photographs, and hand-written scores. In Movement 1 "Memory", Raúl/Bernard "accidently" shows the audience David's image just after he displays on the screen Woolf's most frequently reproduced photo (taken in 1902 by George Charles Beresford, when the writer was in her twenties). In the subsequent Movements, we learn that similarly to Woolf, David committed suicide – and Movement 4 "Absence" becomes a meditation about their decisions, deaths and people they left behind. Bucknam was a mentoring figure for Esperza and Gwon – and hence they continue his artistic endeavour: Raúl impersonates Bernard, as David did in 1990; Adam restores his musical scores and writes additional music. There are also strong emotional ties – Raúl/Bernard confesses that as a young man he was in love with David, and his feelings became intertwined with Woolf's novel that he was then reading.

In its multiplying form, *The Waves in Quarantine* imitates the ephemeral nature of the theatre: with each performance gone in the very movement of its unfolding. As this work gravitates towards *mise-en-abyme*, the audience may discover yet other parallel characters, frames and embedded stories – as in the scene of Carmen/Jinny's dance, in which her silhouette is accompanied by a pair of female dancers, evoking the narrated past moment, in which Rhoda and Susan danced together (cf. fig. 2), or when Woolf's works briefly emerge on the screen, from the collection of her autobiographical writings *Moments of Being* to the feminist essay-lecture *A Room of One's Own* to volumes of her letters.

By portraying a group of contemporary actors who take on the roles of Woolf's characters, Peterson was able to span a whole spectrum of vulnerabilities and reactions to the Covid-19 pandemic, since "[t]he networks in the fiction represent the protagonists' common humanity through their common susceptibility" (Wald 2008, 54). In *The Waves in Quarantine*, each actor's persona both illuminates a specific vulnerability of their Woolfian inner core and projects its contemporary image.

Several scenes focus on the vulnerabilities of characters resulting from isolation – both as an intrinsic part of human existence and a temporary phenomenon enforced by lockdowns. In Movement 5 "The Sun Cycle", the outsider Manu/Louis takes a solitary winter walk through a deserted Jersey City to the banks of the Hudson River, accompanied only by the choral songs based on Woolf's vignettes describing the coastal landscape transformed by the changing position of the sun. As the sun is hidden behind clouds, a depressed Manu/Louis returns to his quarantined household – his joy at Raúl/Bernard's call and invitation is laced with Louis's fear that he does not truly belong to the circle of his friend and the loneliness experienced by Manu's persona as he moved across the country at the beginning of the pandemic. In the case of Alice/Rhoda, the actress first interprets Rhoda's isolation as her personal trait and wonders "[t]here is an isolation in Rhoda that could be madness. Or... maybe she just has the clearest eyes" (Peterson 2021 Movement 2 [04:42-04:52 min.]). However, as the lockdown continues, Alice's persona comes to a different reflection: "Uh... but... this isolation? There's kind of a beautiful thing, uh, you know. Like this never happened to me before. I've never been through this before, but also this is everybody. This is happening to everybody" (Peterson 2021 Movement 3 [06:37-06:57 min.]), observing that isolation is both an unprecedented experience in her own life and simultaneously a universal phenomenon for all people affected by the pandemic. Yet, a different facet of isolation is revealed by Carmen/Jinny, since Jinny represents embodied experience and perception in Woolf's novel: "My body goes before me, like a lantern down a dark lane, bringing one thing after another out of darkness into a ring of light" (Woolf 2011, 101). Carmen's persona feels alienated in the electronic simulacrum of personal connections created within social media and mediated by smartphones – she confesses "I've been mourning quite, quite some time, even before the pandemic", and then creates a vivid image of a people gaping at their phones in a subway train: "We're all doing this, you know with our phones – 'WAAAAAAA' [pokes out her tongue and imitates writing on a phone screen]. You know just looking at that on the subway, we're like, you know, looking at our phones all the time and… and we're not connecting" (Peterson 2021 Movement 6, 06:30-06:50 min.]). Carmen/Jinny's diagnosis echoes the current debates on the negative impact of social media on personal relationship and social cohesion while her embodiment allows for subtle exploration of new conditions associated with the pandemic, from "screen fatigue" to "touch starvation" that were reported by major newspapers (Leder Mackley/Jewitt 2022, 17, 18) and other media.

The entire Movement 3 "The Female Gaze" focuses on gender disparities and the actresses' interpretations of gender aspects of their Woolfian characters. Each persona represents through a song – based on excerpts from Woolf's novel – a different vision of female identity: Nikki/Susan has a close connection to nature "I think I am the field, I am the barn, I am the trees. I think sometimes I am not a woman, but the light that falls on this gate, on this ground" (Peterson 2021 Movement 3 [00:35-00:56 min.]), Alice/Rhoda focuses on the famous lines from Woolf's *A Room of One's Own*, referring to the necessary material basis of women's creative pursuits, Carmen/Jinny defies the pervasive Victorian cultural ideal of womanhood, shouting "Jinny! She's so FEROCIOUS, I love that! I feel empowered" (Peterson Movement 3 [03:47-03:54 min.]). The personas also express different vulnerabilities: Nikki/Susan grapples with motherhood: "Man, being a mum at quarantine is no joke. I basically have no time to myself" (Peterson 2021 Movement 2 [01:00-01:04 min.]), Alice/Rhoda has doubts about her identity "I do not know if I feel like a woman. Or if Rhoda does" (Peterson 2021 Movement 3 [05:48-05:52 min.]). Nikky/Susan's vulnerabilities represent the rising burden of the female contribution to domestic chores during the pandemic with Woolfian phrases turned into song lyrics: "Yet more will come, more children; more cradles, more baskets in the kitchen and hams ripening; and onions glistening; and more beds of lettuce and potatoes. Until I am glutted with natural happiness" (Peterson 2021 Movement 6 [08:29-08:37 min.]). Though Carmen/Jinny's persona also performs some household work, her struggles focus rather on the vanishing boundaries between her work and private life, brought about by the demands for her social media presence: "I don't do social media, hardly ever. Because… I dunno, I'm for some reason incredibly private about my life. And, and yet I know it's, it's part of what I'm supposed to be doing? You know, all the sudden it's now my job, it is…" (Peterson 2021 Movement 3, [06:08-06:26 min.]). In *The Waves in Quarantine*, the vulnerabilities exposed by the pandemic – such as those arising from isolation and gender inequity – overlap with pre-existing identities and contexts, creating a complex representation of the pandemic social world.

DALLOWAY-ESQUE SUPERSPREADER

On January 25, 2022, and the exact day marking the 140th anniversary of Woolf's birthday, Anna Pook and Talia Argondezzi published a short story "Mrs. Dalloway said she would buy the rapid COVID test herself", with a parodic nod to Woolf's novel *Mrs. Dalloway*. This publication date seems carefully chosen, since Pook announced their story with a tweet "What a laugh! What fun! To co-write this piece with @TaliaArgondezzi for @mcsweeneys. And what an impossible task it is to parody a genius. Happy birthday Virginia Woolf. And apologies in advance" (Pook 2022). The story appeared on the website of McSweeney's, an independent non-profit publishing company based in San Francisco. A social media preview was illustrated with an image that combines a spectral figure of the writer with the notion of multiplicity/replication, since Woolf's iconic 1902 photograph is juxtaposed with three samples of the 15-minute Covid-19 antigen self-test (cf. fig. 3). Shedding light on the origins of her other popular pandemic fiction "Vaccine Side Effect, or Have You Just Been Alive for 40 Years?", Argondezzi (2021) confessed: "I started writing satire right at the beginning of the pandemic because I wanted to cheer myself and other people up, which is a filthily earnest thing to say, but it's true, so it's encouraging to hear when it worked" (par. 'On the audience's reactions'). Both authors focus on parodic and satiric aspects of their Corona Fictions, emphasizing the intended mood-enhancing function of their text. According to mock bios accompanying this story, it was a result of transatlantic French-American cooperation: while Pook (n.d.) describes herself as "a writer and translator, living and working in the suburbs of Paris", emphasizing that "[s]he has never worn a beret. Not even ironically", Argondezzi (n.d.) – in fact, the Director of the Center for Writing and Speaking, Ursinus College – informs with a self-deprecating humour that she "is grateful they let her teach English and writing at Ursinus College", in Collegeville, Pennsylvania. Their story is freely available in its original digital form to global audiences.

Pook and Agondezzi's fiction belongs to a growing number of works that responds to Woolf's iconic *Mrs. Dalloway*. Woolf's 1925 novel focuses on one day of Clarissa Dalloway, an upper-class middle-aged woman, whose life is interwoven with several other characters. The most extended subplot shows Septimus Warren Smith, a traumatized working-class veteran, supported by his wife

Lucrecia. All other characters – including Sally Seton and Peter Walsh, with whom Clarissa was romantically involved in her youth, as well as her husband Richard and friend Hugh – meet at Clarissa's party, where one of the guests, Dr. Bradshaw brings the news of Septimus's suicide. In *Mrs. Dalloway*, Woolf had significantly developed her unique version of the stream of consciousness, in which she masterfully reproduced the mechanism of associative memory. Monica Latham (2021) has described the rich texture of Woolf's fiction as "Dalloway-esque" and has demonstrated how "these narrative, thematic, stylistic and syntactic Woolfian features are used, imitated, extended, transformed or updated" (355) in contemporary postmodern literature. She enumerates among Dalloway-esque characteristics, such elements as "the passage of time, the workings of memory, the meaning of death, the traumatic haunting experiences that lead to diverging choices of life or death" (ibid., 363).

Alhough at first glance, Pook and Argondezzi's story seems like a light reading, this fiction carefully imitates and parodies some "Dalloway-esque" elements and adapts them to the pandemic settings. They imitate Woolf's experimental technique, oscillating between the narrative of ordinary events and the complex workings of the human mind: while "stroll[ing] to the corner pharmacy, herself, for some rapid COVID tests" (Pook/Argondezzi 2022, par. 2), Clarissa analyzes the post-pandemic situation and eulogizes over her ordinary experience of shopping. The short-fiction satirizes Woolf's synesthetic passages that combine kinaesthetic, aural, and visual impressions: "Clarissa tripped in her buoyant, light-heeled way to the pharmacy; soft peals of laughter drifting through the automatic doors; the pharmacy lights dazzling, positively fluorescent" (ibid., par. 3).

Throughout their text Pook and Argondezzi extend 'Dalloway-esque' strategies by employing the viral poetics of repetition and multiplying, signalled with a metafictional comment "the phone greeting repeated like a prayer, like viral RNA replicating in a host cell" (ibid., par. 7). For instance, the authors echo Woolf's memorable exclamations, reflecting Clarissa changing mood, from an enthusiastic praise of a bright and fresh morning, "What a lark! What a plunge!" (Woolf 2015, 1) to a disappointed sigh, "What a waste! What a folly!" (ibid., 41) referring to the life course of her friend Peter Welsh. In Pook and Argondezzi's pandemic narrative, the trajectory of Clarissa's mood goes from an overwhelming joy of "How glorious! What delight!" (Pook/Argondezzi 2022, par. 2), stemming from the prospect of organizing the party preceded by rapid testing (though, as the narrative voice ironically observes these home tests have only "58.1" accuracy) to a frustrated grumbling, "What a farce! What a curse!" (ibid., par. 11) when the protagonist discovers that tests are out of stock not only in the nearby pharmacy but also in internet stores.

In "Mrs. Dalloway said she would buy the rapid COVID test herself", the characters are reduced to staged caricatures of their Woolfian predecessors: Clarissa is a middle-aged housewife, who copes with post-pandemic reality by planning a party while the shell-shocked soldier Septimus evolves into a burned-out pharmacist, traumatized by his 'frontline' healthcare job. In contrast with the careful multiplying of characters used in *The Waves in Quarantine*, Pook and Argondezzi's short-story does not engage deeply with its hypotext. For instance, there are no signs that a modern Clarissa may be a survivor of Covid-19 in parallel to Mrs. Dalloway whose heart was affected by the Spanish flu. Similarly, Smith's dramatic suicide is reduced to a parody of a job resignation: "It was all too much! Septimus flung himself vigorously, violently, past Clarissa, through the open pharmacy door, crying, 'I quit!'" (Pook/Argondezzi 2022, par. 8). The most extensive and nuanced use of Woolf's fiction may be observed in the spectral figure of Evans. In Woolf's novel, he is the friend and commanding officer of Septimus who was killed in WWI and who recurs in Smith's hallucination. In the short story, Evans became for Septimus not only his supervisor but also "Evans whom he'd loved" and "Evans who had volunteered to man the pharmacy phone, never dreaming it would destroy him" (ibid., par. 7) – as the authors developed the romantic bond between two men, only coded in Woolf's novel due to oppressive censorship of non-heteronormative themes in the interwar UK. This emphasis on Septimus's queerness is contrasted with a subdued portrayal of Clarissa's lesbian/bisexual identity (cf. Barrett 1997, Wood 2018) – both her former love interests appear only once in the story: "But what of Peter; he was still frail from his bout of consumption; should one take risks on behalf of others? Yet perhaps the chance of stealing another kiss from Sally Seton in the garden outweighed the dangers?" (ibid., par. 12). However, in the closing, after several futile attempts at obtaining the antigen Covid-19 tests, Clarissa evolves into a female superspreader, a femme fatale, organizing an event, in which many people may be potentially infected: "'Fuck it,' Clarissa Dalloway thought. 'Let's throw the year's first great superspreader'" (ibid., par. 13). Since Clarissa's decision comes just after her imagined reunion with Sally, it may be read as a challenge to socio-cultural norms parallel to Woolf's defiance of heteronormativity in her 1925 novel.

Pook and Argondezzi's story also offers a satiric portrayal of several systemic vulnerabilities exposed by the Covid-19 pandemic. The lack of effective educational strategies results in inadequate attitudes and behaviours, from Septimus's "mask shoved under his chin to better expel viral aerosols throughout the pharmacy" (ibid., par. 6) to Hugh's alleged vaccine skepticism. The inefficient healthcare and medical resources led to the burn-out of healthcare workers vividly portrayed in the figures of Septimus and Evans while the ubiquitous bureaucracy hampering immediate responses to the crisis is metonymically captured as "the seventeen-page form, with receipts" (ibid., par. 9) necessary for the insurance coverage of a Covid-19 test. However, the most persistent vulnerability remains the lack of systematic knowledge about the virus, as Clarissa sighs "what a shambles – an utter mess, as if after two years they'd failed to learn anything about COVID testing. The cases rising, falling, swirling, exploding" (ibid., par. 9). This short Corona Fiction resonates well with the uncertainty of the early 2022 year, oscillating between the hope for the end of the pandemic and the fear of its new waves and Covid-19 variants.

CONCLUSION

This article has explored two Corona Fictions, inspired by Woolf's works – both transform their Woolfian protagonists and re-locate them into the contemporary times. However, these works focus on different aspects of vulnerability, manifested on personal and systemic levels. While the fictional documentary *The Waves in Quarantine* offers a moving and nuanced portrayal of individual vulnerabilities related to isolation and gender inequality, the short fiction "Mrs. Dalloway said she would buy the rapid COVID test herself" becomes a caricature of the insufficient strategies adopted by the healthcare and governmental systems.

Since these vulnerabilities are mediated by the use of Woolfian characters, they become more accessible to diverse audiences on both affective and cognitive levels. As both Woolf and her works have iconic status in the contemporary global culture, readers and viewers are familiar with the basic frameworks and protagonists of her works – some audiences may have also encountered adaptations, biopics and fictions inspired by Woolf's oeuvre. While reading and watching these Corona Fictions, they may take comfort in returning to a well-known work or focus on the first artistic portrayals of the current pandemic – or enjoy them both simultaneously, since the unprecedented aspects of the current pandemic are inscribed into transmedia or transtextual contexts that are recognizable and familiar to the majority of their audiences.

The experimental character of Peterson's work results from her use of digital technologies: the vulnerabilities revealed by actors' persona are doubly mediated: first, by the use of Woolfian characters and second, by the re-scripting of the actors' statements. This video-experiment situates some experience that has been recently equated with the pandemic – loss, isolation, suffering – into a larger existential framework, provided by Woolf's works. Although the short story "Mrs. Dalloway said she would buy the rapid COVID test herself" reduces its transtextual protagonists to caricatures, it also transforms them into the pandemic figures of essential workers, ghosts and superspreaders, offering a sound critique of systemic vulnerabilities. By applying these very different strategies, the authors of the analyzed Corona Fictions transform Woolf's complex protagonists into contemporary figures and depict them in their humanity as exposed to the pandemic stressors, as well as personal and systemic vulnerabilities. Finally, due to their free dissemination and participatory nature, these fictions may offer new adaptive coping strategies to global audiences.

BIBLIOGRAPHY

Corpus Analyzed

Peterson, Lisa (dir.) (2021) *The Waves in Quarantine*, Berkeley Repertory Theatre in Berekely, CA, US, https://www.berkeleyrep.org/shows/the-waves-in-quar antine, 2022-09-15.

Pook, Anna/Argondezzi, Talia (2022) "Mrs. Dalloway said she would buy the rapid COVID test herself", *McSweeney's*, 2022-01-25, https://www.mcsweeneys. net/articles/mrs-dalloway-said-she-would-buy-the-rapid-covid-test-herself, 2022-09-15.

Works Cited

Argondezzi, Talia/McSweeney's (2021) "Behind the Tendency Classics: Talia Argondezzi's 'Vaccine Side Effect, or Have You Just Been Alive for 40 Years?'" [Interview], *Patreon*, 2021-05-18, https://www.patreon.com/posts/ 51362465, 2022-09-07.

Argondezzi, Talia (n.d.) "Articles by Talia Argondezzi", *McSweeney's*, www.mc sweeneys.net/authors/talia-argondezzi, 2022-12-11.

Barrett, Eileen (1997) "Unmasking Lesbian Passion: The Inverted World of *Mrs. Dalloway*", Eileen Barrett, Patricia Cramer (eds.) *Virginia Woolf: Lesbian Readings*, New York, NY, New York University Press, 146-164.

berkeleyrep [Berkeley Repertory Theatre] (2021) "Opening Night Conversation: *The Waves in Quarantine*", https://youtu.be/p7k2tg0eGSY, 2022-08-17.

Butler, Judith et al. (eds.) (2016) *Vulnerability in Resistance*, Durham, Duke University Press.

Catullus, Gaius Valerius (2005) *The Poems of Catullus: A Bilingual Edition*, trans. by Peter Green, Berkeley, CA, University of California Press.

Detloff, Madelyn (2016) *The Value of Virginia Woolf*, Cambridge, Cambridge University Press.

Evans, Elizabeth (2011) *Transmedia Television: Audiences, New Media, and Daily Life*, London, Routledge.

Evans, Elizabeth (2022) "Audiences, Industry, and Agency in Transmedial Character Transformation: Response to Susana Tosca", *Narrative* 30/2, 221-223. DOI: 10.1353/nar.2022.0022.

Froula, Christine (2021) "The Waves in Quarantine", *Virginia Woolf Miscellany* 98, 48-50.

Ganteau, Jean-Michel (2015) *The Ethics and Aesthetics of Vulnerability in Contemporary British Fiction*, London, Routledge.

Godara, Malvika et al. (2022) "The Wither or Thrive Model of Resilience: An Integrative Framework of Dynamic Vulnerability and Resilience in the Face of Repeated Stressors During the COVID-19 Pandemic", *Adversity and Resilience Science* 3, 261-282. DOI: 10.1007/s42844-022-00069-7.

Joseph, Jonathan (2013) "Resilience as Embedded Neoliberalism: A Governmentality Approach", *Resilience* 1/1, 38-52. DOI: 10.1080/21693293.2013.76 5741.

Kindley, Evan (2020) "Why Anxious Readers under Quarantine Turn to 'Mrs. Dalloway'", *The New Yorker*, 2020-04-10, https://www.newyorker.com/books/page-turner/why-anxious-readers-under-quarantine-turn-to-virginia-woolfs-mrs-dalloway, 2022-08-12.

Latham, Monica (2021) "Clarissa Dalloway's Global Itinerary: From London to Paris and Sydney", Jeanne Dubino et al. (eds.) *The Edinburgh Companion to Virginia Woolf and Contemporary Global Literature*, Edinburgh, Edinburgh University Press, 354-370.

Leder Mackley, Kerstin/Jewitt, Carey (2022) "Sociotechnical Imaginaries of Remote Personal Touch before and during COVID-19: An Analysis of UK Newspapers", *New Media & Society*, 1-29. DOI: 10.1177/14614448221113 922.

Madariaga, Aldo (2020) *Neoliberal Resilience: Lessons in Democracy and Development from Latin America and Eastern Europe*, Princeton, NJ, Princeton University Press.

Masten, Ann S. (2021a) "Multisystem Resilience: Pathways to an Integrated Framework", *Research in Human Development* 18/3, 153-163. DOI: 10.1080/ 15427609.2021.1958604.

Masten, Ann S. (2021b) "Resilience of Children in Disasters: A Multisystem Perspective", *International Journal of Psychology* 56/1, 1-11. DOI: 10.1002/ijop. 12737.

Obermayr, Julia/Völkl, Yvonne (2022) "Corona Fictions as Cultural Indicators of Social Cohesion and Resilience in the Wake of the Covid-19 Pandemic", *Momentum Quarterly* 11/2, 129-142. DOI: 10.15203/momentumquarterly.vol11. no1.p129-142.

Outka, Elizabeth (2019) *Viral Modernism. The Influenza Pandemic and Interwar Literature*, New York, NY, Columbia University Press.

Pfaelzer, Johanna/Medak, Susan (n.d.) "Berkeley Repertory Theatre 2020/21 Season Report", https://www.berkeleyrep.org/media/ao4p1wi4/fy2021-seasonreport.pdf, 2022-09-23.

Pook, Anna (n.d.) "Articles by Anna Pook", *McSweeney's*, https://www.mcsweeneys.net/authors/anna-pook, 2022-12-11.

Pook, Anna (2022) "What a laugh!", *Twitter*, 2022-01-25, https://twitter.com/mcsweeneys/status/1486054052538560512, 2022-12-11.

Research Group *Pandemic Fictions* (2020) "From Pandemic to Corona Fictions: Narratives in Times of Crises", *PhiN-Beiheft* 24, 321-344, http://web.fu-berlin.de/phin/beiheft24/b24t21.pdf, 2022-12-11.

Silver, Brenda R. (1983) *Virginia Woolf's Reading Notebooks*, Princeton, NJ, Princeton University Press.

Tosca, Susana (2022) "The Many Faces of Toshizō Hijikata", *Narrative* 30/2, 211-220. DOI: 10.1353/nar.2022.0021.

Wald, Priscilla (2008) *Contagious: Cultures, Carriers, and the Outbreak Narrative*, Durham, Duke University Press.

Wood, Olivia (2018) "A Diamond and a Tropic Gale: Reexamining Bisexuality in *Mrs. Dalloway*", *Journal of Bisexuality* 18/3, 382-394. DOI: 10.1080/15299716.2018.1540374.

Woolf, Virginia (1982) *The Diary of Virginia Woolf. Volume 3: 1925-30*, edited by Anne Olivier Bell, Harmondsworth, Penguin.

Woolf, Virginia (1985) *Moments of Being*, edited by Jeanne Schulkind, New York, NY, Harcourt.

Woolf, Virginia (2001) *A Room of One's Own and Three Guineas*. London, Vintage.

Woolf, Virginia (2011) *The Waves*, edited by Michael Herbert, Cambridge, Cambridge University Press.

Woolf, Virginia (2015) *Mrs. Dalloway*, edited by Anne E. Fernald, Cambridge, Cambridge University Press.

IMAGES

Figure 1: Recorded and transcribed Zoom conversations have been scripted and reworked into a film collage

Top row, left to right: Carmen Cusack (Carmen/Jinny), Manu Narayan (Manu/Louis), and Raúl Esparza (Raúl/Bernard/Associate Director). Bottom row, left to right: Darius de Haas (Darius/Neville), Nikki Renée Daniels (Nikki/Susan), and Alice Ripley (Alice/Rhoda) in Berkeley Rep's production of The Waves in Quarantine, directed by Lisa Peterson. Source: Photo courtesy of Berkeley Repertory Theatre.

Figure 2: The Waves in Quarantine *gravitates towards mise-en-abyme, as in the scene of Carmen/Jinny's dance. Carmen Cusack (Carmen/Jinny) in Berkeley Rep's production of* The Waves in Quarantine, *directed by Lisa Peterson*

Source: Photo courtesy of Berkeley Repertory Theatre.

Figure 3: A social media preview of Anna Pook and Talia Argondezzi's short story "Mrs. Dalloway said she would buy the rapid COVID test herself", illustrated with samples of the Covid-19 antigen self-test and Virginia Woolf's iconic photograph taken in 1902 by George Charles Beresford

Source: McSweeney's Twitter @mcsweeneys.

'¿Te importa?' Entre soledad y olvido: la representación de los ancianos en el teatro español durante la pandemia de COVID-19

Luana Bermúdez (Université de Genève)

Abstract

In recent years, the Covid-19 pandemic has become a subject suitable for reflection – and social criticism – that has nourished Spanish dramaturgy.

In the present study, we will analyze the representation of the elderly in some short plays written in the context of the pandemic, namely "Balada triste para armónica" (2020) by Sebastián Moreno, "Machu Picchu" (2020a) by Jerónimo López Mozo and "Justo en la noche" (2020) by Raúl Hernández Garrido. As we shall see, despite the aesthetic differences dictated by the playwrights' choices, these plays present the characters through similar strategies. Thus, the protagonists (undefined, helpless and often anonymous) are locked in claustrophobic spaces (apartments, rooms or isolated residences). On some occasions, their speeches become alternating monologues – even soliloquies – that speak of illness, fear of contagion and, above all, loneliness. At other times, their speeches denounce the lack of listening and the abandonment of the authorities. Ultimately, these texts give the floor to the elderly, one of the most vulnerable groups in the face of Covid-19, and become memorial reflections on the importance of rescuing them from oblivion.

INTRODUCCIÓN

A finales de diciembre de 2019 aparecieron las primeras noticias sobre la propagación de una extraña neumonía en la ciudad de Wuhan (cf. Calvo et al. 2020, 241). En apenas un mes, el nuevo virus ya se había extendido a otros 18 países (O.P.S./O.M.S. 2020). El 11 de marzo de 2020, el director general de la O.M.S.

declaró que la COVID-19 debía catalogarse como pandemia (Ghebreyesus 2020). Poco tiempo después, empezaron los días de confinamiento: calles vacías, didáctica a distancia, eventos celebrados a través de las plataformas digitales... Las secuelas físicas y psíquicas de la pandemia y del consiguiente encierro se han visto tempranamente reflejadas en forma de entradas de blogs, fotos de costumbres domésticas albergadas en perfiles Instagram y numerosos libros de autoayuda.[1] Tampoco faltaron videos compartidos una y otra vez que retrataban cómo se construyó un hospital en tan solo diez días en pleno Wuhan, o cómo, la silenciosa noche del 19 de marzo, una caravana de camiones militares salía de la ciudad de Bérgamo cargada de ataúdes (Hebrero 2020).

Por su parte, la literatura que, desde siglos, ha retratado grandes plagas como la peste negra o la gripe española, también ha captado los cambios provocados por la pandemia de coronavirus, unas veces reinventándose a través de las nuevas tecnologías y la mezcla genérica, otras, inspirándose en el éxito de propuestas –no tan– antiguas. Así, muchas obras acerca de epidemias (tanto reales como imaginarias) se han convertido en una verdadera mina de argumentos y de estrategias literarias en la que los autores contemporáneos han podido basarse. Basta pensar en el *Decameron* de Giovanni Boccaccio y en sus personajes que, tras huir de una Florencia asolada por la peste, buscaban maneras de entretenerse;[2] en los *Diarios* (1660-1669) de Samuel Pepys y el *Diario del año de la peste* (1722) de Daniel Defoe, donde nos topamos con la presencia insistente de estadísticas mortíferas; en *I promessi sposi* (1827) de Alessandro Manzoni y *La peste* (1947) de Albert Camus, cuyas páginas hablan del miedo al contagio y al confinamiento; en *Los ojos de la oscuridad* (1981), de Dean Ray Koontz, sobre un misterioso virus llamado "Whuan-400" y la psicosis que se derivó de su propagación, o en *Ensayo sobre la ceguera* (1995), del portugués José Saramago, acerca de una ceguera tanto física como metafórica.[3]

---

1 Basta pensar en títulos como *Ansiedad en tiempos de coronavirus: pierde el miedo a enfermar y mejora tu sistema inmunológico* (2020) de Fabiola Cuevas, o *Tu «Nueva A-Normalidad»: 5 pasos para salir con fuerza del Coronavirus* (2020) de Cantabrana Ruiz Larrinaga.

2 En numerosas obras sobre la pandemia de COVID-19 los personajes protagonizan todo tipo de actividades para no pensar en la crisis sanitaria. Así lo percibimos, por ejemplo, en *Nadie duerme* (2020), de Gracia Morales, en la que vemos cómo intentan distraerse buscando recetas culinarias, navegando por las redes sociales o refugiándose en el sexo.

3 Esta lista de obras no es exhaustiva. Para más informaciones acerca de los textos literarios que han retratado distintas epidemias, remitimos a los estudios de Zurita (2020), De Arriba Iglesias e Hidalgo Balsera (2021).

En lo que a España se refiere, las creaciones literarias sobre la pandemia de COVID-19, las Corona Fictions (cf. Research Group *Pandemic Fictions* 2020, 322-323), se han ido multiplicando a lo largo de los últimos años, pues contamos con varias novelas,[4] propuestas gráficas canónicas e incluso otras más excéntricas, como las aleluyas de la pandemia.[5] Tampoco faltan diarios de confinamientos de distinto tipo y tono, entre los que cabe mencionar *Parte de mí* (2021), de Marta Sanz o *Diario de un confinamiento* (2020), relato autobiográfico firmado por Eduardo Galán. Por su parte, en el panorama dramatúrgico, las compañías de teatro tuvieron que anular sus talleres, cancelar sus espectáculos o, en el mejor de los casos, reinventarlos y difundirlos a través de las nuevas tecnologías (Romera Castillo 2020a, 2020b, 2020c; Oñoro Ontero 2020). Como señalan los informes oficiales y abundantes artículos en periódicos digitales, esto supuso importantes secuelas para el ámbito teatral (Muro 2020, González 2021). Ahora bien, más allá de las repercusiones nefastas para el sector, la pandemia se ha convertido asimismo en un tema apto para la reflexión –y la crítica social– que ha nutrido la dramaturgia española actual. Pensemos en *La pira* (2020), proyecto del Centro Dramático Nacional compuesto por nueve textos breves de distinta autoría;[6] en la antología *De los días sin abrazos. 25 obras de teatro para un confinamiento* (2020), coordinada por Alberto de Casso y Julio Fernández, que recoge propuestas de varios autores de habla hispana; en *COVID-451*, de Sergio Blanco, escrita en 2020 y estrenada en el mismo año en el Teatre Lliure de Barcelona,[7] o en el volumen colectivo *Teatro para una crisis* (2021), fruto del proyecto #yomequedoencasahaciendoteatro, que reúne 83 textos teatrales. Juan Mayorga, Alfredo Sanzol, Jerónimo López Mozo, Gracia Morales, Paloma Pedrero, Sebastián Moreno y Raúl Hernández Garrido son solo algunos dramaturgos que se han dedicado a escribir no solo en marco de la pandemia, sino también sobre ella. Según creemos,

---

4 Nos referimos a *Behetría y miedo* (2021), de Vicente Martín Crespo, o *Volver a dónde* (2021), de Antonio Muñoz Molina.

5 Pensemos, entre otras, en los dos cómics *NoPanicovid* (2020), de Paloma Fernández Corcuera y Julio Serrano. En cuanto a las aleluyas, cabe señalar que la Diputación Provincial de Huesca celebró un concurso titulado "Aleluyas de la pandemia" a finales de 2020, en el que participaron varios autores cuyas propuestas hablaban de varios aspectos relacionados con la pandemia de COVID-19.

6 La obra se estructura en tres secciones tituladas *La conmoción*, *La distancia*, y *La incertidumbre*, que se representaron en *streaming* respectivamente el 26 de junio de 2020, desde el Teatro María Guerrero, el 3 de julio desde el Teatro Valle-Inclán y el 10 de julio de 2020, desde el Teatro María Guerrero.

7 Para más informaciones acerca de esta obra remitimos al estudio de Prieto Vidal (2021).

en las obras resultantes destacan varios rasgos comunes más allá del tema del que parten, como la forma de representar a los personajes ancianos y el objetivo crítico que estas persiguen, pues retratan tanto ejemplos de solidaridad hacia los mayores como de discriminación por parte de los grupos menos vulnerables.[8]

En una charla impartida en Ginebra en marzo de 2020, Rosa Kornfeld-Matte, Experta independiente de las Naciones Unidas, afirmaba que "las noticias sobre ancianos abandonados en asilos o el hallazgo de cadáveres en residencias de la tercera edad resultan escandalosas" (Hassine 2020). En cuanto a los mayores confinados en espacios domésticos, "el confinamiento en casa" –apunta Pinazo-Hernandis– "tiene muchas consecuencias negativas: afectación del estado emocional y anímico, con un aumento de la sintomatología depresiva; falta de contacto con red social y soledad. La soledad aumenta el riesgo de sedentarismo, la enfermedad cardiovascular […] y el riesgo de muerte" (Pinazo-Hernandis 2020, 250). Volviendo al ámbito dramatúrgico notamos que, en algunas ocasiones, esta preocupación por los ancianos –o, incluso, la denuncia de su situación– se plasma en la ausencia –tanto física como metafórica– de dichos personajes, pues solo se mencionan en los parlamentos de los protagonistas. Así sucede, por ejemplo, en "Mi ciudad en 97 m²" (2020), de Laura Aparicio, en "Mientras Duermes" (2020) de Carmen Abizanda, o en "Y tu entraña quemada" (2020), de Ruth Gutiérrez, donde los mayores solo están presentes a través del soliloquio de sus hijos que se desplazan sobre las tablas. De esta manera, en el texto de Aparicio, la madre con la que Silvia parece hablar por teléfono está ingresada en una UCI, por lo que toda la obra es, en realidad, la grabación de una nota audio que la anciana no puede escuchar. Por su parte, en la propuesta de Abizanda, el personaje del ABUELO ya ha muerto del coronavirus antes de que empiece la obra, y HOMBRE lo rememora en un amplio monólogo dirigido a su hijo enfermo. Así sucede también en el texto de Gutiérrez, ya que la protagonista de la obra, HIJA, da vida a un largo soliloquio en el que pretende hablar con su difunta madre. En otras ocasiones, en cambio, los ancianos ya no son personajes ausentes, sino que se convierten en los verdaderos protagonistas de los textos literarios.

En las líneas que siguen nos centraremos en este último caso y analizaremos la representación de los mayores en algunas obras de teatro breve escritas en el marco de la pandemia del COVID-19, a saber, "Balada triste para armónica", de Sebastián Moreno (2020), "Machu Picchu" (2020a), de Jerónimo López Mozo, y

---

8   Nos referimos al "edadismo" o "viejismo". Sobre este asunto, ver Rico (2020), Mediavilla (2020), Mansilla (2020) y Pinazo-Hernandis (2020).

"Justo en la noche" (2020), de Raúl Hernández Garrido.[9] Como veremos, pese a las diferencias estéticas dictadas por las elecciones de los dramaturgos, dichos textos presentan a los personajes mayores a través de unas estrategias similares. Así, los protagonistas (indefinidos, desamparados y, a veces, anónimos), se encuentran encerrados en unos espacios inhóspitos (pisos, habitaciones o residencias incomunicadas). En algunas ocasiones, sus diálogos se convierten en monólogos alternados que nos hablan de enfermedad, miedo al contagio y, sobre todo, soledad. En otras, sus discursos denuncian la falta de escucha y el abandono de las autoridades. En última instancia, estos textos ceden la palabra a los ancianos, uno de los grupos más vulnerables ante la COVID-19, y se convierten en reflexiones memorialísticas sobre la importancia de rescatar del olvido sus historias cotidianas.

BALADA TRISTE PARA ARMÓNICA, DE SEBASTIÁN MORENO: PRISIONEROS EN CASA

Inspirada en una noticia real sobre el calvario de una pareja octogenaria durante la pandemia, "Balada triste para armónica", de Sebastián Moreno, reconstruye de manera anti cronológica los últimos días de vida de Hermann, anciano enfermo de Alzheimer y contagiado por la COVID-19, y de Esperanza (en la vida real, Tamara), quien intenta cuidar de él a lo largo de los seis cuadros en los que se articula el texto teatral.[10] Esta peculiar estructura permite dividir la obra en tres partes distintas: la primera, que corresponde al momento posterior a la muerte de Hermann, la segunda, que coincide con su contagio, y la última, centrada en los días previos a la infección, donde el miedo a la pandemia ya se percibe en las réplicas de los personajes. Por lo tanto, el virus y sus consecuencias se convierten en un verdadero hilo conductor que atraviesa todas las escenas: antes del luto, como tema del que hablar y del que protegerse a nivel psicológico; durante la enfermedad, como problema del que curarse a nivel físico, y, después de ella, como causa directa del duelo.

Tal como indica el título que encabeza la primera sección de la obra, a saber, "Último día de confinamiento: cenizas", la propuesta de Moreno empieza al final

---

9   Todas estas obras forman parte de la antología *De los días sin abrazos. 25 obras de teatro en confinamiento* (2020), publicada en Madrid por Ediciones Invasoras.

10 La historia de la pareja se editó en varios periódicos españoles y no tardó en dar la vuelta al mundo. Para más informaciones acerca de la vida y la muerte de Hermann Schreiber, el 'alemán de la armónica', ver los artículos de Junquera (2020) y de Currás (2021).

del encierro forzado. El marbete, que en un primer momento parece indicar algo positivo, preanuncia la entrega de la urna con las cenizas de Hermann a Esperanza. Se trata, pues, de una treta del dramaturgo para romper con las expectativas del lector y hacer énfasis desde el principio en la tragedia vivida por el personaje anciano, condenado a muerte desde el principio. Cuando se abre el telón sorprendemos a Esperanza, sola, en un espacio doméstico. Según sugiere la acotación, estamos ante un escenario vacío, indefinido, en el que ella se encuentra confinada, donde solo destacan los accesorios que tienen que ver con el contexto pandémico –a saber, "guantes", "gafas protectoras", "mascarillas"[11] (Moreno 2020, 149)–, y el único mueble visible en las tablas es una mesa sobre la que colocará los restos mortales de él. Por ende, a través de la construcción del escenario, el dramaturgo pretende concentrar la atención del lector hacia el resultado mortífero de la enfermedad, al igual que lo hacen otras propuestas teatrales articuladas en torno al tema pandémico.[12] Volviendo a la obra de Moreno observamos que, lejos de ser un escenario acogedor, el espacio doméstico en el que se desenvuelve el personaje femenino aparece antropomorfizado y la asusta, pues según leemos el timbre, en un primer momento "tímido", luego suena "como una lengua inflamada. Tumefacta […], como un grito ahogado" (Moreno 2020, 149). Por lo tanto, la casa –escenario privilegiado de muchas obras teatrales sobre la crisis sanitaria[13]–, se convierte en un lugar que intimida y oprime a los protagonistas, opresión que se acentúa al descubrir que estos personajes particularmente vulnerables ni siquiera salen a aplaudir al balcón.[14]

---

11 En los textos sobre la pandemia de COVID-19 la presencia de este tipo de accesorios es frecuente, basta pensar en "Mi ciudad de 97 m²" (2020), de Laura Aparicio. Allí, la protagonista se dedica a desinfectarse las manos y la ropa antes de entrar en casa, y el dramaturgo salpica las acotaciones con elementos como "spray", "guantes", "lejía", etc.

12 Así, por ejemplo, en "Mientras duermes" (2020), de Carmen Abizanda, la breve acotación que inaugura la obra dirige nuestra mirada hacia una cama presente en el centro de un cuarto, prolongación escénica de la enfermedad del niño: "Una habitación de reducidas dimensiones en una vivienda de un edificio de ciudad. Una cama en el centro que ocupa el cuerpo de un niño de diez años" (Abizanda 2020, 15).

13 Pensemos en "El rincón de sol" (2020), de Laura Garmo; "Y tu entraña quemada" (2020), de Ruth Gutiérrez; en "Mientras duermes" (2020), de Carmen Abizanda y "Mi ciudad en 97 m²" (2020), de Laura Aparicio, todas editadas en la misma antología.

14 En la obra, leemos: "Fuera, el resto de vecinos sale a sus balcones a aplaudir en homenaje a los sanitarios que andan combatiendo la pandemia con fuerza y pocos recursos. […] Hermann enrojece, mira *hacia* la ventana [la cursiva es nuestra]" (Moreno 2020, 152).

La soledad y el abandono a los que debieron enfrentarse los ancianos y sus cuidadores a lo largo de la crisis sanitaria –y que el dramaturgo intenta denunciar[15]– se notan no solo a través de la construcción escénica del texto literario, sino también a partir del sucinto reparto de personajes que habita(ba)n ese lugar inhóspito, a saber, dos. Estos se reducen simplemente a "los ojos de Esperanza" y "los ojos de Hermann" (ibid.), como si se hubieran fragmentado a raíz de la crisis y de la obligación de llevar mascarilla.[16] Un tercer personaje, es decir, un funcionario ausente de la *dramatis personae*, asoma en la primera sección para desaparecer de la obra sin dejar huella, pues su función solo consiste en traerle la urna a Esperanza y subrayar su aislamiento. Así lo percibimos en la acotación inicial, que insiste en la ausencia de comunicación entre ellos –no solo verbal sino también corporal, ya que incluso sus ojos *callan*–, provocada por el distanciamiento obligatorio:

> [Esperanza] Se cubre con una mascarilla, y abre. La luz natural entra a través del rellano, y se despliega sobre el funcionario, que cubierto en ropas blancas y asépticas, como un Dios profiláctico, le hace entrega de una urna. Cenizas. Se miran. […] Es curioso cómo han involucionado los sentidos durante el encierro. […] Los ojos del funcionario callan detrás de unas gafas protectoras. Cierra la puerta. (ibid.)

En la parte central de la obra nos encontramos en el mismo espacio cerrado, pero volvemos atrás en el tiempo y asistimos a la progresión de la enfermedad de Hermann, empezando por el momento clímax en el que "se lo llevan en una camilla" (ibid., 150). Tal y como sucedía en la primera escena protagonizada por el funcionario, volvemos a hallar a unos personajes anónimos que, en este caso, se llevan al enfermo sin comunicar con Esperanza. En esta sección, central desde el punto de vista estructural, se insiste en la omnipresencia del virus y en el miedo que se deriva no solo a través de los títulos que encabezan las secciones, sino también por medio de las acotaciones. En cuanto a los títulos, notamos que están centrados en los órganos afectados por el virus o en los síntomas que presenta Hermann (a saber, "Segundo miércoles de confinamiento: la tos"; "Segundo lunes de confinamiento: los pulmones"; "Primer domingo de confinamiento: la fiebre"). Por su

---

15 Esta denuncia se nota en partes de las acotaciones, donde leemos reflexiones como: "Parece que pronto, todo volverá, paulatinamente a la normalidad. Al menos para unos cuantos; es imposible determinar si para unos muchos o unos pocos" (Moreno 2020, 149).

16 Estamos ante una estrategia que vuelve a aparecer en otras obras, como en "(Silencio)" (2020), de Elena González-Vallinas, donde los protagonistas se llaman simplemente "A" y "B".

parte, en las acotaciones, los síntomas parecen cobrar vida, pues aparecen personificados, como si se describieran a través de los ojos de Esperanza: "Es una tos amarga, endemoniada, que, maleducada, interrumpe la música que libera un viejo tocadiscos" (ibid.). Así se sugiere también cuando se nos cuenta cómo ella le cura la fiebre, ya que las acotaciones se asemejan a instrucciones que Esperanza, asustada, se repite de manera obsesiva: "Treinta y ocho con siete. Un trapo húmedo y un poco de presión en la frente. [...] Y un trapo húmedo, bajo las manos [...]. Bajo sus guantes. Sobre la frente de HERMANN. Bajo sus guantes. [...] Treinta y ocho con seis. Al escurrir el trapo, parece que chisporroteara destilando fiebre y otros *miedos* [la cursiva es nuestra]" (ibid., 151). Este miedo silencioso parece verbalizarse a través de las breves réplicas desarticuladas de Hermann que interrumpen la acción, en las que se repiten adjetivos como "solo", sustantivos como "miedo", e interjecciones coloquiales como "Bu" (ibid.).

Las últimas dos secciones de la obra nos hablan del comienzo de un confinamiento que acentuará la situación de soledad e incomunicación inicial en la que se hallan los personajes, no solo frente a la sociedad, ya que Esperanza debe cuidar sola de él,[17] sino también entre ellos. En efecto, en la acotación que inaugura la quinta sección se recalca la distancia que separa a los protagonistas desde el comienzo de la historia, a pesar de que compartan el mismo espacio vital. Según se nos dice, él se asemeja a una celda a la que la cuidadora no logra acceder, por lo que se acentúa la situación de aislamiento de él: "Esperanza lo mira desde la distancia. Se le acerca, como el que se aproxima a una celda, a una coraza, a un despertar. Como si cada vez, fuera la primera vez" (ibid., 152). Esta separación se confirma al leer sus diálogos –o, mejor dicho, sus monólogos alternados–, puesto que los personajes nunca entablan una verdadera discusión debido al Alzheimer que padece Hermann. Por ende, el anciano no parece comprender la explicación del virus proporcionada por ella, a pesar de que se lo describa con unas imágenes banales y comparaciones sencillas –las únicas, quizás– que él aún puede reconocer. Así lo percibimos cuando el personaje femenino le dice que "el virus está de gira" (ibid., 153) ya que él "solo recuerda palabras de urgencia en alemán, balbuceos y notas de armónica" (ibid., 150). Conforme a lo que sucede en otras obras centradas en la pandemia y sus secuelas, notamos que Esperanza intenta proteger al anciano: busca actividades para entretenerse ("nos entretendremos con otras cosas", ibid., 153), procura que no le lleguen las noticias dolorosas ("no veremos mucho la tele", ibid.) y matiza su marginalización por medio de la imaginación,

---

17 Según indica el texto, Esperanza solo recibe apoyo de un médico por vía telefónica. Esta situación llama a la memoria situaciones reales recopiladas en el informe de Amnistía Internacional España (2020).

pues le hace creer que los aplausos son para su concierto de armónica ("El aplauso dura unos minutos. Hermann enrojece, mira hacia la ventana. Se lleva la mano al pecho, toca algunas notas más y saluda", ibid., 152). A esta lista de acciones se suma también una serie de precauciones físicas que ella toma –en balde– para evitar el contagio ("haremos ejercicios. Llevaré guantes y mascarilla", ibid., 154).

Mostrando la progresiva desaparición de Hermann, la propuesta de Moreno remarca el aislamiento y el abandono a los que debieron hacer frente los ancianos y sus cuidadores durante la pandemia, al igual que sugiere la necesidad de recordar a los mayores que murieron en sus domicilios y no siempre fueron contabilizados en las cifras oficiales (cf. BBC News Mundo 2020; Sosa Troya 2021). Por ende, el Alzheimer del protagonista se convierte también en una enfermedad metafórica contra la que hay que luchar: en palabras del propio dramaturgo, "escribo […] para lanzar preguntas para las que no tengo respuestas […] Para colocar un espejo turbio al lado de la polis. Para dar voz y memoria a quienes la perdieron" (Otheguy Riveira 2021).

MACHU PICCHU, DE JERÓNIMO LÓPEZ MOZO: RESIDENCIAS, INCOMUNICACIÓN Y MUERTE

Según Alberto de Casso y Julio Fernández, "Machu Picchu", de Jerónimo López Mozo, se inspira en la obra *Venecia*, de Jorge Accame, representada en la sala Cuarta Pared de Madrid en el año 2000 (cf. Casso/Fernández 2020, 117). Esta cuenta que el personaje principal, llamado la Gringa, quiere viajar a Venecia para volver a ver a Don Giacomo, coprotagonista de un amor juvenil sin final feliz. En el momento presente, la mujer –anciana, ciega y enferma–, logra conocer el destino anhelado gracias a tres prostitutas que trabajan para ella. De manera parecida a lo que sucederá en la obra del dramaturgo español, estas transforman sillas y accesorios cotidianos en un supuesto barco, y la transportan a los canales venecianos por medio de su imaginación. A pesar de este elemento común, el objetivo del viaje descrito por López Mozo no es recuperar un amor adolescente, sino huir del encierro al que se enfrentaron los ancianos en los hogares para personas mayores. Así pues, con su texto, López Mozo nos coloca directamente dentro de una residencia, otro escenario privilegiado para representar y denunciar la situación de este grupo vulnerable durante la pandemia de COVID-19. Allí encontramos a Encarna, personaje indefinido del que solo sabemos que "pasa de los ochenta" (López Mozo 2020a, 119), y a Raúl, asistente social que se ocupa de ella. Tras una serie de preguntas sobre la pandemia a las que, según sugieren las acotaciones,

Raúl no quiere responder para protegerla,[18] Encarna le pide llevarla a Machu Picchu, lugar desde donde su nieto le ha mandado una postal. Después de intentar explicarle que se trata de un viaje imposible y, sobre todo, luego de conmoverse al ver su reacción desesperada, el asistente decide usar la imaginación para sacarla de allí. Acto seguido, construye un avión en el balcón del cuarto y finge trasladarla al destino deseado.

Tal como ocurre en "Balada triste para armónica", "Machu Picchu" se divide en varias secciones que delimitan la vida y la muerte de la protagonista anciana. En este caso, la primera corresponde a "la realidad" vivida por Encarna dentro del hogar para personas mayores, compuesta por preguntas, noticias dolorosas y alusiones al encierro; la segunda constituye un puente entre la realidad y la ficción, la vida y la muerte de la protagonista, y la última corresponde al viaje imaginario hacia Perú y al momento en el que fallece Encarna. Como también sucede en la obra de Moreno, la soledad, el abandono y la incomunicación a la que se enfrentaron los mayores —en este caso, en las residencias— se sugieren gracias a la peculiar construcción escénica. Al comienzo de la obra, nos encontramos ante un escenario prácticamente vacío, indefinido y cerrado. En este caso, el espacio se reduce todavía más, pues no estamos en un piso, sino solamente en "una habitación" de una residencia anónima. Los escasos objetos visibles encima de las tablas —y que, por ende, cobran protagonismo— son una silla y una mesilla de noche en la que se encuentra la postal, única huella del cariño familiar con el que cuenta la protagonista. Según el informe redactado por Mediavilla, colaborador de Amnistía Internacional, "las residencias se convirtieron en los días más críticos de la pandemia en auténticos lugares de encierro, con sus residentes bajo confinamiento durante semanas en sus habitaciones" (Mediavilla 2020). En nuestra opinión, López Mozo intenta plasmar ese "lugar de encierro" no solo a través del escenario en el que desarrolla la historia, sino también por medio de las breves réplicas de Encarna, en las que pregunta de manera reiterada "¿Por qué no puedo salir de mi habitación? ¿Qué pasa ahí fuera?" (López Mozo 2020a, 119). Esta misma idea parece resurgir en otras obras de teatro protagonizadas por personajes ancianos, como vemos en "Importuna lluvia de batracios…" (2020), de Amelie Blume, donde el protagonista mayor —reducido a simple VOZ en la *dramatis personae*— afirma ser un "Liberado de las residencias para la tercera edad" (Blume 2020, 36).[19]

---

18 En el texto, leemos: "ENCARNA: ¿Y a él dónde lo han llevado? RAÚL: (*Tarda en decirlo*) Rafael ha muerto [la cursiva es nuestra]" (López Mozo 2020a, 120).

19 El anciano que protagoniza la obra completa esta idea poco después, reproduciendo los diálogos de los demás personajes que le traen la compra: "VOZ: (*Cantando*): Para no

La única forma de salir de ese universo cerrado es a través de la representación de un guion inventado por Raúl, como si de una obra de teatro se tratara, con su respectivo cambio de escenario, de vestuario y de guion. Así, en la parte central de la obra, titulada "Intermedio", asistimos a la creación de un escenario alternativo dentro de la residencia, constituido por "un par de sillas, otros tantos cajones, algunas tablas y un ventilador" (López Mozo 2020a, 122). El propio Raúl –ahora, el "Aviador Jorge" (ibid., 123)– se cambia de ropa y se prepara al viaje imaginario en un avión llamado significativamente "Clavileño". En palabras de Julia Nawrot, la intertextualidad caracteriza buena parte de la dramaturgia de López Mozo sobre la pandemia (cf. Nawrot 2021, 179-181).[20] Esta reflexión se aplica también a "Machu Picchu", ya que solo entendemos la envergadura de la tragedia final si tomamos en cuenta la referencia a las aventuras que viven Sancho Panza y don Quijote durante el capítulo titulado *De la venida de Clavileño, con el fin desta dilatada aventura*. En efecto, tras la descripción del viaje por parte de Raúl –que calca las palabras de Sancho– Encarna parece captar la cita literaria. Por consiguiente, la anciana entiende que el vuelo hacia Machu Picchu solo será imaginario –al igual que su fuga de la residencia–:

> RAÚL: El motor. Ya vamos por los aires, rompiéndolos con más velocidad que una saeta. El viento es tan recio que parece que con mil fuelles nos están soplando.[21]
> ENCARNA: Que bonitas frases. Parecen del Quijote. Aunque no se siente que nos movamos de donde estamos […]
> RAÚL: La residencia. Cada vez más pequeña. […] Llegamos, doña Encarna. Machu Picchu a la vista. ¡Impresionante! Empezamos a bajar. ¿Me oye? ¿Me oye, doña Encarna?
>
> *RÁUL la mira. ENCARNA no respira.* [cursiva del original]
> (López Mozo 2020a, 124)

---

contaminar / me dejan la comida y el agua en el ascensor / y las medicinas / […] Ahí estás bien / mejor que en la residencia / me dicen / Desde luego / No es un hotel de cuatro estrellas / pero es lo que hay" (Blume 2020, 39).

20 Como señala Nawrot, López Mozo ha abarcado la pandemia de COVID-19 en cinco obras de teatro breve reunidas bajo el rótulo *Desde mi celda* (2020b), aún sin editar (cf. Nawrot 2021).

21 En el capítulo XLI de la *Segunda parte del ingenioso caballero don Quijote de la Mancha*, Sancho afirma que "por este lado me da un viento tan recio, que parece que con mil fuelles me están soplando" (Cervantes 2004, 973).

Según Manuela Fox, en las obras de López Mozo destacan "dos principales líneas creativas", una, "centrada en el compromiso político y civil, que abarca temas de la historia reciente o de la actualidad para llegar a una reflexión ideológica y ética sobre la sociedad, […] la segunda, orientada hacia la investigación metateatral" (Fox 2019, 148; cf. Nawrot 2021, 179). En esta misma línea, "Machu Picchu" propone una reflexión crítica sobre la manera en la que los ancianos vivieron la pandemia desde los cuartos de las residencias, al igual que muestra que el teatro sirve como medio de evasión momentáneo, como instrumento apto para protegerse del dolor. Así parece sugerirlo el desenlace de la obra: antes de que se cierre el telón, Raúl opta por seguir interpretando durante unos minutos el papel del "aviador Jorge" para evitar sufrir por la muerte de Encarna: "RAÚL: Lo primero que haré cuando regrese es decirle a Raúl que Encarna ha llegado bien" (López Mozo 2020a, 124).

JUSTO EN LA NOCHE, DE RAÚL HERNÁNDEZ GARRIDO: ENTRE MEMORIA Y OLVIDO

"Justo en la noche", de Raúl Hernández Garrido, nos sitúa en un lugar abierto, precisamente en una "plazoleta, en la noche" (Hernández Garrido 2020, 103). Allí, sentado en un banco, un anciano enfermo y anónimo –"HOMBRE de unos 90 años" (ibid.)– presencia el intercambio de réplicas rápidas entre dos personajes jóvenes, a saber, CHICA (una prostituta) y CHICO (un ladrón). Tras descubrir que el anciano está escuchando su conversación, CHICA lo interpela y le da la posibilidad de expresarse. La pregunta desencadena el largo monólogo de él, en el que les cuenta su fuga de una residencia de ancianos.

A pesar de situarnos en un espacio abierto y no en uno cerrado –como sucedía en los textos de Moreno y López Mozo–, el escenario que elige Hernández Garrido es igual de intimidador que los anteriores. La ubicación espacial, bastante vaga (solo hay un banco), se completa con datos temporales concretos y agobiantes: estamos en "los tiempos de coronavirus", precisamente durante "la primavera *negra* de 2020 [la cursiva es nuestra]" (Hernández Garrido 2020, 103). Esta impresión negativa se confirma unas líneas después, al explicitar por medio de las palabras y los gestos abruptos de los personajes que estos se sienten amenazados:

> Una CHICA llega a la plaza. […] Se pasea por la plazoleta, como esperando algo.
> Llega alguien, apresurado. La chica se detiene, asustada.
> CHICA: ¿Quién está ahí?

> El que ha llegado, un CHICO, se para en seco. No contesta. La CHICA se detiene, intentando protegerse de un posible ataque. (ibid.)

Como sucede en varias obras de teatro escritas durante la pandemia de COVID-19, los espacios abiertos son lugares tan inhóspitos y claustrofóbicos como los cerrados, ya sean habitaciones, pisos enteros o residencias. Así lo vemos, por ejemplo, en "La espantapájaros" (2020) de Paloma Pedrero, donde la protagonista trabaja de estatua viviente en la plaza de Lavapiés de Madrid y le grita a un policía "¡Sáquenme de aquí, sáquenme de esta pesadilla! ¡No puedo respirar! ¡Necesito una ventana!" (Pedrero 2020, 161).[22] De esta manera, la "plazuela" al aire libre de Moreno se convierte en un espacio parecido a la residencia de la que se ha escapado HOMBRE, pues como él mismo dirá, en ambos lugares se siente desamparado, carece de interlocutores que lo escuchen y el miedo al contagio está omnipresente.[23] Así, a través de sus palabras, descubrimos que el hogar para ancianos es un espacio donde los mayores se encuentran solos y completamente aislados del mundo exterior.[24] Según el informe de Amnistía Internacional España, a las personas mayores ingresadas en residencias "no se les explicó lo que estaba pasando y muchos pensaron que se les estaba castigando" (Amnistía Internacional España 2020, 55). De la misma manera, en el texto literario, la desaparición repentina de sus compañeros resulta tan inexplicable que HOMBRE se ve obligado a robar un periódico durante una consulta con su médico para descubrir qué sucede:

> Esto fue demasiado rápido. Paco. Luego, Ramona. [...] Dejaron de ponernos la televisión. Dijeron que la residencia se había comprado el plus con series, y que eso era mejor para nosotros. No volvimos a ver noticias. [...] Un día tuve cita con el médico. [...] Me escondí el periódico. [...] Me dirigí a la habitación y encontré lo del virus. [...] Y me di cuenta de lo que ocurría en la residencia. (Hernández Garrido 2020, 106)

---

22 Ocurre algo parecido en "Mikel y la conmoción" (2020), de Alfredo Sanzol, donde la calle se caracteriza por "un silencio tenso, un silencio de amenaza" (Sanzol 2020, 15).

23 En la obra, leemos: "El hombre tose. Los otros dos dan cada uno un paso atrás. CHICO: ¿Qué? ¿Quiere infectarnos?" (Hernández Garrido 2020, 105).

24 En su monólogo, HOMBRE dirá: "Le pregunté a Judit, la cuidadora morenita. [...] No volvió a responder a mis preguntas. [...] Me crucé con la directora, le dije adiós. Ella apenas me contestó. [...] Saludé a todos, no me hicieron caso. [...] Salí y caminé, a mi paso, sin apresurarme. Nadie me siguió" (Hernández Garrido 2020, 106f.).

El anciano, sin hogar al que acudir ni personas a las que contactar tras su huida,[25] se aferra a sus únicas pertenencias (metonimias de sus vínculos familiares) para intentar sobrellevar la dolorosa situación en la que se halla, al igual que lo hacían los protagonistas de López Mozo y Moreno. En este caso, a la fotografía de su mujer fallecida, en el de López Mozo, a una postal que representa el cariño de un nieto, y en el de Moreno, a las notas de armónica que Hermann aún recuerda, pues en palabras de Esperanza "Tu hija fue tu profesión. Tu hija fue la música" (Moreno 2020, 153). Sin embargo, contrariamente a los textos previamente analizados, y de la misma manera que ocurre en obras como *¡Que revienten los viejos! (El depósito de cadáveres vivos)*, de Jerónimo López Mozo,[26] la propuesta de Hernández Garrido critica la completa falta de solidaridad hacia los mayores. Así se sugiere al final de "Justo en la noche", cuando CHICA y CHICO –posiblemente, cualquiera– abandonan el escenario y, por ende, al anciano. Al encontrarse ante unas tablas desiertas y una oscuridad cada vez más metafórica, a HOMBRE solo le queda preguntarle a su interlocutor ausente si le importa su situación:

> *Suena una sirena de un coche policía, aproximándose.*
>
> CHICO: Será mejor que nos vayamos.
> CHICA: ¿Y ese?
> CHICO: ¿Te importa?
> *El CHICO se va. La CHICA mira al viejo. El HOMBRE no le mira. La CHICA sale. El HOMBRE carraspea.*
> HOMBRE: ¿Te importa? ¿Te importa? ¿Te importa? [cursiva del original]
> (Hernández Garrido 2020, 107)

En una entrevista fechada en agosto de 2020, Hernández Garrido afirmaba que no "es indiferente al tema social en plena pandemia. [...]. Hago obras que son reflexiones sobre lo que está ocurriendo", y concluía indicando que la pandemia es una "enfermedad social" (El Teatro 2020 [22:13-24:30 min.]). Por ende, "Justo en la noche" revela uno de sus síntomas –uno más– como la falta de solidaridad hacia los más vulnerables.

---

25 "HOMBRE: Mi casa. Si supiera a dónde ir. Mi casa. No puedo volver atrás. ¿Para qué? Ya no está Carmen allá" (Hernández Garrido 2020, 105).

26 Para más informaciones acerca de esta obra, remitimos al estudio de Nawrot (2021).

CONCLUSIONES

Como hemos visto a lo largo de este breve recorrido por tres obras de teatro sobre la COVID-19, los personajes ancianos y, en parte, sus cuidadores, han atraído la atención de numerosos dramaturgos españoles. Sus textos –a menudo inspirados en noticias y datos reales– se convierten en reflexiones sobre las situaciones –positivas y, sobre todo, negativas– que los mayores vivieron durante la pandemia. En algunas obras, los ancianos solo aparecen de manera marginal, evocados en los parlamentos de los verdaderos protagonistas, casi para plasmar su aislamiento y marginalización por parte del resto de la sociedad durante la pandemia de CO-VID-19; en otras, estos personajes –a menudo indefinidos, solos y anónimos– toman la palabra y denuncian ellos mismos su aislamiento. Para llevar a cabo esta denuncia, los dramaturgos los sitúan en espacios distintos, pero igualmente asfixiantes: no solo residencias incomunicadas y plazas vacías por el toque de queda obligatorio, sino también casas o habitaciones sin balcón para evitar desenlaces trágicos, como sugiere el protagonista anciano de "Importuna lluvia de batracios…" (2020), de Blume: "VOZ: Muchas gracias por todo / La habitación está genial / sin balcón / para que no haga tonterías" (Blume 2020, 39). En sus textos, los dramaturgos insisten en la incomunicación que padecieron las personas de esta franja etaria también a través de la ausencia de un interlocutor activo, de la construcción de sus parlamentos –compuestos por réplicas entrecortadas, frases interrumpidas por puntos suspensivos o exclamaciones desesperadas–, y de su contenido. Por ende, no debe sorprendernos que los personajes mayores repitan de manera casi obsesiva palabras como "soledad" o "miedo", y subrayen una y otra vez su "encierro", al igual que lo hace "VOZ" en el texto de Blume: "Tómate la vitamina D / que el único sol que vas a ver / durante mucho tiempo es / el que se cuela por entre las ranuras de las persianas bajadas y clausuradas en candado / A través de esas ranuras veo el cielo…" (ibid.).

En última instancia, estos textos teatrales ceden la palabra a uno de los grupos más vulnerables ante la COVID-19 y, de esta forma, establecen a los ancianos como protagonistas pandémicos. Las obras se convierten, pues, en reflexiones sobre la importancia de rescatar a estas víctimas del olvido, insertarlas dentro de las estadísticas oficiales en las que no siempre aparecen, y reflexionar en torno a una "sociedad [que] se ha anestesiado ante la tragedia" (Altares, 2021). Por lo tanto, cuando se cierra el telón, le toca al público contestar a la pregunta reiterada de HOMBRE que, al final de "Justo en la noche", nos pregunta: "¿Te importa?" (Hernández Garrido 2020, 107).

BIBLIOGRAFÍA

Bibliografía primaria

Abizanda, Carmen (2020) "Mientras duermes", Alberto de Casso/Julio Fernández (eds.) *De los días sin abrazos. 25 obras de teatro en confinamiento*, Madrid, Ediciones Invasoras, 13-18.

Aparicio, Laura (2020) "Mi ciudad en 97 m²", Alberto de Casso/Julio Fernández (eds.) *De los días sin abrazos. 25 obras de teatro en confinamiento*, Madrid, Ediciones Invasoras, 27-31.

Blume, Amelie (2020) "Importuna lluvia de batracios…", Alberto de Casso/Julio Fernández (eds.) *De los días sin abrazos. 25 obras de teatro en confinamiento*, Madrid, Ediciones Invasoras, 33-40.

Garmo, Laura (2020) "El rincón de sol", Alberto de Casso/Julio Fernández (eds.) *De los días sin abrazos. 25 obras de teatro en confinamiento*, Madrid, Ediciones Invasoras, 63-70.

González-Vallinas, Elena (2020) "(Silencio)", Alberto de Casso/Julio Fernández (eds.) *De los días sin abrazos. 25 obras de teatro en confinamiento*, Madrid, Ediciones Invasoras, 79-86.

Gutiérrez, Ruth (2020) "Y tu entraña quemada", Alberto de Casso/Julio Fernández (eds.) *De los días sin abrazos. 25 obras de teatro en confinamiento*, Madrid, Ediciones Invasoras, 87-94.

Hernández Garrido, Raúl (2020) "Justo en la noche", Alberto de Casso/Julio Fernández (eds.) *De los días sin abrazos. 25 obras de teatro en confinamiento*, Madrid, Ediciones Invasoras, 101-108.

López Mozo, Jerónimo (2020a) "Machu Picchu", Alberto de Casso/Julio Fernández (eds.) *De los días sin abrazos. 25 obras de teatro en confinamiento*, Madrid, Ediciones Invasoras, 117-124.

López Mozo, Jerónimo (2020b) "¡Que revienten los viejos! (El depósito de los cadáveres vivos)", *Cartas desde mi celda* (manuscrito).

Morales, Gracia (2020) "Nadie duerme", Alberto de Casso/Julio Fernández (eds.) *De los días sin abrazos. 25 obras de teatro en confinamiento*, Madrid, Ediciones Invasoras, 139-146.

Moreno, Sebastián (2020) "Balada triste para armónica", Alberto de Casso/Julio Fernández (eds.) *De los días sin abrazos. 25 obras de teatro en confinamiento*, Madrid, Ediciones Invasoras, 147-154.

Pedrero, Paloma (2020) "La espantapájaros", Alberto de Casso/Julio Fernández (eds.) *De los días sin abrazos. 25 obras de teatro en confinamiento*, Madrid, Ediciones Invasoras, 155-162.

Sanzol, Alfredo (2020) "Mikel y la conmoción", *La pira. La conmoción. La distancia. La incertidumbre*, Madrid, Centro Dramático Nacional, 9-22.

Bibliografía secundaria

Altares, Guillermo (2021) "La muerte sin duelo: cómo la pandemia ha transformado la percepción del fallecimiento", *El País*, 2021-08-29, https://elpais.com/sociedad/2021-08-29/la-muerte-sin-duelo-como-la-pandemia-ha-transfor
mado-la-percepcion-del-fallecimiento.html, 2022-08-07.

Amnistía Internacional España (2020) *Abandonadas a su suerte. La desprotección y discriminación de las personas mayores en residencias durante la pandemia Covid-19 en España*, Madrid, Amnistía Internacional España.

BBC News Mundo (2020) "Coronavirus: las muertes de miles de ancianos que no están siendo contabilizadas en las estadísticas de los fallecidos por covid-19 en Europa", *BBC News Mundo*, 2020-04-14, https://www.bbc.com/mundo/noticias-52283394, 2022-08-08.

Boccaccio, Giovanni (1989 [~ 1349-1353]) *Decameron*, editado por Vittore Branca, Milán, Mondadori.

Calvo, Cristina/García López-Hortelano, Milagros/De Carlos Vicente, Juan Carlos/Byrne Vázquez Martínez, José Luis (2020) "Recomendaciones sobre el manejo clínico de la infección por el «nuevo coronavirus» SARS-CoV2. Grupo de trabajo de la Asociación Española de Pediatría (AEP)", *Anales de Pediatría* 92/4, 241.e1-241.e11. DOI: 10.1016/j.anpedi.2020.02.001.

Camus, Albert (1947) *La Peste*, París, Gallimard.

Cervantes, Miguel de (2004 [1605/15]) *Don Quijote de la Mancha*, editato por Florencio Sevilla Arroyo, Barcelona, Lunwerg.

Cuevas, Fabiola (2020) *Ansiedad en tiempos de coronavirus: pierde el miedo a enfermar y mejora tu sistema inmunológico*, Barcelona, Grijalbo.

Currás, Victor P. (2021) "Muere Hermann Schreiber: 'el alemán de la armónica' que emocionó a Vigo durante el confinamiento", *Faro de Vigo*, 2021-09-04, https://www.farodevigo.es/gran-vigo/2021/09/04/muere-hermann-schreiber-aleman-armonica-56936373.html, 2022-08-09.

De Arriba Iglesias, Sara/Hidalgo Balsera, Augustín (2021) "Similitudes y diferencias entre *El diario del año de la peste* y la enfermedad por COVID-19", *Revista de Medicina y Cine* 17/4, 315-335. DOI: 10.14201/rmc2021174315335.

De Casso, Alberto/Fernández, Julio (eds.) (2020) *De los días sin abrazos. 25 obras de teatro en confinamiento*, Madrid, Ediciones Invasoras.

Defoe, Daniel (2020 [1722]) *Diario del año de la peste*, traducido por Carlos Pujol, Barcelona, Alba Editorial.

El Teatro (2020) "Los Ingleses Dicen Calm! - Raúl Hernández Garrido [EP10]", https://youtu.be/MIIXdvjse7k, 2022-08-02.

Fernández Corcuera, Paloma/Serrano, Julio (2020) *NoPanicovid*, Barcelona, El Jueves.

Fox, Manuela (2019) "Jerónimo López Mozo, compromiso y metateatralidad", *Acotaciones: Revista de investigación teatral* 42, 147-184. DOI: 10.32621/aco taciones.2019.42.06.

Galán, Eduardo (2020) *Diario de un confinamiento*, Madrid, Éride ediciones.

Ghebreyesus, Tedros Adhanom (2020) "Alocución de apertura del Director General de la OMS en la rueda de prensa sobre la COVID-19 celebrada el 11 de marzo de 2020", *Organización Mundial de la Salud*, 2020-03-11, https://www.who.int/es/director-general/speeches/detail/who-director-general-s-open ing-remarks-at-the-media-briefing-on-covid-19---11-march-2020, 2022-12-02.

González, Raúl (2021) "El sector cultural pierde un 70% de la recaudación como consecuencia de la pandemia", *El País*, 2021-10-19, https://elpais.com/cul tura/2021-10-19/el-sector-cultural-pierde-un-70-de-la-recaudacion-como-con secuencia-de-la-pandemia.html, 2022-03-03.

Hassine, Khaled (2020) "Experta de Naciones Unidas califica de 'inaceptable' el abandono de las personas de edad, que corren riesgos más graves por el COVID-19", *Naciones Unidas. Derechos humanos*, 2020-03-27, https://www.ohchr.org/es/2020/03/unacceptable-un-expert-urges-better-protection-older-persons-facing-highest-risk-covid-19, 2022-08-08.

Hebrero, Virginia (2020) "Coronavirus: La siniestra caravana de camiones militares cargados de féretros en Bérgamo", *Diario de Sevilla*, 2020-03-19, https://www.diariodesevilla.es/sociedad/Coronavirus-siniestra-caravana-milita res-Bergamo_0_1447655661.html, 2022-12-03.

Junquera, Natalia (2020) "Hermann, la mentira piadosa que se hizo realidad", *El País*, 2020-03-25, https://elpais.com/sociedad/2020-03-25/la-mentira-piado sa-que-se-hizo-realidad.html, 2022-06-05.

Koontz, Dean (2020 [1981]) *Los ojos de la oscuridad*, traducido por Lorenzo Cortina, Barcelona, Diagonal.

Mansilla, José (2020) *La pandemia de la desigualdad. Una antropología desde el confinamiento*, Madrid, Bellaterra.

Manzoni, Alessandro (1993 [1827]) *I promessi sposi*, Milán, Mondadori.

Martín Crespo, Vicente (2021) *Behetría y el miedo*, Barcelona, Tregolam.

Mediavilla, Manu (2020) "Residencias en tiempos de Covid", *Amnistía Internacional*, 2020-12-03, https://www.es.amnesty.org/en-que-estamos/reportajes/residencias-en-tiempos-de-covid-personas-mayores-abandonadas-a-su-suerte/, 2022-09-09.

Muñoz Molina, Antonio (2021) *Volver a dónde*, Barcelona, Seix Barral.

Muro, Robert (2020) *Informe sobre las artes escénicas en España: distribución, programación y públicos (2020)*, Madrid, Colección Estudios.

Nawrot, Julia (2021) "La mirada costumbrista de Jerónimo López Mozo sobre la pandemia COVID-19", *Romanica Cracoviensia* 3, 177-185. DOI: 10.4467/20 843917RC.21.018.14190.

Oñoro Ontero, Cristina (2020) "Y la ciudad se volvió teatro. Reflexiones sobre paseos y teatro deambulatorio en tiempos de pandemia", *Acotaciones* 45, 521-527.

O.P.S./O.M.S. (2020) "La OMS declara que el nuevo brote de coronavirus es una emergencia de salud pública de importancia internacional", *Organización Panamericana de la Salud*, 2020-01-30, https://www.paho.org/es/noticias/30-1-2020-oms-declara-que-nuevo-brote-coronavirus-es-emergencia-salud-publi ca-importancia, 2022-12-02.

Otheguy Riveira, Horacio (2020) "Teatro para leer: *Nana de la desaparición*, de Sebastián Moreno, maravilla y horror en la jungla de Borneo", *Culturamas*, 2021-08-04, https://www.culturamas.es/2021/08/04/teatro-para-leer-nana-de-la-desaparicion-de-sebastian-moreno/, 2022-07-07.

Pepys, Samuel (1944 [1660-1669]) *Diarios*, traducido por Milli Dandolo, Milán, Bompiani.

Pinazo-Hernandis, Sacramento (2020) "Impacto psicosocial de la COVID-19 en las personas mayores: problemas y retos", *Revista española de geriatría y gerontología* 55/5, 249-252. DOI: 10.1016/j.regg.2020.05.006.

Prieto Vidal, Ana (2021) "*Covid-451*, de Sergio Blanco: una alterficción en tiempos de pandemia", *Acotaciones* 46, 183-203. DOI: 10.32621/ACOTACIO NES.2021.46.07.

Research Group *Pandemic Fictions* (2020) "From Pandemic to Corona Fictions: Narratives in Times of Crises", *PhiN-Beiheft* 24, 321-344, http://web.fu-ber lin.de/phin/beiheft24/b24t21.pdf, 2022-10-10.

Rico, Manuel (2020) *¡Vergüenza! El escándalo de las residencias*, Barcelona, Planeta.

Romera Castillo, José (2020a) "Semiótica, pandemia, COVID-19 y teatro", *Signa* 31, 27-37. DOI: 10.5944/signa.vol31.2022.32184.

Romera Castillo, José (2020b) "Teatro y coronavirus", *Ideal de Granada* 21, 2020-08-27, https://academiadebuenasletrasdegranada.org/wp-content/uploa ds/2020/12/de-buenas-letras-20-08-27.pdf, 2020-10-10.

Romera Castillo, José (2020c) "Teatro, pandemia y salas virtuales", *Ideal de Granada*, 2020-10-08, https://academiadebuenasletrasdegranada.org/wp-content/ uploads/2021/01/de-buenas-letras-20-10-08.pdf, 2021-07-07.

Ruiz de Larrinaga, Cantabrana (2020) *Tu «Nueva A-Normalidad»: 5 pasos para salir con fuerza del Coronavirus*, s.l., Koro Cantabrana Ruiz de Larrinaga.

Sanz, Marta (2021) *Parte de mí*, Barcelona, Anagrama.

Saramago, José (2022) *Ensayo sobre la ceguera*, traducido por Basilio Losada Castro, Madrid, Alfaguara.

Sosa Troya (2021) "El Gobierno certifica que 29.408 personas han muerto por coronavirus en residencias desde el inicio de la pandemia", *El País*, 2021-03-02, https://elpais.com/sociedad/2021-03-02/en-espana-han-muerto-29408-mayores-que-vivian-en-residencias-desde-el-inicio-de-la-pandemia.html, 2022-08-08.

VV.AA. (2020) *La pira. La conmoción. La distancia. La incertidumbre*, Madrid, Centro Dramático Nacional.

VV.AA. (2021) *Teatro para una crisis*, Sevilla, Junta de Andalucía.

Zurita, Carlos (2020) "La realidad, la ficción. Apuntes sobre pestes y plagas en la literatura", *Trabajo y Sociedad* 21/35, 203-208, https://dialnet.unirioja.es/ejemplar/556034, 2022-12-02.

Immunity and Community:
The Role of Immune Protagonists
in Saramago's *Ensaio sobre a Cegueira* (1995)
and Roth's *Nemesis* (2010)

Louis Mühlethaler (CRAL, Paris)

Abstract

This article focuses on the immune protagonists in *Ensaio sobre a Cegueira* (*Blindness*) and *Nemesis*, portrayed as resistant to the epidemic at the center of each novel. While the doctor's wife in Saramago's novel remains mysteriously immune to blindness, Bucky Cantor, in *Nemesis*, ends up contracting polio. Even though the two immune protagonists seem not to be physically affected by the 'plague', they strive to be heavily involved in the struggle for a better life for the community. Their involvement in the community tests their immunity. The apparently heroic function of the immune protagonists is an indication of this test, but the crucial dilemmas that they face appear to be significant for the question of how to live and survive together. The individual 'self-blinding' in *Nemesis* is negative for Bucky Cantor, while the 'struggle-for-survival' of the doctor's wife in *Blindness* is eventually constructive. It is thus not only the real physical resistance against the 'plague' that asserts itself as positive: it is also the way in which immunity turns into symbolic autoimmunity (*Nemesis*) or into an immunity of the community (*Blindness*).

[O]nce its negative power has been removed, the immune is not the enemy of the common, but rather something more complex that implicates and stimulates the common. The full significance of this necessity, but also its possibility, still eludes us.[1]

Look at her. She thinks she is different from the rest of us. She thinks she's got immunity. But when they come here, they won't make any exception for her.[2]

Partis d'un système immunitaire conçu comme un moyen de protéger l'organisme contre les autres, nous arrivons à un système qui lui permet de vivre avec les autres.[3]

INTRODUCTION: IMMUNITY AND COMMUNITY

In his last novel *Nemesis*, Philip Roth fictionalizes the aftermath of the polio epidemic in Newark. The epidemic takes place in a realistic frame of reference that differs from the dystopian and post-apocalyptic frame of *Ensaio sobre a Cegueira*. In both cases, the epidemic can be read as an 'outbreak narrative', according to the term coined by Priscilla Wald (2008).[4]

In *Blindness*, the immune protagonist is an anonymous woman identified by her social position: 'the doctor's wife'. In *Nemesis*, he is a young man named Eugene (Bucky) Cantor. In Saramago's novel, the immune protagonist remains

---

1   Esposito 2011, 18.
2   McMullen 1983 [00:25:00-00:25:11 min.].
3   Daëron 2021, 334; "From an immune system conceived as a means of protecting the organism from others, we arrive at a system that enables it to live with others" (author's translation).
4   In the following, I will use the letter *N* for quotations from *Nemesis* and *B* for quotes from Saramago's novel in Giovanni Pontiero's translation; for original quotations from *Ensaio sobre a Cegueira*, inserted in footnotes, I will use *EC* (all in parentheses, followed by the page number). Unless indicated otherwise, all italicized emphases are in the original.

uninfected by the 'virus' of blindness, and in Roth's he resists polio up to a certain point. Nevertheless, both immune protagonists are primarily concerned with the distressed and sick community.

Neither of the two protagonists has a direct or natural remedy for the ills afflicting the community:[5] they merely attempt to alleviate them. In both novels, the immune protagonists are the only characters who seriously 'resist' oppression that comes about in response to the epidemic. Thus, a significant difference is to be emphasized from the outset: in Saramago's text, the doctor's wife remains mysteriously immune from the outbreak of the epidemic until its end, whereas, in Roth's novel, the fight against polio ultimately fails. Roth's protagonist Bucky Cantor *seems* immune to polio until the fateful day when he realizes through a test that he may have been "a healthy infected carrier" (*N* 236). He then blames himself throughout his life for the infections he may have caused and for the death of a child under his care. It turns out that Bucky Cantor is not an 'immune protagonist' in the strict sense of the word for two reasons. First, he is not the only character unaffected by the disease (several characters other than Bucky Cantor do not contract polio); second, while in *Nemesis*, polio affects the whole community, "the chances [of dying from polio] are slight overall in the community, in the city" (*N* 113). However, Roth's protagonist is portrayed as a resister and a resilient defender of children in the community throughout much of the novel. I shall argue that Bucky Cantor also embodies the vulnerability of a man who could be infected at any time. However, there is another notable difference between the two stories. While the doctor's wife partially succeeds in restoring the society that has been blinded – and thus, in a sense, restoring sight to the population – Bucky Cantor fails to protect the community he is supposed to defend. The fact that he is eventually infected is a sign that his role as protector has failed miserably.

Despite these differences, there are also many similarities between the two protagonists: because of the equally heroic qualities that the story bestows on him (integrity, a sense of fairness and responsibility), Bucky Cantor can be considered as being very similar to the (truly) immune protagonist that is the doctor's wife. I will thus treat both the protagonists of the two novels under study as 'the immune protagonists'.

---

5   In each novel, the 'plague' (in the figurative sense of the epidemic) has an unknown origin, a scenario that occurs in some epidemic narratives (and also in pandemic fiction). Moreover, as Doctor Steinberg says to Bucky Cantor: "We don't know who or what carries polio, and there's still some debate about how it enters the body" (*N* 104). In Saramago's novel, there is a similar absence of knowledge about the contagion.

My hypothesis is that the community tests the immune protagonists' immunity. The symbolically heroic function of the immune protagonists in the narrative and the path they take within the narrative framework are the indication of this test.

The conceptual relationships between community and immunity are complex, as the contentious debates over herd immunity and vaccination during the Covid-19 pandemic have demonstrated.[6] Although to some extent, these concepts can be viewed as inversions of each other, as Esposito (cf. 2002, 3-61) suggests, the concepts of community and immunity are interrelated. According to Esposito, immunity belongs primarily to the lexical domain of legal-political privilege or exemption, while what characterizes community corresponds to the notion of the *gift* and thus to what connects us to one another. But the concept of immunity cannot be understood only as the exact opposite of community. I shall argue that there seems to be a link between purely medical immunity and a properly legal-political immunity which would correspond to a kind of 'privilege- immunity'. However, the model of immunity that I uncover in my reading of these texts is a rather different one: it concerns the political and ethical *resistance* that the immune characters pass on to the dominated, enclosed or suffering communities.

I use a comparative study approach to examine these two immune protagonists: I will describe, analyze and interpret the pertinent similarities and differences between the two narratives. I will thus divide the study in two main parts: I will study the immune protagonists, first, on an individual level as mere characters and, second, on both an individual and collective level as embodiments of collective resistance (that is, of the resistance but also the failures of the community). After having examined to what extent the *immune* protagonists can be deemed heroic characters (first section), I shall consider the politics of community and the dilemmas at play in both novels (second section). Finally, I will extend my interpretation by analyzing two main types of immunity – the overprotective type of 'self-blindness' (third section) and the type of collective resilience (fourth section). This will eventually allow me to conceive a literary[7] theory of resilience and symbiotic immunity.

---

6   The fact that a community seeks immunity in a pandemic context demonstrates that the two concepts cannot be considered separately. This critical issue of herd immunity was raised during the Covid-19 pandemic. For a detailed analysis of the damaging consequences of the ideology inspired by the notion of herd immunity and by social Darwinism, see Marie-Laure Salles-Djelic (2020) "Quand l'idéologie avance masquée. Immunité collective, néolibéralisme et darwinisme social".

7   On the very notion of the "immunity of literature", see Johannes Türk's book (2011).

HEROIC IMMUNITY?
FROM *'PRIVILEGE'* TO *RESISTANCE*

The immunity of the immune protagonists may appear as an individual 'privilege', but at the same time, they are 'naturally *immune*'.[8] One might think that the first striking thing about the two immune protagonists is their (medically) natural ability to overcome 'disease', be it blindness or polio. However, they fear being infected by blindness or the virus at every turn, but they also fear constantly for the well-being of the community.

In both novels, the immune protagonists, despite their guaranteed immunity, risk exposure to the disease that afflicts the rest of society. In *Nemesis*, Bucky Cantor is personally legitimized by a doctor himself to "contribut[e] to the welfare of the community" (*N* 105). In *Blindness*, the doctor's wife is described by the narrator as "[…] a kind of natural leader, a king with eyes in the land of the blind" (*B* 256).[9] The privilege of 'not being blind' in Saramago's text (of not having succumbed to the contagion of blindness) is not, however, used by the female protagonist to exert authority over the blind: although she might have the upper hand in the asylum where they are locked up, she chooses not to exercise her exemption to dominate the others.

One of the dilemmas that might arise for the two immune protagonists is the question of how to protect others without exercising too much authority. However, the immune protagonists not only have a privilege with regard to the disease, they are also the driving force of resistance to the disease and its negative consequences. The doctor's wife, for example, is not afraid to declare herself blind: when the ambulance comes to pick up her already blind husband, she pretends to go blind so as not to abandon him.[10]

The immune protagonists are in a way considered role models by a portion of the community. But it is important to identify which characters make up the community in each book. On the one hand, in *Nemesis*, this community consists of the boys of the Weequahic neighbourhood of Newark. It is these boys and their sports camp that Bucky Cantor is supposed to watch over. He is very concerned about his duty as a man of integrity and has an excessive sense of "responsibility"

---

8   Because they have this immunity without any need for vaccination, the two immune protagonists can be considered 'naturally' immune to the disease.

9   "Uma espécie de chefe natural, um rei com olhos numa terra de cegos" (*EC* 245).

10 First, the doctor's wife just wanted to protect her husband. She was not thinking of the community. Later, in the asylum, she had no other choice. She did not choose her role of resister and helper; she arrived there by accident.

(*N* 101): in this sense, he has much in common with the antihero of Albert Camus's novel *La Peste* (1947), Dr. Rieux. On the other hand, the community corresponds in Saramago's novel to the oppressed blind people confined to an asylum
and separated from already contaminated (but not yet blind) people. However, the
protected community, at the beginning, composed of the six main characters of
Blindness that we follow from the beginning to the end of the book, soon expands:
"For the moment there are only six of us here, but by tomorrow we shall undoubtedly be more; people will start arriving every day" (*B* 46).[11]

Both protagonists have extraordinary qualities that make them in some way
heroic characters. The doctor's wife holds a leadership role. Not only is she the
only woman who can see, but her visual immunity remains secret. Apart from her
husband, the doctor-ophthalmologist, no one knows about her "sixth sense, some
sort of a vision without eyes [...]" (*B* 201).[12] Moreover, "[...] it is quite extraordinary how she manages to [...] orient herself [...]" (*B* 81):[13] that ability proves
crucial in the continuation of the story; she not only orients herself, she also orients
the others.

The immune protagonists embody a particular form of *care*. Not only are they
listened to (unlike the doctors in each novel), but they also tend to take precedence
over medical authority. Even if the immune protagonists are not medical professionals (a fact they are constantly reminded of), they seem to be the only characters
that can be trusted: the doctor's wife and Bucky Cantor are both close to the medical function from a narratological perspective. There is a complex relationship
between the immune protagonists, medicine itself and its practitioners. Nevertheless, the protagonists also embody 'political' and 'ethical' resistance. They try to
take care of others. In *Blindness*, the doctor's wife quickly replaces her husband
with that of a 'caregiver' (cf. Tronto 1993). If the immune protagonists are heroes,
it is only in the sense that they represent a heroic figure for the community of
children (*Nemesis*) and for the oppressed blind people (*Blindness*).

Two types of defence – medical self-defence and the resistant defence of the
community – are linked in the two novels. The immune protagonists' first function
is not primarily self-defence but co-resistance, that is ethical and political 'resistance'. Both immune protagonists help to facilitate the resistance of the community, a form of resistance that counters both the virus and hostile controlling forces

---

11 "[...] Por enquanto só estamos aqui estes seis, mas amanhã de certeza seremos mais,
virá gente todos os dias [...]" (*EC* 53).
12 "[...] ela deve ser dotada de um sexto sentido, algum tipo de visão sem olhos [...]"
(*EC* 196).
13 "[...] é extraordinário como ela consegue [...] orientar-se [...]" (*EC* 87).

that attempt to mitigate its spread. To enable resistance, however, they must also at times defend themselves. Being forced into self-defence, Bucky Cantor and the doctor's wife face dilemmas through their resistance.

FACING DILEMMAS THROUGH RESISTANCE

One model of immunity that emerges in literature (cf. Türk 2011) is that of an immune character who *resists* for and with others, thus transmitting their resistance to the community members. This resistance concerns a significant part of the community that tries to defend itself and thus to promote self-defence against 'evil'.

Nevertheless, in a very similar way, the two immune protagonists face 'dilemmas' involving the complex relationships between immunity and community. At least four dilemmas arise for the immune protagonists, each of which I will now describe. These dilemmas – sometimes presented as tragic (*Nemesis*) and other times as parabolic (*Blindness*) – may recall ethical and sociopolitical dilemmas encountered during the Covid-19 pandemic.

Dilemma n° 1: *How to avoid ('the evil' of) contagion? Between the biopolitical paradigm and the consideration of the community*
In *Nemesis*, polio does not affect most of the population. As a leader and a driving force of the diegesis, Bucky Cantor feels responsible for the spread of the contagion. Even if he was not watching the children, they would still run the risk of contracting the disease; they would not be protected in any way and could be contaminated. He thus asks Dr. Steinberg, the father of Bucky Cantor's bride-to-be Marcia, if he has succeeded in "kill[ing] the polio germs" (*N* 104) through sanitary measures:

> [W]hat's important is that you cleaned up an unhygienic mess and reassured the boys by the way you took charge. You demonstrated your competence [...] your equanimity – that's what the kids have to see. Bucky, you're shaken up by what's happening now, but strong men get the shakes too. [...] To stand by as a doctor unable to stop the spread of this dreadful disease is painful for all of us. (*N* 104)

Dr. Steinberg is reassuring. He gives Bucky legitimacy in his mission to take good care of the children: "To the contrary, you're making things better. You're doing something useful. You're contributing to the welfare of the community" (*N* 105).

In Saramago's novel by contrast, blindness affects most of the population. The fight against the 'virus' is organized in a much more repressive way. The government in *Blindness* quickly views the fight against the virus under a warlike paradigm. It seeks to exert control over people's lives and introduces extremely authoritarian measures: "[…] the Government regrets having been forced to exercise with all urgency what it considers to be its rightful duty, to protect the population by all possible means in this present crisis" (*B* 42).[14]

Although it is impossible, in Saramago's novel, to avoid the contagion, everything is done to *fight* it, as is shown by the presence of the military forces dedicated to 'control' blind people. If the shift from relative freedom to a political regime characterized by violent measures of overtly military and even biopolitical control[15] may have been brought about by the epidemic of blindness, the question for the doctor's wife is: *how to find a solution to fight social chaos while not resorting to violence?* This is the second dilemma that I will study.

Dilemma n° 2: *How to protect the community while not resorting to violence?*
The question facing the immune protagonists in the context of enemies to defeat is crucial in both novels. Nevertheless, it manifests in different ways. In Roth's novel, the virus is described as an "invisible" (*N* 271) enemy that must be defeated by the "invincible" (*N* 280) figure of Bucky Cantor. In *Blindness*, the doctor's wife is tested by the divisions within the community, especially between the two Wards. Women are forced to surrender sexually to get food (they are raped and used as sex slaves), but the doctor's wife does not force anyone to submit to this cruel law. Commenting on this very dilemma, Monika Kaup (2021, 191) notes that "[i]n the asylum, the collective decisions, first, to agree to the criminals' demand for sex slaves, and next, to attack the criminals in self-defence are reached via a tense debate in each case". After facing a profound moral dilemma, the doctor's wife kills the oppressive leader (the man with the gun) and feels no guilt afterwards. She has fallen into violence, but violence was necessary: the community eventually regulates the actions of the doctor's wife.

---

14 "[...] O Governo lamenta ter sido forçado a exercer energicamente o que considera ser seu direito e seu dever, proteger por todos os meios as populações na crise que estamos a atravessar" (*EC* 73).

15 In the film adaptation of *Blindness* directed by Fernando Meirelles, interestingly, the voiceover says "that the disease was immune to bureaucracy" (Meirelles 2009 [00:41:09-00:41:14 min.]). It showcases that, as in the novel, the spread of blindness is unstoppable: all authoritarian and repressive efforts made to stop it are in vain.

Dilemma n° 3: *How to reconcile individual and collective well-being* (in *Nemesis*)?[16]

In *Nemesis*, Bucky Cantor is caught between several obligations. He must comply with the moral imperative to do his job fairly and ethically – *taking care* of the children of the Weequahic playground and 'caring' for his own well-being. Roth's immune protagonist fails to embody the resistance of the community. Indeed, as the polio epidemic reaches its peak, a reinforcement of public health measures leads to the closure of the playground. Bucky Cantor has to symbolically concede defeat in *"his* war" (*N* 174) against the virus:[17] "Yet he *had* been given a war to fight, the war being waged on the battlefield of his playground [...]" (*N* 173). Taking advantage of the post vacated by one of his classmates who has left for the war, Bucky Cantor sets out to find his beloved Marcia. He seizes the opportunity to get engaged, escaping the contagion of polio in Indian Hill, a heavenly place apparently devoid of any harm.[18] Before he accepts, he is confronted with a profound dilemma. Has he failed in taking care of the children? If he owes many people, according to the notion of moral debt, he must nevertheless first think of his own happiness. This leads to another dilemma that can be found in the two novels: *How to be responsible and not feel guilty?*

Dilemma n° 4: *How to be responsible and not feel guilty?*

Although Saramago's protagonist feels guilty at certain points in the story, she manages to overcome her guilt, which is a crucial difference between the two novels, both characterized by the "Judeo-Christian guilt"[19] and the attribution of the

---

16 Saramago's novel also raises the question of the balance between collective and individual well-being. However, I preferred not to deal with this question so as not to weigh down the comparative approach. To these four dilemmas, one could have added a more crucial one in *Blindness*: 'how to survive together?' – I will talk about this at the end of this article, but from a biological perspective.

17 Another war – World War II – is at play in Roth's story, which is set in 1944. However, Bucky Cantor does not fight in that (real) war because he has been exempted from fighting in it – another privilege for him, though he would have liked to fight in that war.

18 Villate Torres (2018) suggests about Indian Hill, in which Bucky Cantor joins his beloved and wife-to-be Marcia: "Un lieu aussi pur apparaît aux yeux de Bucky comme immunisé contre la polio. [Such a pure place appears to Bucky to be immunized against polio]" (301; author's translation).

19 Seth (2020) suggests: "Paradoxalement, en refusant Dieu, Cantor est victime de la vieille notion de culpabilité si profondément ancrée dans la tradition judéo-chrétienne.

disease to the will of God. As a "maniac of the why" (*N* 265), Bucky Cantor "has to convert tragedy into guilt" (ibid.):

> He has to find a necessity for what happens. There is an epidemic and he needs a reason for it. He has to ask why. [...] That it is pointless, contingent, preposterous, and tragic will not satisfy him. That it is a proliferating virus will not satisfy him. Instead he looks desperately for a deeper cause, this martyr, this *maniac of the why*, and finds the why either in God or in himself or [...] in their dreadful joining *together as the sole destroyer*. (ibid., my emphasis)

When he leaves Newark, Bucky Cantor is berated as an "opportunist" (*N* 138) by O'Gara (who heads the playground of Weequahic) not without anti-Semitism – he deliberately calls him "*Cancer*" instead of "*Cantor*": "All you're doing is running away, *Cancer*, a world-champion muscleman like you. You're an opportunist, *Cancer*. [...] And then, with revulsion, he repeated, '*An opportunist*,' as though the word stood for every degrading instinct that could possibly stigmatize a man" (*N* 138, my emphasis). The accusation of being an "opportunist" can be read literally. O'Gara accuses Bucky Cantor of taking advantage of the privilege and opportunity afforded him to have a wife from a wealthy social class and seek her out in a polio-free land. However, if we ignore the anti-Semitism of the insult, we can also read the word 'opportunist' with a *biological* frame of reference. That is, we can understand that the opportunist (who possesses a kind of 'privilege-immunity') is associated with a disease (cancer) and seen thus as a kind of opportunistic disease. If we take seriously this association of illness and opportunism, we could say that, like an 'opportunistic infection' – i.e. a disease caused by relatively unaggressive germs that exploit a weakness of the immune system to survive – Bucky Cantor may have symbolically taken advantage of a kind of failure in the community's 'immune system'. To his great misfortune, by fleeing his (vain) moral duty, he has 'attacked' (on a literal medical level) the natural defences of a child weaker than himself: Donald Kaplow. As Seth (cf. 2020, 39) states, Bucky Cantor turns from defender into contaminator in an unexpected reversal. His falsely strong health has infected the one who, above all, should not have been contaminated – the child that he was supposed to protect. He has precisely the narrative function of an 'opportunistic disease' – an apparently harmless disease for a healthy immune system – in that his deceptively unaggressive privileged health may have infected the young child.

[Paradoxically, by denying God, Cantor falls victim to the old notion of guilt so deeply rooted in the Judeo-Christian tradition]" (40; author's translation).

Bucky Cantor, the champion of hygiene, integrity, health and protection, has indeed found in Indian Hill the realization of carnal desire with Marcia. The fact that he contracts polio, according to Cantor's own interpretation, may be seen as a punishment for escaping far from Newark and not demonstrating his sense of Judeo-Christian sacrifice to the end.

I have been arguing that the narrative paints Bucky Cantor – by way of a biological reading – as a kind of opportunistic disease. I will now extend this argument by showing how the reversal of the protective logic becomes a kind of auto-immune logic (on the symbolic level) for Roth's (no longer) immune protagonist.

SELF-BLINDNESS AS A COUNTER-MODEL OF IMMUNITY

In *Nemesis*, many members of the community accuse Bucky Cantor of not having made the right decision. Many, like O'Gara, make him a kind of 'scapegoat'. Bucky Cantor thus reveals the weaknesses, failures and successes of the community. He embodies the risk of the overprotective paradigm, the risk that the community will find scapegoats[20] (Jews, for example) for symbolic and real ills of the community. Bucky Cantor's immunity (i.e. his own self-protection and the fact that he wants to protect others) turns against him by way of a self-defeating logic.

After he contracts polio, Marcia still wants to marry him, but he runs away from her. In their last conversation, Marcia accuses him of "finding [...] comfort in castigating himself" (*N* 139). As an ultimately defenceless man, who is now "against [him]self [...] making things worse by scapegoating [him]self" (*N* 272), he only wants to protect himself from the woman he is destined to marry. He also enjoins her "to save [her]self from [him]" (*N* 260) because he is now disabled. Marcia analyzes Bucky Cantor's tendency for overprotection as a delusion and a

---

20 The 'logic of scapegoating' is developed by René Girard (cf. 1982) and taken up by Roberto Esposito with regard to community self-immunization. Esposito argues that, in times of crisis, the community is forced to 'operate and divide itself' (cf. Esposito 2002). The logic of scapegoating is also to be found in Saramago's work but in a different way. In *Ensaio sobre a Lucidez*, which is a sequel to *Ensaio sobre a Cegueira*, the former heroes also become scapegoats. As Vieira (2011, 123) notes, "[in *Ensaio sobre a Lucidez*,] the protagonists of *Ensaio sobre a Cegueira*, [...] are used as scapegoats for the situation. Since she did not go blind, the doctor's wife is identified as the head of the supposed conspiracy behind the wave of blank votes and the novel ends with her assassination, together with that of the dog of tears".

self-blinding with regard to the ability they still have to be happy, despite polio and the resulting disability: "You're speaking nonsense! [...] By telling me to leave you alone. Oh, Bucky, you're being so blind!" (N 259). The logic of the self-blindness of the hero seems very close to that of symbolic self-protection that provokes self-destruction.[21] However, as he becomes a kind of tragic hero in his own eyes – his failure as an infected man fulfilling his sense of the tragedy of the community as well as the vanity of self-sacrifice – Marcia decides to leave him; she considers that "[t]he only way to save a remnant of his honor was in denying himself everything he had ever wanted for himself" (N 262). Bucky Cantor's guilt complex is simultaneously self-protective and – from the point of view of his own happiness – self-destructive: his self-protection leads (on the psychic level) to his self-destruction.

Noteworthy, then, is the connection between symbolic self-destruction and self-blinding[22] from the perspective of the paradigm of rationality. Self-blindness and blindness can be conceived as a partial failure on the part of the immune protagonist in Roth's novel to protect the community and its cohesion. It is possible to extend this self-destructive logic of opportunistic disease which I analyzed in the previous part, to that of autoimmunity. 'Self-immunization' (i.e. self-destructive self-protection) is linked to the philosophical logic of Jacques Derrida (cf. 2001 and 2003) and Roberto Esposito (cf. 2002). Drawing a parallel between philosophical and biological (or immunological) theories of living, Derrida defines self-immunization as the tendency of an auto-protective impulse to be self-

---

21 As Giannopoulou (2016, 29) notes, "[m]oral earnestness to the point of self-destruction is a staple of Roth's characters". She quotes an interview with Philip Roth by Georges Searles, in which Roth asserts: "I have concerned myself with men and women whose moorings have been cut, and who are swept away from their native shores and out to sea, sometimes on a tide of their own righteousness or resentment" (Searles 1992, 55).

22 As Fastelli (cf. 2021, 3-13) points out by drawing a connection between pandemic and blindness in the work of Saramago and Roth, and as John Maxwell Coetzee (cf. 2010, 12-15) and – in his wake – Giannopoulou (cf. 2016, 15-31) had already suggested, Philip Roth's protagonist was in a way self-blinding man: both compare him to the tragic figure of Oedipus. In my analysis, I take from Giannopoulou's commentary this emphasis on Bucky Cantor who is blind to his own rational blindness.

destructive as well.[23] This paradigm may also apply to the self-destructive self-protection of the community.[24]

So, what defines self-blinding (in its philosophical sense), if not the propensity to self-destruct of that which is *immune*? I argue that blindness, self-blindness and self-destruction are 'counter-models' that represent the limits of the "immunization paradigm" (cf. Esposito 2002, 3-61). Thus, the anti-heroic fallibility of Roth's character and the way he turns into a negative character (first and foremost in his own eyes),[25] can be correlated to the symbolic self-blinding of his auto-immunization.

The paradigm of self-blindness leads me to propose an interpretation of blindness at the core of Saramago's novel. I argue that there is a connection between natural blindness and blinding oneself that has to do with a self-destructive tendency. In Saramago's novel many, sometimes contradictory, thoughts about blindness are propounded by the protagonists and the secondary characters. I will focus only on those of the doctor, who is a kind of philosopher and often reflects on the 'wisdom of blindness'. In the doctor's view, blindness has a philosophical primacy over being blind: "[…] it even used to be said there is no such thing as blindness, only blind people when the experience of time has taught us nothing other than that there are no blind people, but only blindness" (*B* 324).[26] The doctor hints at a possible connection between natural blindness and blinding oneself, which also has to do with voluntary self-deception: "[…] Let's open our eyes, We can't, we are blind, said the doctor, It is a great truth that says that the worst blind person was the one who *did not want to see* […]" (*B* 298, my emphasis).[27]

---

23 We could also cite the idea of *apoptosis*, or programmed cell death, described by Jean-Claude Ameisen (1999; cf. also Vitale 2018).

24 "Community as common *auto-immunity*. No community is possible that would not cultivate its own auto-immunity, a principle of sacrificial self-destruction ruining the principle of self-protection" (Derrida 1998, 51); "Communauté comme com-mune (sic.) *auto-immunité*: nulle communauté qui n'entretienne sa propre auto-immunité, un principe d'autodestruction sacrificiel ruinant le principe de protection de soi" (Derrida 2001, 59).

25 Despite (and perhaps, mainly because of) his failure, he arouses the reader's empathy.

26 "[…] costuma-se até dizer que não há cegueiras, mas cegos, quando a experiência dos tempos não tem feito outra coisa que dizer-nos que não há cegos, mas cegueiras" (*EC* 309).

27 "[…] Abramos os olhos, Não podemos, estamos cegos, disse o médico, É uma grande verdade a que diz que o pior cego foi aquele que *não quis ver* […]" (*EC* 283, my emphasis).

The connection between self-blinding – whether it is voluntary or not – and self-destruction,[28] under the paradigm of rationality and enlightenment, is of paramount importance but too complex to be conceptualized here in detail. I can at least assert that the application of some biological theories, such as autoimmunity, to literature can be useful for seeing – at a philosophical level – the complex relations between community and immunity. At a more general level of reflection, we can say that self-blindness and blindness in a crisis can be seen as negative counter-models of the community's immunity, a kind of symbolic 'autoimmunity of the community'.

Self-blindness, when it concerns the whole community, is highly negative. The question then arises of creating another mode of rationality that conceives of immunity as convincing and non-authoritative impulse implying collective resilience. The fundamental difference between the two novels is not indeed whether the protagonist remains immune to the 'plague' until the end of the story. The difference lies rather in the way the two characters deal with symbolic violence. In *Nemesis*, the symbolic violence of the community turns against the protagonist Bucky Cantor, who is not resilient, unlike the novel's narrator Arnie Mesnikoff who also contracted polio but managed to live with his disability. In *Blindness*, the symbolic violence eventually subsides: it is averted by the resilience of the doctor's wife who guides the collective resilience that leads to collective immunity, i.e. immunity of the community.

HOW TO SURVIVE TOGETHER?
(COLLECTIVE RESILIENCE IN *BLINDNESS*)

One of the questions that *Blindness* raises is: how can we organize ourselves to survive together? How can we deal with the 'struggle-for-survival'?[29] To put it in the words of the female immune protagonist in *Blindness*:

---

28 The link between reason and destruction has already been brought to light by Horkheimer and Adorno (cf. 1944), through the dialectic of enlightenment to which Saramago seems to allude when speaking – in the last sentences of his 1998 Nobel lecture of "the monsters generated by the blindness of reason" (Saramago 1999, 9).

29 Monika Kaup (cf. 2021, 144-195) suggests that "[t]he small collective of survivors tracked in post-apocalyptic fiction is formed by the peculiar logic through which the respective catastrophes unfold, in this case the first to be quarantined" (ibid., 177). The question of organization for survival is crucial in almost all epidemic (or pandemic) narratives – whether post-apocalyptic or not.

[I]f we stay together we might manage to survive, if we separate we shall be swallowed up by the masses and destroyed, [...] I don't know to what extent they are really organised, I only see them going around in search of food [...] nothing more [...].[30] (*B* 256)

This necessity for a 'struggle-for-survival' is primarily a matter of concrete material survival: it implies the need for self-organization on the part of people who want to find food and who, instead of fighting, choose the path of harmony by organizing themselves: "[...] And how can a society of blind people organise in order to survive, By organising itself, to organise oneself is, in a way, to begin to have eyes [...]" (*B* 296).[31] This crucial struggle-for-survival leads to the necessity not of separation but of self-organization. As Monika Kaup (cf. 2021, 144-195) suggests in her commentary on *Blindness*, self-organization is the *way* for the newly blind to survive. But it must be thought of at the very level of their representation of the world:[32] "Newly sightless, they must find a new type of cognitive organisation that allows them to know their world, a process in which neither blind minds not [sic] worlds are pre-given but [...] are brought forth in the process of living" (ibid., 185). Applying the autopoietic and enactive theories of Maturana and Varela[33] (which mainly involve self-organization) to her reading of Saramago, Kaup observes that the immune doctor's wife enables the six other protagonists and survivors to orient themselves. There exists among the six protagonists who survive from Ward One – until the end of the story – a kind of co-resistance:

---

30 "[...] Voltemos à questão, disse a mulher do médico, se continuarmos juntos talvez consigamos sobreviver, se nos separarmos seremos engolidos pela massa e destroçados, [...] Não sei até que ponto estarão realmente organizados, só os vejo andarem por aí à procura de comida e de sítio para dormir, nada mais [...]" *(EC* 245).

31 "[...] E como poderá uma sociedade de cegos organizar-se para que viva, Organizando-se, organizar-se já é, de uma certa maneira, começar a ter olhos [...]" (*EC* 281f.).

32 I do not go into the details of Kaup's admirable and compelling analysis. However, I would like to point out that the necessity of self-organization and enaction of blind people is both phenomenological (involving "the co-constitution of blind minds and worlds" (Kaup 2021, 185)) and social ("[i]t is social coupling and linguistic coupling among the blind that results in the formation of blind collectives, as well as their coordinated drift via collective ontogenies" (ibid.)).

33 Maturana and Varela (cf. 1980 and also 1987) developed the concept of autopoiesis (i.e. self-organization) to explain and describe the property of living organisms to generate their own structural and functional organization, in permanent interaction with their environment.

> Notably, because the group of survivor protagonists includes the woman who can see, they are *exempted from the disorientation that defines the universal condition in the city of the blind.* While the doctor's wife and her group enjoy the relative safety of their real home, conditions in the entire city of the blind reach an apocalyptic state [...]. But just when the city seems on the brink of an outbreak of new infectious diseases such as cholera and typhoid, the blindness pandemic ends as miraculously as it began. (Kaup 2021, 187, my emphasis)

The doctor's wife, then, provides the impetus and direction that will enable part of the blind community to be resilient. The protagonist's sight, however, cannot replace the strength of the bonds that unite those who share the 'vulnerability of blindness' and yet seem to have 'nothing in common'.[34] What they have in common is the true bond of the community that gives them resilience – while not making them immune to blindness – and the strength to learn to live together again.

In so far as she is inseparable from the community, the immunity of the doctor's wife is not as stable as one might think. At the end of the story, she orients the blind members of the small blind community but she no longer *leads* them. When all the blind people regain their sight, she feels as if she has gone blind. This ending is enigmatic, as enigmatic as her tears in the middle of the story, which make her believe that she is really blind. Should we see in the nostalgia of the doctor's wife a nostalgia for the bonds of the *community*? Is it an act of mourning a community that, once immune to blindness, shall no longer be able to forge solid human bonds? At the very least, we could say that the character supposed to represent immunity may be in the grip of nostalgia for the community. Conversely, when the community is led by immunity (for instance, the doctor's wife who *orients* the others in the last part of the narrative), the members of the community strive to become immune to their blindness. It is especially when the relationship between the community and immunity is out of balance that there is a risk of symbolic or real violence. Community and immunity must remain interrelated, for better or worse.

CONCLUDING REMARKS

The models or counter-models of immunity embodied by the immune protagonists in *Blindness* and *Nemesis* are very different. In Roth's novel, the logic of

---

34 Having "nothing in common" is the very definition of "community" according to Alphonso Lingis (cf. 1994), on whom Patrícia Vieira builds her interpretation (cf. 2011, 99-124) of Saramago's narrative, as well as that of Roberto Esposito (cf. 2002).

overprotection eventually prevails. Contrary to all expectations, it is ultimately the opposite that happens in Saramago's novel.

Both immune protagonists *represent* the critical issues of the community. They remain highly vulnerable and cannot directly resolve the tensions within the community. They are neither exempt from the 'evils or ills' of the community nor from its self-destructive slippages (when immunity is disrupted on the symbolic level and leads to autoimmunity). By facing these misfortunes, bearing them to the highest degree and embodying the interrelationships and entanglements between community and immunity, the immune protagonists offer solutions of temporary resilience that do not always find a way out.

Used moderately, immunization can lead to a shared life that seeks to build on the resilience of the community. This should lead us to the notion of a shared immunity or a "co-immunity",[35] an immunity that intertwines ethical and political issues.

BIBLIOGRAPHY

Corpus Analyzed

Roth, Philip (2011 [2010]) *Nemesis*, London, Vintage Books.
Saramago, José (1995) *Ensaio sobre a Cegueira*, Lisbon, Caminho.
Saramago, José (1999 [1995]) *Blindness*, trans. by Giovanni Ponticro, New York, NY, Harcourt Brace.

Works Cited

Ameisen, Jean-Claude (1999) *La Sculpture du vivant. Le suicide cellulaire ou la mort créatrice*, Paris, Seuil.
Camus, Albert (1995 [1947]) *La Peste*, Paris, Gallimard.
Coetzee, John Maxwell (2010) "On the Moral Brink", *The New York Review of Books*, 2010-10-28, 12-15, https://www.nybooks.com/articles/2010/10/28/moral-brink/, 2023-01-15.
Daëron, Marc (2021) *L'immunité, la vie. Pour une autre immunologie*, Paris, Odile Jacob.

---

35 I refer here to the concept coined by Peter Sloterdijk (cf. 2009, 699-714).

Derrida, Jacques (1998) "Faith and Knowledge: The Two Sources of 'Religion' at the Limits of Reason Alone", Jacques Derrida/Gianni Vattimo (eds.) *Religion*, Cambridge, Polity Press, 1-78.

Derrida, Jacques (2001) *Foi et Savoir*, Paris, Éditions du Seuil.

Derrida, Jacques (2003) *Voyous: deux essais sur la raison*, Paris, Galilée.

Esposito, Roberto (2002) *Immunitas: protezione e negazione della vita*, Turin, Einaudi.

Esposito, Roberto (2011 [2002]) *Immunitas: The Protection and Negation of Life*, trans. by Zakiya Hanafi, Cambridge, Polity Press.

Fastelli, Federico (2021) "Incarnare il contagio. Destino e colpa nella letteratura della pandemia", *Lea* 10, 3-13. DOI: 10.13128/LEA1824-484x-12839.

Giannopoulou, Zina (2016) "Oedipus Meets Bucky in Philip Roth's *Nemesis*", *Philip Roth Studies* 12/1, 15-31. DOI: 10.5703/philrothstud.12.1.15.

Girard, René (1982) *Le bouc émissaire*, Paris, Grasset.

Horkheimer, Max/Adorno, Theodor W. (2002 [1944]) *Dialectic of Enlightenment, Philosophical Fragments*, Stanford, CA, Stanford University Press.

Kaup, Monika (2021) *New Ecological Realisms, Post-apocalyptic Fiction and Contemporary Theory*, Edinburgh, Edinburgh University Press.

Lingis, Alfonso (1994) *The Community of Those Who Have Nothing in Common.* Bloomington, IN, Indiana University Press.

Maturana, Humberto R./Varela, Francisco J. (1980), *Autopoiesis and Cognition. The Realization of the Living*, Dordrecht, Reidel.

Maturana, Humberto R./Varela, Francisco J. (1987) *The Tree of Knowledge. The Biological Roots of Human Understanding*, trans. by Robert Paolucci, Boston, MA, New Science Library.

McMullen, Ken (dir.) (1983) *Ghost Dance*, Great Britain/Germany, Looseyard Production.

Meirelles, Fernando (2008) *Blindness*, Brazil/Japan/Canada, Andrea Barata Ribeiro, Niv Fichman et Sonoko Sakai.

Salles-Djelic, Marie-Laure (2020) "Quand l'idéologie avance masquée. Immunité collective, néolibéralisme et darwinisme social", Marc Lazar/Guillaume Plantin/Xavier Ragot (eds.), *Le monde d'aujourd'hui. Les sciences sociales au temps de la Covid*, Paris, Presses de Sciences Po, 293-307.

Saramago, José (1999) "The Nobel Lecture", *World Literature Today* 73/1, 5-10.

Saramago, José (2004) *Ensaio sobre a Lucidez*, Lisbon, Caminho.

Searles, George J. (1992) *Conversations with Philip Roth*, Jackson, MS, University Press of Mississippi Print.

Seth, Catriona (2020) "Quand Philip Roth raconte la contagion", *En attendant Nadeau. Journal de la littérature des idées et des arts* 101, 39-40, https://www. en-attendant-nadeau.fr/2020/03/31/roth-raconte-contagion/, 2020-08-08.

Sloterdijk, Peter (2009) *Du musst dein Leben ändern. Über Anthropotechnik*, Frankfurt am Main, Suhrkamp.

Tronto, Joan C. (1993) *Moral Boundaries. A Political Argument for an Ethic of Care*, New York, NY, Routledge.

Türk, Johannes (2011) *Die Immunität der Literatur*, Frankfurt am Main, S. Fischer.

Vieira, Patrícia I. (2011) *Seeing Politics Otherwise. Vision in Latin American and Iberian Fiction*, Toronto, ON, University of Toronto Press.

Villate Torres, Lina Patricia (2018) *De la maladie contagieuse à la fin des temps dans 'La Montagne magique', 'La Peste', 'L'amour aux temps du choléra' et 'Némésis'*, Doctoral Thesis, Strasbourg, University of Strasbourg, https:// www.theses.fr/2018STRAC032, 2022-05-14.

Vitale, Francesco (2018) *Biodeconstruction. Jacques Derrida and the Life Sciences*, Albany, NY, State University of New York Press.

Wald, Priscilla (2008) *Contagious: Cultures, Carriers, and the Outbreak Narrative*, Durham, NC, Duke University Press.

The Crowd as a Pandemic Character: Determinism, Entertainment and Transgression in Literature

Aureo Lustosa Guerios (Independent scholar, São Paulo)

Abstract

This chapter discusses the portrayal of crowds as a pandemic character. It focuses on the paradoxical perception of the masses as both the main target and the root cause of the cholera outbreaks of the 1800s. First, it presents historical reasons for the emergence of the public tumults. Then, it tackles the literary imagination of crowds, seen as an entity in itself, homogeneous and unchanging. Fictional crowds customarily laugh and drink without considering risks, with outbreaks erupting in their midst almost as a punishment for their lack of restraint. Texts mentioned at this point include Heine's *The Cholera in Paris* (1832), Belli's *Er Còllera Mòribbus* (1835), Lambruschini's *Il Choléra a Roda* (1835) or De Roberto's *San Placido* (1887). Finally, I consider how the crowds are seen as ignorant and destructive by nature. They are taken as an embodied expression of the outbreak; yet, if cholera is intangible and mysterious, crowds can be easily observed, explained and held accountable.

INTRODUCTION

Cholera has exerted an enormous influence in recent history. Since it first reached continental proportions in the early 19th century, it has caused seven pandemics that resulted in millions of deaths and has influenced almost every aspect of life. Cholera induced economic and political instability, disrupted human displacement patterns (military action, pilgrimage, tourism), and encouraged major changes in culture (personal hygiene), society (public health campaigns, sanitation, re-urbanization) and science (germ theory of disease).

Cholera also gave rise to tumults and riots all around the world. In previous centuries, other contagious diseases – above all plague and smallpox –, had proved capable of unleashing turmoil. However, the cholera riots are set apart for two reasons. First, they were remarkably consistent not only in space and time, but across different cultures and political systems. Second, they were unprecedented in the consistent attacks against authorities, which they provoked: whereas previous riots motivated by epidemics tended to persecute marginalized groups, the cholera riots overwhelmingly targeted the rich and powerful (government, aristocrats, religious leaders) (cf. Cohn Jr. 2017). As such, cholera riots were feared as a political force to be reckoned with, not least for their potential to foster revolutions (cf. Evans 1992, 152).

Critics have pointed out how the French Revolution was vital for the emergence of crowds as a literary character (cf. Tumeo 2011, 44; Matucci 2003, 15). Crowds appear constantly in 19th century fiction and the literary representation of the crowd has been indispensable for the formation of 'crowd psychology' as a field of study. As Dufief remarks, besides drawing from history, psychology and sociology, the *psychologie des foules* also kept in constant dialogue with literature (1990, 21f.):

> Le Bon [...] was an attentive reader of Zola; writers, in their turn, wrote novels in which they limit themselves on occasion to recopying Le Bon, as Rosny was to do in *The Red Wave*. Politicians served as models for writers and sociologists; Barrès, just like Le Bon, was interested in Boulanger.[1, 2]

In this chapter, I analyze the representation of crowds in a few literary texts featuring cholera, most of which belong to Italian literature, hoping to demonstrate how and why pandemic narratives employ large groups as a single character. I start with a brief discussion of historical reasons for the emergence of cholera riots. Next, I tackle some recurrent characteristics of tumults in literature: uniformity, determinism, unison. I then investigate how crowds are represented as fearless and irresponsible; they laugh and drink in times of epidemics without considering

---

1   Unless indicated otherwise, all translations of foreign-language quotations and italicized emphases are by the author. Original quotations are cited after each translation in the footnote.

2   "Le Bon [...] a été le lecteur attentif de Zola; les écrivains, de leur côté, écriront des romans où ils se contentent parfois de recopier Le Bon, comme le fera Rosny dans *La Vague Rouge*. Les hommes politiques servent de modèles aux écrivains et aux sociologues; Barrès, tout comme Le Bon, s'intéressera à Boulanger" (Dufief 1990, 21f.).

risks. Their search for hedonism is framed as a transgression that invites for some kind of supernatural punishment. Finally, I consider how, in their cultural context, crowds are seen as ignorant and destructive by nature. They are taken as human equivalents to the epidemic, but differ from it to the extent they can be seen, touched and imbued with intention. Thus, crowds stand opposite to the randomness of disease for being easy to understand and blame.

HISTORICAL RESPONSES TO THE ARRIVAL OF CHOLERA

Diseases are more than biomedical phenomena; they are also social and cultural constructions that are imbued with meaning through multi-layered narratives. Since knowing the root-cause of the problem is essential for treating or coping with most medical conditions, diseases naturally call for narratives of origins that may offer insights, meaning and a sense of control. This is particularly true in the case of contagious diseases, for its gratuity and randomness defy many of our beliefs about the world. Furthermore, epidemics are invasive by definition, and expectedly give rise to questions like *"where did it come from?"*, *"how did it get here?"* or *"who is to blame?"*.

In the case of the cholera pandemics, European sources have routinely attributed these to Asia since at least the 16th century – although, as shown by recent scholarship (cf. Hamlin 2009, 39-50), upon scant and problematic evidence. The cholera *vibrio* kills through severe dehydration: an infected person suffers from uncontrollable diarrhoea and vomiting, which results in weakness and lethargy. It also causes the victim to look 'mummified' through apparent sudden weight loss, sunken eyes, leathery and wrinkled skin and a bluish colouring of the face, hands and feet. If not treated, it can cause death in up to 50% of cases. To put it simply, in the 19th century, cholera was a humiliating and terrifying condition.

Cholera's assault on the digestive system and its spread via the faecal-oral route make it a disease of poverty. Its transmission relies on defective sanitary infrastructures and contaminated food and water. Furthermore, it targets the undernourished and those with compromised immune-systems (the young, the old or the sick). This means that the poor are more likely to develop an infection and less likely to recover from it – and this was especially the case in the 1800s, when sanitary standards in overcrowded cities were notoriously low. A few statistics can prove this point: if, during the Naples outbreak of 1836, casualties among 'the affluent and property owners' accounted for 9.5% of deaths, but 87.8% among 'artisans, traders and others' (cf. Tognotti 2000, 151). Similarly, during the

Hamburg outbreak of 1892, people earning 800 to 1 000 marks were twelve times more likely to die than those with an income of 50 000 or more (a death rate of 62‰ against 5‰) (cf. Evans 2017, ch. 4).

Both rich and poor were quick to understand that cholera preferred the socially vulnerable but they interpreted the phenomenon in quite different ways. The bourgeoisie saw their resistance as a biological counterpart to their economic privilege, in some instances even exaggerating their advantage to claim immunity. For instance, a Parisian newspaper asserted in 1832 that "*all the men* stricken with this epidemic … come from the class of the people" (Kudlick 1996, 55); while the chronicler Raffaello Mastriani, declared in 1836 that the populace of Naples had reasons to fear, "because this evil raged *exclusively* among the miserable" (Mastriani 1836, 63).[3] The belief in the invulnerability of the upper classes was disseminated enough for Octave Mirbeau to satirize it in *L'Épidemie* (1898), in which a so-called "anti-scientific" event takes place: "Gentlemen… an unbelievable novelty… frightful … overwhelming! […] A bourgeois has died!" (27).[4] Furthermore, cholera's humiliating symptoms encouraged affluent families to keep silent about it and, if there were deaths, to attribute the *causa mortis* to other more respectable conditions – that is likely the case of Leopardi, who allegedly died of digestive complications during the Naples outbreak of 1837 and whose body went notoriously missing.

On the other hand, the poor, horrified by cholera and suspicious of government action, interpreted the health inequalities as intentional and designed. Widely disseminated rumours claimed that outbreaks were, in fact, the result of poisoning campaigns devised by states to control the growth of the population. Such conspiracy theories sprang spontaneously around the world and shared remarkable similarities in their composition and scope, even if they were not connected in any way (cf. Cohn Jr. 2017). Indeed, multiple factors gave credence to such beliefs in an age when the very concepts of public health and scientific medicine were still in the making. By the time the pandemic arrived in Europe, Malthusian ideas about demographic control had been in circulation for over three decades. Additionally, government actions often came across to the populace as arbitrary and excessively harsh – forced hospitalizations or confiscation of dead bodies were not uncommon, for example. Furthermore, private physicians regularly fled or even denied

---

3 "[...] ben n'avevan d'onde, inferocendo il male esclusivamente fra la misera gente, più necessariamente priva di mezzi, mancante di ogni agio del comun vivere, pascentesi per necessità di malsani cibi" (Mastriani 1836, 63).

4 "Messieurs... Une nouvelle incroyable... affreuse... foudroyante ! [...] Un bourgeois est mort!" (Mirbeau 1898, 27).

assistance for fear of contagion (cf. Sorcinelli 1986, 63-88). The poor also suffered the most with the reverberations of preventive strategies (restricted mobility, product shortages, economic losses), while social inequality and corruption meant that rules would apply differently to different social groups. Moreover, conspiracy theories were generally well received because they were built upon deeply-rooted beliefs about secret groups willingly trying to damage society (plague-spreaders, witches, Jews).

Once conspiracy theories collided with the general feelings of fear, helplessness and abandonment, riots swiftly followed. The first of these took place in the Russian countryside as soon as the pandemic reached Europe in 1830 and 1831; and continued to flare up from this point onwards. Samuel Cohn Jr. (2017, 164) calculates that, in a timespan of only fourteen months, at least seventy-two cholera riots took place in the United Kingdom alone. In Canada, in 1832, the police had to summon the military after an unruly crowd dismantled Quebec City's hospital (ibid., 169). In Paris, the carnival and riots attracted enormous international attention, in part for the city's revolutionary history and cultural relevance as the *ville lumière*, but in part also due to a vivid journalistic description by Heinrich Heine that had circulated broadly around the continent. Riots spiked in the 1830s, and continued to emerge until the end of the century, especially in Italy.

LITERARY RESPONSES TO CHOLERA: DETERMINISM, GROUP UNISON AND PEDAGOGY

These disturbances intrigued literary authors who felt an immediate urge to describe and explain them in narratives. A great number – if not a majority – of the cholera texts I have identified elsewhere (cf. Guerios 2021) feature crowds and tumults in some form or another. That happens to such an extent, that texts rarely focus on convalescence itself; rather, cholera is a social ailment that usually serves to create a tumultuous background against which characters can be tested. Once that happens, they can triumph – as Angelo in *Le Hussard sur le toit* or the physician Axel Munthe in his *Letters from a Mourning City* – or fall – as Lydgate in *Middlemarch* or Aschenbach in *Death in Venice*. Thus, cholera is overwhelmingly portrayed as a disease of the social body, quite unlike tuberculosis or cancer, which are generally seen as conditions of the individual. That is already evident in the titles: instead of focusing on individuals – *Dombey and Son*, *La Dame aux camélias*, *The Death of Ivan Ilyitch* –, texts about cholera usually name the disease, its location and time.

These texts are usually interested in exploring the outbreak as a collective problem, trying to embrace the epidemic as a phenomenon in itself, instead of adopting the partial perspective of one single character. As we shall shortly observe, some of them are entirely constructed around collective characters, sometimes lacking individual ones altogether. That applies to contagious diseases in general – plague, yellow fever, typhus, influenza – and encompasses many canonical epidemic narratives, including Thucydides' description of the Plague of Athens, the prologue of the *Decameron*, or Defoe's *A Journal of the Plague Year*, all of which describe a mosaic of human reactions towards pestilence without following anyone in particular. Plague images (triumphs of death, *dances macabres*) are also cases in point, since they commonly portray the demise of large groups of anonymous individuals who personify entire social groups.

Investigating the representation of riots in fiction, Birchall (2015, 57) shows how violent crowds are repeatedly described from the outside by an external observer who takes a position of distance from it. Main characters rarely mix with the anonymous group and, when they do, are taken aback by its irrationality, drunkenness and cruelty. That is very much the case for the cholera riots too. All the texts I could locate treat the theme by simplistic oppositions between civilization and barbarity, notwithstanding their occasional acknowledgement of the populace's suffering and despair. Even when no violence takes place – as is the case of the *partying crowds* –, individuals within the group are dehumanized and prove incapable of identity and thought. Moreover, despite emerging spontaneously and proving impossible to calm down, crowds are, at the same time, manoeuvred by malicious agitators who stir them into violence. If rare voices of dissent arise, they are either ignored or attacked by the 'fanatics'. For example, in Verga's *Quelli dei Colèra* (1887), a "good soul" gets ahead of the crowd to urge the soon-to-be-killed actors to escape.[5] Later, yet another effort to prevent violence makes the narrator to comment as if in surprise: "there were also some good souls in that mob. But the others did not want to hear reason".[6] In other words, crowds can be directed only towards 'evil': if they are *partying crowds* they tend towards recklessness and debauchery; if *rioting crowds*, towards violence and destruction.

A key mechanism to build such representations is to treat conspiracy theories and riots as inevitable repercussions of outbreaks; ones which are unchanging and

---

5 "Un'anima buona si mise le gambe in spalla, e corse [...] a dirgli che scappasse" (Verga 1887, 295).

6 "—No! no! non li ammazzate ancora! Vediamo prima se sono innocenti! vediamo prima se portano il colèra! [sic] — C'erano pure delle anime buone in quella ressa. Ma gli altri non volevano intender ragioni" (Verga 1887, 296).

constant throughout history. For instance, in *I Misteri di Napoli* (1870) by Francesco Mastriani, it is said that *"wherever* a plague erupted, the people believed in poisoning" (185);[7] in *L'Esercito Italiano Durante il Colèra del 1867* (1869), De Amicis reports that "superstition, fear and misery, are assiduous company to the great dying *in all peoples and in all ages*" (286);[8] while in *Contes Nouveaux* (1833), Jules Janin laments that "[t]he crowd is so cruel and so stupid! *Everywhere and always* the same, in London, in Saint Petersburg, in Paris; *always the same*" (63).[9] Given that the populace is inherently credulous, and that tumults are among an outbreak's inescapable consequences, no further analysis is necessary. There is no need to address the situation beyond dispersing groups by force.

Another way to naturalize tumult is to pretend the crowd is capable of single and unified speech. This is achieved by group members somehow speaking in unison, similar to the implementation of the *chorus* in classic tragedy. That is the case of the *Quadri Storici del Cholera di Napoli* (1837), which was published by the Count Sterlich immediately after the disease subsided. The text presents itself as a historical chronicle, even if its brief chapters are anecdotal and rarely reference any sources. In his account, once cholera reaches Naples, "a chorus of four hundred thousand voices echoed in unison" and screamed "'the Cholera!'" (19).[10] The statement can only be taken as figurative, since it is clearly impossible for individuals to tacitly coordinate themselves on a scale such as this. Authors often count on the good will of the public to accept some freedom of expression: readers are expected to understand that not everybody is actually pronouncing words at the same time; this is a textual liberty, which is nevertheless supposed to encapsulate the crowd's 'true spirit'. Readers should accept that as part of the fictional pact – and the pattern is so widespread that one presumes they often did. As Birchall noticed, "[i]f such depictions [of crowds] appeal to readers, it is because they comfort them by confirming and flattering prejudices they already hold" (2015, 56). This effect is even more remarkable if we consider this trope's

---

7   "Dovunque scoppiò una peste, il popolo credé agli avvelenamenti" (Mastriani 1870, 185).

8   "Ma per quanto fossero disposti a fare pel bene del paese l'esercito e i cittadini animosi ed onesti, tre grandi forze nemiche dovevano rendere per molta parte e per lungo tempo inefficace l'opera loro: la superstizione, la paura, la miseria, assidue compagne della morìa presso tutti i popoli e in tutti i tempi" (De Amicis 1869, 286).

9   "Elle est si cruelle et si stupide, la foule! Partout et toujours la même, à Londre, à Saint-Pétersbourg, à Paris; toujours la même" (Janin 1833, 63).

10 "— Il cholera! — era l'eco di quattrocentomila cittadini, era l'unisono d'un coro di quattrocentomila voci. — Il cholera!" (Sterlich 1837, 19).

presence in many non-fictional and journalistic discourses that have presumably, a different relationship to truth.

These tendencies can also be spotted in Luigi Settembrini's autobiography *Ricordanze della mia Vita* (written in 1849-1851, published in 1879). It contains a chapter dedicated to cholera, which starts by avowing that "*Always and anywhere it has been a plague not previously known, the people* [...] *always* believe that it is poison, and accuse its enemies" (38).[11] It proceeds to describe how "finding myself helpless in the midst of so many who wanted to shoot cholera" (80),[12] Settembrini tried to reason with the crowd, hoping to appease the spirits by quoting from Thucydides and Manzoni. They answer as one (*mi rispuosero*) and, when they start to speak, their individual sentences are reported in bulk without any differentiation. This common strategy serves the purpose of maintaining the individual identity as opaque and imprecise as possible:

> They were reasonable people, but spoke as if they were mad: their faces were transformed, their eyes wide open. "I saw a dog die ten minutes after a woman threw him a piece of bread." "And the woman?" "She was already gone." "Here is a letter from Cosenza: 'Dearest friend, beware because our enemies want to poison us like rats. [...]" "I spoke to a man of standing who [...] saw a man [throw a white matter into the fountain]" "Fool! when you see him flee, shoot him [...]".[13] (80f.)

---

11 "Sempre e dovunque è stata una peste non conosciuta prima, il popolo che vede in un subito morire e non sa come e perché, crede sempre che sia veleno, e ne accagiona i nemici, se ne ha, o quelli che egli odia. Il nostro popolo credette che fosse veleno e che il governo lo facesse spargere, mandandone le casse agl'intendenti, e questi lo dividessero tra i loro cagnotti i quali lo gittavano nella acque" (Settembrini 1964, 38).

12 "Trovandomi inerme in mezzo a tanti che volevano fare a schioppettate col cholera, io mi provai una volta a dire [...]" (Settembrini 1964, 80).

13 "Erano uomini di senno, e parlavano come matti: avevano le facce trasformate, gli occhi spalancati. «Ho visto io morire un cane dieci minuti dopo che una donna gli ha gittato un pezzo di pane». «E la donna?». «Era giá scomparsa». «Ecco qui una lettera da Cosenza: 'Amico carissimo, guardatevi perché i nostri nemici ci vogliono attossicare come topi. Moriamo almeno con le armi in mano'. E chi mi scrive non è uno sciocco». «Ho parlato con un proprietario il quale co' suoi guardiani è andato in campagna, ed ha veduto un uomo vestito come un calderaio che beveva a una fontana: egli ha sospettato, ha detto: 'ferma lá', e quegli è fuggito come una lepre. Hanno guardato l'acqua, e v'era una materia bianca gettatavi da colui». «Sciocco! quando lo vedi fuggire, tiragli una fucilata, e fallo cadere. Se m'accade a me, io gli tiro al volo»" (Settembrini 1964, 80f.).

On occasion, the group is capable of acting together, as if its individual members were a single organic entity with multiple legs and arms. That is how De Amicis portrays the attack on a soldier who was believed to be spreading poison:

> He was reached, *seized by ten hands*, [...] [and] threatened with death. — Where do you keep the poison? — *ten voices asked in one*. — I have no poison... — the soldier stammered, white as a corpse. — Where do you keep the poison? — insisted the others menacingly.[14] (317)

These characteristics are also evident in the short story *Il Cholera a Roda* (1835) by Raffaello Lambruschini. The text was published independently in Florence in the year Italy experienced its first outbreaks. It tells the story of how a small town in the outskirts of Barcelona was afflicted by violence. In a preface addressed 'To the Tuscan people', the author attests that his story is based on actual events and he urges his fellow citizens to avoid repeating these by uniting, trusting God and respecting the authorities. Moved by the sudden multiplication of riots, the author decides to write a short moral tale, which he hopes, might help prevent havoc in Tuscany. His aim is to achieve this by means of education, as evident in the text's subtitle: *racconto istruttivo* (an instructive story). As if speaking with disorderly children, Lambruschini tries to convince the populace to behave: "[Tuscan people,] I wanted to teach you (*ammaestrare*), so that you do not let yourself be seduced, should it ever happen that anyone proclaims the same nonsense among us. Learn, oh good and docile people [...]" (3).[15] The paternalistic tone is reinforced by the choice of the verb: instead of the more common and neutral *insegnare* (to teach), the author prefers *ammaestrare*, that can also mean 'to tame or train animals' – in effect, crowds are regularly compared to flocks of animals in the cholera texts. Despite presenting itself as a preventive strategy, the story engages very much with the *topoi* of unison and determinism. The author treats 'the people' as a single entity and, if he hopes to prevent turmoil, is precisely because he believes it is forthcoming.

---

14 "Fu raggiunto, afferrato da dieci mani, tradotto dietro una casa romita, messo colle spalle al muro, minacciato di morte. — Dove tieni il veleno? — gli domandarono dieci voci in una. — Io non ho veleno... — rispose balbettando il soldato, bianco come un cadavere. — Dove tieni il veleno? — insistettero gli altri minacciosamente" (De Amicis 1869, 317).

15 "io ho voluto ammaestrarti, perché tu non ti lasci sedurre, se avverrà mai che alcuno spacci tra noi le medesime assurdità. Impara, o popolo, buono, docile, [...]" (Lambruschini 1835, 3).

The development of the story is in harmony with the didacticism of the preface. The first paragraph offers all the required background information – time, place, the anomalous event – by following the conventions of fairy tales. Then, the narrator turns to the "malevolous fools" spreading rumours of poisoning to the multitude, who "immediately believe whatever is said to them, and never reflect whether it can or cannot be" (6).[16] Then, the crowd unifies and sparks out of control as a force of nature – another common trope:

> "We are poisoned, we are poisoned," was a voice that burst out like thunder that spread over everything and gradually increased, like the flood of a river, which swells when it receives the waters of the ravines, and roars and breaks the banks and floods and deserts a country. "We are poisoned, we are poisoned" – and woe to anyone who dared to answer "but who said so? how do you know?" Reason was not followed; they screamed, cursed and sought nothing but the poisoner.[17] (6f.)

The emotional contagion is irresistible to every member who blindly follows the group's least reasonable actors. Their identities dissolve within this uniformed mass, so much so that their screams are described in Italian by impersonal verb constructions (*si urlava, si bestemmiava*), a nuance which can not be immediately rendered into English. If translated word for word, the structure would be similar to those that express weather ('it rains'), yet it would result in the ungrammatical formulation "it screamed, it cursed", in which the pronoun 'it' would not designate a subject but rather the lack of one.

CHOLERA, DRINKING AND CARNIVAL

Not all literary tumults are violent, though. When cholera first appeared, a part of the population was not afraid of it. Many doubted it could even reach Europe, belittled its seriousness, or thought they could prevent it (cf. Guerios 2022).

---

16 "Gli ignoranti han questo difetto che credono subito qualunque cosa è detta loro, e non riflettono mai s'ella possa o non possa essere [...]" (Lambruschini 1835, 6).

17 "— Siamo avvelenati, siamo avvelenati, — fu una voce che scoppiò come un tuono, e si sparse per tutto, e s'accrebbe via via, come la piena d'un fiume, che ingrossa al ricevere giù le acque de' borri, e mugghia e rompe gli argini e allaga e diserta un paese. — Siamo avvelenati, siamo avvelenati: — e guai a chi avesse ardito rispondere «ma chi l'ha detto; come lo sapete?» Non si intendeva ragione; si urlava, si bestemmiava, e non si cercava d'altro che dell'avvelenatore" (Lambruschini 1835, 6f.).

Effectively, innumerable physicians and politicians were certain that the continent would evade the second cholera pandemic (1826-1838), as it had already done during the first (1817-1824). The so-called 'Asiatic' or 'Indian' cholera was perceived as Tropical and – as its very name ensured – would not thrive in the European colder climate. One such reassuring prediction is found in a letter from Leopardi to his sister; he mentions that "in here, the physicians laugh [at the prediction that cholera could enter Italy] because they don't believe it" (Tognotti 2000, 28).[18] Not only that, but even after outbreaks erupted, governments would deny or downplay its seriousness as a way to prevent panic.

Additionally, many people both within and without medicine believed that contagion could be avoided by strong alcohol. The idea captured the popular imagination because it promised to combine prevention and entertainment. Many caricatures explored the theme humorously (cf. Guerios 2021, 163-166), and so did G. G. Belli in *Er Còllera Mòribbus, Converzazzione a l'osteria de la ggènzola indisposta e ariccontata co ttrentaquattro sonetti, e tutti de grinza* (written in 1835). This is a cycle of thirty-four sonnets written in the Roman dialect. It aims at creating a panorama of popular opinions by presenting the reader with a cacophony of unidentified voices – as stated in the subtitle, "dialogues in a tavern by the indisposed people". The commoners who speak are seen with a certain paternalist sympathy, yet are also derided at the same time. Their opinions are often based on absurd assumptions, and arguments are presented using defective grammar and vocabulary – as such, readers are invited to laugh *with* and *at* the characters. The text seems to be conceived as a sort of anthropological document, which, despite containing fictional dialogues, is truthful to the 'spirit of the masses'. Hence, it is unsurprising that it follows a similar pattern to others already mentioned. The first poem denies the existence of the disease ("this epidemic in my view, / is not among us, if it exists at all") (848),[19] while another builds up tension by assuring that "a rumour spreads that cholera is nothing less / than the effects of poison" (845).[20] However, rather than violence, the speaker instigates laughter by

---

18 "L'altra sera parlai colla commissione medica mandata da Roma a complimentare il Cholèra a Parigi, la quale ci promette la venuta del morbo in Italia: predizione di cui ridono i medici di qui, perché non ci credono" (Foschi 1983, 161 and Tognotti 2000, 28).

19 "che sta pidemeria sarvo me tocco, / cqua da noi nun ce viè, sippuro è vvera" 1749. [Er còllera mòribbus] 1°.

20 "curre la sciarla mó ggnente de meno / ch'er collèra è l'affetto d'un veleno" 1756. [Er còllera mòribbus] 8°.

concluding: "to water, they can do as they wish, / on condition that they do not poison my wine" (845).[21]

There is a long cultural tradition that sees epidemics and festivities in relationship to one another: the *Decameron* is notoriously filled with stories and banquets; Brueghel's paintings of plague and public celebrations are astoundingly similar; while medieval plague masks have turned from medical instruments into carnival costumes. A great majority of epidemic texts feature at least one party and some, as Pushkin's *A Feast During the Plague* (2000 [1830]), are entirely built around the subject. The search for pleasures during a serious crisis comes across in these narratives as signs of natural irresponsibility and supernatural provocation. The festive behaviour, we are led to believe, calls for heavenly retribution; and, in fact, punishment usually arrives to those involved without delay. An illustration of this is found in Poe's *The Mask of the Red Death* (1850 [1842]), a short story that was based on written cholera sources, as well as in the author's own experience with the 1832 outbreaks in Boston and Philadelphia. In it, Prince Prospero hopes to escape the deadly pestilence by remaining isolated in a monastery with a thousand of his court nobles. They throw decadent feasts and masked balls every day; until, the Red Death itself appears at the party, and all revellers fall dead without exception. The dialect of transgression and retribution could not be clearer.

Interestingly, stories of the same kind are found in non-fictional reports. This is the case with Chateaubriand's autobiography *Mémoires d'outre-tombe* (1900 [1849-1850]), which includes descriptions of the first Paris outbreak of 1832. Chateaubriand decries "the indifference of the crowd" because adults kept attending theaters during the crisis and children "played cholera, which they called the *Nicolas Morbus* and the *scoundrel Morbus*" (emphasis by Chateaubriand) (486).[22] He even claims to have witnessed the strangest of deaths: "I saw drunkards at Barrière Street, sitting in front of a tavern door, drinking on a small wooden table and saying as they raised their glasses, 'To your health, *Morbus*!' Morbus, out of gratitude, rushed up, and they fell dead under the table" (486).[23] The description is certainly exaggerated, if not completely made up. We can declare that with

---

21 "Sull'acqua ponno fà cquanto j'aggrada, / purché nun zia d'avvelenamme er vino" 1756. [Er còllera mòribbus] 8°.

22 "Les enfants jouaient au choléra, qu'ils appelaient le *Nicolas Morbus* et le *scélérat Morbus*" (Chateaubriand 1900, 486).

23 "Et chacun continuait de vaquer à ses affaires, et les salles de spectacle étaient pleines. J'ai vu des ivrognes à la barrière, assis devant la porte du cabaret, buvant sur une petite table de bois et disant en élevant leur verre: « À ta santé, *Morbus*! » Morbus, par reconnaissance, accourait, et ils tombaient morts sous la table" (Chateaubriand 1900, 486).

confidence because the narrated facts are not consistent with biology. Cholera is abrupt and swift, to be sure, but even in the worst cases it requires a timespan of at least a few hours to kill. Moreover, symptoms only begin after an incubation period of between 18 to 120 hours (cf. Sack et al. 2004, 224). It is simply not possible for people to drop dead on the spot, struck down by it as if from a heart attack. Rather than describing a true event, this anecdote serves the purpose of conveying a just and immediate punishment for a transgression. Besides, it also evinces the temerity and irresponsibility of the drunkards – who appear to see little value in their own lives – and also bestows authority upon the alleged eyewitness.

The pattern of hedonistic behaviour followed by instant punishment surfaces quite often in pandemic narratives when the origins of an outbreak is brought to the fore – in what Priscilla Wald (2008) has defined as the 'outbreak narrative'. In this particular case, the punishment goes beyond the irresponsible revellers, because the epidemic continues to spread after they die. Thus, this type of origin myth is used in both a direct and indirect way to blame, at least partially, certain behaviours, individuals or groups as being responsible for the outbreak.

The best example of that is found in Heinrich Heine's so-called *The Cholera in Paris* (letter *VI*, dated April 19th 1832), part of a series of nine long journalistic texts that circulated in a German newspaper in 1831 and 1832, and achieved great acclaim when published in book form in 1833, both in German (*Französische Zustände*) and French (*De la France*). These were 'letters to the public' that commented on French politics and society by combining different elements of travel narratives, cultural essays and epistolary novels. Heine's status as a privileged observer allowed him to report events as they unfold, presumably for being an eyewitness. Indeed, he says he was present in many instances, but in others he only refers to rumours and in some – as in the one we are about to discuss – he says nothing about his sources.

Heine describes the Paris outbreak in over twenty pages, from the moment it officially started to a mid-way point into the epidemic, about three weeks later, when no resolution is yet in sight. The letter contains many bleak passages of suffering and death, but they are accompanied with Heine's characteristic irony, which occasionally creates humorous effects. The text follows a similar pattern of development to those already discussed: the great anxiety of contagion – or the lack of it –; references to Thucydides and Boccaccio – whom Heine mockingly promises to surpass –; and the unidentified crowd – the "merry people" from the week before, had now given way to "grim indifference", "most terrible voices", and "sorrowful faces" (Heine 1893, 163).

From the beginning, cholera is portrayed in relationship to the French Revolution in Heine's letters: the disease is "a masked executioner who passed through

Paris with an invisible *guillotine ambulante*" (ibid., 162) and its "reign of terror [was] far more dreadful than the first, because the executions took place rapidly and mysteriously" (ibid.). Such comparisons made sense in view of recent events – cholera did spread during the *Age of Revolutions* (cf. Evans 1992) – but they also tackled deeper fears of the poor, of instability and social change.

According to Heine, apprehension in the population was initially not particularly great, because the London outbreak was said to have been mild and because the spring weather was sunny with clear skies, with the assumed result that the noxious clouds of miasmas were nowhere in sight. Consequently, Parisians celebrated the traditional carnival of the *Mi-Carême*, and merrily took to the streets "where one could even see maskers, who in caricatures of livid colour and sickly mien, mocked the fear of the cholera and the disease itself" (Heine 1893, 167). A sense of transgression is already noticeable in these remarks, and it only grows as the dancing and music begin:

> That night the balls were more crowded than usual; excessive laughter (*übermütiges Gelächter*) almost drowned the roar of music; people grew hot in the *chahut*; a dance of anything but equivocal character; all kinds of ices and cold beverages were in great demand – when all at once the merriest of the harlequins felt that his legs were becoming much too cold, and took off his mask, when, to the amazement of all, a violet-blue face became visible. (Heine 1893, 166f.)

The amusement is portrayed as excessive and overconfident, even if it is not clear why. Hitherto, no cases had been reported, so laughter itself seems to be the problem. That is proven by the prompt collapse of the "merriest" – i.e., most accountable person. His transgression is presumably an offense against cholera itself, who punished the misdeed on the spot. It is very relevant that this is a *harlequin*: the mask prevents the formation of a personal identity by conjuring up the collective identity of a John Doe – and this harlequin is indeed accompanied by others. Besides, the *Arlecchino* also embodies the common folk in general since he is a servant and the trickster of the *Commedia dell'Arte*. Not only that, but the mask originally personified a demon – as the devil *Alichino*, who Dante sees brawling in *Inferno XXII* –, so it is transgressive in itself (cf. Scuderi 2000).

The infection erupts dramatically: the reveller has a bout of diarrhoea and, in an instant, unmasks himself to reveal a countenance already tainted by blue. As in the case of Chateaubriand, it is simply not possible for cholera to do so much harm in so little time. At best, the episode was exaggerated for theatrical effect, but it is most likely apocryphal. To the best of my knowledge, no other chronicler reports this story and Heine does not claim to have been present, nor does he mention any viable source. Rather, the narrative is simply given as a fact from a bird's-eye view; a problematic stance for a text posing as 'truth' – and Heine certainly expects his letter to be taken "as a source of history" in the future; he even claims in the preface, that this is already being "extensively" done "by French historiographers" (Heine 1893, 26f.). More importantly, however, is that the pattern fits the literary imagination of cholera to perfection. Immediate changes in colour, especially in the face, are relatively common in fictional texts, with death quickly following – as in this case (cf. Guerios 2021, 200-206). Not only that, but Heine's description of the reveller's diarrhoea as being a 'refreshment' is unmistakably sarcastic, and turns the joke against the joker. The idea of a *contrapasso* – punishment by means somehow related to the sin itself – is already strong and it becomes even more pronounced as cases inexplicably multiply in the following instants:

> It was at once seen that there was no jest in this; the laughter died away, and at once several carriages conveyed men and women from the ball to the *Hôtel Dieu*, the Central Hospital, where they, still arrayed in mask attire, soon died. [...] it is said that these dead were buried so promptly that even their fantastic fools' garments were left on them so that as they lived they now lie merrily in the grave. (Heine 1893, 167)

The harlequin gives way to a large and unspecified mass of people, who are rushed into the hospital just in time to die. The text emphasizes the displacement (*from the ball into the hospital*) to, again, highlight the transgression. Shortly afterwards, all these victims die; an occurrence that starkly contradicts the statistics, which would predict a recovery rate of at least half – and most likely more. Not only that, but they all expire while still in costume, as is remarked twice in the text. Finally, the supernatural retribution is further emphasized by a last ironic remark that, almost bordering on the glee of *schadenfreude*, directly links their exultation at the party to their 'merry' disposition – that is, 'dressed in costume' – at their graves.[24]

Heine seems to be building upon other examples of *hubris* avenged by pestilence that are found in the classical and Christian traditions. In the *Second Book of Samuel* and *First Chronicles*, for instance, God exhorts David to choose the ways of his own demise: three years of famine, three months pursued by an enemy, or three days of plague. David chooses the latter. In the *Iliad*, Apollo punishes the

---

24 The parallelism of this final comment is even more pronounced in German, since it repeats the word 'merry' (*lustig*) and also has an interesting cadence and assonance (*haben, Grabe*): "und lustig, wie sie gelebt haben, liegen sie auch lustig im Grabe" (Heine 1833, 152f.).

Greeks with pestilence due to Agamemnon's rebuttal of the rescue offer made by Chryses. In *Oedipus the King*, Oedipus' inadvertent misdeeds are responsible for unleashing the Plague of Thebes. However, these transgressions are committed unknowingly, and in all cases, the punishment goes way beyond the individual to afflict the entire society. What is more, those who perish are the thousands of the general populace and not those guilty individuals who summoned pestilence in the first place.

In Heine's description, this dialect is transformed because the Parisian revellers neither offended the gods nor broke any taboo. Their guilt appears to lie in their simply having fun, even if the text itself admits there were no particular reasons for fear – quite the contrary. Nevertheless, retribution is instantaneous and unforgiving and it seems designed to blame the party goers for their own demise. Here the social body is portrayed as 'having brought disgrace upon itself', in the very same way that syphilis is often seen in literature as just retribution for an individual's sins (cf. Schonlau 2005). In this way, the revellers unleash an almost supernatural force that kills them as punishment, but which despite this job done, subsequently continues to spread through society as a whole. What is more, given that the revellers are a collective entity that symbolizes 'the populace' at large, it can be concluded that the population is itself responsible for the epidemic to which it falls prey.

Tropes of this kind appear repeatedly in later pandemic texts. In De Roberto's short story *San Placido* (1891 [1887]), a crowd threatens the mayor who wishes to cancel the feast of the city's saint as a preventive sanitary measure: "We want the feast!... Long live the feast! ... Long live San Placido, or we'll burn down the townhall!" (99);[25] as a consequence, an outbreak of cholera erupts at the height of the celebration. In Bruno Jasieński's futurist novel *I Burn Paris* (2017 [1928]), people fall down killed by the plague while others continue dancing in a carnival frenzy. In Lúcio Cardoso's *Maleita* (1934), a smallpox outbreak erupts during a play in the theatre when the lead actor collapses on stage. This trope is also used in cinema. In the first scenes of Murnau's *Faust* (1926), Mephistopheles kindles a plague in a city, and its first victim is a circus acrobat who collapses during the spectacle. The public rushes on stage to help but, after taking his mask off and looking at his face, runs out in alarm. The scene is remarkably similar to the one described by Heine, with the focus on the face arguably relating to cholera and not to the plague: if the buboes that are characteristic of the plague appear only in the

---

25 "Vogliamo la festa!... Viva la festa!... Viva San Placido, o diamo fuoco al Municipio!..." (De Roberto 1891, 99).

neck, armpit or groin, it is cholera that normally leaves its victims with blueish tinted faces – but not instantaneously.

CHOLERA, CROWDS AND DEBAUCHERY

This pattern is taken one step further in Thomas Mann's *Death in Venice* (2004 [1912]). In the novel, a cholera outbreak erupts in a swampy and insalubrious Venice, and serves as a symbolic background for Aschenbach's infatuation – which the narrator calls "absurd", "perverse" and "ridiculous" (ibid., 96) – with a fourteen-year-old boy. Yet, the epidemic is not caused by ordinary cholera, but by an alleged rare variant called *cholera sicca*, in which fluids accumulate in the intestines to cause death by dehydration yet without any diarrhoea or vomiting. Despite being found in medical treatises of the 19th century, this variant is likely a fictional creation resulting from the will to preserve the honour of victims – the depiction of cholera as 'dry' seeming a simple inversion of its main symptom. As demonstrated by Otis (2000, 148-167), Mann was aware of *cholera sicca*'s questionable scientific status, but opted for it as a way to bypass the presence of bodily fluids. In the text, Aschenbach is struck down in an instant and without a trace of diarrhoea, in similar fashion to Chateaubriand's drunkards.

Before his downfall, Aschenbach had been warned in conspiratorial tones by an English Clerk, who had access to privileged information, presumably, due to England's colonial ties to India. The clerk stresses that, given the variant's "utmost ferocity", "[r]ecovery was rare" (Mann 2004, 121f.). Not only was the mortality rate significantly higher than usual ("eighty out of a hundred"), but a "patient would shrivel up and choke" to the point that those who "fell into a deep coma" should consider themselves "fortunate" (ibid.).

It is important to note that Mann's novella is set at the turn of the 20th century, a period when the vibrio and its contagion mechanism were already known and effective prevention strategies could – and had already been – implemented. In the context of such knowledge, one might expect cholera to be less rather than more menacing. Yet, the clerk does not provide a biological reason for this burst in virulence; instead, he immediately describes the social disturbances which accompany the outbreak:

> The populace knew all this [the cover-up of the epidemic], and corruption in high places together with the prevailing insecurity and the state of emergency into which death stalking the streets had plunged the city led to a certain degeneracy among the lower classes, the encouragement of dark, antisocial impulses that made itself

felt in self-indulgence, debauchery, and growing criminality. There was an unusu-
ally high number of drunkards abroad in the evening; vicious bands of rabble were
said to make the streets unsafe at night; muggings were not uncommon and even
murders, for it had been shown that on two occasions people who had allegedly
fallen victim to the epidemic had in fact been done in, poisoned, by their relatives;
and prostitution now assumed blatant and dissolute forms hitherto unknown here,
at home only in the south of the country and the Orient. (ibid., 122f.)

The clerk's fearmongering about crime takes place immediately after his alerts
about the disease's severity. This overlapping implicitly suggests that the higher
virulence was caused by the 'degeneracy' of the populace – in particular as a result
of the absence of medical justifications. In the eyes of the clerk, 'the lower classes' – understood as an unidentified and homogeneous group – are inclined to
moral failings of all sorts (dissipation, violence, prostitution). And this in turn,
seems to augment the virulence of the pathogen in some mysterious way. The fact
that sexual mores 'deteriorate' into forms only known "in the South [of Italy] and
in the Orient" – precisely those areas which are traditionally associated with the
disease and which were mentioned shortly before when the itinerary of the pandemic was described – suggests a parallel connection between the two.

Under these lights, the epidemic and the crowd are both a cause and an effect:
the disease prompts the poor to follow their base instincts, which, in turn, somehow augments the infection's ferocity. If in the narratives of Heine or De Roberto
the crowds were responsible for the final arrival of a much-anticipated epidemic,
in *Death in Venice*, they go beyond this by sustaining and catalysing its deadliness.

Ultimately, crowds as pandemic characters are used to embody disease: they as-
sign to the invisible germs not only faces and bodies, but also intentionality. It
follows that the capriciousness of the epidemic can be explained in simple terms
of transgression and punishment; narrative tropes which have a long history that
expands well beyond literature to embrace various forms of storytelling in folklore, religion, myth and so forth. In this way, these collective characters can be
seen as coping mechanisms aimed at explaining biological randomness by appeal-
ing to the social and cultural.

As repeatedly shown by medical anthropology, individuals and societies often
interpret diseases within moral, cultural or spiritual frames. At the individual level,
it is not uncommon for life-threatening diagnoses to be accompanied by existential
questions ('why me?', 'what have I done?', 'how could I have prevented it?') and
this may result in feelings of blame and guilt. When epidemic outbreaks are the
issue at hand, such questions are not individual, but collective; and in literary texts,

they may be answered via festive or violent crowds that act in a predictable – if irresponsible – fashion.

BIBLIOGRAPHY

Corpus Analyzed

Belli, Giuseppe Gioachino (1998 [1866]) *Tutti i Sonetti Romaneschi*, edited by Marcello Teodonio, Roma, Newton.

Chateaubriand, François-René de (1900 [1849-1850]) *Mémoires d'outre-tombe, vol. 5*, edited by Edmond Biré, Paris, Garnier Frères.

De Amicis, Edmondo (1869) "L'Esercito Italiano Durante il Colèra del 1867", *La Vita Militare*, Firenze, Successori le Monnier.

De Roberto, Federico (1891 [1887]) "San Placido", *La Sorte*, Milano, Galli.

Heine, Heinrich (1833) *Französische Zustände*, Hamburg, Hoffmann und Campe.

Heine, Heinrich (1893) *The Works of Heinrich Heine, vol. 8*, trans. by Charles Godfrey Leland, London, William Heinemann.

Janin, Jules (1833) *Contes Nouveaux*, Paris, Fonderie de A. Pinand.

Lambruschini, Raffaelo (1835) *Il Choléra a Roda: racconto struttivo*, Florence, Tipografia Galileiana.

Mann, Thomas (2004 [1912]) *Death in Venice: A New Translation*, trans. by Michael Henry Heim, London, Perfect Bound.

Mastriani, Francesco (1870) *I Misteri di Napoli, vol. 2*, Naples, G. Nobile.

Mastriani, Raffaele (1836) *Relazione della Peste di Firenze del 1348 di G. Boccaccio, di Quella di Milano del 1630 di A. Manzoni, dell'Altra di Napoli del 1656 di C. Botta, e del Colera di Quest'Ultima Città nel 1836 di Raffaele Mastriani*, Naples, Rafaelle de Stefano e Socii.

Mirbeau, Octave (1898) *L'épidémie. Pièce en un acte*, Paris, Charpentier et Fasquelle.

Settembrini, Luigi (1964 [1879]) *Ricordanze della Mia Vita, vol. 1*, Milan, Rizzoli.

Sterlich, Cesare de (1837) *Quadri Storici del Cholera di Napoli*, Naples, Tipografia Flautina.

Verga, Giovanni (1887) "Quelli del Colèra", *Vagabondaggio*, Firenze, G. Barbèra.

Works Cited

Birchall, Ian (2015) "Imagined Violence: Some Riots in Fiction", Keith Flett (ed.) *A History of Riots*, Cambridge, Cambridge Scholars Publishing, 39-58.

Boccaccio, Giovanni (2015 [1348-1353]) *Il Decameron*, Milan, Mondadori.

Cardoso, Lúcio (1934) *Maleita*, Rio de Janeiro, Schmidt.

Cohn Jr., Samuel K. (2017) "Cholera Revolts: A Class Struggle We May Not Like", *Social History* 42/2, 162-180. DOI: 10.1080/03071022.2017.1290365.

Defoe, Daniel (1994 [1722]) *A Journal of the Plague Year*, London, Everyman.

Dickens, Charles (1848) *Dombey and Son*, London, Bradbury and Evans.

Dufief, Pierre (1990) "La figure des meneurs et l'image de la foule dans le roman français de 1870 à 1914", *Littérature et Nation* 1, 2nd series, 21-42.

Dumas, Alexandre (1848) *La Dame aux camélias*, Paris, Gustave Harvard.

Eliot, George (1872) *Middlemarch: A Study of Provincial Life*, London, William Blackwood.

Evans, Richard J. (1992) "Epidemics and Revolutions: Cholera in Nineteenth-century Europe", Terence Ranger/Paul Slack (eds.) *Epidemics and Ideas: Essays on the Historical Perception of Pestilence*, Cambridge, Cambridge University Press, 149-174.

Evans, Richard J. (2017) *The Pursuit of Power: Europe 1815-1914*, New York, NY, Penguin, epub.

Foschi, Franco (1983) *Epidemie nella terra di Leopardi*, Roma, Bulzoni.

Giono, Jean (1951) *Le Hussard sur le toit*, Paris, Gallimard.

Guerios, Aureo Lustosa (2021) *Cholera and the Literary Imagination in Europe, 1830-1930*, Doctoral Thesis, Padua, University of Padua.

Guerios, Aureo Lustosa (2022) "Three Facets of the Literary Imagination of Cholera: Hysteria, Ridicule, and the Rise of Bacteriology", Sathyaraj Venkatesan/Antara Chatterjee/A. David Lewis/Brian Callender (eds.) *Pandemics and Epidemics in Cultural Representation*, Singapore, Springer, 65-79. DOI: 10.1007/978-981-19-1296-2_5.

Hamlin, Christopher (2009) *Cholera: The Biography*, Oxford, Oxford University Press.

Jasieński, Bruno (2017 [1928]) *I Burn Paris*, trans. by Soren Gauger, Prague, Twisted Spoon Press.

Kudlick, Catherine (1996) *Cholera in Post-revolutionary Paris: A Cultural History*, Berkeley, CA, University of California Press.

Matucci, Andrea (2003) "La folla nel romanzo storico italiano da Manzoni a Pirandello", *Laboratoire Italien. Politique et société* 4, 15-36. DOI: 10.4000/laboratoireitalien.320.

Munthe, Axel (1887) *Letters from a Mourning City: Naples, Autumn, 1884*, London, John Murray.

Murnau, Friedrich Wilhelm (1926) *Faust*, Babelsberg, UFA.

Otis, Laura (2000) *Membranes: Metaphors of Invasion in Nineteenth-Century Literature, Science, and Politics*, Baltimore, MD, Johns Hopkins University Press.

Poe, Edgar Allan (1850 [1842]) "The Mask of the Red Death", *The Works of the Late Edgar Allan Poe, vol. 1*, New York, NY, J. S. Redfield, 339-345.

Pushkin, Alexander (2000 [1830]) "A Feast during the Plague", *The Little Tragedies*, trans. by Nancy K. Anderson, New Haven, CT, Yale University Press, 95-105.

Sack, David/Sack, R. Bradley/Nair, G. Balakrish/Siddique, A. K. (2004) "Cholera", *Lancet* 363, 223-233. DOI: 10.1016/S0140-6736(03)15328-7.

Schonlau, Anja (2005) *Syphilis in der Literatur: Über Ästhetik, Moral, Genie und Medizin, 1880-2000*, Würzburg, Königshausen & Neumann.

Scuderi, Antonio (2000) "Arlecchino Revisited: Tracing the Demon from the Carnival to Kramer and Mr. Bean", *Theatre History Studies* 20, 143-155.

Sorcinelli, Paolo (1986) *Nuove Epidemie, Antiche Paure: uomini e colera nell'Ottocento*, Roma, Franco Angeli.

Thucydides (2009 [~ 431-400 *BCE*]) *The Peloponnesian War*, Oxford, Oxford Classics.

Tognotti, Eugenia E. (2000) *Il Mostro Asiatico: Storia del Colera in Italia*, Bari, Laterza.

Tolstoy, Leo (2008 [1886]) *The Death of Ivan Ilyitch*, trans. by Anthony Briggs, London, Penguin.

Tumeo, Antonio Casamento (2011) *The Rebel Crowds in the 19th Century's Italian Literature*, Doctoral Thesis, Grenoble/Padua, University of Grenoble/University of Padua.

Wald, Priscilla (2008) *Contagious: Cultures, Carriers, and the Outbreak Narrative*, Durham, NC, Duke University Press.

'C'était quelqu'un de toute façon' : les personnages humains et non humains dans le roman animaliste *Les Métamorphoses* de Camille Brunel[1]

Fleur Hopkins-Loféron (CNRS/THALIM, Paris)

Abstract

The 'roman animaliste' *Les Métamorphoses* (2020), written by French author Camille Brunel, narrates an irrepressible transformation of men and women into animals of all kinds. Written just before the Covid-19 pandemic, this novel strongly resonates with the philosophical questions that occupied the political scene and the activist world during the outbreak, as public opinion became more aware of the responsibility of humans in the destruction of ecosystems and questions of societal collapse came to the forefront of French public debate. More than that, the novel aims to deconstruct the usual societal conceptions regarding non-human animals, while the author underlines their individuality and confers on them the status of characters, and by extension of persons. Far from writing an anti-humanist pamphlet, since humanity is not extinguished but is transformed for the benefit of the enrichment of the living, Brunel reminds us that anti-speciesism is conceived as an ecologism conscious of the interactions of the living within the Earth system.

---

1   Je remercie la Fondation pour les Sciences Sociales d'avoir permis la concrétisation de mes recherches portant sur les liens entre Covid-19 et science-fiction, dans le cadre de son édition 2021 consacrée aux Pandémies.

INTRODUCTION

Quelques mois après le début de la pandémie de Covid-19, de nombreux articles ont familiarisé le public avec la notion de 'zoonose', maladie infectieuse émergente passée de l'animal à l'humain sans que l'agent zoonotique, qualifié de 'réservoir naturel', soit nécessairement infecté. Le SARS-CoV-2 n'est pas le premier virus à intégrer un animal dans la chaîne de contamination. Plusieurs études consacrées à l'épidémie de SRAS en 2002-2004 ont déjà pointé du doigt le rôle joué par la civette, vendue sur les marchés de Canton, ou dans le cadre de l'épidémie d'Ebola en 2013-2016, celui de la chauve-souris roussette, chassée par les populations autochtones. Cependant, à la différence des articles évoquant ces zoonoses ou les épizooties touchant les animaux d'élevage lors des décennies précédentes (encéphalopathie spongiforme bovine des vaches, grippe aviaire des oiseaux, grippe porcine des porcs, etc.), les papiers grand public touchant à la pandémie de Covid-19 ont souvent choisi de personnifier les porteurs, 'suspects numéro un' (Belin 2020), comme le pangolin, soupçonné d'être un hôte intermédiaire, ou la chauve-souris, espèce réservoir. Ils leur accordent même parfois une volonté de nuisance, voire un désir de « vengeance » (Dussol 2020), comme si le franchissement de la barrière d'espèce était prémédité et servait de représailles envers l'effondrement de la biodiversité. S'il se garde bien de recourir à cette anthropomorphisation des animaux, le professeur de bioéthique et philosophe utilitariste de la condition animale Peter Singer (2020) a lui aussi souligné combien la pandémie de Covid-19, née au sein des *wet markets*[2] de la ville de Wuhan, devait pousser à repenser de manière éthique nos relations aux animaux, dans le but de prévenir d'autres zoonoses, mais aussi de protéger la planète contre le désastre écologique en marche.

C'est au croisement avec ces deux perspectives – personnification de l'animal et remise en question de sa place dans la chaîne du vivant – que se situe le second roman de l'auteur français Camille Brunel, publié en août 2020 et dont les dernières lignes ont été écrites alors que débutait la pandémie de Covid-19. Ses *Métamorphoses* empruntent de toute évidence leur titre au poème antique d'Ovide, qui décrit les transformations, subies ou désirées, des grandes figures de la mythologie gréco-romaine. Certaines se changent en animaux pour tromper les humains (Zeus en cygne ou en taureau) ou sont punies par une divinité courroucée (Arachné

---

2   Un *wet market* est un marché à ciel ouvert au sein duquel le client peut choisir l'animal vivant, mammifère, gallinacé, reptile, poisson ou même sauvage – comme sur le marché de Wuhan – qu'il souhaite que le vendeur abatte devant ses yeux dans le but de le consommer ultérieurement.

en araignée, Callisto en ourse). D'autres deviennent des végétaux afin d'échapper aux ardeurs d'un dieu (Daphné en laurier, Syrinx en roseau). Brunel imagine quant à lui, dans un monde pré-Covid-19, une maladie sans virus qui provoque une irrépressible transformation en animal, parfois domestique, parfois sauvage, chez celui ou celle qui ressent un pic de désir sexuel ou d'amour inconditionnel. Rien ni personne ne parvient à endiguer cette pandémie, que la protagoniste humaine Isis n'interprète pas tant comme une punition châtiant la destruction des écosystèmes, que comme une bénédiction annonçant une nouvelle ère. À ce titre, Brunel emprunte aussi à Ovide le récit filé des transformations que le monde connaît à travers le temps. Les animaux prospèrent, plutôt que prolifèrent, au milieu des ruines de la civilisation, vidées de toute présence humaine, et la Terre semble entrer dans un cycle de floraison nouvelle.

En revisitant un motif littéraire bien connu, celui de la métamorphose en un autre être vivant, Camille Brunel se place sensiblement dans la lignée de Franz Kafka (1915) et sa vermine, d'Eugène Ionesco (1959) et du rhinocéros, du Comte de Lautréamont (1868) et du pourceau, ou encore de Jean-Charles Rémy (1976) et de l'arbre. La nouveauté apportée par l'auteur est visible dans le nom donné à sa 'pandémie de tératomorphoses'. Ce néologisme (terato-, du grec ancien monstre, et morphose, du grec ancien mise en forme) suppose que les humains se transforment en monstres, à la manière de loups-garous. Ce devenir animal ne rime pourtant ni avec sauvagerie, ni avec régression et il est définitif. Brunel, qui a été candidat en 2022 aux élections législatives sous la bannière du Parti Animaliste[3] et est depuis de longues années engagé auprès des mouvements de libération animale, incarne un genre de littérature émergent, que l'on pourrait qualifier de 'roman animaliste'. Cette veine, qui se compose d'auteurs tels que Vincent Message ou Jean-Baptiste Del Amo, proche de l'association L214,[4] met en scène les relations et interactions entre les hommes et les animaux afin d'interroger le principe idéologique d'asservissement du vivant qui régit notre société occidentale. Si Del Amo (Règne animal, 2016) et Message (Défaite des maîtres et possesseurs, 2016) ont recours à la fresque balzacienne ou à la fable écologique pour raconter le

---

3   Le Parti Animaliste est un parti politique français fondé en 2016 qui met au centre de son programme l'intérêt des animaux, afin que la question animale soit davantage prise en compte dans les décisions politiques.

4   L'association française L214 Éthique et Animaux, fondée par Brigitte Gothière et Sébastien Arsac en 2008, a pour but la protection des animaux, en particulier d'élevage, et la prise en compte de leur sensibilité, donnant lieu à des campagnes tant welfaristes qu'abolitionnistes. Elle s'est faite connaître du grand public pour son rôle de lanceur d'alertes grâce à des enquêtes menées au sein de plusieurs abattoirs français.

rapport d'exploitation qui unit les hommes aux animaux, Brunel construit, depuis son premier roman publié en 2018 (*La Guérilla des animaux*), une œuvre littéraire totale, qui emprunte au mythe sa fonction téléologique et exégétique : expliquer ce qui est et ce qui sera si les humains ne réforment pas leurs conceptions. Dans *Les Métamorphoses*, l'auteur expose une nouvelle fois sa philosophie antispéciste,[5] laquelle prône de considérer les animaux comme des protagonistes de roman, mais plus encore comme des personnes, des 'sujets-d'une-vie' (Regan 2004). Ainsi, à la différence des écrits de ses confrères, Brunel ne réduit pas les animaux à leurs fonctions d'outils, d'accessoires ou d'objets, mais à la manière de Joseph Andras (*Ainsi nous leur faisons la guerre*, 2021) s'interroge sur l'histoire et la culture des animaux, indépendamment du prisme humain par lequel ils sont toujours perçus.

En suivant comme fil rouge l'idée d'animaux à la fois personnages, personnes (cf. Francione 2008 ; Morizot 2020) et victimes d'oppressions systémiques (cf. Torres 2009 ; Nibert 2013), le présent article s'interrogera sur la double appellation qui accompagne le travail de Camille Brunel, tantôt qualifié de roman « animalier » ou « animaliste ». En effet, si la veine « animalière » de Brunel se ressent par le souci quasi-documentaire accordé à la vie émotionnelle et cognitive des bêtes qui peuplent ses pages, l'engagement « animaliste » de l'auteur passe par un discours idéologique assumé, qui dispute la nécessité de prendre en compte les intérêts singuliers et les droits des animaux. Aussi, en considérant *Les Métamorphoses* comme partie d'un tout cohérent, l'article préférera avancer le terme de roman « antispéciste » pour qualifier la production de Brunel puisque la question de la convergence des luttes antiracistes, environnementales, féministes ou anticapacitistes agitent le mouvement antispéciste, au sein duquel de nombreuses voix (cf. Kemmerer 2011 ; Adams/Gruen 2014 ; Boutet 2021) font valoir la nécessité de lutter contre toutes les formes d'oppressions et de dominations. À cet égard, l'œuvre de Brunel esquisse timidement une utopie féministe lesbienne biraciale, écosophie qui prendra de l'ampleur dans son roman à paraître, *Ecatepec* (2023).

---

5   Il n'existe pas de définition fixe de l'antispécisme, que certains considèrent comme une philosophie morale, d'autres comme une pensée politique, d'autres encore comme une continuité des luttes antisexistes et antiracistes. Jérôme Segal, par exemple, en parle comme d'une « volonté politique de prendre en compte les intérêts des animaux dans l'organisation de la cité » (Segal 2020, EPUB non numéroté).

UN ROMAN ÉCOLOGISTE :
LES HUMAINS, SPECTATEURS DE L'EFFONDREMENT

Pour donner à lire la richesse de la vie émotionnelle des animaux, Brunel dépeint par contraste l'appauvrissement de la vie intérieure des humains, obnubilés par la gratification immédiate que leurs procurent les réseaux sociaux. Spectateurs passifs de ces mondes virtuels, ils sont sourds à l'effondrement du monde qui les entoure.

Réseaux sociaux et désagrégation du tissu humain

Brunel dépeint la place que l'univers virtuel occupe dans les constructions mentales, en accord avec ce que le sociologue Gérald Bronner qualifie d'« apocalypse cognitive » (2021), à savoir l'omniprésence des écrans dans nos vies. Ces derniers, mitraillant à chaque instant leurs détenteurs d'informations, déhiérarchisent ce qui est essentiel de ce qui ne l'est pas, expliquant l'aveuglement des personnages à l'effondrement qui se lit en arrière-plan du roman. Les écrans font office de miroirs magiques, destinés à conforter leur détenteur sur ses atours chaque fois qu'il reçoit une réaction à l'une de ses publications, mais aussi de surface déformante, puisqu'Isis en parle comme d'une barrière : « Du côté du miroir où je vivais encore » (*LM* 48).[6] Très tôt, l'auteur donne à voir l'omniprésence des réseaux sociaux dans la vie d'Isis et de sa famille, laquelle s'accompagne d'une forme de paralysie de l'esprit critique et d'une uniformisation de la pensée. Incapable de détacher ses yeux du flot incessant d'actualités sur la *timeline* de ses divers comptes sociaux, elle est comme hypnotisée.

Ce monde virtuel symbolise le premier stade de la transformation en animal puisqu'Isis compare son addiction au digital à une forme de « désagrég[ation] » (*LM* 20) qui lui fait perdre pieds dans ce monde de nulle part, alors même qu'elle sait que cette « mémoire numérique » (*LM* 21) n'a rien de pérenne. Son être est comme morcelé, anticipant les scènes frappantes de métamorphoses lors desquelles les humains se transforment par fragments. Au ciel des oiseaux, omniprésent dans le roman, répond ce *cloud* humain. Par le parallèle qui est fait avec les grues qui sillonnent le ciel dès la première page, Brunel critique, en regard, la limitation de l'univers mental humain, mû non plus par la force magnétique du

---

6   La pagination a été réalisée d'après l'édition EPUB. Désormais, toute citation tirée du roman *Les Métamorphoses* sera indiquée par *LM* entre parenthèses, suivi du numéro de la page.

globe et par l'instinct, mais conditionné par le numérique au point de ne réagir que par émoticônes, présumés capables d'exprimer une pensée complexe :

> [Isis] ajouta même un emoji malheureux sous un article consacré au génocide des Premières Nations brésiliennes par Jair Bolsonaro, et un autre, énervé celui-ci, sous un article [...] qui mentionnait un accord ratifié par la France donnant les coudées franches aux destructeurs de la forêt amazonienne. (*LM* 45)

En mettant en scène des réactions quasi pavloviennes chez l'humain, avide de gratifications (un article triste provoque un symbole montrant un visage qui pleure, tandis qu'un article révoltant entraîne un visage colérique), l'auteur entame sa déconstruction de la supposée supériorité humaine.

L'effondrement pour décor

Camille Brunel se réfère explicitement au champ de recherche transdisciplinaire de la collapsologie (cf. *LM* 38), théorisé par l'ingénieur-agronome Pablo Servigne et son collègue Raphaël Stevens (2015) comme étant l'étude de l'inévitable « effondrement » (*LM* 35) de notre civilisation industrielle mondialisée et plus largement du système-Terre, causé par les interdépendances et vulnérabilités trop fortes entre les différentes infrastructures. De fait, plutôt que de proposer de réparer le monde, à renfort de croissance verte et d'écologie marchande, la collapsologie invite les humains à réfléchir au monde d'après. À bien y regarder, le récit de Brunel se pose autant en pamphlet antispéciste qu'en discours écologique. L'auteur approche la fin du monde vivant tel que nous le connaissons aujourd'hui, laquelle s'accompagnera d'un renouveau pour ces mêmes écosystèmes, exploités et souillés par les hommes.

À la manière des militants comme Greta Thunberg ou du mouvement Extinction Rebellion qui multiplient manifestations et actions directes pour dénoncer l'urgence climatique et condamner l'immobilisme des gouvernements, Brunel suppose que la pandémie de tératomorphoses aurait dû être prévisible puisque, si elle n'est explicitée qu'à la page 51 (de 167 pages), de nombreux signes avant-coureurs, ces fameux 'signaux faibles' étudiés par les prospectivistes, auraient dû alerter les humains sur l'effondrement imminent du monde : explosion d'un barrage (cf. *LM* 13), pollution aux algues (cf. *LM* 25), explosion d'une plateforme pétrolière (cf. *LM* 35), éruptions volcaniques (cf. *LM* 78). La pandémie de tératomorphoses se signale aussi par des indices, chaque fois rapportés sur le régime de l'extraordinaire puisqu'au début du roman il est rare de rencontrer des animaux sauvages en liberté et que chaque rencontre furtive avec l'un d'eux provoque

sidération chez les humains, alors qu'elle est le signe d'une accélération, percep-
tible dans la brièveté des chapitres. Dès lors, Brunel nous fait comprendre que les
humains, responsables de l'anthropocène, ne sont plus que les spectateurs passifs
d'un monde mourant et qu'il leur faut devenir animaux pour pouvoir réintégrer le
temps long du vivant, et non plus celui immédiat des interactions humaines.

UN ROMAN ANIMALIER :
ANIMAUX HUMAINS ET NON HUMAINS

Les penseurs de la condition animale ont pour habitude de faire la distinction entre
'animaux non humains' [*non-human animals*] et 'animaux humains' [*human animals*], le terme 'animal' présent dans les deux expressions ayant pour effet de
revendiquer une égalité de traitements malgré la singularité des espèces. Comme
le rappellent Axelle Playoust-Braure et Yves Bonnardel (2020) dans leur essai
Solidarité animale, cette égalité consiste à apporter la même considération aux
intérêts de chacun : « Il ne s'agit pas de dire que les individus *sont* égaux, mais de
considérer de façon égale les intérêts de tous [...]. Il s'agit d'accorder les droits
qui permettent de défendre les intérêts réels des individus [en italique dans
l'orig.] » (idem. 2020, 40-41). Si certains accordent des droits supérieurs aux animaux non humains dotés de capacités cognitives plus développées (cf. Singer
2011), comme les grands singes ou les cétacés, le roman de Brunel a pour effet de
faire imploser ce point de tension – qui perpétue une forme de hiérarchie de valeur
au sein des animaux – puisqu'il intègre à son bestiaire les animaux les plus divers :
reptiles, insectes, cétacés, mammifères et les grands oubliés de la cause animale,
les poissons.

De plus, la pandémie de tératomorphoses ne correspond pas tout à fait à ce que
Shravanthi, l'amoureuse d'Isis, appelle abusivement « darwinisme inversé »
(*LM* 156). La vague associe en effet au hasard une nouvelle forme animale à un
individu, sans le besoin d'aucune prédisposition génétique ou traits de caractère
marqués. Ainsi, la grand-mère d'Isis, un peu sénile, se fait veuve noire ; son oncle
aviné devient hirondelle ; sa mère, amoureuse des grands espaces et persuadée
qu'elle sera baleine, prend la forme d'un okapi. Brunel chamboule l'arbre phylo-
génétique des espèces, qui ordonne et donc classe le vivant en dehors des équi-
libres des écosystèmes. Son geste déclassificatoire ne suit plus l'évolution naturelle. Ce grand chambardement rappelle au genre humain qu'il n'est jamais qu'un
animal.

Les animaux, êtres sentients

Dès l'*incipit* de son roman, Camille Brunel fait comprendre que les pages qui suivent seront le lieu d'un renversement des forces. En effet, Isis, commentant le vol des grues au-dessus de sa maison, souligne qu'elle ne représente pour elles qu'une « plante » (*LM* 8) et donc que ces animaux négligent les humains dans le paysage en contrebas, mais, plus encore, ne leur reconnaîtraient pas même d'aptitude intellectuelle. Au fil des chapitres, l'auteur alterne entre focalisations internes et externes, proposant même une forme de roman choral alors qu'il donne au lecteur la possibilité d'occuper, un court instant, les pensées d'un animal. Ce jeu sur les focalisations sert le propos général du roman : il permet de souligner le caractère situé de l'anthropocentrisme, en suggérant que le point de vue humain sur toute chose n'est pas central, seulement dominant car culturel.

L'auteur donne aussi à voir une palette d'émotions animales, d'abord sous la forme d'anecdotes éthologiques, ensuite sous la forme d'une descente dans le corps d'un animal, jamais édulcorée. Brunel, en effet, a puisé dans l'essai *Qu'est-ce qui fait sourire les animaux ?* de Carl Safina (2018) l'envie d'explorer la vie émotionnelle des animaux. Plutôt que de relever de l'anecdote touchante ou amusante, à la manière des vidéos qui inondent les réseaux sociaux, ou de la personnification des animaux à la Walt Disney, ces éléments de savoir ont pour but d'asseoir l'argument souterrain du livre, à savoir la richesse de la vie mentale et émotionnelle des animaux. Par cette rigueur dans la description animalière, Brunel souligne que l'animalisme se conçoit comme l'aboutissement d'un cheminement intellectuel humain, devant l'abondance de preuves d'ordres divers (éthologie, paléoanthropologie, neurosciences, etc.) qui vont dans le sens d'une sentience[7] du vivant.

Les animaux humains et leur univers mental

L'une des questions pressantes parmi les protagonistes humains qui ne se sont pas encore transformés est de savoir si, une fois animaux, ils conserveront quelque souvenir de leur vie passée, et notamment leur amour pour leurs proches. Ainsi, Tobias croit voir dans la patte tendue de la veuve noire devant lui la preuve que sa femme le reconnaît. Cette question va de pair avec la dépréciation sociale du genre animal. C'est parce que les humains accordent peu d'importance à l'existence

---

7   Le terme 'sentience', traduit de l'anglais *sentient*, désigne la capacité d'un animal à ressentir des sensations, des émotions, des envies, bonnes comme mauvaises. Voir sur le sujet Estiva Reus (2005).

d'une vie intérieure chez les animaux qu'ils craignent que la transformation s'accompagne de l'effacement de leurs souvenirs, mais aussi d'une forme de néant émotionnel. En ce sens, la transformation symbolise ce qu'Yves Bonnardel qualifie d'animalisation (Playoust-Braure/Bonnardel 2020), à distinguer de l'animalité : « On ne naît pas animal (au sens social), on ne l'est pas par nature ou par essence, on le devient » (ibid., 47). L'animalisation désigne, de fait, le processus politique et social par lequel l'humanité distingue le non humain de l'humain et place, à la fois, en retrait, mais aussi dans une position de dominé, l'animal. Brunel critique vivement cette conception en donnant à voir à de multiples reprises la richesse du monde intérieur des animaux.

UN ROMAN ANIMALISTE :
LES ANIMAUX COMME PERSONNES

Les Métamorphoses mettent en présence Isis, végane et antispéciste, avec le milieu clos de sa famille, puis avec les changements qui s'opèrent dans le monde. Cela permet à l'auteur de construire un discours filé en faveur de l'animalisme. Ce dernier entend, dans un premier temps, questionner le carnisme[8] et la mentaphobie[9] des humains ; dans un second temps, faire valoir sentience et capacités cognitives des animaux, tout comme la richesse de leur vie mentale (cf. Sigler 2018).

Un pamphlet animaliste

Les trois romans animalistes de Camille Brunel, à savoir *La Guérilla des animaux* (2018a), *Les Métamorphoses* (2020) et *Après nous, les animaux* (2020) se proposent comme des fables philosophiques destinées à penser la condition animale, mais surtout la responsabilité humaine dans l'effondrement des écosystèmes et l'extinction de masse. *La Guérilla des animaux*, qui met en scène un militant de la cause animale recourant à l'action directe, pose de manière provocante la question suivante : faut-il faire disparaître le genre humain pour que les animaux soient enfin préservés ? Dans *Les Métamorphoses*, Isis se pose à son tour en anti-héroïne, parfois antipathique. Elle sert de figure repoussoir, tout comme l'est à ses yeux sa cousine Carolina, « militante fatigante » (*LM* 28) qui ne cesse de relayer sur les

---

8   Le 'carnisme', expression diffusée par Melanie Joy (2019), désigne le fait de penser que manger de la viande est naturel et nécessaire à l'espèce humaine.

9   David Chauvet (2016) emploie le terme de 'mentaphobie' pour désigner le fait de craindre de reconnaître chez l'animal des capacités cognitives.

réseaux sociaux des contenus virulents, voulant éveiller ses amis à la réalité de l'exploitation animale par des formules chocs.

Pourtant, Isis, fait, elle aussi, figure de militante, puisqu'elle intègre constamment à son monologue intérieur de courtes anecdotes invitant un hypothétique lecteur à reconsidérer ses conceptions de l'animalité alors que les animaux sont capables de deuil (cf. *LM* 46), de tristesse (cf. *LM* 65), de reconnaître un visage (cf. *LM* 66), d'apprendre des mots (cf. *LM* 104), de comprendre le principe d'Archimède (cf. *LM* 115). Là où certains lecteurs de l'œuvre pourraient y voir un militantisme forcené de la part de l'écrivain, qui confondrait tract et roman, il semblerait qu'il faille plutôt y lire, à la manière des rapports du GIEC (Groupe d'experts intergouvernemental sur l'évolution du climat) et de ses prévisions, ignorées pendant longtemps par les hommes politiques, une mise en garde : si les humains ne changent pas leur manière de vivre, ils finiront par disparaître.

Nuisibles, familiers ou sauvages

Comme le confirme Camille Brunel (2022), l'ouvrage *Zoopolis* des philosophes canadiens Sue Donaldson et Will Kymlicka (2016) a eu une influence déterminante sur la genèse des *Métamorphoses*. Cet essai développe une nouvelle manière de cohabiter avec les animaux, sans les exploiter ou leur nuire et imagine pour chaque catégorie – « domestique », c'est-à-dire dépendants de nous comme le sont les animaux de compagnie ou le bétail ; « sauvage » car ils vivent en des territoires propres comme les ours ou les loups, « liminaire », qui vivent auprès de nous pour leurs subsistances comme le pigeon ou le hérisson – un modèle de vivre-ensemble qui lui est propre : citoyenneté, souveraineté, résident. Pourtant, par l'effacement total de la présence humaine dans l'épilogue du roman, Brunel abandonne une lecture politique des relations de l'humain à l'animal, puisque le second se substitue entièrement au premier.

Isis, vers la fin du roman, espère devenir chatte, pour pouvoir ronronner de plaisir avec celle qui partage sa vie. Elle deviendra genette et continuera son existence auprès de son ancienne compagne. Certains humains se changent en animaux domestiques, comme ce pitbull aperçu à bord d'un train pour Toulouse, mais nombre d'entre eux prennent la forme d'animaux sauvages, à l'image de ce marcassin effrayé dans le couloir du train, ancien adolescent qu'aucun passager ne veut accueillir car il n'est pas un familier. Brunel cherche à mettre le lecteur face à l'aporie de ce travail classificatoire, qui distingue les animaux entre eux en les qualifiant de nuisibles, de familiers, de domestiques, ou encore de sauvages, dans un monde en sursis. Prenant par surprise son lecteur, Brunel souligne que l'animal n'a pas besoin de l'humain pour déterminer son statut d'individu. Ainsi, quand

Ariane souhaite garder son mari auprès d'elle, bien qu'il soit devenu python, elle finit dévorée parce qu'elle s'est changée en koala. Scène surréaliste qui pastiche celle du *Petit Prince* d'Antoine de Saint-Exupéry (1943), elle pousse dans ses retranchements la pensée animaliste : chercher à savoir si l'animal est une personne n'a de sens que dans une société humaine et le serpent n'a ici que faire du statut qu'il possède auprès de son ancienne femme.

UN ROMAN ANTISPÉCISTE : ESQUISSE ÉCOFÉMINISTE

En esquissant à la fin de son roman une utopie féministe et en plaçant, à l'inverse, dans la bouche d'Isis une forme de naturalisation de la condition féminine, Brunel étend son propos animaliste (libérer les animaux de la domination humaine) aux transformations qui ont lieu au sein-même du mouvement antispécisme (dialogue avec les autres luttes en faveur de la justice sociale).

La fin de l'androcène

Fin août, la députée écologiste et écoféministe Sandrine Rousseau a fait couler beaucoup d'encre en affirmant, lors des Journées d'Été d'Europe Écologie-les Verts, qu'il existait une corrélation entre virilisme et consommation de viande : « Il faut changer de mentalité pour que manger une entrecôte cuite sur un barbecue ne soit plus un symbole de virilité » (2022). Elle signifiait par-là que les hommes sont, dans les cultures occidentales, de plus gros consommateurs de viande que les femmes, et qu'il leur fallait faire preuve de sobriété écologique puisque l'industrie de la viande est polluante et gourmande en eau. Si son propos a été critiqué par les figures politiques de droite et conservatrices, elle reflète une opinion déjà défendue dans la pensée antispéciste (cf. Adams 1980), ainsi que dans l'ouvrage de Bon, Roudeau et Rousseau (2022) *Par-delà l'androcène*, lequel emprunte son concept-clef aux chercheuses qui l'ont popularisé, Myriam Bahaffou et Julie Gorecki (cf. 2020, 8). Selon les dernières, nous ne polluons pas tous de la même manière et, à ce titre, le plus gros pollueur est indéniablement l'homme viril et le continuum de ses exactions (sexisme, racisme, colonialisme, capitalisme, extractivisme, etc.).

Quelques mois à peine avant *Les Métamorphoses* et avant la pandémie de Covid-19, Christina Sweeney-Baird (2019) publie le roman *The End of Men*, dans lequel une mutation du virus de la grippe, survenue en 2025, cause la disparition de 90% des hommes à la surface du globe. Camille Brunel avance la même proposition provocante dans son roman : et si les hommes étaient condamnés à disparaître et, par la même occasion à libérer la société de l'hégémonie masculine ?

La fin du roman est pourtant sans appel : les femmes, comme les hommes, devien-nent animaux. Certaines femmes se transforment en végétal, sans qu'il ne soit per-mis de savoir si Brunel symbolise là leur capacité à ensemencer le monde au moyen des spores et des graines, ou l'habitude culturelle occidentale d'associer le végétal au féminin.

Autodétermination féminine

Si dans les dernières pages Shravanthi invite Isis à la suivre jusque dans un gyné-cée, la disparition brutale des deux amoureuses empêche de savoir exactement comment fonctionne ce modèle de gynarchie ou gynocratie, qui supposerait que les femmes redeviennent pleinement maîtresses de leur existence. Si le terme n'est pas utilisé par l'auteur, le modèle décrit, microsociété de femmes n'autorisant pas les hommes en leur sein, clamant leur supériorité sur eux et la nécessité d'établir une domination féministe, pose le problème évident d'une nouvelle forme d'es-clavage, cette fois imposé au sexe masculin.

Aurait-il été une occasion supplémentaire pour Camille Brunel de développer le parallèle entre les sociétés animales et humaines, en comparant par exemple le gynécée à une ruche, où chacun possède un rôle bien précis, ou à une meute de lionnes, qui écartent volontairement les mâles pour assurer la survie des petits ? Quelles formes de féminités se seraient développées avec le temps, ou plutôt dé-construites, à mesure que le *male gaze* (Mulvey 1975) n'opérait plus son travail d'injonction et de conditionnement ?

Le devenir lesbien

Depuis quelques années, plusieurs militantes trans, lesbiennes et féministes (cf. Coffin 2020 ; Drouar 2021 ; Letourneur 2022) dans la continuité de Monique Wit-tig (2018), en appellent au lesbianisme politique pour sortir de la naturalisation de l'hétérosexualité, qui va de pair avec domination masculine et patriarcat. Si Brunel ne se réfère jamais explicitement à ce projet, il n'en propose pas moins, dans les derniers chapitres de son roman, un séparatisme radical puisque non seulement les femmes se réunissent dans des gynécées, mais elles entendent également utiliser une méthode de fécondation nouvelle qui permet d'emprunter, à parts égales, le code génétique des deux mères. Cette utopie matriarcale ne s'arrête pas là. Les femmes décident de ne plus laisser naître de sujets masculins, grâce à la sélection génétique, sinon en leur offrant une éducation entièrement nouvelle. Le lecteur ne saura jamais si ce projet est mené à bien puisque la métamorphose d'Isis, puis de sa compagne, rebat les cartes. Cependant, il aurait été intéressant de savoir si l'exploration de l'auteur se prolonge jusque dans la question de l'identité de genres, en dehors de la répartition binaire et cis-genre soutenue tout au long du roman.

UNE ÉCOSOPHIE : PENSER LE MONDE PRÉSENT

Loin de démobiliser les humains, les théories de collapsologie ouvrent la porte à de nouveaux possibles sous la forme de prospective, de prophétie ou de science-fiction (cf. Li Vigny et al. 2022). Brunel propose un exercice un peu différent de celui de la Red Team, *think tank* français d'auteurs et d'artisans de l'imaginaire en appui au Ministère de la Défense, qui travaille à des scénarios crédibles, anticipant sur les menaces technologiques, géopolitiques ou culturelles qui pourraient survenir à l'horizon 2030-2060. Sa pandémie de tératomorphoses se pose en effet comme un évènement poétique extraordinaire face à l'ordinaire de la fin, assez proche en cela du film *The Lobster* (2015) de Yórgos Lánthimos. En inventant un monde d'après dans lequel la vie prolifère plus que jamais, qui détonne des récits post-apocalyptiques racontant la difficile survie des survivants humains, Brunel ne propose ni un récit d'anticipation, ni un récit de science-fiction, mais plutôt une forme d'écosophie, philosophie d'harmonie écologique.

Si certains commentateurs du roman ont parlé de « virus » (Bini 2020) pour expliquer l'origine des transformations qui touchent les hommes, l'auteur ne donne jamais de raison scientifique au phénomène. Il parle bien d'une « pandémie sans virus » (*LM* 111) et récuse sa contagiosité (cf. *LM* 86), dont il souligne la nature imprévisible, à mesure que des transformations sont géographiquement localisées (les hommes deviennent insectes aux Îles Féroé ou bien le gouvernement français est changé en chiens). À aucun moment non plus ne suggère-t-il que la Terre aurait pu vouloir se venger des humains qui l'exploitent sans relâche. La métamorphose, comme processus dont on n'en connaît ni l'origine, ni la modélisation, ni le point d'aboutissement, s'apparente alors à un coup de dés lancé par l'auteur, sans logique autre que sa force créatrice comme en témoigne l'arbitraire de la transformation de fillettes en végétal à la fin du roman. De fait, il apparaît que *Les Métamorphoses* ne se posent pas comme un scénario catastrophe, mais est prétexte à rebattre les cartes de l'altérité sous la forme d'une expérience de pensée qui souligne la place toute relative du genre humain au sein du vivant.

Multiplication *vs* prolifération

Avant-même les métamorphoses d'humains, c'est la mise en présence inattendue avec un animal sauvage qui étonne les citadins. Isis, par exemple, rencontre une grue antigone dans son jardin, animal migratoire qui ne devrait pas se trouver là. Si sa bienveillance naturelle lui inspire un sentiment de ravissement devant ce spectacle, sa famille a une toute autre interprétation du phénomène : les animaux viennent sur le territoire des hommes parce qu'ils pensent y trouver de la nourriture et peut-être même une forme de confort. Loin d'être anodine, cette affirmation pose la question des lieux et espaces d'existence des animaux sur une planète dominée par l'humain, mais aussi celle de la responsabilité que les humains ont envers eux, dès lors qu'ils sont à la source de la raréfaction de leurs environnements, voire de leur asservissement. Ainsi, les animaux, comme nous l'avons vu, sont classés en catégories (familier, domestique, bétail, sauvage) et à chaque qualificatif est associé un lieu de vie ou de détention qui lui est propre (maison, volière, zoo, cirque, laboratoire, hangar, nature). De cette répartition spatiale imposée aux animaux par l'extension des villes et par l'anéantissement des milieux naturels naît une nouvelle catégorie classificatoire, celle de l'animal « fugitif » (*LM* 17), animal en fuite qui n'a nulle part où aller et tente seulement d'échapper à l'exploitation humaine. Aussi, cette rencontre singulière avec l'animal se prend au piège de rester dans l'individualisation d'une espèce, au détriment de la notion de personne et d'individu, centrale à la compréhension de l'œuvre de Brunel, qui fait dire à Isis, au sujet de la mort d'un lapin dans un incendie, qui a peut-être été autrefois humain : « C'était quelqu'un de toute façon » (*LM* 72).

Brunel évoque avec humour une invasion zombie (cf. *LM* 102) comme contrepied des tératomorphoses qui s'inscrit dans un processus de réensauvagement, de repeuplement aléatoire du monde. Normalement guidée de main d'hommes, alors que des écosystèmes sont reconstruits en les soustrayant de l'activité humaine, la multiplication des animaux ne suit aucune logique. Elle frappe parfois des groupes d'individus (des policiers deviennent chiens de prairie ou des touristes, mygales) ou une personne en particulier (Beyoncé en ara).

Recomposition du paysage

Lors du repas familial de baptême qui occupe de longues pages dans le roman, les opinions s'affrontent au sujet de la condition animale et plus spécifiquement du rapport des humains aux animaux. Habitué à s'opposer à des penseurs de l'exploitation animale, comme la zootechnicienne Jocelyne Porcher (2014) qui se positionne en faveur d'une relation de travail entre les animaux et les hommes et suggère qu'il est possible de leur donner une « bonne mort » (ead. 2016), Brunel met dans la bouche de la cousine Carolina une proposition étonnante, en décalage avec sa pensée végane : et si les vaches étaient considérées comme des employées et non comme des possessions ? Plutôt que de reposer sur une critique marxiste du travail, à la manière de Fahim Amir (2022) ou de Donna Haraway (2008), Carolina occulte la réalité du système de domination de l'industrie bouchère et laitière (vaches inséminées de force, veaux séparés de leurs mères à la naissance et destinés à la production de cuir, etc.). Elle rêve un monde impossible puisqu'une vache ne donne pas son consentement pour la traite, l'insémination ou la séparation d'avec sa progéniture, et qu'il n'existe pour elle pas d'autre retraite que l'abattoir.

Peupler le monde d'après

En bon cinéphile qu'il est, Camille Brunel a vu *The Fountain* de Darren Aronofsky (2006) qui raconte la recherche, à travers l'espace et le temps, de Tommy pour un remède afin de sauver sa femme atteinte d'un cancer (cf. Brunel 2018b). Dans une scène saisissante, l'une de ses incarnations, à savoir un *conquistador* espagnol en quête de l'Arbre de vie, se transforme en parterre de fleurs dans un dernier râle d'agonie. À cet égard, Brunel présente le même principe de vie inhérent à l'apparente destruction du genre humain. L'épilogue se clôt sur la disparition de Shravanthi et des nièces d'Isis, toutes transformées en arbres, nouvel acte transformatoire qui dit à la fois la nécessaire disparition des hommes et des femmes et la possibilité d'une acceptation de cette fatalité, si elle signifie la pérennité de l'écosystème planétaire. Surtout, si cet épilogue est moins funeste que poétique, c'est parce que jamais l'auteur ne donne corps à l'accusation caricaturale affublée au mouvement antispéciste, celle de vouloir l'extinction de l'humain (cf. Sugy 2021). La forme humaine disparaît, certes, en tant que domination et exploitation du vivant, mais les individus continuent d'exister, sous une forme nouvelle, animale ou végétale, au sein d'une autre dynamique. C'est ce que signifie l'image du lapin Suraj, frère autiste de Shravanthi qui avait des difficultés relationnelles, grignotant à présent paisiblement l'herbe aux côtés des nouveaux végétaux formés par sa sœur et par les enfants. La place accordée au végétal, dans les dernières pages du roman, apporte d'ailleurs une nuance nouvelle à la réflexion de Brunel sur l'individualité des animaux non-humains. En écho aux travaux de la philosophe du vivant Florence Burgat (2020), Brunel s'éloigne de l'anthropomorphisation des végétaux, qui a fait le succès de Peter Wohlleben (2017) pour introduire l'altérité radicale de la vie végétale, qui vit sur un autre temps que les animaux non humains, qui partagent avec les animaux humains le tragique de la finitude.

Dès lors, le mot « FIN » (*LM* 167) qui clôt le roman, se pose comme un profond paradoxe : Camille Brunel ne nous rapporte ni le récit de la fin des hommes, ni celui du monde d'après, mais plutôt un bond vers une autre forme d'être au monde, qui doit être concevable dès à présent pour le lecteur, pour peu qu'il se familiarise avec la pensée animaliste. De même, Brunel n'a pas consigné la mémoire de la fin du monde, mais celle d'un bouillonnement de vie, où animaux, végétaux et micro-organismes vont continuer l'histoire des peuplements, sans que la présence du lecteur soit requise. En cela, il serait trompeur de considérer que *Les Métamorphoses* concrétisent le projet fou de l'idéaliste Isaac du premier roman de Brunel, *La Guérilla des animaux* (2018a), à savoir effacer l'humain de la surface du globe. L'auteur se détourne en effet de l'une des accusations posées à l'animalisme par ses détracteurs, celui d'être un antihumanisme désirant l'extinction du genre humain. *Les Métamorphoses* invitent plutôt à une prise de conscience globale des interactions, et non plus de la place, des êtres au sein du vivant, ce que révèle par exemple Isis quand, devenue genette, elle voit seulement l'enfant blond devant elle comme un « bipède » (*LM* 162), susceptible de la faire remarquer par la meute de loups.

CONCLUSION

Les Métamorphoses, bien davantage qu'un roman animaliste, se posent comme récit mythique, partagé entre sa dimension anticipatrice, pour ne pas dire science-fictionnelle (utopie matriarcale basée sur la viande de culture et l'eugénisme des naissances) et prédictive (les comportements humains seront, à termes, responsables de l'extinction du vivant). En effet, elles se donnent plutôt à lire comme un mythe téléologique qui explique la disparition supposée des hommes par des raisons non pas scientifiques mais symboliques, provoquée par une puissance incompréhensible. En écrivain militant passant ses idées par le filtre du roman, Brunel cherche à se dégager d'une parole catastrophiste qui culpabiliserait les lecteurs, pour plutôt ouvrir le champ des possibles aux autres manières de percevoir le monde, faisant évoluer son roman vers un récit antispéciste et non plus seulement animaliste. C'est le même processus qui est présenté dans son troisième roman *Après nous, les animaux* (2020), publié quasi simultanément. Dans ce roman jeunesse, l'espèce humaine a presqu'entièrement été décimée par des fléaux venus des insectes et le lecteur suit une meute incongrue d'animaux, traversant des paysages déserts, en quête de leur mémoire à eux, des mythes qui les ont entourés en des temps reculés, mais aussi à la recherche des derniers humains qui peupleraient le monde, dont ils conservent en eux la mémoire. En cela, Brunel s'attache à la question complexe de l'existence d'une civilisation et d'une histoire animale.

Ainsi, l'auteur représente une voix singulière dans le paysage des auteurs 'animaliers', 'animalistes' ou 'antispécistes', cette dernière étiquette nous paraissant mieux s'accorder avec son projet. Dans chacun de ses romans, ce qu'il appelle une « force compensatrice » (*LM* 40), selon qu'elle prenne la forme de la violence d'Isaac, de la sexualité d'Octavio ou de l'amour paternel débordant du père d'Isis, sert à combattre l'incrédulité systématique qui paralyse ses personnages et, par extension le lecteur. Force libératrice, elle doit amener ce dernier à déconstruire l'endoctrinement social qui lui a fait, d'abord, considérer les animaux comme dénués de sentience et de sensibilité ; encore, les approcher dans une relation utilitariste qui détermine leur intérêt en fonction de leur exploitation ; enfin, amène à généraliser l'existence animale seulement au travers de ses interactions avec l'homme. Ainsi, l'animal passe de personnage à personne, puis individu, sans que le qualificatif employé pour le définir importe à présent puisqu'il existe en propre, dans un monde neuf.

BIBLIOGRAPHIE

Œuvre analysée

Brunel, Camille (2020) *Les Métamorphoses*, Paris, Alma Éditeur.

Ouvrages cités

Adams, Carol J. (2016 [1980]) *La Politique sexuelle de la viande*, Lausanne, L'Âge d'homme.
Adams, Carol J./Gruen, Lori (2014) *Ecofeminism. Feminist Intersections with Other Animals and the Earth*, New York, NY, Bloomsbury Academic.
Amir, Fahim (2022) *Révoltes animales*, Paris, Éditions Divergences.
Andras, Joseph (2021) *Ainsi nous leur faisons la guerre*, Arles, Actes Sud.
Aronofsky, Darren (dir.) (2006) *The Fountain*, United States, Warner Bros.
Bahaffou, Myriam/Gorecki, Julie (2020) "Préface", Eaubonne, Françoise d', *Le Féminisme ou la mort*, Paris, Le Passager clandestin.
Belin, Mathilde (2020) "Coronavirus : pourquoi le pangolin est-il devenu le nouveau suspect numéro un ?", *L'Express*, 2020-02-07, https://www.lexpress.fr/monde/coronavirus-pourquoi-le-pangolin-est-il-devenu-le-nouveau-suspect-numero-un_2117667.html, 2022-12-26.

Bini, Christine (2020) "Les Métamorphoses : Darwinisme inversé et littéraire", *La Règle du jeu*, 2020-09-22, https://laregledujeu.org/2020/09/22/36533/les-meta morphoses-de-camille-brunel, 2022-11-19.

Bon, Adélaïde/Roudeau, Sandrine/Rousseau, Sandrine (2022) *Par-delà l'andro-cène*, Paris, Seuil.

Boutet, Marilou (2021) *(V)égaux : vers un véganisme intersectionnel*, Montréal, Éditions Somme Toute.

Bronner, Gérald (2021) *L'Apocalypse cognitive*, Paris, PUF.

Brunel, Camille (2018a) *La Guérilla des animaux*, Paris, Alma Éditeur.

Brunel, Camille (2018b) *Le Cinéma des animaux*, Paris, UV Éditions.

Brunel, Camille (2020) *Après nous, les animaux*, Bruxelles, Casterman.

Brunel, Camille (2022) Échanges électroniques répétés avec l'auteur.

Brunel, Camille (2023) *Ecatepec*, Paris, Alma Éditeur.

Burgat, Florence (2020) *Qu'est-ce qu'une plante ? Essai sur la vie végétale*, Paris, Seuil.

Chauvet, David (2016) *Contre la mentaphobie*, Lausanne, L'Âge d'homme.

Coffin, Alice (2020) *Le Génie lesbien*, Paris, Grasset.

Del Amo, Jean-Baptiste (2016) *Règne animal*, Paris, Gallimard.

Donaldson, Sue/Kymlicka, Will (2016) *Zoopolis. Une théorie politique des droits des animaux*, Paris, Alma.

Drouar, Juliet (2021) *Sortir de l'hétérosexualité*, Paris, Binge Audio Éditions.

Dussol, Alexis (2020) *Covid-19, la vengeance du pangolin : les 180 jours qui ébranlèrent la planète*, Paris, Fauves Éditions.

Francione, Gary (2008) *Animals as Persons. Essays on the Abolition of Animal Exploitation*, New York, NY, Columbia University Press.

Haraway, Donna (2008) *When Species Meet*, Minneapolis, MN, University of Minnesota Press.

Ionesco, Eugène (1959) *Rhinocéros*, Théâtre de Dusseldorf.

Joy, Melanie (2019) *Powerarchy. Understanding the Psychology of Oppression for Social Transformation*, San Francisco, CA, Berrett-Koehler Publishers.

Kafka, Franz (1915) *Die Verwandlung*, Leipzig, Kurt Wolff Verlag.

Kemmerer, Lisa (2011) *Sister Species. Women, Animals and Social Justice*, Chicago, IL, University of Illinois Press.

Lánthimos, Yórgos (dir.) (2015) *The Lobster*, Ireland, Element Pictures.

Lautréamont, Comte de (1868) *Les Chants de Maldoror*, Paris, Gustave Balitout, Questroy et Cie.

Letourneur, Daisy (2022) *On ne naît pas mec. Petit traité féministe sur les masculinités*, Paris, La Découverte.

Li Vigny, Fabrizio/Blanchard, Enka/Tasset, Cyprien (2022) "Theories of Global Collapse: Closing Down or Opening Up the Futures?", *Journal of Future Studies* 27/1, 1-14. DOI: 10.6531/JFS.202209_27(1).0001.

Message, Vincent (2016) *Défaite des maîtres et possesseurs*, Paris, Éditions du Seuil.

Morizot, Baptiste (2020) *Manières d'être vivant : enquêtes sur la vie à travers nous*, Arles, Acte Sud.

Mulvey, Laura (1975) "Visual Pleasure and Narrative Cinema", *Screen* 16/3, 6-18. DOI: 10.1093/screen/16.3.6.

Nibert, David Alan (2013) *Animal Oppression and Human Violence. Domesecration, Capitalism, and Global Conflict*, New York, NY, Colombia University Press.

Ovide (1992) *Les Métamorphoses*, Paris, Gallimard.

Playoust-Braure, Axelle/Bonnardel, Yves (2020) *Solidarité animale. Défaire la société spéciste*, Paris, La Découverte.

Porcher, Jocelyne (2014) *Vivre avec les animaux, une utopie pour le XXIe siècle*, Paris, La Découverte.

Porcher, Jocelyne (2016) "Une mort digne des animaux d'élevage, c'est possible", *Libération*, 2016-03-30, https://www.liberation.fr/debats/2016/03/30/une-mort-digne-des-animaux-d-elevage-c-est-possible_1442895/, 2022-12-26.

Regan, Tom (2004) *The Case for Animal Rights*, updated with new preface, Berkeley, CA, University of California Press.

Rémy, Jean-Charles (1976) *L'Arborescence*, Paris, Denoël.

Reus, Estiva (2005) "Sentience !", *Cahiers antispécistes* 26, http://www.cahiers-antispecistes.org/sentience/, 2022-12-26.

Rousseau, Sandrine (2022), rapporté par Moulinier, Ève (@EveMoulinier), Tweet posté dans le cadre des Journées d'Été d'Europe Écologie-les Verts, 2022-08-27, https://t.co/aQGh1MNtW9, 2022-12-26.

Safina, Carl (2018) *Qu'est-ce qui fait sourire les animaux ? Enquête sur leurs émotions et leurs sentiments*, Paris, Librairie Vuibert.

Saint-Exupéry, Antoine de (1943) *Le Petit Prince*, New York, NY, Reynal et Hitchcock.

Segal, Jérôme (2020) *Animal Radical. Histoire et sociologie de l'antispécisme*, Montréal, Lux Éditeur.

Servigne Paul/Raphaël Stevens (2015) *Comment tout peut s'effondrer. Petit manuel de collapsologie à l'usage des générations présentes*, Paris, Seuil.

Sigler, Pierre (2018) "La vie mentale des animaux", Yves Bonnardel/Thomas Lepeltier/Pierre Sigler (eds.) *La Révolution antispéciste*, Paris, PUF, 77-117.

Singer, Peter (2011) *Practical Ethics*, 3rd edition, Cambridge, Cambridge University Press.

Singer, Peter/Cavalieri, Paola (2020) "The Two Dark Sides of COVID-19", *Project Syndicate*, 2020-03-02, https://www.project-syndicate.org/commentary/wet-markets-breeding-ground-for-new-coronavirus-by-peter-singer-and-paola-cavalieri-2020-03, 2022-12-26.

Sugy, Paul (2021) *L'Extinction de l'homme. Le projet fou des antispécistes*, Paris, Tallandier.

Sweeney-Baird, Christina (2019) *The End of Men*, New York, NY, G.P. Putnam's Sons.

Torres, Bob (2009) *Making a Killing. The Political Economy of Animal Rights*, San Francisco, CA, AK Press.

Wittig, Monique (2018) *La Pensée straight*, Paris, Éditions Amsterdam.

Wohlleben, Peter (2017) *La Vie secrète des arbres : ce qu'ils ressentent, comment ils communiquent, un monde inconnu s'ouvre à nous*, traduit par Corinne Tresca, Paris, Les Arènes.

The Role of Animals in Pandemic Narratives: Forewarning Disaster, Causing Outbreaks, Conferring Immunity

Ana Carolina Torquato (MECILA, São Paulo/University of Cologne),
Aureo Lustosa Guerios (Independent scholar, São Paulo)

Abstract
In this chapter, we explore the role of animals in pandemic narratives. We start by discussing how animals often serve as harbingers of disaster in literature and culture. We use Raphael's *Il Morbetto* and Shelley's *The Revolt of Islam* as case studies to illustrate how they are often imagined to die before humans as a signal of the impending tragedy. Next, we argue animals may be perceived as aggravating the epidemic by reversing to a wild state – as happens in Teófilo's *A Fome* or Giono's *Le Hussard sur le toit*. We then analyze how they become agents of contagion following the discovery of animal vectors in the late 19th century. This is what happens in Murnau's *Nosferatu*, where rats and the rodent-like Nosferatu are taken to cause the outbreak. Finally, we investigate the representation of animals as agents conferring immunity in *I Am Legend* and *Y: The Last Man*, in which animals grant the main characters with anomalous and unanticipated resistance to disease.

INTRODUCTION

Animals have always had an important place in the cultural imagination of epidemics: dogs are blamed for rabies in Ancient Akkadian literature; diseases and animals placed side by side in Biblical plagues; while many medieval sources imagine serpents and frogs as the root causes of plague outbreaks.

In this article, we study the representation of animals in pandemic fiction. We argue that animals perform a recurrent role as 'expository characters', standing at the beginning of a chain of events and at the same time, help to clarify and explain it. Without these expository animal characters, the action would not unfold in the same way. By drawing examples from various media, we suggest that animals perform three main recurrent functions, all of which vary in accordance with developments in science and medicine. In all of them, animals are vital to: (1) forewarn disaster is approaching, (2) worsen the outbreaks or cause it directly or (3) confer immunity to other characters.

ANIMALS FOREWARNING DISASTER

Prior to the discovery of animal vectors in the 19th century, animals were rarely considered relevant for the eruption and maintenance of epidemics – apart from the associations of dogs with rabies and snakes with poison. Far from being seen as potential disease-spreaders, non-human animals were commonly depicted as companions in misfortune who suffered from the same ailments as humans. This perception reflected human-animal relationships established before the Industrial Revolution, when humans had a much closer relationship with and relied far more on animals for food, transport and the production of goods, which in turn, ascribed a higher symbolic and spiritual meaning to many animals (Thomas 1983).[1]

In the influential essay, *Why look at animals?* (1980), John Berger notes the fascination that animals exerted on humans before the advent of industrial production. In his view, their special capabilities – strength, speed, dexterity, sensitivity to smells or sound and so forth – induced an admiration and respect which, albeit irretrievably lost today, were previously constant throughout human history.

On these grounds, animals were understood as more perceptive and, therefore, more connected to 'the natural world'. As such, they are frequently depicted in

---

1   As a field, the Animal Studies engages transdisciplinary approaches drawn from Zoology, History, Law, Literary Studies, Anthropology, Philosophy and others, to study both animal life in itself and the relationship between human and non-human animals. It seeks to offer new light on both broader and specific understandings of animals as living beings and it also aims to critically probe the dominance of anthropocentrism in Western culture (cf. Waldau 2013). Some of the field's key areas of investigation are: animal agency; animal welfare and ethics; the cultural imagination of animals; human-animal relationships; animal rights; among others. The terminology *human* and *non-human animals* is used within the field to emphasize the – often overlooked – fact that human beings are also part of the animal world, and also that non-human animals share similar characteristics with their human counterparts.

folklore, fiction and even some historical chronicles, as able to sense that danger is approaching, sometimes intuitively, even before any signs are available. They may flee before a storm approaches, for example, or behave oddly prior to an earthquake. One such case is found in Pliny the Elder, who asserts that, before earthquakes, "birds don't remain sitting quietly" (Tributsch 2013, 278) – in fact, such anecdotal evidence is recurrent enough to be taken seriously by present scientific research (cf. Wikelski et al. 2020). Not all occurrences are necessarily tied to natural disasters; human action may also be predicted by animals, and it is a common trope in literature and film for animals to notice a threat before it is evident in anyway. In some cases, a paranormal element seems to be implied in this perception, for instance, when dogs bark insistently at a character who will turn out to be a serial-killer, a vampire, a demon, etc. As such, animals often occupy the narratological function of forewarning the immediate future and thus, in the case of natural catastrophes such as epidemics, they become harbingers of disaster.

Homer is a case in point. At the start of the *Iliad* (I, v. 69-72), Apollo sends a pestilence to the Greek camp as punishment for Agamemnon's refusal to return prisoners of war. Albeit the retribution is aimed at humans, the text makes clear that animals are struck first, with the Greeks following suit:

> On mules and dogs the infection first began;
> And last, the vengeful arrows [of pestilence] fix'd in man.
> For nine long nights, through all the dusky air,
> The pyres, thick-flaming, shot a dismal glare. (ibid. 1909, 35)

In a similar take, Thucydides seems to suggest in *The Peloponnesian War* that nature may foretell calamity, since during the conflict, "eclipses of the sun, [were] occurring more frequently than in previous memory; [as well as] major droughts in some parts, followed by famine [...]" (2009 [c. 431-400 *BCE*], 13). Later, when describing the Plague of Athens, he notices an odd event: the "notable disappearance of carrion birds, [which were] nowhere to be seen in their usual or any other activity" (ibid., 98). The anomaly is concomitant with the outbreak, which was called before "one of the most destructive causes of widespread death" (ibid., 13). He also remarks that some animals died immediately after feeding on the bodies of the plague victims (ibid.). The assertion is possibly an overstatement designed to create a Homeric intertext. Few pathogens kill several species aimlessly at once; besides, bioarchaeology identifies the Plague of Athens as caused by *Salmonella typhi*, for which animals can be carriers, but it is not ordinarily lethal to them in large numbers (cf. Papagrigorakis et al. 2006).

Regardless of that, Thucydides is likely followed by Boccaccio in *The Decameron*, which was written between 1348-1353. The Italian author claims to have seen pigs die moments after having sniffed the garments of plague victims. The anecdote is possibly apocryphal or exaggerated since *Yersinia pestis* requires a few days of incubation before any symptoms surface. Nonetheless, it serves the narratological purpose of illustrating the seriousness of the menace faced by humans. The expiring animals are a sort of prelude for a greater tragedy in the making.

That is also the role Percy Shelley imputes to animals in the narrative poem *The Revolt of Islam* (1818). It narrates the story of Laon and Cythna as they initiate a rebellion against the tyrant Othman to free the allegorical Golden City. In the poem, animals are the first to be stricken by the disease, and as such, they anticipate the plague and famine that are about to erupt. After Othman's army violently supresses a popular revolt, the bodies of humans and animals are left to rot. The fumes exuding from the corpses unleash a plague that grows by following a clear pattern:

> First Want, then Plague came on the beasts; their food
> Failed, and they drew the breath of its decay.
> [...]
> In their green eyes, a strange disease did glow,
> They sank in hideous spasm or pains severe and slow.
> The fish were poisoned in the streams; the birds
> In the green woods perished; the insect race
> Was withered up; the scattered flocks and herds
> Who had survived the wild beasts' hungry chase
> Died moaning, each upon the other's face
> In helpless agony gazing; round the City.
> (Canto Tenth, XIV to XV) (Shelley 1818, 219)

The plague strikes animals in a hierarchical way, moving bottom-up in a scale that implies a human-centred distinction between lower and higher life forms. The "strange disease" hits fish first, then birds, insects, and finally, reaches mammals, mostly cattle and sheep. The hierarchical order in which the animal victims are organized suggests that the next prey will notedly be human beings. This use of animals as announcers of death creates an atmosphere of suspense that prepares the way for the looming catastrophe.

An analogous case is found in the plagues of Egypt as described in the *Book of Exodus*, where animals suffer alongside humans in most cases: they are all infected by lice (3rd plague); slain by wild beasts (4th); tormented by festering boils (6th); killed by a storm of hail and fire (7th); and starved after a cloud of locusts devastates the land (8th). If that was not enough, the fifth plague consists of a pestilence that decimates only livestock; that is to say, animals die as a means to punish humans indirectly. The shared retributions and the co-suffering reveal a profound connection between the fate of human and non-human animals. And even if many plagues are somehow related to disease, they do not imply any kind of contagion, as animals are not seen as causing or worsening the calamity in any way. Moreover, even when animals are part of the problem, as during the multiplication of frogs (2nd plague), they are considered more of a practical nuisance rather than a health menace – as their common association with toxicity could suggest.

A comparable portrayal is also found in the Renaissance print *Il Morbetto* (c. 1515) (cf. fig. 1), produced by the Italian engraver Marcantonio Raimondi after sketches by Raphael known as *The Plague of Phrygia* (c. 1512-1514) (cf. Boeckl 2000, 48-51 and 91-106). It depicts a city ravaged by pestilence through a combination of public and domestic scenes. A large dark cloud looms on the horizon in an unmistakable allusion to miasmas, the foul odours which were taught to cause epidemics by medical theories of the time. A woman has just died in the foreground, and her suckling infant still tries to drink her milk. A few individuals come to their aid, but all shudder at the view and the stench. A man moves the baby's face away while covering his nose to avoid inhaling the noxious fumes. A related scene is found to the left, where a man holding a torch discovers the bodies of three dead calves – a dead horse is also visible to the right in the background. Nearby, a sickened cow observes the dead calves, in what can be interpreted as a reversed parallel of the dead mother's scene. A fourth calf sniffs its dead companions, thus completing the action from which the baby was precluded. The dialogue and overlap between the scene performed by humans and that performed by the cow and the calves serve as another indication that, in times of pestilence, animals are thought of as victims and co-sufferers, rather than originators or spreaders.

The affinity between human and animal distress is further highlighted by the Latin phrase inscribed in the monument that separates the two scenes: *linquebant dulcis animas aut aegra trahebant corpora*. The sentence is taken from a passage of Virgil's *Aeneid*, and it translates as "People let go of the sweet breath of life or they dragged ailing bodies / painfully" (2007 [29-19 BCE], 58). The description is part of a scene referred to as 'the plague of Pergamea'. Aeneas misinterprets an oracle from Apollo and tries to fulfil his mission of founding a great city in Crete, rather than Italy. Due to the mistake, he, his men and their animals and crops are punished by a pestilence. As in the Bible, the problem is ultimately caused by the human failure to obey the commands of God. Animals do not contribute to the transgression in any way; but nevertheless they must innocently share the fate of humans.

Moreover, the status of the animals as 'collateral damage' reveals that, culturally, there were no fundamental divergences between understandings of human and animal health. In effect, prior to the germ theory of disease and the consequent scientificization of medicine in the late 19th and early 20th, the division between human and veterinary medicine was less pronounced. As Rudolf Virchow – who made numerous contributions to pathology and social medicine but repeatedly dismissed the Germ Theory of Disease – still remarked in 1872: "Between animal and human medicines there are no dividing lines – nor should there be. The object is different, but the experience obtained constitutes the basis of all medicine" (Saunders 2000, 203).

ANIMALS WORSENING AND CAUSING OUTBREAKS

After the turn of the 19th century, Italian scientist Agostino Bassi (1773-1856) would show in his widely circulated essay *Del mal del segno* (1835) how disease in silkworms was both contagious and caused by microorganisms. A decade later, he would expand his ideas in *Del Contagio in Generale* (1844), arguing that animalcules could be responsible for human maladies too. Concomitantly, in 1847, Ignaz Semmelweis (1818-1865) established the statistical correlation between unwashed hands and puerperal fever (cf. Carter 2017, 28-32 and 44-61).

These early propositions were followed by the meteoric rise of the Germ Theory of Disease after the 1860s. This new understanding of disease ushered a revolution whose profound consequences went well beyond science and medicine to influence nearly all areas of life. A series of significant breakthroughs bacteriologists demonstrated how the *animalcules* – which were now increasingly being termed *microbes* – were responsible for illnesses in plants, animals and humans. Louis Pasteur (1822-1895) proved that microorganisms spoiled milk, wine and beer. Gerhard Hansen (1841-1912) discovered that the bacterium *Mycobacterium leprae* caused leprosy in 1873, thus identifying the first human pathogen (Worboys, 531). Little after, Robert Koch (1843-1910) established the link between *Bacillus anthracis* and anthrax in cattle and sheep (cf. Blevins/Bronze 2010). In the early 1880s, Pasteur and Émile Roux would successfully develop vaccines against anthrax and rabies, solving in the process the mystery of how Jenner's vaccination against smallpox worked (cf. Bazin 2011). In the meantime, in 1882 and 1883, Koch would discover the pathogens that caused tuberculosis and cholera, the two major infections of the century (cf. Blevins/Bronze 2010).

These findings offered visibility to the formerly unseen threat posed by the microbial world. As a result, they provided a solid and robust rationale for the urban and social reforms which sanitarians had advocated since the 1840s. Foreseeably, sanitarians quickly updated their reliance on miasmas to adopt the new concept of microbes (cf. Latour 1993). Yet, since microscopic life was described for over two centuries as composed of 'tiny animals', many cultural discourses were naturally built around the animalization and anthropomorphizing of germs (cf. King 2014, Tomes 1999). As such, threatening bacteria were often imagined in newspapers, caricatures and fiction, as minuscule insects, reptiles or chimaeras (Stones et al. 2022, 107-113). If animalcules had been interesting oddities before, they now turned into villains responsible for immensurable death and suffering.

These were not the only cultural perceptions to shift, for research increasingly revealed the role of animals in disseminating germs. Malaria, for example, was linked to mosquitos in the 1890s by Ronald Ross and Giovanni Battista Grassi (Worboys, 514). The exact relationship with mosquitos was established for yellow fever by Carlos Juan Finlay in 1881 and later confirmed by Walter Reed in the early 1900s (ibid.). To make a few other examples: rats were identified as the vectors of plague by Paul-Louis Simond in 1898 (Simond et al. 1998); shortly followed by the connection of African sleeping sickness to the tsetse fly by David Bruce in 1903; or of Chagas' disease to the barber bug by Carlos Chagas in 1908 (ibid., 527-530).

These ties between certain animals and particular diseases were a novelty. Traditionally, humans primarily categorized animal species based on their perceived utility or threat: wild or tame, edible or inedible, useful or useless (cf. Thomas 1983, 47-55). Those creatures which served as transportation, or which provided nourishment and work power were regarded with appreciation and concern – which is not to say that cruelty to animals was not equally rife. Certain species were interpreted as menacing to human life and others to human subsistence for consuming crops and spoiling food. The first groups included wolves, bears and wild boars, while the latter comprised the so-called 'vermin': insects, rats, foxes and certain birds. Creatures appertaining to these groups were often persecuted and exterminated (ibid., 58).

Nonetheless, persecutions were carried out because of the perceived threat to people and their property by direct action, not by means of diseases – with the eventual exception of rabid dogs and 'poisonous creatures'. Every so often, animals could be considered an indirect danger to health due to their power to generate miasmas, either through excrement or by their decomposition after death. This was the reason why laws regulating butchery and the disposal of offal and animal carcasses in the open air were created (cf. Carr 2008, 451). Yet, the inner workings of contagion were not explicitly tied to animals; they resulted instead from all types of decaying matter, including human and even plant materials. Given that miasmas could originate from any of the abundant and ubiquitous organic sources, there was no systematic effort to inculpate non-human animals for their existence.

These perceptions slowly started to change with the rise of sanitary movements; yet major cultural transformations only took place after the breakthroughs of bacteriology after the 1880s. In that regard, the successive discovery of animal vectors had significant importance. Once that link was established, pre-existing notions of 'vermin' could be updated to include this new biological peril. Such was the case of rats and mice: even though they had been despised and considered symbols of evil for long – and had been, on occasion, indirectly linked to miasmas and the plague (cf. Cole 2010; Biehler 2013, 113) –, it was throughout the 1800s that rats and mice were increasingly equated with disease. At first, they were generally paired to filth and squalor, just to become the quintessential emblem of plague by the turn of the century after their identification as a vector. Then, controlling the rat population became a major strategy used to curb plague outbreaks in Rio de Janeiro (1900), Sidney (1900) or San Francisco (1900-1904), among others.

These transformations were also noticeable in literature too, where the advent of animals as disease-spreaders took hold after the beginning of the 1900s. Rats appear abundantly in Bram Stoker's *Dracula* in a meaningful relationship with the Count. They convey old ideas about 'vermin' and, hence, serve to highlight his parasitic reliance on human blood. After being severely injured, Renfield reveals to Drs. Seward and Van Helsing a vision in which Dracula summons "Rat, rats, rats! Hundreds, thousands, millions of them, and everyone a life; and dogs to eat them, and cats too" (1983 [1897], 279). Then, he conjures up a dark mist in which "there were thousands of rats with their eyes blazing red – like His, only smaller. He held up His hand, and they all stopped" (ibid.). Dracula is akin to these animals and can control them.

Nevertheless, the rats do not invoke ideas of plague here for two reasons. Firstly, *Dracula* was serialized in 1897 and published in book form in the following year. Therefore, it slightly pre-dates Simond's discovery of the role played by rodents in the transmission of plague. Secondly, these rats seen in a vision are offered to Renfield as a reward to be presumably consumed as food.

This is not to say that the narrative disregards medical discourses. The threat of looming biological invasion appears metaphorically throughout the entire novel. Dracula is himself linked to epidemic diseases: his victims become frail and feverish; he can infect others with vampirism; he is a tall and pale noble, and his mouth is eventually tinged with blood – as in the case of stereotypical tuberculosis patients –; he invades a major urban center to feed preferably on sensible and refined women – in the same way that tuberculosis was imagined as doing (cf. Byrne 2011, 124-149) –; he can summon a cloud of mist before landing in England or invading Nina Harker's room – very much like miasmas –; he comes from a barbaric and loosely defined 'East' – in the same way as *Asiatic* cholera or *Oriental* plague. In this way, the Count is depicted in two complementary ways which do not intersect directly. On the one hand, he is related to rats, which are understood as disgusting parasites and symbols of corruption. On the other, he is seen as an invasive biological force in the guise of the numerous epidemics of the 19th century.

Nevertheless, in our interpretation, these two co-existent views do not interact to create a third relationship that sees rats as vectors of plague or dogs and bats as vectors of rabies. Rats were chosen due to their rich symbolic charge, which is undoubtedly related to decay and filth – and consequently to disease –, yet still it is less direct than our present-day sensibility would suggest. By the same token, dogs or bats are employed in the narrative not so much for their ties with rabies but rather for being an allegory of evil (dogs) and feeding on blood (bats).

Yet, that relationship changes completely in *Nosferatu: A Symphony of Horror*, the cinematic version of the novel directed by Murnau in 1922. In the film, the Count is directly and inextricably linked to the bubonic plague by means of rats. This is obvious from the moment the coffins loaded with accursed earth are dispatched by ship to Germany. When the port authorities inspect one of them, they discover they are all teeming with rats. In the following scenes, the imminent arrival of the Count is announced by his insane follower, at the same instant in which, a professor compares carnivorous plants and microscopic 'polyps' to vampires during the course of a lecture. The superposition of a macroscopic menace (Nosferatu) and also a microscopic one (*Yersinia pestis* delivered by means of rats) is quite evident. A little later, the newspapers are shown announcing that "a plague epidemic has broken out in Transylvania" and its "victims appear to have strange scars on their necks" (Murnau 1922 [00:46:41 min.]), an ambiguous reference to the vampire's bite as much as to the plague's buboes which customarily erupt in the area. In the meantime, a sailor falls sick in the ship and realizes in his delirium Nosferatu's presence. The sailor soon dies and is shortly followed by the rest of the crew, all of whom are explicitly decimated by "the epidemic on board" (ibid. [00:49:15 min.]). The Count and his mischief of rats are inseparable: they leave Transylvania, get out of the coffins on the ship, and disembark in Germany always at the same time. Once the ghost ship is inspected, politicians read about the plague on its registers and immediately sound the alarm of a "plague threat" (ibid. [01:03:51 min.]).

Interestingly, on hearing the terrible news, many politicians cover their noses to avoid miasmas, thus confusing the current and the discarded mechanisms of contagion. A plague outbreak erupts from this point onwards, with a vast number of citizens perishing and houses being marked with characteristic white crosses. Seemingly, these individuals genuinely die of the plague since the Count pays no attention to the surrounding chaos; he is all too busy preparing an attack against Ellen, the virtuous wife of his real estate agent about whom he obsesses.

In this fashion, Murnau's *Nosferatu* constructs a tripartite relationship in which vampire, rats and plague are indissociably linked. However, this interaction emerges only partially in *Dracula*, where rats appear less extensively and are not considered vectors of plague; instead, they are loosely linked to disease in general by eliciting ideas about filth. These changes reveal the new perspectives about animals as vectors that circulated in the twenty-five years, which separate the publication of the novel (1897) and the making of the film (1922).

Another example of animals acting to worsen a natural disaster is found in the Brazilian naturalist novel *A Fome* (*Hunger*), published by Rodolfo Teófilo in 1890. It describes the deadliest natural catastrophe in Brazilian history: the Great Drought of 1877-1878, which caused a third of the population of the Northeast region to succumb to hunger or to a concomitant outbreak of smallpox; an overall loss of life equated to 5% of the Brazilian population at the time (cf. Mota et al. 2021).

The novel follows a family of formerly rich farmers who migrate to the coast searching for better life conditions. Their future sufferings are foretold before their departure by the sudden death of their cattle due to "epizootics of various nature" and the "microbe of anthrax" (Teófilo 2011 [1890], 22; authors' translation).[2] Moreover, when they start the quest, the migrant family discovers the hinterlands are startlingly silent: "[n]ão se ouvia o trinar de uma ave, o zumbir de um inseto!" (ibid., 30).[3] In both cases, the death or disappearance of animals serve to forewarn disaster.

---

2   "Epizootias de diversas naturezas se desenvolveram e faziam diariamente centenas de vítimas. O micróbio do carbúnculo, embora fosse enterrado não morria, ressuscitaria nas ervas do campo levado pelas minhocas, quando chovesse" (Teófilo 2011 [1890], 22).

3   "Not the twitter of a bird, not the chirp of an insect could be heard!" (authors' translation).

Along the way, besides suffering from hunger and illness, the migrants are constantly attacked by ravenous animals, who – like the smallpox outbreak on the making – seem to thrive in the desolate conditions. Such is the case of the New World vultures (*urubus*), whose imagery is used to stage the overall human misery and death but also to engender a gothic atmosphere:

> Os urubus, pousados aos milhares nos galhos das árvores num crocitar constante, tornavam a solidão tétrica e pavorosa. De uma gula insaciável, espreitavam as vítimas, que caíam aos centos mortas de fome e de peste, e banqueteavam-se naquele repasto de pelangas. A atmosfera que enchia os campos era deletéria e podre.[4] (ibid., 22)

In the passage, the vultures gather around on the trees waiting for their next prey. They are very numerous and noisy and consequently stand in stark contrast to the barren and silent surroundings. In addition, they act in consort with natural catastrophes, waiting for weakened victims to succumb to hunger or to plague (*peste*) – a word which is carefully chosen to refer to a collection of diseases, rather than to bubonic plague itself. The stench referred to in the last sentence is yet another invocation of miasmas. However, it is also used to reveal the combined burden of disease, hunger and now, animal aggression: if the adjective 'deleterious' could be interpreted as referring mostly to the plague – in Portuguese, it is nearly always used in the expression 'deleterious to health' –, the smell of 'rotten' cadavers is tied to the vultures, who, as the text suggests, devour their victims still alive. The passage thus makes clear that hunger and disease may impair the health, but it is the vultures that come in for the kill at the end.

Proof of that is a later scene in which a woman, too weak to protect herself, is eaten alive by the birds:

> [...] uma mulher tão magra como uma múmia, era devorada ainda viva pelos urubus. Banquete horrível! Como o Prometeu, imóvel e sem ação, sente rasgarem-lhe as entranhas as garras e os bicos acerados das aves malditas! Vivia, ainda, quando

---

4   "The vultures made the loneliness gloomy and dreadful with their constant caw while perched by the thousands on the tree branches. With insatiable gluttony, they were on the lookout for victims, who fell dead of hunger and plague by the hundreds, and they feasted on that pasture of flesh. The atmosphere that filled the fields was deleterious and rotten" (authors' translation).

estas, que das alturas devassavam a terra, procurando repasto à fome, vêem-na e descem sobre ela.[5] (ibid., 67)

Bats are also portrayed by Teófilo as parasites working in tandem with disease. Early on in the novel, they are called 'stinking' animals and are compared with rats infested by fleas – which they pass over to one of the characters. Later on, the main character witnesses a grotesque scene in which a frail baby is bled dry by hundreds of bats. He tries to scare them away, but the bats pay no attention to him and, without regard for personal safety, continue to attack the child. In fact, the narrator remarks that they were already so full with blood that they could no longer fly (ibid., 58). Instants before, the character had been attacked by a dog that was in such a frenzy it had to be put down with axe blows. The savagery and temerity of the animals – whose aggression can be only avoided by extermination – is consistent with the symptoms of rabies; besides, dogs and bats are its stereotypical vectors. In this way, certain non-human animals are used in the narrative to add up to a Gothic panorama of disease and decay; their status as contagious vectors is not stated directly, but it is understood tacitly.

Another example of how animals may worsen an epidemic is found in Jean Giono's *Horseman on the Roof* (*Le Hussard sur le toit*, 1995 [1951]). In the novel, we accompany the wanderings of the officer Angelo Pardi through Provence in 1832, at the height of a cholera outbreak. At the very start of the book, Angelo enters a village whose entire population has been exterminated by cholera. That comes across as an enormous exaggeration of historical fact, since despite its seriousness, cholera rarely caused more than 5% of the population to die (cf. Guerios 2021, 100; Hays 2005, 229-331). Given that some persons may carry cholera vibrios with only mild or asymptomatic infections, and also that mathematical models predict them to be at least three times more numerous (cf. King et al. 2008, 878; Sack et al. 2004, 224), even in the worst-case scenario, only a third of the population would fall seriously ill at any given time – let alone die from the infection.

This information was probably accessible to the author, so in our reading, the epidemic's augmented ferocity seems to be intentional. Giono seems to be modelling cholera on the plague, with its pulmonary and septicaemic forms that are indeed deadly in a hundred per cent of cases (cf. Moss 2008). In addition, the

---

5   "[…] a woman as thin as a mummy was devoured alive by vultures. Horrible feast! As Prometheus, motionless and actionless, she feels the claws and sharp beaks of the cursed birds tearing her entrails! She was still alive when the birds which were ravaging the earth from above, seeking food out of the famine, saw her and descended on to her" (authors' translation).

Provence region is notable for its plague outbreaks, especially the much-publicized Plague of Marseille of 1720-22. The manipulation of the mortality rate results in a gothic atmosphere, and one which is particularly frightful since it is allegedly based on historical facts.

Angelo wanders around against this dramatic background and his interaction with the epidemic is mediated by various animal encounters, which work, in some instances, as harbingers of disaster and in others as disease spreaders. Before realizing that the city was stricken with pestilence, Angelo notes that "the roofs of the houses were covered with birds" (Giono 1995 [1951], 28). He wonders if something is wrong and his suspicion grows when he listens to "a dense chorus of asses braying, horses neighing, and sheep bleating" (ibid., 29). The entire setting seems unnatural to him and the animals sound "as if somebody were cutting their throats" (ibid.).

Next, the presence of disease is revealed theatrically when "his horse suddenly shied as a huge clump of crows flew up to reveal a body lying across the track" (ibid., 29). It was the partially-devoured corpse of a woman. Shocked, Angelo tries to disperse the birds that are not intimidated; they fly off only in the last instant and shortly after, regroup and return to stand against him. The crows "stank like stale syrup" (ibid.), just like the corpse which "smelled appallingly" (ibid., 30). Immediately after the confrontation, Angelo feels the urge to throw up – a typical cholera symptom –, as if he had been metaphorically contaminated by the birds.

However, he manages to control himself and continues to roam around, slowly grasping that all of the inhabitants died from cholera. In the process, he encounters a succession of animals – and is attacked by most of them. A dog "leaped at his stomach and would have bitten him badly had he not instinctively hurled it back" (ibid., 30). As the dog continues to strike, Angelo notices its "strange eyes" and "a muzzle smeared with nameless gobbets" (ibid.), both of which indicate ferociousness and, possibly, rabies. Furthermore, the dog – like the crows – was feeding on the corpse of the cholera victim; that seems to indicate a degree of contagiousness, as if the animals had turned rabid after consuming the contaminated flesh.

The scene is repeated once Angelo enters a house to find a few partially eaten bodies, including a baby. They have all died of cholera: "[the bodies] were blue, their eyes sunk deep in the sockets, and their faces, reduced to skin and bone, thrust out enormous noses, thin as knife blades" (ibid., 32). Angelo then notices the presence of rats that also seem malicious and threatening:

> He found there a fourth body, naked, very thin, quite blue, curled up on the bed
> amid copious evacuations of milky curds. Some rats that were busy eating the

shoulders and arms jumped aside when Angelo parted the curtains. He wanted to kill them with the spade, but he would have had to strike the corpse, too; besides, they were watching him with inflamed eyes, they were grinding their teeth, crouching on all fours as if to spring. (Giono 1995 [1951], 33)

A clear link is established between the rats and cholera: they move around amid the victim's evacuations, precisely the mechanism of contagion for the infection. Again, the animal's defiance suggests they are somehow rabid. Moreover, the plague is also invoked by the presence of the rats – cholera is effectively referred to as 'plague' several times along the novel.

Once more, Angelo "was nearly bitten by two of the animals, which flung themselves at his boots" (ibid., 33). He kills one of the rats, but the other, in yet another reference of the miasmas, "raised a stench so horrible that Angelo had to get out of the house as fast as he could" (ibid.). In the following scenes, Angelo continues to meet cats who look like foxes, horses and goats who are maddened by hunger, and pigs that were "voracious beasts" (ibid., 38) and "mad with rage" (ibid., 39), and "had charged the man like a bull" (ibid.).

When combined, these scenes reveal the author's intention of creating the feeling of a 'total outbreak': a perfect storm that combines cholera and numerous animal attackers – crows, dogs, rats, pigs – that, in turn, are symbolically tied to rabies, the plague and filth in general. Interestingly, cholera, which follows the faecal-oral route, cannot be spread by animal vectors. However, the fact is manipulated in the novel precisely to create a gothic atmosphere in which non-human animals turn upon humans.

Such framing of animals as disease vectors seems to respond to the scientific discoveries of the late 19th century, as well as the wish to create human-centered narratives. At a later date, with the reappearance of vector-born diseases in the 21st century, animals will turn into real *epidemic villains* in modern fiction, as in the formulation of Christos Lynteris. As he puts it: "No longer seen as mere reservoirs or spreaders of disease, but as the very ground where new pathogens emerge, non-human animals are today conceived as the incubators of existential risk for humanity" (Lynteris 2019, 1). In this sense, a few selected animals – bats and rodents especially – are listed as an epidemiological danger to society, a pattern which has circulated far and wide during the Covid-19 pandemic.

ANIMALS CONFERRING IMMUNITY

The 20th and 21st centuries have been profoundly impacted by advances in medical science which resulted in an unprecedented rise in life expectancy. The creation and distribution of vaccines have been an important part of this development: vaccines have saved the lives of millions and even achieved the extinction of a human and an animal disease – smallpox (1977) and rinderpest (2011), respectively (cf. Greenwood 2014).

However, vaccines have raised a lot of controversy throughout history, and have always stirred up resistance from different groups in different societies. The reasons for this vary widely, but in 19th century Europe especially, it was commonly related to its animal origins (cf. Bennett 2016). The word 'vaccine' was coined by Edward Jenner in 1796 from the Latin word for cow, *vacca*. The name referred to the cowpox virus which was used to inoculate humans against smallpox. At the time, the vaccination procedure was achieved through a close human-animal link: pus was collected from infected cows and administered to humans via scratches on the skin; then, after a few days, the matter produced by this individual could be used to immunize a second person and the vaccination chain could continue this way.

In the 1880s, rabbits also became part of the picture, after Pasteur and Roux discovered how to attenuate the rabies virus via 'animal filters'. They would contaminate rabbits one after another to obtain a progressively weakened version of the infection (Bazin 2011). In 1885, after Pasteur successfully immunized a nine-year-old boy who had been bitten by a rabid dog, the rabies vaccine became a popular sensation in France (cf. Wasik/Murphy 2013, 137-148). Consequently, rabbits became linked in the popular imagination with vaccine development and Pasteur started to appear in images alongside various animals. In 1887, for instance, he was celebrated in a drawing by Théobald Chartran published in *Vanity Fair* which was part of the series "Men of the Day" (cf. fig. 2). The image is entitled "Hydrophobia" – the historical name for rabies – and in it Pasteur poses with two rabbits in his arms – one of them even looks directly at the viewer. The complete absence of dogs in a drawing that portrays rabies demonstrates the rabbits' new iconic status.

Several other examples are available at the Pasteur Institute's website.[6] In a caricature by Moloch published in *La chronique Parisienne* in 1885, for instance, the scientist is portrayed while ostentatiously cooking two rabbits as if he was a *chef de cuisine*. In another, drawn by F. Graetz and published in *Revue encyclo-*

---

6   Cf. "Caricatures de Louis Pasteur" in: https://phototheque.pasteur.fr/, 2023-01-23.

pédique ten years later, Pasteur vaccinates himself in his laboratory 'against the Prussian Order of Merit' and is surrounded by both caged and uncaged animals: dogs, rabbits, various types of rats and mice, and even a horse. The association between non-human animals and vaccine development is explicit.

In literary narratives, such a link between animals and development of immunity against one disease also emerges occasionally, especially when the diseases depicted in the story happen to be new. One example is found in the popular novel *I Am Legend* (1995 [1954]) by Richard Matheson. In the narrative, all humans were transformed into vampires after a new and strange disease emerged. The only exception is Robert Neville, who lives by himself in this post-apocalyptic world. At the start of the narrative, Neville has been isolated for a long period of time, and he struggles daily to gather goods and repel vampire attacks, amid an unsettling environment of collapse and loneliness. The story does not provide much detail on to how the pandemic started, but it is clear that vampirism is contagious and that Neville is immune to it for some mysterious reason.

The novel explores two possible relationships between human and non-human animals: companionship and immunity. The first one unfolds when the character comes across a dog that is equally untouched by the disease. The animal is the first living creature to come near Neville and he changes his behaviour entirely after the appearance of the dog. If previously his only concerns were to survive the vampire attacks, now Neville's whole existence centres around his non-human companion. Their relationship is an affectionate one and it offers them both a much-needed psychological relief from constant persecution and a secluded life. As noted by Donna Haraway, dogs can "become therapists, companions, students and inmates in the world of prison cells" (2008, 63).

Besides representing an affectionate solace in the character's lonely life, the dog's immunity also suggests that there might be other survivors after all. However, the hope does not last for long: the dog eventually falls sick and Neville, in despair over the possible loss of his companion, commits himself to finding a cure. Previously, Neville had studied the disease and had actually discovered the pathogen responsible for it: it was a type of bacteria – which he names the *vampiris bacillus* – that was capable of dividing into many spores. These spores were dispersed by the wind during dust storms – yet another conjuring of miasmas – and entered the victims' bodies via "minute skin abrasions" (Matheson 1995 [1954], 88). All of that was achieved "without bats fluttering against state windows, all without the supernatural" (ibid.). After the progress, Neville hits a wall and gives up on the effort. Now, however, he restarts his investigations, but the dog dies before he was able to make any substantial progress.

Over two years later, he meets yet another survivor, this time a woman called Ruth. Neville is suspicious at first and subjects her to a few tests, some of which she fails. Still, he eventually starts to trust her and, unknowing of her real intentions of spying on him, answers to all her queries, including his conjectures about why he is immune:

> "Then why are we immune?" she asked.
> For a long moment he looked at her, withholding any answer. Then, with a shrug, he said, "I don't know about you. As for me, while I was stationed in Panama during the war I was bitten by a vampire bat. And, though I can't prove it, my theory is that the bat had previously encountered a true vampire and acquired the *vampire's* germ. The germ caused the bat to seek human rather than animal blood. But, by the time the germ had passed into my system, it had been weakened in some way by the bat's system. It made me terribly ill, of course, but it didn't kill me, and as a result, my body built up an immunity to it. That's my theory, anyway. I can't find any better reason". (ibid., 144)

Contrasting with the negative representations discussed before, bats are not the vector of contagion here but confer immunity via a sort of 'natural vaccination'. By a fortunate chain of events, the bat became an 'animal filter', attenuated the pathogen very much like Pasteur's rabbits. In *I Am Legend*, bats are not only dismissed from having any role in the spread of vampirism, but in Neville's case even become an agent of immunization. The novel was published in the mid-20th century and at this point in history, numerous advances in immunology were already consolidated. Thus, it is not surprising that the key to the novel is also tied with scientific developments.

A similar connection between human-animal immunity and an epidemiological threat appears in *Y: The Last Man* a series of comics by Brian Vaughan and Pia Guerra (2002-2008). It depicts the aftershock of a pandemic that killed all mammals possessing a Y chromosome, that is to say, every single human and non-human male in the planet. The only exception to the rule is the story's main character, Yorick Brown, and his capuchin monkey, Ampersand. In the series, Yorick is an unremarkable young man in his early twenties, who suddenly finds himself to be extremely valuable for being humankind's only chance of long-term survival. Given his special status, Yorick becomes the focus of a secret governmental mission mobilized by his mother, who is a member of the United States House of Representatives. A geneticist, Dr. Allison Mann, is part of this mission and she hopes to discover what is the source for Yorick's immunity.

In their quest, the team will eventually discover that Ampersand, the protagonist's monkey, used to be a laboratory animal. He had been injected with a special chemical designed by a scientist trying to sabotage Dr. Mann's experiments with cloning. The compound was intended to infect and kill her developing clones. Yet, it does not behave as expected and ends up by protecting Ampersand from the forthcoming plague. In addition, the monkey does not reach his final destination in Dr. Mann's lab, but is mistakenly delivered to Yorick instead. Once they get together, Yorick keeps in close contact with Ampersand by feeding him and cleaning his faeces and urine. Later on, it will be revealed, that in this process the monkey probably infected Yorick – who was asymptomatic – and thus, conferred immunity on him. It was Dr. Mann who first suspects of this chain of events: "Something *inside* of Ampersand *masked* you to the effects of the plague [italics in orig.]" (Vaughan/Guerra 2005, 147). Trying to explain to Yorick how this process could have taken place, she mentions vaccines and highlights again that "something in your pet produced a kind of antibody that sparred him from extinction" (ibid., 149). Similarly to *I am Legend*, the interspecific contact boosted the immune system of the human protagonists, in a reversal of the common depiction of animals as vector which contribute with disease spread. Dr. Mann also emphasizes that in the comic: "I mean, diseases like AIDS probably started with Ampersand's *ancestors*. Isn't it reassuring to think that nature might balance things out by providing his species with a cure to a *different* syndrome? [italics in orig.]" (ibid., 149). In the story, this discovery of the mechanism of immunization is remarkable because it might bring them "closer to discovering what *caused* the plague [italics in orig.]" (ibid.).

CONCLUSION

We argued in this chapter that, throughout history, non-human animals play different roles in pandemic narratives, some of them can be negative, when animals are perceived as worsening or causing disease outbreaks; while others can be positive, when animals forewarn about imminent disasters or confer immunity on humans.

This perspective contrasts sharply with modern views that often consider animals to be reservoirs and disseminators of infection, or, in Christos Lynteris' formulation, "as the very ground where new pathogens emerge" (2019, 1). That was evident recently in 2020, when 17 million minks were killed in Denmark after the authorities concluded that they could act as vectors for the coronavirus and, therefore, posed a threat to public health (cf. BBC News 2020).

We proposed that a fundamental step in this transformation was the discovery that germs cause diseases and that animals may function as vectors that spread pathogens. This realization had profound consequences that far surpassed science boundaries and influenced societies on political, economic, cultural and artistic levels. These discourses would later play a significant role in the rise of totalitarian regimes in the 1930s and they are still present today – although in different form – in contemporary debates about climate change or the Covid-19 pandemic.

BIBLIOGRAPHY

Works Analyzed

Boccaccio, Giovanni (2015 [1348-1353]) *Il Decameron*, Milan, Mondadori.
Giono, Jean (1995 [1951]) *The Horseman on the Roof*, trans. by Jonathan Griffin, London, Harvill Press.
Homer (1909 [c. 600 *BCE*]) *The Iliad*, trans. by Alexander Pope, London, Cassel and Co.
Matheson, Richard (1995 [1954]) *I Am Legend*, New York, NY, ORB.
Murnau, Friedrich Wilhelm (1922) "The Plague Scene", *Nosferatu – Eine Symphonie des Grauens*, Germany, Prana Films.
Raimondi, Marcantonio/Raphael (c. 1512-15) *The Morbetto, or The Plague of Phrygia*, Italy (Art Institute Chicago, Chicago, https://www.artic.edu/art works/61969/the-morbetto-or-the-plague-of-phrygia).
Shelley, Percy Bysshe (1818) *The Revolt of Islam*, London, C. and J. Ollier.
Stoker, Bram (1983 [1897]) *Dracula*, Oxford, Oxford University Press.
Teófilo, Rodolfo (2011 [1890]) *A Fome: cenas da seca do Ceará*, São Paulo, Tordesilhas.
Thucydides (2009 [c. 431-400 *BCE*]) *The Peloponnesian War*, trans. by Martin Hammond, Oxford, Oxford Classics.
Vaughan, Brian K./Guerra, Pia (2005) *Y: The Last Man, vol. 5*, New York, DC Comics.
Virgil (2007 [29-19 *BCE*]) *Aeneid*, trans. by Frederick Ahl, Oxford, Oxford University Press.

Works Cited

Bazin, Hervé (2011) "Pasteur and the Birth of Vaccines Made in the Laboratory", Stanley A. Plotkin (ed.), *History of Vaccine Development*, New York, NY, Springer Science & Business Media, 33-45.

BBC News (2020) "Denmark to Cull up to 17 Million Mink amid Coronavirus Fears", *BBC*, 2020-11-05, https://www.bbc.com/news/world-europe-54818615, 2021-04-01.

Bennett, Michael (2016) *The War against Smallpox: Edward Jenner and the Global Spread of Vaccination*, Cambridge, Cambridge University Press.

Berger, John (1980) "Why Look at Animals?", *About Looking*, New York, NY, Pantheon Books, 1-26.

Biehler, Dawn Day (2013) *Pests in the City: Flies, Bedbugs, Cockroaches, and Rats*, Seattle, WA, University of Washington Press.

Blevins, Steve M./Bronze, Michael S. (2010) "Robert Koch and the 'Golden Age' of Bacteriology", *International Journal of Infectious Diseases* 14/9, 744-751. DOI: 10.1016/j.ijid.2009.12.003.

Boeckl, Christine M. (2000) *Images of Plague and Pestilence: Iconography and Iconology*, Kirksville, MO, Truman State University Press.

Byrne, Katherine (2011) *Tuberculosis and the Victorian Literary Imagination*, Cambridge, Cambridge University Press.

Carr, David R. (2008) "Controlling the Butchers in Late Medieval English Towns", *The Historian* 70/3, 450-461. DOI: 10.1111/j.1540-6563.2008.00218.x.

Carter, K. Codell (2017) *The Rise of Causal Concepts of Disease: Case Histories*, Abingdon, Routledge.

Cole, Lucinda (2010) "Of Mice and Moisture: Rats, Witches, Miasma, and Early Modern Theories of Contagion", *Journal for Early Modern Cultural Studies* 10/2, 65-84. DOI: 10.1353/jem.2011.0007.

Greenwood, Brian (2014) "The Contribution of Vaccination to Global Health: Past, Present and Future", *Philosophical Transactions of the Royal Society B* 369/1645. DOI: 10.1098/rstb.2013.0433.

Guerios, Aureo Lustosa (2021) *Cholera and the Literary Imagination in Europe, 1830-1930*, Doctoral Thesis, Padua, University of Padua.

Haraway, Donna Jeanne (2008) *When Species Meet*, Minneapolis, MN, University of Minnesota Press.

Hays, J. N. (2005) *Epidemics and Pandemics: Their Impacts on Human History*, Santa Barbara, CA, ABC-Clio.

King, Aaron A./Ionides, Edward L./Pascual, Mercedes/Bouma, Menno J. (2008) "Inapparent Infections and Cholera Dynamics", *Nature* 454/7206, 877-880. DOI: 10.1038/nature07084.

King, Martina (2014) "Anarchist and Aphrodite: On the Literary History of Germs", Thomas Rütten/Martina King (eds.), *Contagionism and Contagious Diseases: Medicine and Literature 1880-1933*, Berlin, De Gruyter, 101-130. DOI: 10.1515/9783110306118.10.

Latour, Bruno (1993) *The Pasteurization of France*, Cambridge, Harvard University Press.

Lynteris, Christos (2019) *Framing Animals as Epidemic Villains: Histories of Non-Human Disease Vectors*, London, Springer Nature. DOI: 10.1007/978-3-030-26795-7.

Moss, Sandra W. (2008) "Bubonic Plague", Joseph P. Byrne (ed.), *Encyclopedia of Pestilence, Pandemics, and Plagues*, London, Greenwood Press, 74-76.

Mota, Camilla Veras/Costa, Camilla/Tombesi, Cecilia (2021) "500 mil mortos: a tragédia esquecida que dizimou brasileiros durante 3 anos no século 19", *BBC News Brasil*, 2021-06-06, https://www.bbc.com/portuguese/resources/idt-5ef 8617a-d045-4f5e-932d-d41d9292ee51, 2022-04-09.

Papagrigorakis, Manolis J./Yapijakis, Christos/Synodinos, Philippos N./Baziotopoulou-Valavani, Effie (2006) "DNA Examination of Ancient Dental Pulp Incriminates Typhoid Fever as a Probable Cause of the Plague of Athens", *International Journal of Infectious Diseases* 10/3, 206-214. DOI: 10.1016/j.ijid.2005.09.001.

Sack, David A./Sack, Bradley/Nair, G. Balakrish/Siddique, A. K. (2004) "Cholera", *Lancet* 363, 223-233. DOI: 10.1016/s0140-6736(03)15328-7.

Saunders, Leon Z. (2000) "Virchow's Contributions to Veterinary Medicine: Celebrated Then, Forgotten Now", *Veterinary Pathology* 37/3, 199-207. DOI: 10.1354/vp.37-3-199.

Simond, Marc/Godley, Margaret L./Mouriquand, Pierre D. E. (1998) "Paul-Louis Simond and His Discovery of Plague Transmission by Rat Fleas: A Centenary", *Journal of the Royal Society of Medicine* 91/2, 101-104. DOI: 10.117 7/014107689809100219.

Stones, Catherine/Stark, James/Rutter, Sophie/Macduff, Colin (2022) "The Visual Representation of Germs: A Typology of Popular Germ Depictions", *Visual Communication* 21/1, 97-122. DOI: 10.1177/1470357219896055.

Thomas, Keith (1983) *Man and the Natural World*, New York, NY, Pantheon Books.

Tomes, Nancy (1999) *The Gospel of Germs: Men, Women, and the Microbe in American Life*, Cambridge, Harvard University Press.

Tributsch, Helmut (2013) "Bio-Mimetics of Disaster Anticipation-Learning Experience and Key-Challenges", *Animals* 3/1, 274-99. DOI: 10.3390/ani3010 274.

Waldau, Paul (2013) *Animal Studies: An Introduction*, New York, NY, Oxford University Press.

Wasik, Bill/Murphy, Monica (2013) *Rabid: A Cultural History of the World's Most Diabolical Virus*, New York, NY, Penguin Books.

Wikelski, Martin/Mueller, Uschi/Scocco, Paola/Catorci, Andrea/Desinov, Lev V./ Belyaev, Mikhail Y./Keim, Daniel/Pohlmeier, Winfried/Fechteler, Gerhard/ Mai, P. Martin (2020) "Potential Short-Term Earthquake Forecasting by Farm Animal Monitoring", *Ethology* 126/9, 931-941. DOI: 10.1111/eth.13078.

Worboys, Michael (2013) "Tropical Diseases", Roy Porter/W. F. Bynum (eds.), *Companion Encyclopedia of the History of Medicine*, Abingdon, Taylor and Francis, 512-536.

IMAGES

Figure 1: Sketch by Raphael known as The Plague of Phrygia *(c. 1512-1515)*

Source: Raimondi, Marcantonio/Raphael (c. 1512-1515) *The Morbetto*, or *The Plague of Phrygia*, Italy, Chicago, Art Institute Chicago, https://www.artic.edu/artworks/61969/the-morbetto-or-the-plague-of-phrygia, 2022-11-18.

Figure 2: Pasteur with two white rabbits in his arms as one of the "Men of the Day" in Vanity Fair (1887)

Source: Chartran, Théobald (1887) "Hydrophobia", *Vanity Fair*, n°372, 8 jan. 1887, Wellcome Collection, https://wellcomecollection.org/works/tme22wja, 2023-01-27.

Germs as Social Protagonists: (In)visible Enemies and the Fear of Epidemic Invasion in Classical Hollywood Cinema

Claire Demoulin (Yale University)

Abstract

Two of the *biopics* directed by William Dieterle – *The Story of Louis Pasteur* (1936) and *Dr. Ehrlich's Magic Bullets* (1940) – depict fathers of the advent of bacteriology. However, the story of their life journeys is intertwined with major epidemics of the 19th century (rabies, syphilis, diphtheria). Therefore, these two movies face the challenge of giving face to crucial invisible epidemic protagonists such as microbes and germs. This paper aims at exposing how these *biopics* implement visual and narrative strategies to reveal the instrumental role of the microbes and the fear they embody in classical Hollywood storylines. Making the spirochete or other germs actual pandemic protagonists ultimately enhances the type of war rhetoric that characterizes the treatment of viruses as invading enemies to be fought.

INTRODUCTION

During the Covid-19 pandemic, many political leaders characterized the campaign against the virus as a war on an invisible enemy, a fight against clandestine and invasive forces. War metaphors and military rhetoric have proliferated in media descriptions of the pandemic situation (cf. Demoulin 2020), with health workers on the front lines often being portrayed as engaged in a heroic battle against an enemy in the form of a microbe, the unique danger of which hinges on one crucial aspect: its invisibility. Such tropes also figured prominently in 1930s cinematic depictions of epidemiological diseases and the "microbe hunters"[1] who strove to combat them. But how does cinema, a primarily visual art, represent invisible protagonists? And what might be the political and ideological consequences of a fixation on a metaphorical enemy who is both everywhere and nowhere?

In this context I will focus primarily on *Dr. Ehrlich's Magic Bullet*, a 1940 biographical film directed by William Dieterle, which he made on the heels of *The Story of Louis Pasteur* (1936), another film dealing with a notable scientific researcher. These two films are representative of a broader trend in 1930-1940s Hollywood films: the journey of scientists who contributed to humanity by eradicating epidemics (e.g. Custen 1992). Dieterle, who made a name for himself in the *biopic* genre, encapsulated this trend by drawing particular attention to scientific professions with a strong humanist tone. Indeed, many of Dieterle's movies depict doctors, nurses, biologists – including the founders of the science of bacteriology – as heroic 'germ killers' and narrate the course of 19th century epidemics, such as anthrax and rabies in *The Story of Louis Pasteur*, typhus and cholera in *The White Angel*, and diphtheria, tuberculosis and syphilis in *Dr. Ehrlich's Magic Bullet*.[2]

The challenge is twofold: in addition to representing invisible germs, *Dr. Ehrlich's Magic Bullet* also had to wrestle with the challenge of naming the unnameable, i.e. venereal disease (VD). Germs are crucial actors in all of these stories, and each film evolves a representational strategy to depict not only their reality but their *agency*.[3] Giving bacteria a visible form and allowing them to move on-screen brings with it an interaction between visible and invisible protagonists. But how can the presence of this dreadful invisible agent be evoked? What formal or narrative strategies make them protagonists in spite of their visual absence? And, lastly, what are the potential political and ideological repercussions of such strategies?

To address the double issue of representability of the invisible (visual figuration and censorship constrains), I will first resort to film analysis in order to dissect

---

1   The expression refers to the title of Paul de Kruif's bestseller of 1926. The novel popularizes the scientific journey of several 19th century fathers of bacteriology.

2   Dieterle's biographical films belong to the "microbe hunter" genre of the 1930s, alongside John Ford's *Arrowsmith* (1931, bubonic plague), *The Prisoner of Shark Island* (1936, yellow fever) and George Seitz's *Yellow Jack* (1938, yellow fever again).

3   The term *agency* is here considered as the capacity of agents or specific groups, thanks to their free will, to interpret their social environment and to concretely act within this context. This is the meaning given by the father of the Birmingham School, such as historian Edward Thompson, from which the *Cultural Studies* emerged and made *agency* one of their key concept.

the audio and visual ways to giving shape to the hidden or unspoken. Borrowing to the tools of *Cultural Studies* in analyzing the production as the reception of representations, I will articulate my film analysis to an examination of the discourses which are formulated in the movies and put them in perspective of their cultural context. Such a method will expose how microorganisms become the protagonists of a story that characterizes them with respect to a certain war lexicon and employs novel formal strategies to give them a visual presence. As their existence got progressively recognized in the 19th century, germs became social agents in society and appeared consequently as social protagonists in the cinematographic storyline and other cultural forms.

THE POLITICAL CHALLENGE OF PORTRAYING GERMS

What do germs and cinema have in common? Both have been sources of the collective fear of invisible contamination. "Germ panic", to use a phrase of the historian Nancy Tomes (1998, back cover; see also Nancy Tomes 2000), can arise as a result of the perceived inability to control the circulation of deadly microbes that spread in society in unperceived ways. As for film, cinephobic discourses of the early 20th century portrayed cinema as a space of 'contamination' of minds and morals where images deliver subconscious ideas that influence the audience and shape their behaviours. It led to a wide range of essays written in the 1920s associating cinema with anxieties, disorders or even pathologies (cf. Casetti 2018). Here comes the analogical phobia of cinema itself as an uncontrolled way to display a specific subject with respect to language and content.

At the time of the making of *Dr. Ehrlich's Magic Bullet* at the end of the 1930s, the representation of venereal disease onscreen was a vexed proposition. Under section II.7 of the so-called Hays Code, which began to be rigidly enforced in 1934, depictions of sexual disease in film were completely prohibited. The contemporary discourse around the film was thus characterized by evasions and circumlocutions. In a pre-release interview for *Film Survey*, for example, director William Dieterle referred to syphilis as the "*shshsh* disease" (Commons 1939, 7), while in his 1965 autobiography, Jack Warner remembers having produced a film about a "closet disease" (Warner 1965, 259). In this context, how does one make a film about a disease that cannot be named but that must, at the same time, educate the public about the dangers of contracting and spreading it? I posit that the way silence is used, as part of the mise-en-scène, becomes one of the fundamental features of this strategy.

The opening sequence of *Dr. Ehrlich's Magic Bullet* immediately evokes some of these dichotomies: what is spoken versus what must be left unspoken, what can be shown versus what must remain hidden. The film starts by introducing the main character – Doctor Paul Ehrlich, played by Edward G. Robinson – in consultation with a patient at the hospital where he works (cf. Dieterle 1940 [01:26-05:05 min.]). The consultation follows a seemingly routine protocol: Ehrlich checks the patient's sight, interprets his symptoms, and prescribes medication to treat his skin lesions. At the same time, we observe a discrepancy between the doctor's nonspecific comments ("a disease like many others", he calls it, "transmitted by inanimate objects" and for which there is a cure) and his injunction forbidding the patient to marry, followed by the suicide of the young patient. The disease in question is never explicitly named, nor is it explained how it is contracted and transmitted. In short, everything is left unsaid; the audience only knows that the young patient is now forbidden to marry.

This scene represents a typical example of how the audience can create a discourse out of specific tropes, symbols, images, and is able to act on changing its meaning. Theories on encoding/decoding strategies are indeed fundamental to understand that the processes of producing and receiving messages are not identical (e.g. Stuart Hall 1980). In this scene audiences in 1940 would have created sense out of the reference to syphilis based on the symptoms described and the prohibition against marriage, although the name of the disease is never mentioned. This ban on marriage echoes the narrative models of films in the previous decade, when syphilis and social responsibility shaped the intrigue around the consequences on marriage for people with the disease. The latter ban is based on the 'premarital examination laws' that were being drafted throughout the United States in the 1930s, which gave doctors the power to prevent a couple from marrying if one of them had contracted syphilis (cf. Shafer 1954, 488). Of course, this legislation is an anachronism in relation to the historical Ehrlich's life (he died in 1915), but such a conflation allows the film to overcome the obligation of silence by constructing a typical situation that implied the disease in question.

In other words, the film tries to subvert a silence imposed by society on pandemic VD protagonists that the contemporary scientific public authorities condemned more generally. Contemporary scientific authorities made indeed common cause with the film in condemning such enforced ignorance. Roosevelt's surgeon general, Thomas Parran, who was employed as a scientific consultant on the film, decried the "conspiracy of silence" (N.N. 1936, 23) – a phrase often reused since (cf. Brandt 1988, 378; Walters/Masel Walters 1991) – and supported popular initiatives in the arts and media to break the taboos and improve the level of public education. He believed that *Dr. Ehrlich's Magic Bullet*, by confronting the audience with images and representations of the germ responsible for syphilis, was an important part of this awareness campaign. But this controversial situation paved the way to diverse figurative and narrative patterns suggesting a form of imposed silence. The 1938 play *Spirochete*, by Edward Arnold Sundgaard, that Parran also supported, subverts in its morbid poster an artistic view of this 'conspiracy of silence'. A woman, whose profile is divided in two – the left-hand side with regular features while the right-hand exposes her skeleton – is looking at us with her finger in front of her mouth asking for silence. This example shows a figurative tradition of gestures associated with the motives of silence and which echo forms of conspiracy. As I have just described in a more implicit way with the opening scene of *Dr. Ehrlich's Magic Bullet*, we can find in the film many variations on these subversive motives, as also in the trailer, which points out the irony of imposed silence. One aspect of a syphilis narrative is the silent progression of its VD germs, both linked to their unspeaking quality, but also because of a social injunction against their expression. Silence and invisibility are two key aspects in portraying a germ invasion.

MAKING THE INVISIBLE ENEMY VISIBLE

In its capacity to render visible what is invisible, i.e. microscopic microbes, cinema, employing the technologies of science, is uniquely qualified to represent epidemiological protagonists. The microscope allows the camera to disclose things hidden to the naked eye, such as wriggling masses of spirochetes, giving them a visual as well as narrative identity. Through images, and with the alliance of science, the fear of contagion takes shape, can be visualized through different apparatus: various images or avatars indeed contribute to represent microbes, be it the spirochete, the germ of syphilis or the recent avatar of Covid-19. By doing so, cinema portrays pandemic protagonists. But how to endow bacteria with a cinematographic presence? Both *Dr. Ehrlich's Magic Bullet* and *The Story of Louis Pasteur* employ metonymic figures to stand in for the germs themselves. In *The Story of Louis Pasteur*, the seemingly empty bottle the scientist is holding embodies its microbial abundance.[4] This container is valuable for its microbiota reality. As long as they live in the tube in which they are trapped, the bacteria present no danger. Yet, he must handle them with care, otherwise the invisible marauders can quickly prove fatal. This is precisely the warning addressed to Ehrlich in the first

---

4   Pasteur's poses in the film reference have been borrowed from Albert Edelfelt's 1885 painting of the scientist in the Musée d'Orsay, Paris.

half of the movie. In an early scene in *Dr. Ehrlich's Magic Bullet*, as fellow microbiologist Robert Koch hands Ehrlich a container of tuberculosis bacteria, he warns him of the dangerous nature of its contents (cf. Dieterle 1940 [17:04-19:45 min.]). His forewords underline the metonymy conveyed by the dispenser: what is inside is as aggressive as it is invisible. And indeed, after a few experiments using this sample, Ehrlich starts coughing violently as if he has contracted the disease. The invisible danger has been spread through the vehicle of Robert Koch's container.

Dr. Ehrlich's Magic Bullet employs diverse visual figurations of disease-causing agents. In one scene, as Robert Koch is describing his discovery of the bacillus to his peers in a classroom setting, we see a rendering of a bacterium drawn on a blackboard in the background. The sketch allows the hitherto invisible enemy to take shape, representing the seemingly unrepresentable. The expansion of microbes can also be quantified, or modelled, through different sketching: another scene makes use of a similarly audience-oriented mise-en-scène to this purpose. Ehrlich draws a curve on the ground in order to illustrate to his assembled colleagues how microorganisms reproduce themselves. By representing invisible microbes in images, the film deploys formal strategies akin to those elaborated in the educational films of the previous decade, using graphs, sketches, teaching settings, etc., to give the germs form and transform into visible protagonists of some sort (cf. Ostherr 2005).

In another sequence in the film, Ehrlich presents his theories by sketching images of bacteria on a tablecloth while dining with prestigious guests at Baroness Speyer's house (cf. Dieterle 1940 [01:14:40-01:15:15 min.]). Historically, drawings often accompanied theoretical discussion in scientific publications. Indeed, the historical Paul Ehrlich himself used plates resembling the diagram shown in the film at his famous conference in London in 1900 where he introduced his side-chain theory, a precursor of modern immunology (cf. Ehrlich 1900). The sequence in the film, showing bacteria multiplying on the tablecloth via a time-lapse effect, is in fact an accurate representation of the antigen-antibody chain reaction.[5] That the scene takes place in the midst of a crowded, elegant dining setting almost seems to suggest that the germs too are invited guests, underscoring their easy communicability in the midst of even the most refined of settings. And yet by showing Ehrlich's hand sketching their multiplication, the sequence also emphasizes how microbial spread is still subject to human control. He both conjures the

---

5   Filmmakers in Hollywood productions paid careful attention to scientific accuracy in such sequences of scientific biographies and often recruited scientific experts for assistance during filming (cf. Kirby 2010).

enemy into being and contains it. In other words, microbes are never left alone in a Hollywood storyline, they are objectified, and therefore subjected to the human eye and control.

Dr. Ehrlich's Magic Bullet also showcases the then-novel technique of micro-cinematography in order to show Ehrlich working on his theory of staining germs (for which he earned a Nobel Prize). This method made invisible microorganisms visible by isolating them using individually targeted colour staining. Though colour could not be visually conveyed in a black-and-white film, of course, by showing the technique, the film gives bacteria another attribute: it turns them into moving entities. What cinematographic fiction brings to the construction of pandemic protagonists is the possibility of a movement. Not only do we see what these organisms look like, we can also observe their behaviour on the screen.[6] "Microbes Caught in Action" (N.N. 1909, 3), as one *New York Times* headline from 1909 put it, referring to French scientist Jean Comandon's 'moving pictures' of microorganisms.

GERMS AS SOCIAL PROTAGONISTS

Rendered visible, germs become social agents. In these Hollywood *biopics*, the exposure of germs turns microbes into disturbing actors. The visualization techniques I previously demonstrated contribute to the process of identifying a social presence, especially through their movement. By their behaviour, they become protagonists in their own right, active agents of our environment. Commenting on Ehrlich's technique of staining bacteria in his book *The Pasteurization of France*, the sociologist and anthropologist Bruno Latour (1988) describes how isolating and identifying the germs turns them into social protagonists:

> Isolated from all the others, microbes grow enthusiastically in these media,[7] which none of their ancestors ever knew. They grow so quickly that they *become visible* to the eye of an agent who has them trapped there. [...] This event completely modifies both the agent, which has become a microbe, and the position of the skillful strategist who has captured it in the gelatine [italics in orig.]. (Latour 1988, 82)

---

6   For a focus on micro-cinematography and the movement of bacteria, see Delahaye 2020.

7   "Media" has been used to translate the original word "milieu" in the French edition. Latour refers more specifically to the "gelatine milieu".

Latour also argues that Pasteur turned germs into social agents via what he calls the 'theater of proof' (cf. Latour 2001, 140): even though they are invisible, germs must still be socially acknowledged, which is why such experiments were carried out in public. In Latour's analysis, germs occupy conflictual roles: on the one hand, they are 'isolated', 'trapped'; on the other, they are invisible and thus could be anywhere. This duality is particularly suited to classical Hollywood cinema, given that such neat oppositions lend themselves to the trope of heroes confronting villains, even invisible ones.

Microbes become dramatic protagonists when placed in the context of combat with scientist-heroes. In the words of Doctor Gustav Sondelius in John Ford's *Arrowsmith* (1931), the "doctors of an older time" have been replaced by these new "heroes of health" [21:06 min.], waging war on bacteria with all the tools of modern science. Two entities are now opposed: 'germ-killers' doctors and their 'germs-enemy'. These roles recall the archetypes of Vladimir Propp's narratology (1928): Pasteur and Ehrlich are the *acting* and *resisting* protagonists, devoting their lives to the service of a noble cause; the microbes are the *opposing* ones. In deploying such vivid archetypes, these films drew on the popularity of *Microbe Hunters*, Paul de Kruif's 1926 best-selling account of heroic medical breakthroughs. The two *biopics* on Pasteur and Ehrlich follow the vivid tone of Paul de Kruif's novel, the rhythm of actions, as well as the depiction of an overwhelming historical epidemiological context. This contrast between protagonists and contextual background, both playing a key role, has been commented by Bertolt Brecht in his in-depth analysis of Dieterle's *biopics*. In *Wilhelm Dieterles Galerie grosser buergerlicher Figuren* [*A Gallery of Grand-Bourgeois Figures*] (c. 1944), Brecht writes:[8]

> The element of conflict in these bourgeois biographies derives from the opposition in which the hero stands vis-à-vis the dominant opinion, i.e., vis-à-vis the dominant class. This is Ibsen's type of the enemy of the people. Society views the mere growth in productive forces as a cancer. [...] Pasteur is portrayed as a Galileo of medicine, he too risks jail. [...] Dieterle's film biographies, progressive and humanist and intelligent – which alone marks them as a kind of rebellion within the commercial movie industry in America – were also ground-breaking in a dramaturgical sense. [...] In Dieterle's films the historical background moved into the foreground and introduced itself as the protagonist. [...] Now it became among other

---

8   Brecht was close friends with the Dieterles, who helped him to emigrate to the United States in 1941 and settle in California.

things a matter of dramatizing the microbes. The hero was a hero in the struggle against them, just as he was a hero in the struggle against people. (Brecht 2015, 19)

Three elements of this critique are significant for our analysis. First, for Brecht, Dieterle's doctors embody a solitary scientific voice confronting the ignorance of the Establishment. The Marxist subtext is clear: the hero denounces the interests of the ruling powers and rails against "dominant opinion" (ibid.). Dieterle's Pasteur is reminiscent of the Galileo of Brecht's *The Life of Galileo*, a contrarian struggling doggedly against the obscurantist authorities of his time.

Second, Brecht emphasizes the importance of historical context: "the historical background moved into the foreground and introduced itself as the protagonist" (ibid.). Epidemics are not just part of the environmental backdrop; they are key players acting on history, transforming nations and entire civilizations. For historian Frank Snowden, pandemics are the historical acting forces that can be assumed to reverse the power between men and epidemics (cf. Snowden 2019, 2).

Dieterle's biographies make the environmental context a central actor via the representation of newspaper headlines and press releases. In order to punctuate the historical chronology with the life story of the main scientist, close shots of headlines relaying epidemiological developments regularly stop the flow of action in order to put the scientist's deeds in a wider social perspective.

Lastly, Brecht speaks of the films' "dramatizing [of] the microbes" (Brecht 2015, 19). The effects microbes can have are numerous and range from killing a flock of sheep (in Pasteur's experiments) to decimating whole populations. Because the adversary is invisible, its actions can only be seen through their effects on the body of the persons or animals that have been infected. In *The Story of Louis Pasteur*, the moment when young Joseph Meister writhes in pain represents bacteria in action. Back inside the semi-darkness of the laboratory, the camera shows a close-up of the vaccine bubbling away, in a tumultuous fight against infection, giving it a whistle that suggests the noise the enemy is making [57:50-58:47 min.]. The dramatic representation of germs in this manner suggests they can be overcome and hunted down. Laboratories become the new battlefields through visual parallels linking the scientific imaginary with bellicose associations.

THE MAKING OF EPIDEMIOLOGICAL ENEMIES

In equating harmful bacteria with an invisible enemy through visual associations, these films, whether implicitly or explicitly, often deploy the rhetoric of wartime.

This in turn leads to contextualizing the wartime rhetoric associated with science and diseases. Referring to germs as threatening invaders began in popular culture in the late 19th century in such works as H. G. Wells's *The Stolen Bacillus* and Thomas Mullett Ellis's *Zalma*, and scientists, like the forefather of bacteriology, also began to use military terminology when describing their own professional activities. According to James Stark and Catherine Stones (2019), "[s]uch representations of germs – as hostile invaders – arguably owed more to the investigative strategy of Robert Koch and other so-called 'microbe hunters' active around the turn of the twentieth century" (307). Scott Montgomery (cf. 1996, 170-187) associates the research of Pasteur with the origins of 'bio-militarism' and notes increasing use of the language of war by scientists. Both films and science then, have long made metaphoric use of a military vocabulary when speaking about contagion and disease.

Hollywood continued along this line of comparison, adopting the metaphoric repertory of the science-war association. In its very title, *Dr. Ehrlich's Magic Bullet* clearly establishes the metaphoric association of microbiology with a kind of violence. By using the word 'bullet', he associated a doctor's immunological research with a firearm, aiming it at germs to destroy them. In the film, while Ehrlich was experimenting a treatment for diphtheria, he described his search for the "magic bullet" as the attempt to "eradicate and destroy the infectious microorganisms," which "is the promise of modern medicine" [52:19-52:22 min.].

In the press, this warlike rhetoric was linked to the visual evidence of contagion through the use of scientific images. In a contemporaneous article in *Life* magazine about the film, for example, the accompanying caption reads, "Imperceptible but mortal enemies of mankind are the germs of syphilis, diphtheria and tuberculosis [...], which Dr. Paul Ehrlich helped vanquish" (N.N. 1940).

This recurrence is typical of the visual and narrative forms of the interwar years. Priscilla Wald (2008) has analyzed the association between disease and war in media in her essay on the outbreak narrative. In the case of typhoid, she points to a 1913 article in *National Geographic* magazine that presents the disease as a "military disaster – literally, a threat to the security of the nation. The title [...], 'Our Army Versus a Bacillus,' drives home the point, which surfaces throughout typhoid literature, that hygiene is a military issue" (Wald 2008, 82). In classical Hollywood cinema, the fight against the invisible enemy inevitably takes the form of combat. The doctors and soldiers on the Island of Cuba in the film *Yellow Jack* (1938), for example, explicitly associate the eradication of germs with military operations. Doctor Walter Reed saves the island from yellow fever thanks to the sacrifice of some American soldiers on the army base. These "Conquerors of Yellow Fever", to use the title of the 1939 painting by Dean Cornwell, accomplish their mission in the manner of a manhunt, going from door-to-door to eradicate the enemy and free the island from its invaders.

In *The Story of Louis Pasteur*, laboratory battles and actual battles blend together: against a background of images of the Franco-Prussian War, we see the face of Pasteur surrounded by a micro-cinematographic shot of teeming microbes along with the caption "While men fought and killed one another, Pasteur was fighting microbes – the real enemy of mankind" [13:22 min.]. The two battles are joined by a double exposure. These biographies prolong the combination of rhetorical styles, sealing in the association between enemies and bacteria both in text and images.

Metaphorical combat in laboratories and military confrontations on the field of battle thus share the same modes of expression. According to Judy Segal (2005), "[t]he metaphor *medicine is war* still informs a great deal of common parlance about medicine. *Invading* microbes are resisted by the body's *defense* mechanisms [...]; in the *battle* with cancer, we *bombard foreign* cells, and we *fight* for our lives [italics in orig.]" (123). At the intersection of a visual, popular and scientific culture, the visual construction of germs in this war on microbes is used and reused, partly supported and henceforth fashioned by the mass media.

This enemy-bacteria association produces a kind of reversible, transitive metaphor. Interweaving the terms reinforces both the representation of germs as enemies and its converse: political enemies as diseases to be fought. This linkage is clearly stated in the last scene of *Dr. Ehrlich's Magic Bullet* as Ehrlich musters all his strength for his final speech:

> The magic bullet will kill thousands. But there can be no final victory over the diseases of the body unless the diseases of the soul are also overcome. They feed upon each other. [...] In the days to come, there will be epidemics of greed, hate, ignorance. We must fight them in life as we fought syphilis in the laboratory. (Dieterle 1940 [01:39:25-01:41:32 min.])

The film ends with the idea of an association between syphilis germs and fascism, suggesting that the latter spreads much like the former and that the virtues typical of the fight against syphilis – sacrifice, perseverance – can also be found in the fight against the social diseases of political obscurantism and fascist blindness. The "diseases of the soul" (ibid.; i.e. fascism) can be fought in the same way that scientists fight the "diseases of the body" (ibid.). The film makes a connection often found in the visual culture of the period, such as in the poster by Philip

Mendoza that likens Hitler's war to germs infecting a wound.[9] The connection between fascism and disease was further underscored in World War II propaganda posters that linked the fight against venereal disease with that against Hitler or Hirohito (Brandt 1987, 164f.).

The metaphor of the political enemy as biological enemy can be seen in post-war films as well. *Invasion of the Body Snatchers* (1956), for instance, portrays an alarming 'contamination' of a small American community from a mysterious source. A parallel between communist and bacteriological models gradually suggests itself, representing the passage from one zone of conflict to another. In such films, the specific nature of the enemy varies, from fascists to communists, but the use of the disease-war analogy remains the same. The forms of assimilation and exploitation of bacteria as an invisible enemy, exacerbated in times of political upheaval, convey very specific ways of resolving conflicts. The treatment of germs as invisible enemies in these films shows how fears – whether implied, projected, apprehended or exorcized by mass media – are also linked to the linguistic and political contexts of their formulation.

CONCLUSION

Classical Hollywood movies of the 1930s such as *Dr. Ehrlich's Magic Bullet* and *The Story of Louis Pasteur* deal with the difficult task of representing invisible germs at the outset of pandemics or epidemics. Through diverse visual and textual devices, cinema has the ability to give a shape to microorganisms, and consequently, to introduce them within the storyline by developing the action around their thread. As microbes become protagonists in their own rights through both a visual and a textual presence, they are treated as invisible enemies and addressed with a war lexicon. Thus, the battle is led by prophetic figures – such as Ehrlich or Pasteur – whose tasks include unveiling the enemies and targeting them to protect a collective good. The entire infrastructure of the movies embraces the effort of bringing together the spectators to the battlefield by instrumentalizing fear and resolving it through a belligerent lexicon on the one side, and by calling for the defense of mankind and collective good in a dichotomizing depiction of reality and human beings on the other side. Putting these movies in the perspective of their historical context, the belligerent lexicon employed by the mass media in the

---

9   "A finger-wound being attacked by germs represented by German soldiers in World War II. Colour lithograph after Philip Mendoza", 1940, 680216i, Wellcome Collection Library, [Online], https://wellcomecollection.org/works/cetv9anw, 2023-01-08.

fight against germ contamination created a climate in which audiences became inured to a wartime discourse. The leap from the battle against the invisible germ-enemy to the visible threat of war is short, and a 'war-educated' audience is expected to be an easy target for this second call to arms. By the outset of World War II, the equation of microbes with the 'enemy', a dynamic that had been reinforced by the 1930s films, had become reversed: the most perilous contamination was now political, in the form of fascism and later, communism, rather than a biological threat.

BIBLIOGRAPHY

Corpus Analyzed

Dieterle, William (dir.) (1936) *The Story of Louis Pasteur*, USA, Warner Bros.
Dieterle, William (dir.) (1940) *Dr. Ehrlich's Magic Bullet*, USA, Warner Bros.

Works Cited

Brandt, Allan M. (1987) *No Magic Bullet. A Social History of Venereal Disease in the United States since 1880*, Oxford, Oxford University Press.
Brandt, Allan M. (1988) "The Syphilis Epidemic and Its Relation to AIDS", *Science* 239/4838, 375-380. DOI: 10.1126/science.3276007.
Brecht, Bertolt (1980) [1940]) "Life of Galileo", John Willett/Ralph Manheim (eds.) *Bertolt Brecht: Plays, Poetry and Prose, Volume 5*, London, Methuen.
Brecht, Bertolt (2015 [1944]) "Wilhelm Dieterle's Gallery of Grand-Bourgeois Figures", Marc Silberman (ed.) *Bertolt Brecht on Film and Radio*, London, Bloomsbury Methuen Drama, 19-20.
Casetti, Francesco (2018) "Why Fears Matter. Cinephobia in Early Film Culture", *Screen* 59/2, 145-157. DOI: 10.1093/screen/hjy017.
Commons, David (1939) "A Talk with Dieterle", *Film Survey*, Dec. 1939, 7-8.
Custen, George F. (1992) *Bio/Pics. How Hollywood Constructed Public History*, New Brunswick, NJ, Rutgers University Press.
De Kruif, Paul (1926) *Microbe Hunters*, San Diego, CA, Harcourt Inc.
Delahaye, Lydie (2020) "Micrographia ou le spectacle de la nature", *Les cahiers du musée national d'art moderne* 152, 36-49.
Demoulin, Claire (2020) "Drôle de déclaration de guerre", *Libération*, 2020-03-19, s.p.
Dieterle, William (1936) *The White Angel*, USA, Warner Bros.

Ehrlich, Paul (1900) *On Immunity with Special Reference to Cell Life*, London, The Royal Society of London.

Ellis, Thomas Mullett (1895) *Zalma*, London, Tower Publishing Company Limited.

Ford, John (1931) *Arrowsmith*, USA, United Artists.

Ford, John (1936) *The Prisoner of Shark Island*, USA, Twentieth Century Fox.

Hall, Stuart (1980) "Encoding, Decoding", Stuart Hall/Dorothy Hobson/Andrew Lowe/Paul Willis (eds.) *Culture, Media, Language*, London, Hutchinson, 128-138.

Kirby, David (2010) *Lab Coats in Hollywood. Science, Scientists, and Cinema*, Cambridge, MA, MIT Press.

Latour, Bruno (1988) *The Pasteurization of France*, Cambridge, MA, Harvard University Press.

Latour, Bruno (2001) *Pasteur: Guerre et paix des microbes*, Paris, La Découverte.

Montgomery, Scott (1996) *The Scientific Voice*, New York, NY, The Guilford Press.

N.N. (1909) "Microbes Caught in Action. Moving Pictures of Them a Great Aid in Medical Research", *The New York Times*, 1909-10-31, 3.

N.N. (1936) "Wider Drive Urged on Social Disease. 'Conspiracy of Silence' Scored as Chief Drag on Program to Combat Syphilis", *The New York Times*, 1936-01-16, 23.

N.N. (1940) "Movie of the Week: Magic Bullet. Film Tells Story of Doctor Who Found Cure for Syphilis", *Life*, 1940-03-04, 74-77.

Ostherr, Kirsten (2005) *Cinematic Prophylaxis. Globalization and Contagion in the Discourse of World Health*, Durham, NC, Duke University Press.

Propp, Vladimir (1968 [1928]) *Morphology of the Folktale*, Austin, TX, University of Texas Press.

Segal, Judy Z. (2005) *Health and the Rhetoric of Medicine*, Carbondale, IL, Southern Illinois University Press.

Seitz, George (1938) *Yellow Jack*, USA, MGM.

Shafer, James K. (1954) "Premarital Health Examination. History and Analysis", *Public Health Report*, Centers for Disease Control and Prevention 69/5, 487-493.

Siegel, Don (1956) *Invasion of the Body Snatchers*, USA, Allied Artists/Walter Wanger Productions.

Snowden, Frank (2019) *Epidemics and Society, from the Black Death to the Present*, New Haven, CT, Yale University Press.

Stark, James/Stones, Catherine (2019) "Constructing Representations of Germs in the Twentieth Century", *The Journal of the Social History Society* 16/3, 287-314. DOI: 10.1080/14780038.2019.1585314.

Sundgaard, Edward Arnold (1938) *Spirochete: A History*, Federal Project Theater, Living Newspaper Series, USA.

Tomes, Nancy (1998) *The Gospel of Germs: Men, Women and the Microbe in American Life*, Cambridge, MA, Harvard University Press.

Tomes, Nancy (2000) "The Making of a Germ Panic, Now and Then", *American Journal of Public Health* 90/2, 191-198. DOI: 10.2105/ajph.90.2.191.

Wald, Priscilla (2008) *Contagious: Cultures, Carriers, and the Outbreak Narrative*, Durham, NC, Duke University Press.

Walters, Timothy/Masel Walters, Lynne (1991) "The Conspiracy of Silence. Media Coverage of Syphilis, 1906-1941", *American Journalism* 8/4, 246-265. DOI: 10.1080/08821127.1991.10731384.

Warner, Jack L. (1965) *My First Hundred Years in Hollywood: An Autobiography*, New York, NY, Random House.

Wells, H. G. (1895) *The Stolen Bacillus*, London, Methuen & Co.

Human-Viral Hybrids as Challenge to the Outbreak Narrative and Neo-Liberal Biopolitics[1]

Małgorzata Sugiera (Jagiellonian University, Kraków)

Abstract

The article starts with Jean-Luc Nancy's recent supposition that the Covid-19 pandemic has revealed the precarious foundations of the Western developed and progressive societies, laying bare the mechanism of their biopolitical regime. Following Nancy's argument, the article draws first on the example of a few recently published French Corona Fictions which depict contagion as one of many, tightly entangled factors, mostly of an anthropogenic nature. From this perspective, the article then offers a close reading of two speculative pandemic fictions fabulations of the turn of this century: the novel *The Blood Artists* (1998) by American novelist and screenwriter Chuck Hogan, and *Rifters* trilogy (1999-2005) by Canadian SF author Peter Watts. Both revisit and morph the outbreak narrative, introducing a new type of protagonist – the human-viral hybrid – to reveal the workings of biopower and geontopower as yet another form of structural violence inherent in the late liberalism.

1   The article was written within the framework of the project 'Epidemics and Communities in Critical Theories, Artistic Practices and Speculative Fabulations of the Last Decades' (UMO-2020/39/B/HS2/00755), which was funded by the Polish National Science Centre (NCN).

AN ALL-TOO-HUMAN-VIRUS

It is not without reason that Jean-Luc Nancy entitled his small volume *An All-Too-Human Virus* (2022), with intentional reference to Nietzsche's well-known book *Human, All Too Human* in which the German philosopher explained that phenomena once thought to be of divine origin had been revealed as all too human in the second half of the 19ᵗʰ century (cf. Nietzsche, in Nancy 2022, 10). The volume was published in June 2020, at the end of the first period of lockdown in France. It gathers the French philosopher's recent interventions, mostly posted online, which focus on the way the Covid-19 pandemic, which at the beginning froze the whole world in place,[2] brought to light and "revealed – indeed, deconstructed – the fragile and uncertain state of our rational and smoothly functioning civilization" (Nancy 2022, ix). Thus, to put it differently, the pandemic as well as the containment and mitigation measures against its spread have performed as a kind of magnifying glass which enlarged most of the basic contradictions, fault lines, injustices and limits of our (Western) developed and progressive societies. As Nancy argues further, the pandemic soundly attests that humans "get bogged down in a humanity that is surpassed by the events and the situation it has produced" (ibid., 11). Moreover, under these conditions, he explains that when both life and politics visibly defy humans, we gain a better understanding that the widely used term 'biopolitics', which refers to political mechanisms and strategies controlling and managing the basic biological features of the human species, totally fails to grasp the situation in which we find ourselves at the beginning of the second decade of the 21ˢᵗ century. When both our scientific knowledge and our technical power bring with them mostly uncertainty, we have lost our sense of self-sufficiency, and have been forced to finally discover how interdependent we are in the world we so long believed to be fully under our (colonial and scientific) control. It is in this sense, emphasizes Nancy, that today Nietzsche's expression rings true to us, Westerners, who are no longer unquestionable masters of the universe and ourselves.

What is even more important in the context of this article, in an intervention which gives Nancy's volume its title, he addresses a key-difference between pandemics of the past and the Covid-19 pandemic. As a rule, the former, as sickness

---

2   Although well over 100 countries worldwide had instituted either a full or partial lockdown and many others had recommended restricted movement for some or all of their citizens by the end of March 2020, not all of the world 'froze' in the same way, see e.g. https://www.bbc.com/news/world-52103747 or https://ourworldindata.org/covid-stay-home-restrictions, 2022-11-29.

in general, were recognized as 'divine' or 'natural' disasters, and therefore exogenous to the social body, even if they spread through social interaction. In contrast to that "[t]oday the majority of sicknesses are endogenous, produced by our living conditions, food supply and indigestion of toxic substances" (Nancy 2022, 10). That is why, as Nancy stresses in another intervention in the volume, we can be sure "of only one thing: of the enormous ecological or 'econological' difficulties that await us regardless of the outcome of the pandemic" (ibid., 19f.). A couple of years and a few waves of the Covid-19 pandemic later, we are in a better position to understand the French philosopher's insistence on the practical irrelevancy of the outcome of the recent outbreak. Firstly, to the majority of us it has already become evident that the ever-changing, ever-evolving nature of viruses not only seriously undermines the optimistic technocratic vision of controlling – or even of putting an end to – most of contagious diseases through vaccination. But also, we have no longer reason to believe in the capacity of scientists to detect patterns and determine probabilities of any future pandemic that will give us enough time to apply some pre-emptive measures. Secondly, the notion of emerging viruses, which used to naturalize the idea of their permanent thread, has recently revealed its anthropogenic genesis. Global warming causes glaciers and permafrost to melt, liberating ancient viruses and bacteria at the same time when mining, plantation farming and lumber depletion turn stressed animals into chronically feverish bioreactors through destroying their habitats, opening new chains of transmission of zoonotic pathogens to humans. Therefore, contagious diseases, their outbreaks and spreads are no longer seen as exogenous to the human body and independent of human agency. Because all recent epidemics and pandemics have been generated by intrinsic interactions between human biology and more-than-human, albeit often human-caused environmental factors, pathogens have been increasingly recognized as one among many such factors, tightly entangled, interdependent and equally threatening.

The best proof of these more and more evident changes are not only scholarly books and articles, Nancy's volume included, but also recent Corona Fictions that either aim at depicting the Covid-19 pandemic realistically or that speculatively fabulate future ecological and economic catastrophes in which a fictional contagion plays its deadly part along and together with other disasters. It suffices to recall some of the novels written shortly before or during one of the first waves of the ongoing pandemic. In June 2020 when Nancy's volume *An All-Too-Human Virus* was published, a young protagonist of Tom Connan's *Pollution* (2022) starts a first-person account of his daily life in a manner of Michel Houellebecq's characters. Although well-educated, David is only partly employed in a start-up because of the Covid-19 pandemic and he is deeply disappointed by life in France, which he overtly refers to as an underdeveloped though once well-developed country. That is why at the outset of the novel he leaves Paris for an experience of woofing at an organic farm on the Cotentin peninsula in Normandy. Seeking a place free of the pandemic and pollution to recover from a deepening depression, unexpectedly he finds himself at the very center of a serious health crisis of unknown cause(s). Significantly, because of their focus on the pandemic neither government and responsible health agencies nor nation-wide media have taken any interest in the death of local children, farmers and farm animals. Contrary to typical outbreak narratives, no real cause of this health crisis will be sought and found in Connan's *Pollution*. Furthermore, it remains unclear whether the novel's protagonist will still need to cope with a next coronavirus's mutation or already with multiple epidemics causing similar symptoms as cough and impeded breathing. Interestingly, the author moves the action of the last part of his novel into the very near future, to autumn 2023. Then shortly after the sixth lockdown, literally on the last pages of the book the critical situation becomes even more complicated through a grave leakage in a nuclear power plant near Cherbourg, the biggest town of the region. Clearly, although *Pollution* realistically depicts the situation in France after the first lockdown, it is not a novel specifically about the Covid-19 pandemic. Its main aim is rather to demonstrate to what extent the virus has worked as a catalyst, unleashing an economic, social and ecologic dynamic that has already been long in the making. In this respect, Connan shows both humans helpless in the face of tightly entangled crises and the virus as an all-too-human phenomenon as Nancy does.

It is not only in realistic Corona Fictions similar to Connan's that characters have to get by surrounded by rumors, partially verified or fake news. Many of newly published speculative fabulations do not show decision-making governmental bodies or representatives of national health agencies experimenting with new vaccines or fighting fictional pandemics by other means. They focus rather on grass-roots communities, which are afraid and/or uninformed of the real nature of the threat, and therefore react blindly to events that surpass their understanding. Some protagonists do not even notice the quickly rising death toll. A case in point is a reclusive London painter in Oana Aristide's debut novel *Under the Blue* (2021), set in the summer months of 2020. Seeking refuge in his studio from all-too-present environmental destruction, the melting of the polar icecap, eco-terrorism, and TV news about yet another epidemic in a distant Siberia, the painter does not even notice that after two weeks the Russian contagion started to ravage London and the entire world. Importantly, Aristide intermingles two plotlines in her novel. The second one, which starts already in 2017, is a story of two computer scientists who in a remote Arctic location feed data to an advanced AI program, starting from the beginning of written history. They expect it to predict what should happen next to the human species, so that adequate pre-emptive measures can be introduced on time. As it turns out, although the AI was able to predict faultlessly all historical catastrophes and crises, the situation of the late 2010s is, however, too multipronged and complicated to envisage the pandemic which will shortly wipe out the whole world, as Aristide's protagonist witnesses during his trek across post-pandemic Europe and northern Africa beneath the eponymous blue. The failure of cutting-edge AI is not only the best and anticlimactic proof that humans have lost their mastery over the world. It is also a significant signal of entangled paradigmatic shifts which the Covid-19 pandemic has made apparent, affecting fictional imagery in its turn.

Another proof of the recent changes in our understanding of pathogens and epidemics as one of environmental factors is the new hierarchy of protagonists in recently published Corona Fictions. It was long heroic scientists and physicians who frequently played the primary role in outbreak dramas.[3] They did it even in virocentric mockumentary narratives of the last decades such as Richard Preston's *Dark Biology* series (1994-2019) or David Quammen *Spillover* (2012). Now however, their relevance for and function in the novel's plot has changed distinctively.

In Aristide's *Under the Blue*, shortly after the painter had left the city for his cottage in Devon, he is visited by his London neighbour and her older sister who happens to be a doctor. Although she worked in one of the capital's hospitals during the outbreak, the doctor seems to be too traumatized to speak about a probable source and course of the pandemic even from her limited but still better-informed perspective. Thus, the reader of the novel will never learn about what caused the apocalyptic catastrophe of which multiple traces the three protagonists see each day on their road trip to Africa. The situation of non-knowledge, in which the reader finds herself, is clearly intended by the author. When compared to typical outbreak narratives premised on Conan Doylean detective stories, the denouement in Aristide's novel demonstrates exemplarily how the imaginary of contagious diseases has recently changed. Significantly, even when doctors do not remain silent after traumatizing events, their accounts have nothing to do with an expected scientific, medicalized approach, which the reader expects and knows so well from earlier pandemic fictions.

---

3   A formulaic plot that Priscilla Wald calls 'the outbreak narrative' in her *Contagious* (2008), chronicles epidemiological work from the identification of an emerging disease to its containment. Therefore, as a rule it shows scientists and physicians as its protagonists. A good case in point are *Contagion* (1995) and *Pandemic* (2019) by Robin Cook, a prolific writer, credited in popularizing the medical thriller.

A case in point is Valérie Clo's novelette *Gaïa* (2022). It offers a personal testimony of two sisters who kept putting down their impressions almost each day during a terrible hurricane which wiped out an entire region of France in the mid-21st century in a culmination of multipronged climate changes. While the pregnant Mel stays in a small organic village, her sister and physician Laura tries to alleviate the suffering of patients in a city hospital. Indeed, she does exactly this – she tries to alleviate their suffering because she is altogether unable not only to treat their diseases but also to adequately identify the cause of their suffering. There are simply too many and too tightly entangled causes for what overwhelms and exhausts the body's immune defenses, beginning with different ongoing viral epidemics, and finishing with insupportably high summer temperatures and other weather phenomena. Desperately frustrated by her total helplessness, Laura decides eventually to leave her patients in the hospital and join her sister. Hence, both Aristide's and Clo's examples demonstrate that – traumatized in silence or not – doctor protagonists of recent Corona Fictions, which combine the topics of epidemic outbreak and climate change, stand often in a clear contradiction to their heroic predecessors who skillfully exercised their expertise because they have to live in the same situation of non-knowledge as their (potential) patients do. Therefore, they clearly belong to those humans who, as Nancy commented, "get bogged down in a humanity that is surpassed by the events and the situation it has produced" (2022, 11).

In what follows, my aim is not, however, to enlarge the corpus of the newly published Corona Fictions to further support this point. I will rather take a step back to demonstrate that from today's perspective some signals of the recent changes in the pandemic imagery may be identified in former fictional, albeit scientifically informed narratives. The two chosen examples – the novel *The Blood Artists* (1998) by American novelist and screenwriter Chuck Hogan, and *Rifters* trilogy (1999-2005) by Canadian SF author Peter Watts – different as they are, both come back to the outbreak narrative as defined by Priscilla Wald in her book *Contagious* (2008) to morph its well-known structure. As Wald explains, in its various scientific, journalistic and fictional incarnations, the outbreak narrative "follows a formulaic plot that begins with the identification of an emerging infection, includes discussion of the global networks throughout which it travels, and chronicles the epidemiological work that ends with its containment" (Wald 2008, 2). In the case of Hogan's novel, Wald writes explicitly that it "offers an especially vivid example – reading almost as a blueprint – of the outbreak narrative" (ibid., 257). However, she focuses on the novel's human-virus protagonists only as deadly disseminators, which embody the urgency of scientific expertise, and does not even mention Peter Watts's trilogy with its specific embodiment of a human-viral hybrid. Both novels, which the article will analyze, focus on the outbreak narrative's key-figure of contagious disease carrier, the Patient Zero, but in my reading they do it rather to complicate and undermine the common qualitative understanding of the pathological body and of pathogens as the main source of contemporary health crises. Thus, a closer look at the novels will support Nancy's main thesis that the Covid-19 pandemic has not so much spotlighted but rather revealed the precarious foundations of the Western developed and progressive societies.

ANOTHER VIRUS

As I have already indicated, it is in the circumstances caused by the recent outbreak of the Covid-19 pandemic that Jean-Luc Nancy recognizes the inadequacy of the term 'biopolitics' to grasp the situation in which both life and politics visibly defy humans who lose their sense of self-sufficiency. A few years before Nancy's recognition, in her *Geontologies* (2016) Elizabeth Povinelli offered another critical look at Michel Foucault's well-known definition of the Western regime of power, inaugurated at the turn of the 19th century and then consolidated during the 1970s, which has turned the basic biological features of the human species into the main object of this regime's political strategy. The strategy focuses on the management of sexuality and health at the level of the individual and population. Alongside biopower, that is a formation of power which works through managing life and death, and aims at normalization of life, Povinelli identifies another entangled regime that has been operating within the framework of contemporary late liberalism, spewing out a plethora of new problems, figures, strategies and concepts. She calls the new regime geontological power, and explains that it "does not operate through the governance of life and the tactics of death but is rather a set of discourse, affects and tactics used in late liberalism to maintain or shape the coming relationship of the distinction between Life and Nonlife" (Povinelli 2016, 17), that means the distinction between the lively (*bios*) and the inert (*geos*). Povinelli links the new regime to the emergence of the geological concept of the Anthropocene and an upcoming ecological catastrophe – the extinction of humans, biological life and possibly the planet itself that urges us to take into account a previously marginalized form of death other than the life and death of individuals and species, that is a kind of an original lifelessness. This relatively novel perspective reveals that Western ontologies are covert bio-ontologies, and effectively subverts the previously stable ordering divisions of Life and Nonlife.

What is important in the context of my argument, is that this new perspective allows Povinelli to propose a set of three figures of geontopower, one of which is the Virus. In contradistinction to the two former figures (the Desert and the Animist), "the division of Life and Nonlife does not define or contain the Virus" (Povinelli 2016, 35f.), because viruses have been recently categorized as lively or inert depending on the stage of their complicated life cycle, which is dependent on other processes. That is why Povinelli sees a close connection between her figure of the Virus and the popular cultural figure of the zombie, "the aggressive rotting undead" (2016, 37). In other words, although the Virus confuses and levels the fundamental distinction between Life and Nonlife, and by this means also shows its limit, it does this only to sustain the late liberalism ideology and governance by restabilizing it as a supposedly vital form of existential crisis. That is why Povinelli links the Virus to the central imaginary of the Terrorist as the external/internal political "Other" – and while both are seen as an ultimate threat to the capitalist system, they also serve as a source of profit.

Significantly, Povinelli came back to her figure of the Virus after the second wave of the Covid-19 pandemic, in November 2020. In her essay "The Virus: Figure and Infrastructure", she emphasizes an important difference between the Virus and the coronavirus. Povinelli makes it clear that while the actual virus becomes a figure of geontological failure to govern, the Virus-as-Terrorist blocks a vital understanding of the current pandemic as yet another form of structural violence, as a manifestation of the ancestral catastrophes of colonialism and slavery. Thus, she points at what she names 'ghoul health' and defines it as the prefigure of the concept of the Virus:

> [It is] the global organization of the biomedical establishment and its imaginary around the idea [of] the big scary bug, the new plague. [...] It is the bad faith of geontopower in which the real threat is not the virus but the contemporary global division, distribution, and circulation of health. (Povinelli 2020)

Therefore, the only way to see that the current pandemic is yet another form of toxicity that colonialism has seeded, bringing along also the Anthropocene, is to differentiate the actual virus from the Virus. I will approach this problem by focusing on the cultural imagery of viruses wherein the Virus materializes as the qualitative difference between the normal and the pathological body, which will then also be demonstrated in my reading of both chosen examples of Hogan's and Watts's novels.

The ontological understanding of the normal and the pathological reaches back to the second half of the 19th century when researchers identified microbial organisms as causative agents of communicative diseases in laboratory experiments (cf. Caduff 2015). It is on these experiments that the qualitative difference between the normal and the pathological is premised. Although the microbiologists of that time were able to see only traces of viral infections, they assumed that also this kind of contagious diseases is caused by specific and external agents, attacking the organism from the outside. The reification of disease as an entity separate from the patient not only simplifies the process of healing which becomes an action of removing a given contagious agent from the body, leaving it as healthy as before. It is also a source of many cultural fabulations in which a doctor or a scientist, often working for a governmental agency, acquires new capabilities of mastering and weaponizing the agent after removing it entirely or temporarily from the diseased body.

The Rain, a three-season Danish series (2018-2020) produced by Netflix, is a case in point, albeit here it is a carrier himself who learns how to manipulate a pathogen that is causing his disease. The action begins rather typically with a prologue when a virus that is carried by a heavy rainfall wipes out almost all humans in a part of Scandinavia which will subsequently be contained by a perimeter watched over by military forces. Six years later, when the virus has also already mutated to become deadly for plants and animals, the siblings Simone and Rasmus who take shelter in a bunker start to search for their father who, as a scientist and microbiologist himself, may provide a cure. As it progressively turns out, Rasmus is a carrier of the original virus with which his father experimented to cure Rasmus's genetic disease. In the second and third season of *The Rain*, Rasmus learns how to extract the virus from his body and use it as a handy weapon against scattered groups of survivors. To demonstrate that the virus is a separate entity, it is made visible as marking Rasmus's body by swelling and bulging veins before leaving it as a black swarm, ready to execute its master command, and then to return. An important development in this is that Rasmus increasingly enjoys the power over the life and death of others, in a sense becoming one with the virus – as the Virus. Though by the end of the third season, he is killed by an extract from a specific flower which also rids the world of the deadly virus, *The Rain* leaves no doubt that it was a proper punishment for Rasmus's transgression of the ontological line between the normal and the pathological; the line which is still fundamental for the biopolitical regime as all three figures identified by Povinelli demonstrate.

Before looking closely at Chuck Hogan's *The Blood Artists* (1998), I have referred to this Netflix series because the figure of Rasmus as the Virus provides a useful background on which better to see how differently a figure of viral-human hybrid functions in Hogan's novel. On the face of it, *The Blood Artists* still reads as an average medical thriller in which events unfold in 2016, a year that was still a near future for the reader at the moment of publication. However, the author skillfully makes use of the well-known detective narrative convention on which modern epistemological discourse is premised (cf. Wald 2008, 157-212) to subvert not only the ontological difference between the normal and the pathological but also between culture/civilization and nature/the Earth. Dr. Maryk from Centers for Disease Control (CDC) in Atlanta, one of the main characters, offers the reader a telling metaphor of what is at stake in the novel:

> We [humans] are a fungus spreading over this planet, colonizing, warring, consuming. The Earth is a cell we are infecting. And nature is the Earth's immune system, just now sensing the threat of our encroachment, and arming itself to fight back. Macro versus micro. Viruses are the Earth's white blood cells. We are the Earth's disease. (Hogan 2009, 181)

Dr. Maryk's words demonstrate that the plot aims at showing vital relations between humans and their environments in a perspective which today may rightly be named planetary (cf. Mann/Wainwright 2018; Chakrabarty 2021). Nevertheless, the action starts to unfold here in a way rather typical of outbreak narratives, that is with a prologue set several years earlier in a small village in Central Africa, near a Congolese wild nature reserve. After an outbreak of an unknown zoonotic retrovirus has been discovered there, the village is ruthlessly bombed out by the US army to prevent the pathogen from spreading. The virus turns out to be deadly not only for humans, but also for all living organisms. What is important, it attacks brain cells, causing permanent personality changes in those who have happened to survive. The specific feature of the virus makes a difference because it causes a pandemic situation different to that in *The Rain*: it induces/causes no longer a battle between the organism and the foreign agent but rather an internal struggle between opposing forces – a narrative element which Wald overlooks in her reading (2008, 257-259). This becomes more and more evident when two years later, there is a new outbreak in the American provincial town of Plainville that gives the virus its name. Thus, the plot is reminiscent of Wolfgang Petersen's *Outbreak* (1995), well-known at the time when the novel was published. Yet, Hogan introduces some changes in the outbreak narrative, which are significant in the context of my argument. Among others, the narrator presents all events in a chronological, linear order. The reader thus comes to know the Patient Zero who has brought the virus to Plainville before being identified by Dr. Maryk and his colleague, Dr. Pearse, both in charge of an epidemiological research program. In this way, the reader can direct all her attention at what constitutes the Patient Zero – a human-viral hybrid as a kind of onto-epistemological scandal which subverts all fundamental binaries: between life and nonlife, substance and process, nature and culture. On those binaries both the outbreak narrative and neo-liberal biopolitics are premised.

In Hogan's novel, the Patient Zero had once been a US-American botanist who carried out his research on an endangered plant species not far from the outbreak location in Central Africa. By chance the botanist met a woman who survived the bombing of the village and in whose body the virus fought an undecided battle with an immuno-serological injection which she had received secretly from Dr. Pearse shortly before fleeing the village. The Patient Zero has not only become a new place of this undecided battle, he also started to experiment with the virus after returning to the US to come up with a mutated version, deadly only for humans. His intention in this was to get rid of the master species in order to effectively slow down the pending ecological catastrophe. The concept of human-viral hybrid forms the core of the novel, which is additionally emphasized by the author's decision to duplicate the phenomenon. It is Dr. Pearse who becomes the second hybrid after being intentionally infected by the Patient Zero who seeks easy access to the CDC bank of all known pathological agents deadly to humans to accelerate a general collapse of civilization as the only efficient means of saving the damaged planet. This time, however, in the form of the first-person narrative, Hogan allows the reader to follow step by step, the process of reaching the dynamic balance between the human and the virus up until the moment of a confrontation of both hybrids – the botanist and Dr. Pearse. Nevertheless, this confrontation does not bring an end to the story as is the case in *The Rain*. In *The Blood Artists* the human-viral hybrid is something more than only an epidemiological singularity. It also functions as a way to reveal a biopolitical mechanism on which the modern epidemiology is premised.

It is not without reason that among the mottoes which open Hogan's novel, there is an anonymous poem of which I would like to quote a fragment:

> A virus does not want to kill.
> It does not even want to harm.
> It wants to change.
> It wants that part of it that is missing.
> It wants to become. (Hogan 2009, 4)

The poem clearly shows that viruses by definition are neither external entities nor human enemies. We are – at least partly – to blame for their becoming dangerous. The Iranian writer and philosopher Fahim Amir explains:

> The connections, similarities, and relationships between our bodies and those of animals are the hinges that open the door to the viral will to reproduce – accelerated by the infrastructures of the world economy and amplified by social inequalities like those in nutrition, healthcare, and housing. (Amir 2021, 162)

To demonstrate this, Hogan's novel introduces yet another human-viral hybrid in a way which links with the prologue in which Dr. Pearse decided to save the life of the aforementioned seemingly healthy African girl. This time it is Dr. Maryk who has to make such a choice. Unlike Dr. Pearse, he did not hesitate from eliminating every possible threat to public health. This time, however, he makes up his mind to save a Plainville epidemic survivor who has been infected anew by the Patient Zero. To save both her life and public health, Dr. Maryk relocates her to a small island to live alone in a wild nature reserve. Thus, it seems that all recent events have convinced him that it is not viruses but rather humans who pose a real threat to the human species. Significantly, Dr. Maryk's decision also demonstrates that against his hope to find a cure it will not be an easy task because after infecting the body the virus becomes one with it.

Yet another point on which the novel's plot is premised should be underlined here. It is not a cutting-edge medical technology that helps fight the Plainville virus in *The Blood Artists*, rather Dr. Maryk himself is a kind of natural wonder. He not only has two hearts but also his blood cells are capable of quickly eliminating every kind of infection. In my reading of the novel, it is therefore the best evidence that the author intended to subvert the fundamental division between culture and nature with only a little help from experimental technology, which allows an effective use of what nature provides. This is worth remembering, because in the *Rifters* trilogy the situation radically changes – the protagonist is rather a specific form of cyborg-viral hybrid which makes the workings of neo-liberal biopolitics more visible.

ANOTHER "TYPHOID MARY"

To shed light on the historical moment when the outbreak narrative in its scientific incarnation was born at the outset of the 20th century, Priscilla Wald in her book *Contagious* critically reads the case of the first known "chronic typhoid germ distributor" (2008, 68). The epidemiological investigation that resulted in the 'discovery' of this person also resulted in various narratives of detection – the basis for what Wald named the outbreak narrative in her book. An Irish immigrant, Mary Mallon, worked as a cook in a summer house on Long Island, and was identified as a "healthy carrier" (ibid., 70) during a typhoid outbreak in 1909. Identifying her was truly a task for a detective, because Mallon was neither displaying any symptoms nor, once identified, did she show willingness to submit to be tested for evidence of the typhoid bacillus. A certain Dr. Soper, an engineer in the U.S. Army Sanitary Corps, had not only located Mallon as the source of infection, but also documented his epidemiological investigations as a narrative of detection which "explained how epidemiological investigation worked, as well as why it was so important. It transformed the thread of Mary Mallon, the healthy carrier, into 'Typhoid Mary,' the symbol of epidemiological efficacy" (Wald 2008, 70). As a result and thanks to the narrative skills of Dr. Soper, Mallon became the infamous "Typhoid Mary" (ibid.), the most invoked – nearly iconic – example of a dangerous carrier of communicable diseases in the history of modern medicine.

A century later, as I have already demonstrated through the example of Hogan's *The Blood Artists*, the figure of an apparently healthy person which could nevertheless transmit a communicable disease returned in a specific variation of a human-viral hybrid in order to challenge both the already established outbreak narrative in cultural (re)presentations and the epidemiological efficacy discourse as a form of neo-liberal biopolitics. My next example, however, does not concentrate on a dynamic coexistence of human and viral entities/features in one hybrid organism. Depicting a healthy carrier as a protagonist who intentionally spreads deadly disease as a form of personal vengeance, Peter Watts's trilogy *Rifters* (1999-2005) focuses rather on what is performed/recognized as human/normal and contagious/pathological in a future world which seems to be born out of Donna Haraway's *A Cyborg Manifesto*, first published in the mid-1980s. Indeed, to read Watts's trilogy in the context of Haraway's essay, which the author called "an ironic political myth" (2016, 6), highlights a neo-liberal entanglement of the trilogy's action that otherwise could have remained unnoticed because of its visible SF features. However, in Watts's version of the myth the outbreak narrative plays an important action-structuring part and a protagonist has been bioengineered prior to becoming infected and thus offering a model-example of a human-machine-viral hybrid in contradistinction to the protagonists of Hogan's novel.

Although a cyborg is often identified as a cybernetic organism, a hybrid of machine and organism, these defining features do not exhaust its basic characteristics. For Haraway stresses that it is also a creature of social reality – lived social relations as a political construction – as well as a creature of fiction which maps our social and bodily reality at the historical moment of the late 20th century. In other words, in *A Cyborg Manifesto* the cyborg through the very fact of its existence transgresses the border between the natural and the artificial, mind and body, self-developing and externally designed. Therefore, Haraway argues: "The cyborg is a matter of fiction and lived experience that changes what counts as women's experience in the late twentieth century" (2016, 6). In a sense, Watts's protagonist of Lenie Clarke does exactly this – she is "a woman turned amphibious by some abstract convergence of technology and economics" (2002, 5). She has to live through an epidemiological scenario in which the role of "Typhoid Mary" was designed for her to play in order not only to deconstruct the outbreak narrative but also to reveal both social relations and psychological/behavioural conditioning as an intended political construction.

Lenie Clarke is one of the workers who run a generating station three kilometers below the surface of the Pacific, close to the Juan de Fuca Ridge. A huge international corporation has developed a facility here to exploit geothermal power. To survive and work on the ocean floor near a hydrothermal vent, various castaways from society were recruited as the crew; those whose histories have preadapted them to dangerous environments, who have got used to broken bodies and chronic stress. Lenie Clarke herself is presented as a childhood abuse survivor, almost addicted to her trauma. The workers have also been bioengineered to withstand the immense pressure in the depths of the ocean, swim in seawater and breathe it. The cutting-edge technology was used to alter them physically by such implants as, for instance, a plastic and metal hydraulic machine in their lungs which can take in water and corneal caps. They were also enhanced on the psychic-behavioural level, by tweaking their genes and neurochemistry, for instance, by induction of genes from a deep-water fish which function as neuroinhibitors whenever they are outside the station. Lenie Clarke aptly sums up all these alternations saying that the crew-people "tended larger machines, stealing power from deep within the earth in the name of supply and demand" (Watts 2002, 17). In the same name of capitalist supply and demand, in which huge international corporations and national states of the future world colonialize deep-oceans in Watts's trilogy, their Western predecessors aimed at terraforming other continents, destroying their ecosystems and unleashing – recently, mostly zoonotic – epidemics. That is why, the events in *Starfish* (1999), the first instalment of Watts's trilogy, develop similarly to the events in the prologue to Hogan's *The Blood Artists*, albeit on a much greater scale. Since after the corporation has discovered that the underwater power station could be contaminated by a contagious agent from one of the hydrothermal vents, the station is bombed out. Then Pacific Rim, inhabited mostly by ecological and economic refugees, is firestormed, which took millions of lives in collateral damage. These measures seem to be somehow understandable since the human civilization has to face a mighty enemy – deadly not only for all living organisms, but capable of reverse-engineering the whole biosphere.

As one of the characters in Watts's novel explains, the contagious agent in question is a pyranosal RNA: "A precursor to modern nucleic acids, pretty widespread about three and a half billion years ago. (...) it would've made a perfectly acceptable genetic template on its own; faster replication than DNA, fewer replication error" (1999, 258). Although strictly speaking it is not a pathogen but rather a kind of soil nanobacterium, it behaves in a competitive way like a virus, seeking to change the life on Earth into its beta version premised on an alternative genetic template. That is why Watts calls it 'βehemoth'. To further complicate the action and stay true to his idea of extrapolating social reality of the outset of our century, the *Rifters* trilogy introduces another actor in the already complex interplay of interests which Hogan neatly avoided in *The Blood Artists*, namely an Internet of the future increasingly pestered by viral infections. To counteract it smart gels, made out of real neurons, are implemented at critical nodes. While fighting viruses on the net, smart gels learn to make a fundamental choice between the simple (files) and the complex (viruses) that unbeknownst to their human masters bias them against everything that is complex. Therefore, when asked to make an objective choice for all humankind between biosphere and βehemoth, smart gels prefer the latter. That is why they help Lenie Clarke not only to escape from the power station before it is bombed out and reach the coast but also to traverse the American continent and to come back home almost untroubled by police and secret agents. Seeking her private vengeance, she also carries βehemoth around with her to punish the world in the name of all social, racial and ethnic castaways and underdogs. Thus, on the one hand, Lenie Clarke becomes a symbolic figure, an incarnation of a revolt against economic and social injustice and for a better world. On the other, she is wanted by governmental health agencies as a materialization of what Povinelli (2020) called the Virus and the Terrorist at the same time. The author of the *Rifters* trilogy, however, knows how to unfold the events to demonstrate that the real threat is not so much βehemoth but rather the contemporary neo-liberal global division, distribution and circulation of power, wealth and health.

Called the Mermaid of the Apocalypse or the Meltdown Madonna, Lenie Clarke quickly becomes an Internet meme and a new incarnation of a female mythical figure who carries the plague around with her. By the end of the second trilogy novel, *Maelstrom*, she asks however: "You kill me for playing Typhoid Mary?" (Watts 2001, 334). There is a reason why she speaks about "playing Typhoid Mary" as both the well-known pathogen carrier and the very symbol of epidemiological efficacy: While checking her health now and again to prove that she really carries βehemoth in her blood, spreading around the disease, Lenie Clarke discovers that she has been not only bioengineered but also surgically, genetically and chemically altered. Furthermore, her entire personality has been changed by Induced False Memory Syndrome. For it was much easier and quicker to engineer a highly specialized expert than to adapt a social castaway to carry out complicated tasks. It is not only Lenie Clarke's childhood abuse trauma that turns out to be fake. Effectively, the same can be said about her vengeance. Indeed, she only played the character of Typhoid Mary, in bad faith following in her footsteps and performing the well-known scenario of the outbreak narrative.

In the third instalment of the *Rifters* trilogy, published in two volumes for commercial reasons, βehemoth is finally contained by a counter-nanobacterium and, therefore, humanity is saved, at least for a moment. Nevertheless, at this juncture even more questions about a real course of the pandemic crop out: Was Lenie Clarke really the Patient Zero who brought βehemoth ashore in her blood? Has someone engineered the original bacterium to make it more resilient and contagious? Were repeated firestorms an effective means to fight off the contagion or rather a way of diminishing the number of refugees and paupers and explaining it away as collateral damage? Those and many other questions undermine not only the figure of Typhoid Mary but also the outbreak narrative as a narrative of detection. By letting Lenie Clarke play a model epidemiological character, Watts created his own version of Haraway's ironic political myth of cyborg as "the illegitimate offspring of militarism and patriarchal capitalism" (2016, 9). By making use of the original story of modern epidemiology, he denunciated not only militarism and patriarchal capitalism but also the two main regimes – biopolitics and geontopolitics – on which they are premised.

CODA

I started my article with Jean-Luc Nancy's supposition that the Covid-19 pandemic has not so much spotlighted but rather revealed the precarious foundations of the Western developed and progressive societies. This resulted, among others, in laying bare the mechanism of the biopolitical regime premised on the divide between life and death, the normal and the pathological body. In support of his argument that today's diseases, contagions included, are symptoms of far deeper crises, I have drawn on the example of a few recently published Corona Fictions in which viral and bacterial infections are depicted as one of many, tightly entangled factors, mostly of anthropogenic nature. Significantly, scientists and physicians who very often played the primary role of heroic agents in the unfolding outbreak drama of pandemic fictions have been replaced here by other protagonists, who are similarly helpless when facing pending disasters. From this perspective, I sought to answer the question about possible causes of such a distinct change by closely reading speculative fabulations from the turn of this century. Both revisit and morph the outbreak narrative and its protagonists of the epidemiologist-detective and the Patient Zero, introducing a new type of protagonist which I call the human-viral hybrid. When analyzed in the context of two paradigmatic neo-liberal figures of the past decades – the Virus and the Cyborg – the hybrid protagonists of Hogan's *The Blood Artists* and Watts's *Rifters* trilogy reveal the workings of biopower and geontopower, making way for a vital understanding of the Covid-19 pandemic and its fictional counterpart as not only a contagion but also yet another form of structural violence inherent in the late liberalism.

BIBLIOGRAPHY

Corpus Analyzed

Aristide, Oana (2021) *Under the Blue*, London, Serpent's Tail.
Clo, Valérie (2022) *Gaïa*, Paris, Buchet Chastel.
Connan, Tom (2022) *Pollution*, Paris, Albin Michel.
Hogan, Chuck (2009 [1998]) *The Blood Artists*, New York, NY, Harper.
Kainz, Kenneth/Arthy, Natasha (dir.) (2018-20) *The Rain* (TV series), Denmark, Miso Film/Netflix.
Watts, Peter (1999) *Starfish*, New York, NY, Tor Books.
Watts, Peter (2001) *Maelstrom*, New York, NY, Tor Books.
Watts, Peter (2004) *βehemoth: β-Max*, New York, NY, Tor Books.
Watts, Peter (2005) *βehemoth: Seppuku*, New York, NY, Tor Books.

Works Cited

Amir, Fahim (2021) "A Touch Too Much: Animals of the Pandemic", trans. by Geoffrey C. Howes. Ekaterina Degot/David Riff (eds.) *There Is No Society? Individuals and Community in Pandemic Times*, Hamburg, Verlag der Buchhandlung Walther und Franz König, 157-172.
Caduff, Carlo (2015) *The Pandemic Perhaps: Dramatic Events in a Public Culture of Danger*, Oakland, CA, University of California Press.
Chakrabarty, Dipesh (2021) *The Climate of History in a Planetary Age*, Chicago, IL, University of Chicago Press.
Cook, Robin (1995) *Contagion*, New York, NY, G.P. Putnam's Sons.

Cook, Robin (2019) *Pandemic. A Novel*, New York, NY, G.P. Puntman's Sons.

Haraway, Donna J. (2016 [1985]) "A Cyborg Manifesto: Science, Technology, and Socialist-Feminism in the Late Twentieth Century", *Manifestly Haraway*, Minneapolis/London, Minnesota University Press, 3-90.

Mann, Geoff/Joel Wainwright (2018) *Climate Leviathan: A Political Theory of Our Planetary Future*, London, Verso.

Nancy, Jean-Luc (2022) *An All-Too-Human Virus*, trans. by Cory Stockwell/Sarah Clift/David Fernbach, Cambridge, Polity Press.

Petersen, Wolfgang (dir.) (1995) *Outbreak*, USA, Punch Productions.

Povinelli, Elizabeth A. (2016) *Geontologies: A Requiem to Late Liberalism*, Durham, NC, Duke University Press.

Povinelli, Elizabeth A. (2020) "The Virus: Figure and Infrastructure", *E-Flux*, 2020-11, https://www.e-flux.com/architecture/sick-architecture/352870/the-virus-figure-and-infrastructure/, 2022-09-13.

Preston, Richard (1994) *The Hot Zone. A Terrifying True Story*, New York, NY, Random House.

Preston, Richard (1997) *The Cobra Event. A Novel*, New York, NY, Random House.

Preston, Richard (2002) *The Demon in the Freezer. A True Story*, New York, NY, Random House.

Preston, Richard (2019) *Crisis in the Red Zone: The Story of the Deadliest Ebola Outbreak in History, and of the Viruses to Come*, New York, NY, Random House.

Quammen, David (2012) *Spillover: Animal Infections and the Next Human Pandemic*, New York/London, W.W. Norton & Company.

Wald, Priscilla (2008) *Contagious: Cultures, Carriers, and the Outbreak Narrative*, Durham, NC, Duke University Press.

Protagonisti in cerca di una nuova *agency*: la pandemia di Covid-19 nella letteratura italiana

Tommaso Meozzi (University of Graz)

Abstract
Through the concept of 'agency', the article analyzes three works published in Italy at the beginning of 2020 which focus on the psychological and social consequences of the Covid-19 pandemic – *Come il mare in un bicchiere* by Chiara Gamberale, the anthology *Andrà tutto bene*, and *Nel contagio* by Paolo Giordano –, highlighting the strategies through which the protagonists try, despite the crisis, to maintain a coherent narrative of themselves that integrates past, present and future.

The following aspects are analyzed in particular: the temporal structure of the narratives, the dialectic between autobiography and references to the dystopian genre, the recovery of a shared symbolic plane and the use of metaphors expressing collective agency.

STRUMENTI TEORICI: SUL CONCETTO DI AGENCY

L'articolo analizza tre opere narrative che hanno al centro le conseguenze psicologiche e sociali del virus Covid-19, uscite in Italia nel 2020, nel momento in cui l'epidemia iniziava a rivelare la sua dimensione pandemica e la popolazione italiana si trovava ad affrontare il primo *lockdown*: si tratta del romanzo *Come il mare in un bicchiere*, di Chiara Gamberale, dell'antologia *Andrà tutto bene*, promossa dal gruppo editoriale GeMS, e del diario-saggio di Paolo Giordano *Nel contagio*.

Come strumento teorico si utilizzerà il concetto di *agency*, particolarmente appropriato per indagare sia i meccanismi di elaborazione di senso messi in atto di fronte alla crisi, che la loro rappresentazione letteraria. Si tratta infatti di un concetto che, pur essendo nato in ambito sociologico, sottolinea l'importanza dell'identità narrativa, vale a dire delle strategie messe in atto dal soggetto per creare una narrazione coerente di sé che unisca le dimensioni del passato, del presente e del futuro.[1] Lontano dal rappresentare una minaccia solo per il corpo o per la psiche di individui fragili, il Covid-19 ha infatti attaccato l'essere umano in quanto produttore di senso,[2] protagonista della propria vita, costringendo ognuno, in modo diverso, a riorientarsi.

Nel loro articolo *What is agency?*, Mustafa Emirbayer e Ann Mische (1998) evidenziano come siano proprio i momenti di crisi – «*emergent events*» (Emirbayer/Mische 1998, 968) – a rendere l'individuo conscio della dimensione temporale, spingendolo a costruire, al di là della *routine*, una nuova narrazione di sé. Al tempo stesso, tuttavia, i due autori non appiattiscono l'*agency* nel suo aspetto proiettivo, rivolto verso il futuro, ma sottolineano come la *routine* stessa comporti un certo sforzo cosciente, e come l'elemento iterativo – «*The iterational element*» (ibid., 971) – dell'*agency*, la riproposizione selettiva di schemi d'azione attinti dal passato, giochi un ruolo importante nel consolidare l'identità e le pratiche di interazione sociale.

Questa concezione complessa dell'*agency* è, nel caso dei cambiamenti sociali indotti dal Covid-19, particolarmente interessante: interrompendo le nostre abitudini e prospettando un futuro incerto, il virus apre la possibilità di nuove rifunzionalizzazioni proiettive dell'esperienza passata. Al tempo stesso, tuttavia, i testi presi in esame hanno al centro il primo *lockdown*,[3] che ha costretto la maggior parte degli individui ad interrompere i propri progetti, facendo i conti con un forzato isolamento sociale e con una limitazione spaziale in cui la *routine*,

---

1 Per quanto riguarda il concetto di *narrative identity*, consultare ad esempio McAdams (2019): «Narrative identities reconstruct the autobiographical past and anticipate the imagined future to provide the self with temporal coherence and some semblance of psychosocial unity and purpose [Le identità narrative ricostruiscono il passato autobiografico e anticipano il futuro immaginato, fornendo all'individuo una coerenza temporale e una certa unità psicosociale e di intenti]» (2; traduzione dell'autore).

2 A questo proposito, Salvadori (2021, 153) parla di una «carenza a livello narrativo-discorsivo, nel senso che l'individuo non ha saputo elaborare e rendere dicibile il trauma, dal momento che il Covid-19 'non si lascia ricondurre a niente di già noto se non per una approssimazione difettosa' (Ronchi 2020)».

3 Il Research Group *Pandemic Fictions* (cf. 2020, 332) ha sottolineato come il *lockdown* costituisca spesso il centro della prima produzione culturale relativa al Covid-19.

l'autodisciplina, hanno giocato un ruolo da non sottovalutare nella preservazione del benessere psicofisico.

La difficoltà di rinunciare all'aspetto proiettivo dell'*agency* emerge con ancora più evidenza se si allarga l'analisi dalla dimensione individuale a quella epocale, e si considera come la società industriale sia caratterizzata dal deciso orientamento verso una razionalità progettuale, sempre alla ricerca dei giusti mezzi per raggiungere nuovi fini (cf. ibid., 985).

L'interruzione della progettualità porta dunque a mettere in discussione anche uno stile di vita improntato alla produttività. Resta il fatto che, dal punto di vista dell'*agency*, l'individuo, qualunque siano gli influssi culturali a cui è sottoposto, è costantemente necessitato, come afferma Dan P. McAdams riprendendo le riflessioni di Marya Schechtman, ad essere protagonista, cioè a sentire di avere un certo controllo sul senso della propria vita (cf. McAdams 2019, 6-7). I testi che prenderemo in esame offrono uno spaccato significativo dei modi in cui i personaggi, nel mezzo di una crisi sconosciuta, di enormi proporzioni, tentano di restare protagonisti, senza rinunciare ad una costruzione di senso.

Confermando la tendenza messa in rilievo dal Research Group *Pandemic Fictions* (2020, 328), l'*agency* si realizza, nelle opere analizzate, attraverso costanti elementi autobiografici. Questa scelta rappresenta il tentativo estremo di restare ancorati ad un'elaborazione razionale della realtà di fronte ad un evento sconvolgente, che apre un vuoto nell'immaginario di proporzioni troppo ampie per essere facilmente metabolizzato. A questo proposito è interessante la sensazione, espressa da molti personaggi, di vivere non nella realtà, ma dentro un film o un romanzo catastrofico. Più volte viene menzionato esplicitamente il genere della distopia: la descrizione immaginaria del peggior mondo possibile. La distopia, genere non estraneo al *mainstream*, mette tra parentesi la realtà consueta, seducendo il lettore o lo spettatore attraverso una complessa combinazione di principio di vita e principio di morte (cf. Meozzi 2017, 117).[4] Tuttavia, nel momento in cui il Covid-19 porta ad un'improvvisa implosione della distanza tra realtà e distopia, quest'ultima tende a perdere il suo aspetto ludico, lasciando il posto ad un'esigenza di realismo. Sarà interessante valutare, nei prossimi anni, se sia riconoscibile, nella produzione letteraria con al centro il Covid-19, un progressivo passaggio dall'autobiografia alla *fiction*, nel caso in cui la situazione pandemica si stabilizzi su un minor livello di allerta.

---

4 Una simile prospettiva è sviluppata anche da Giungato (2020, 107): «[L]a distruzione, dovuta alla guerra o alla pestilenza, conduce all'ineluttabile e catastrofica rottura di tutti i patti sociali, come se l'eccesso di paura conducesse fatalisticamente alla riscrittura in senso regressivo dei legami fra gli individui».

L'esigenza di realismo e il conseguente sviluppo di narrazioni con forte matrice autobiografica apre tuttavia un ulteriore problema, che a sua volta si collega al concetto di *agency*. L'isolamento sociale causato dal *lockdown* provoca infatti al tempo stesso nei personaggi un'idiosincrasia verso la forma autobiografica, che deve confrontarsi con una quotidianità povera di eventi e contatti sociali. Per riuscire, nonostante ciò, a dare voce all'esigenza di realismo a cui si è accennato, la narrazione autobiografica esplora allora un ulteriore aspetto dell'*agency*, che anche Emirbayer e Mische, riprendendo la riflessione di George Herbert Mead, non mancano di sottolineare, quello della proiezione non tanto nel tempo, ma negli altri (cf. Emirbayer/Mische 1998, 988).

La narrazione della propria quotidianità durante il *lockdown* diventa così spesso immaginazione della quotidianità degli altri che, proprio nel momento della loro assenza fisica, si fanno emotivamente presenti.[5] Questo aspetto si ricollega alla già citata interruzione della progettualità produttiva, che lascia il tempo per un recupero della memoria emotiva. Si attua così una ricomposizione simbolica[6] che tenta, nonostante l'isolamento degli individui o dei nuclei familiari, di ricostruire, nella crisi, una solidarietà di base.

LA SUDDIVISIONE TEMPORALE DELLE NARRAZIONI: UN'ANALISI COMPARATA

L'antologia *Andrà tutto bene* offre, in relazione al concetto di *agency* e alle sue realizzazioni narrative, un oggetto di studio estremamente interessante, perché consente di operare un confronto qualitativo tra le strategie adottate da ventisei scrittori a cui il gruppo editoriale GeMS ha chiesto di raccontare il Covid-19.

Un primo elemento che unisce molti dei racconti, evidente da un punto di vista formale, è la difficoltà e al tempo stesso la necessità che gli autori hanno di suddividere la narrazione in paragrafi secondo diverse scansioni temporali. La ricorsività di questo dato strutturale, che non è stato concordato in sede editoriale,

---

5 Il recupero, a livello emotivo, degli 'altri' durante il *lockdown*, è stato sottolineato da Ronchi (2020): «In realtà il distanziamento personale, invece di spegnerlo, ha rafforzato il senso di prossimità, ce ne ha fatto sentire l'urgenza proprio sospendendolo per ragioni di forza maggiore».

6 A proposito della capacità dell'individuo di proiettare se stesso, a livello immaginario, in un ventaglio diversificato di prospettive, Emirbayer e Mische (1998, 989) parlano di «*Symbolic recomposition*».

testimonia come l'orientamento temporale costituisca un problema e una risorsa centrale nel quadro della minaccia pandemica e del *lockdown*.

Ritanna Armeni suddivide il racconto *Un'ora dopo l'altra* in paragrafi indicanti l'ora, che si succedono in ordine cronologico e che coprono una giornata, dal risveglio alla mezzanotte, ora in cui la protagonista si corica. Nonostante gli evidenti richiami autobiografici alla propria attività di scrittrice – «Le hanno chiesto un bel po' di video. Appelli alla lettura, presentazioni online del suo ultimo libro» (Armeni 2020, 17) –, il racconto procede alla terza persona, rispecchiando un'*agency* che, nell'incertezza del futuro, si concentra sul presente, realizzando un'autodisciplina che ha lo scopo principale di non cedere alla disperazione. Il soggetto dell'*agency* diventa così, al tempo stesso, oggetto insensibile, che tenta di anestetizzare la propria naturale spinta proiettiva – l'uso della terza persona esprime chiaramente questo distanziamento –: «non è necessario essere mattiniera al tempo del Coronavirus. Ma vuole che tutto, o almeno quello che è possibile, rimanga come prima» (ibid., 13). Solo nel momento in cui la protagonista entra in contatto con i propri affetti familiari, la voce narrante scivola senza soluzione di continuità alla prima persona: «Eccoli i miei nipoti sullo schermo del computer» (ibid., 18). Tuttavia, al termine della giornata, quando l'autodisciplina si allenta, si intensifica la spinta proiettiva verso un futuro incerto, che si manifesta sotto forma di ansia: «tornano le domande inevitabili: quanto durerà? Resisterò? Resisteremo?» (ibid., 24).

Gianni Biondillo, in *Attraversare il buio*, sceglie invece di interporre allo scorrere cronologicamente lineare della narrazione una temporalità diversa, dal valore simbolico: «*Questa è la storia di un uomo che cade da un palazzo di cinquanta piani*» (Biondillo 2020, 65). La frase, una citazione dalla scena iniziale del film *La Haine* (1995) di Mathieu Kassovitz, viene riportata in corsivo, e i suoi sviluppi, sempre in corsivo, intervengono a sottolineare i momenti salienti della narrazione stessa. Attraverso questa sovrapposizione, adottando una prospettiva per certi versi complementare a quella di Armeni, Biondillo vuole evidenziare i rischi di un'*agency* concentrata esclusivamente sul presente – «Mantieni le abitudini, gli orari, le scadenze» (ibid., 65) –, miope di fronte al fatto che «Stiamo cadendo, tutti» (ibid., 70) e che, riprendendo le parole del film di Kassovitz, «*Il problema non è la caduta, ma l'atterraggio*» (ibid., 74). La difficoltà di elaborare individualmente un evento di proporzioni globali, non ancora codificato socialmente, si esprime attraverso lo sviluppo della narrazione lineare che inizia da un dato personale, ovvero la data del compleanno – «a ogni storia occorre dare un inizio: è il 3 febbraio, insomma, ed è il mio compleanno» (ibid., 65) –, per lasciar convergere solo gradualmente gli eventi della propria quotidianità e l'evolversi della pandemia: «È domenica 8 marzo. Ho tre donne in casa, niente mimose, per nessuna» (ibid., 71); «Poi alla sera del 14 marzo giunge la notizia che hanno ricoverato Claudio. Questa volta non è un anello del pallottoliere, non è un numero in una statistica» (ibid., 77).[7] L'iniziale scetticismo del protagonista di fronte all'allerta generale – «Faccio pure una fotografia al piatto di trippa alla fiamma e la metto su Instagram. Scrivo: 'Coronavirus, io me te magno!'. Probabilmente credo di essere simpatico» (ibid., 77) – matura così nella consapevolezza che, nella minaccia pandemica, ognuno è chiamato ad assumersi una parte di responsabilità: «Stiamo precipitando, tutti, ma ognuno cuce un pezzo di paracadute. Chi lo dice che ci sfracelleremo al suolo?» (ibid., 82).

Anna Dalton, in *Ore 18.00*, suddivide la narrazione in paragrafi dallo stesso titolo, *Ore 18.00*, che, isolando nel fluire temporale un particolare momento della giornata, consentono alla protagonista di analizzare comparativamente l'evolversi della propria condizione psichica durante il *lockdown*. L'aspetto più interessante del racconto di Dalton è la registrazione di una continua oscillazione dell'*agency* che, nella crisi pandemica, fatica a consolidarsi: così, in un primo momento, la protagonista partecipa all'evento musicale a cui un improvvisato dj ha dato vita sul proprio balcone (cf. Dalton 2020, 151); in seguito si sente sdegnata di fronte al facile populismo che sembra non voler affrontare la gravità della situazione: «Sto in cucina come una tigre in gabbia in attesa di potermi sdegnare all'arrivo dell'inno d'Italia» (ibid., 153); si passa poi all'autoconsapevolezza di un'*agency* che oscilla compulsivamente tra il completo assorbimento nel presente e l'angoscia per il futuro:

> Sto cercando di tracciare un grafico del mio umore [...]. Non varia solo di giorno in giorno, ma di ora in ora, a volte di minuto in minuto. Magari faccio qualcosa che assorbe totalmente la mia attenzione, tipo un puzzle, e solo dopo un bel po', guardando le notizie online, ricado con un tonfo nella realtà. (ibid., 155)

In questa condizione, anche la partecipazione ai riti collettivi più populistici diventa un modo per non sentirsi soli e vincere la depressione: «Tre giorni deprimenti di fila non sono accettabili [...]. Appena parte l'inno d'Italia comincio a cantare con tutta la voce che ho» (ibid., 156).

---

7   Giungato (2020, 104) nota come la continua ripetizione delle statistiche sulla pandemia nei *mass media*, anziché evidenziare la gravità del problema, possa contribuire alla sua rimozione: «[S]i è tendenzialmente assistito ad una dinamica generale di *rimozione* delle immagini dei corpi fisici delle vittime in favore di una sorta di sublimazione numerica».

Citiamo infine il racconto di Alessia Gazzola, *My Sweet Quarantine*, suddiviso in paragrafi i cui titoli indicano in ordine crescente il succedersi dei giorni di *lockdown* (*Giorno zero*, *Giorno quattro*, *Giorno cinque*), nel tentativo di mantenere l'orientamento temporale e psicologico. Tuttavia, nel momento in cui la condizione eccezionale diventa una nuova normalità, di cui nessuno può prevedere con certezza la fine, la progressione numerica lascia il posto prima al *Giorno X* e poi all'*Ennesimo giorno X*, indice di una frustrazione dalla quale i protagonisti, ricercatori italiani emigrati negli Stati Uniti, possono uscire solamente proiettando nel futuro un cambiamento radicale delle loro vite: «Io vorrei tornare in Italia» (Gazzola 2020, 229). Emerge così come l'appiattimento dell'*agency* nel presente sia sopportabile solo nel quadro di un periodo di tempo delimitato che comunque prospetta, alla fine, una nuova possibilità di futuro.

AUTOBIOGRAFIA E DISTOPIA

Nella condizione di isolamento sociale, l'autobiografia[8] diventa un modo per comunicare la propria esperienza ed affrontare collettivamente una crisi che, altrimenti, rischia di non trovare il dialogo e la condivisione simbolica necessari all'elaborazione.[9] In questa prospettiva l'*agency* della letteratura consiste nel creare una memoria collettiva e rinegoziare un piano simbolico condiviso (cf. Obermayr/Völkl 2022, 131).

---

8 Utilizziamo un concetto di autobiografia che non si basa sul riscontro della veridicità della narrazione rispetto a dati extratestuali, ma sull'intenzione dell'autore di stabilire con il lettore un preciso 'patto autobiografico'. «L'autobiographie étant un genre référentiel, elle est naturellement soumise en même temps à l'impératif de ressemblance au niveau du modèle, mais ce n'est qu'un aspect secondaire. Le fait que *nous* jugions que la ressemblance n'est pas obtenue est accessoire à partir du moment où nous sommes sûrs qu'elle a été visée. Ce qui importe, c'est moins la ressemblance de 'Rousseau à l'âge de seize ans', représenté dans le texte des *Confessions*, avec le Rousseau de 1728 'tel qu'il était', que le double effort de Rousseau vers 1764 pour *peindre*: 1) sa relation au passé; 2) ce passé tel qu'il était, avec l'intention de ne rien y changer» (Lejeune 1996 [1975], 40).

9 La difficoltà di elaborare, a livello individuale, la crisi pandemica, è così descritta da Ronchi (2020): «Restiamo attoniti, istupiditi, senza un discorso che sia capace di trasformare il colpo subito in un sapere comunicabile. Renderlo comunicabile vorrebbe dire padroneggiarlo, tenerlo a distanza e, in qualche modo, disporne».

Si tratta del resto di una crisi globale che, in modo diverso, influisce sulla vita di ognuno. Sono molte, nelle opere prese in esame, le riflessioni degli autori sulla scrittura stessa e in particolare sull'autobiografia. Scrive a questo proposito Chiara Gamberale, nel suo romanzo *Come il mare in un bicchiere*: «Ed è soprattutto per questo che sto scrivendo senza l'armatura di una storia dentro cui nascondermi. Perché magari qualcuno, proprio adesso, si sta facendo le mie stesse domande» (Gamberale 2020, 91-92).

Anche Paolo Giordano, in apertura del suo *Nel contagio*, riflette sulle ragioni della scrittura:

> Per tenere a bada i presagi, e per trovare un modo migliore di pensare tutto questo. A volte la scrittura riesce ad essere una zavorra per restare piantati a terra. Ma c'è anche un altro motivo: non voglio perdere ciò che l'epidemia ci sta svelando di noi stessi. (Giordano 2020, 5)

L'esigenza di «restare piantati a terra» risponde alla difficoltà di realizzare ciò che sta accadendo, e alla sensazione di vivere come in un romanzo o un film catastrofico.[10] Significativa, a questo proposito, la frequenza dei rimandi al genere della distopia. Federica Bosco, ad esempio, apre così il suo racconto: «Se c'è un genere di film che detesto, sono quelli che nel trailer recitano in un 'futuro distopico'» (Bosco 2020, 95). Tali film trasmettono infatti un'«ansia assoluta» (ibid.), troppo generalizzata per essere velocemente elaborata a livello cosciente: «Ne hai una percezione distaccata, incredula, come se stessi appunto guardando un film su un futuro distopico: non può succedere a te» (ibid., 97). Più si realizza la gravità della situazione, più torna il riferimento al filtro letterario, estremo meccanismo di difesa psicologico contro il dolore: «Non ci voglio vivere in questo futuro distopico» (ibid., 111). Uno stesso meccanismo di distanziazione psicologica attraverso il filtro della finzione è quello che apre il racconto di Marco Buticchi: «È come vivere i convulsi fotogrammi di quei film che non ho mai amato: terremoti, alluvioni, contagi. Forse le sequenze degli avvenimenti attuali ci paiono familiari proprio per quello» (Buticchi 2020, 121). Si tratta di un senso di familiarità perturbante, in cui è sempre latente la consapevolezza che non esiste un eroe protagonista pronto a sciogliere il nodo problematico: «Ma intanto si spera che il film finisca, che l'eroe protagonista trovi il rimedio» (ibid., 122). Attraverso la focalizzazione

---

10 Su questa sensazione si sofferma Salvadori (2021, 158): «Ma è soprattutto il rovesciamento del paradigma apocalittico a farsi preponderante: di un armageddon che nel passaggio dall'immaginazione alla realtà innesca in un vero e proprio trauma da inveramento».

interna del racconto, il personaggio autobiografico si fa protagonista non tanto risolvendo la crisi – come accadrebbe in una distopia a lieto fine –, ma piuttosto concentrando su di sé l'empatia del lettore e non rinunciando a mantenere quel minimo di *agency* che gli è concessa – convincere la figlia, che si trova a Londra, a rientrare a casa, cercare di non disperarsi e di dare coraggio alle persone care. In questa prospettiva la narrazione autobiografica consente una rinegoziazione dell'*agency*, fondata sulla presa di coscienza dei propri limiti e sulla progressiva ricostruzione di senso che non cede a una «nevrosi dell'anticipazione» (Giungato 2020, 109).

L'autobiografia si oppone dunque alla tendenza di derealizzazione che la crisi comporta, e che viene riempita da un immaginario sommariamente catastrofico o salvifico,[11] che non consente l'elaborazione cosciente. Scrive Silvia Truzzi nel racconto *Caro microbo, ti scrivo*, a proposito di un facile populismo: «uscire in strada con tanta altra gente, come alla fine di un film apocalittico (di quale spazzatura si nutre il nostro immaginario…). Non sarà così. Ritorneremo alla vita di sempre per gradi» (Truzzi 2020, 289). Paolo Giordano invece, nella sua ricerca di una scrittura che, come già accennato, si prefigge di «restare piantati a terra» (Giordano 2020, 5), incita a non rimuovere, attraverso teorie complottistiche da film di fantascienza, l'ansia per il futuro e il vuoto di senso: «La soluzione più semplice, quella che comporta meno dispendio di fantasia, è con ogni probabilità quella corretta. Sul laboratorio segreto, magari, faremo un film» (ibid., 54). La tendenza complottistica rappresenta, in questa prospettiva, un movimento opposto, di violenta proiezione simbolica, rispetto a quello di un'*agency* che, nella crisi, rinegozia progressivamente i rapporti sociali fino a raggiungere una nuova unità simbolica.

Tuttavia, la distopia è chiamata in causa non solo come filtro immaginario che impedisce l'elaborazione cosciente della pandemia, ma anche come sistema simbolico che, proprio distaccandosi dalla *mimesis*, evidenza il valore epifanico della pandemia stessa. Ciò può avvenire nel momento in cui si rinuncia a trovare una facile soluzione allo scenario distopico – protagonisti onnipotenti, o antagonisti che incarnano il male –, indagando piuttosto la complessa ridefinizione dei rapporti umani a cui la crisi costringe. Scrive a questo proposito Donato Carrisi nel

---

11 Il nesso tra narrazione apocalittica e immaginario salvifico è descritto efficacemente da Giungato (2020, 116): «Il Covid-19 diviene, così, il catalizzatore dell'ansia millenaristica per una società che piega la narrazione delle vicende che lo investono ad una narrazione apocalittica coerente, attribuendo all'umanità stessa la responsabilità del passaggio verso una prossima Città Celeste e assegnando alla scienza il ruolo di costruttore mitico».

suo racconto *Lettera sul futuro a due bambini*: «Per anni, durante le presentazioni, ho fatto un esempio al pubblico [...]. 'Se una cometa puntasse contro la Terra, cosa faremmo? [...]. Terremmo fede alla nostra indole o ci trasformeremmo approfittando dell'improvvisa anarchia?'» (Carrisi 2020, 144).

Messi di fronte ad una crisi della *routine*, gli individui sono chiamati a scegliere la propria etica comportamentale e dunque ad attuare, nel bene e nel male, le proprie potenzialità.[12] Maria Laakso (cf. 2020, 79) vede proprio nella liberazione di possibilità latenti l'effetto principale della narrazione distopica. Questo movimento verso la differenziazione ne incontra uno complementare, la rivelazione di un'uguale fragilità di fronte alla morte, che si realizza espressivamente attraverso l'implicito riferimento all'immaginario della danza macabra: «casa nostra è diventata terra straniera. Il virus ha compiuto il miracolo di renderci, da questo punto di vista almeno, davvero tutti uguali, ha annullato le differenze di razza, sesso o religione» (Carrisi 2020, 145). Così anche Hans Tuzzi: «Riscoprire valori che esulano dall'asfittico campo delle religioni e toccano la sfera del sacro: della sacralità della vita, tanto più preziosa quanto più soggetta alla morte» (Tuzzi 2020, 309). La distruzione delle gerarchie sociali implicata dalla danza macabra, si trova anche nel racconto di Marco Buticchi: «È un'incertezza comportamentale che travolge tutti: dai potenti agli ultimi, dai sovrani ai senzatetto» (Buticchi 2020, 121). In questa prospettiva, la crisi della pandemia si associa a quello che Bosco, nel suo racconto, definisce «Un restringimento dell'ego» (Bosco 2020, 111).

Nel ventaglio delle diverse reazioni messe in luce dal valore epifanico della pandemia e testimoniate dalle opere narrative prese in esame, si trova tuttavia anche un'eccezione all'alternativa tra ricerca di un facile protagonismo e positiva accettazione della comune impotenza. Nel racconto di Alice Basso, il filtro dell'immaginario distopico non si associa infatti ad un'atmosfera cupa, ma stimola al contrario lo spirito di avventura e un autoironico, nuovo protagonismo finalmente svincolato dalla *routine* della vita quotidiana. Basso crea due personaggi che abitano nella stessa casa: un poliziotto, costretto a lavorare anche durante il *lockdown*, e una «lavoratrice del settore editoriale» (Basso 2020, 38), abituata all'isolamento, che finalmente nella «bizzarra situazione da apocalisse fantascientifica» (ibid., 41) causata dalla pandemia può riscoprire la centralità della propria *agency*. Se infatti il compagno poliziotto ha «la faccia da protagonista di romanzo distopico» (ibid., 45), anche il personaggio femminile vive da protagonista

---

12 A questo proposito, cf. anche le riflessioni di Giungato (2020, 108) sull'etimologia delle parole 'crisi' e 'apocalisse': «L'etimologia della parola *crisi*, infatti, deriva dal greco *krìsis*, ovvero scelta, decisione; mentre l'etimo di apocalisse è *apokàlypsis*, ovvero rivelazione, disvelamento».

un'avventura, aiutando un signore anziano, che ha la moglie a letto malata – forse di Covid? –, a fare la spesa. Dopo aver proclamato «Gliela faccio io la spesa» (ibid., 48), il personaggio si mette ludicamente nei panni dell'eroe distopico – «Noi eroi oscuri mica sorridiamo» (ibid., 49) – ed esce dal supermercato pensando euforicamente al dialogo che avrà con il suo compagno: «lui mi chiederà se ho avuto la mia avventura anch'io» (ibid.). La pressione psicologica che il virus associa ad ogni gesto è così vinta da una nuova centralità acquisita dall'individuo che, nella situazione di crisi, è chiamato a dare il suo contributo e incarnare, nell'immaginario quotidiano, in una sorta di ironica *autofiction*, la figura dell'eroe.

DALL'AUTOBIOGRAFIA AL RECUPERO DEGLI 'ALTRI'

Se la matrice autobiografica è presente nella maggior parte dei racconti, e talvolta esplicitamente dichiarata per sottolineare l'esigenza di condivisione e elaborazione collettiva, altrettanto presente è l'idiosincrasia degli autori verso la scrittura stessa e l'autobiografia di fronte a una catastrofe di proporzioni globali. Così la già citata Ritanna Armeni riflette sul proprio senso di impotenza come scrittrice, chiedendosi se «Davvero un libro può essere una consolazione per i tanti che sono già disoccupati» (Armeni 2020, 17). Le fa eco Barbara Bellomo: «Alcune settimane fa aspettavo con ansia l'uscita del mio nuovo romanzo [...]. Tutto ha perso colore e cambiato valore» (Bellomo 2020, 59). Gianni Biondillo riflette sia sul senso di colpa derivante da uno sfruttamento commerciale, a livello di *fiction*, della catastrofe – «Mi farebbe sentire uno sciacallo» (Biondillo 2020, 71) –, sia sulla difficoltà di creare un resoconto autobiografico, nel momento in cui vengono meno un'*agency* proiettata verso il futuro – «'Scrivi! [...]. Ora hai tutto il tempo che vuoi' [...]. Ma scrivere è un progetto» (ibid., 72) – e «la materia prima, rigenerante per ogni scrittore» (ibid., 73). Il senso di colpa dello scrittore emerge anche nelle parole di Clara Sánchez: «forse a noi scrittori questa clausura pesa meno che agli altri [...]. Una cosa mostruosa, a dire il vero» (Sánchez 2020, 267).

Per sfuggire al solipsismo e alla povertà di eventi, l'autobiografia tende così a decentralizzarsi, soffermandosi, più che sulla voce narrante, sugli 'altri' che dalla narrazione vengono evocati. La catastrofe rivela, come già detto, un ampio ventaglio di reazioni sociali, rappresentato talvolta con un certo perentorio essenzialismo – cf., ad esempio, il già citato racconto di Carrisi: «quel pezzo di roccia incandescente che arriva dalle profondità dello spazio ci rivelerebbe, inevitabilmente, chi siamo» (Carrisi 2020, 144) – che non ammette sfumature e che dà luogo a un'elencazione di tipologie umane. Così, ad esempio la protagonista del racconto

di Armeni, per uscire dalla solitudine del *lockdown*, chiama prima «l'amica vani-
tosa» (Armeni 2020, 21), che approfitta del tempo libero per dedicarsi al *pilates*
online e ai video di massaggi cinesi, poi «l'amica godereccia» (ibid.), che non
rinuncia ad organizzare una cena a casa sua, poi «l'amico che ha sempre una spie-
gazione 'altra' su tutto» (ibid., 22).

A volte l'elenco di tipologie umane riguarda non tanto il carattere, ma le condizioni sociali e economiche che influiscono sugli effetti della pandemia. Così
Massimo Gramellini, in *L'amore ai tempi del coronavirus*, esaminando la casi-
stica delle coppie costrette ad una convivenza forzata a causa del *lockdown* – ad
ogni tipologia è riservato un paragrafo –, si sofferma sui *preoccupanti*, ovvero «le
vittime della violenza domestica [...] che l'isolamento obbligatorio consegna di
fatto ai capricci e ai soprusi del carnefice» (Gramellini 2020, 252). Enrico Galiano,
in *Serendipità*, raccontando la sua esperienza di insegnante di scuola ai tempi del
Covid-19, prima opera una distinzione caratteriale tra i colleghi, distinguendo i
bravi, «che si affrettano a far sapere a tutti di aver già predisposto novantacinque
lezioni online» (Galiano 2020, 205), e *Tutti gli altri*, che agiscono prudentemente,
rinegoziando la loro *agency* con gli studenti, cercando di capire come fare a mantenere un contatto, anche solo emotivo, di fronte alla crisi; poi analizza le conseguenze del Covid-19 sugli studenti, tenendo conto del loro contesto socioecono-
mico: «Adesso spuntano fuori, tutte, le differenze. Fra chi ha i mezzi e chi no. Fra
chi ha i genitori presenti e chi no. Fra chi ha i libri in casa e chi no. Ed è una rabbia
mista a dispiacere» (ibid., 212).

In altri casi, il recupero emotivo e cognitivo degli 'altri' avviene non tanto
attraverso una catalogazione analitica delle reazioni di fronte alla pandemia, ma
grazie ad un'indagine su di sé[13] che approfitta della solitudine forzata per distinguere i rapporti umani emotivamente significativi, la cui assenza è dolorosa, da
quelli solamente strumentali.[14] Emblematico, in questa prospettiva, il romanzo di

---

13 Il percorso autoriflessivo che può essere innescato dall'evento pandemico, è così de-
    scritto dal Research Group *Pandemic Fictions* (2020): «[S]ocial isolation forces the
    protagonists to change their perspective, which can result in a positive focus on oneself
    [L'isolamento sociale forza i protagonisti a cambiare la loro prospettiva, il che può por-
    tare ad un'attenzione positiva su se stessi]» (332; traduzione dell'autore).

14 La diversa prospettiva sul mondo dovuta alla pandemia si fa così, come scrive Federico
    Boni (2020, 4), strumento interpretativo: «[T]anto vale accettare e accogliere proprio
    quello straniante senso di disorientamento che il Covid-19 ha introdotto nelle nostre
    vite e nelle nostre quotidianità: non, quindi, negarlo o annichilirlo, banalizzandone la
    portata così sconcertante – e così planetaria –, ma al contrario adeguarsi allo

Chiara Gamberale. Qui, la protagonista, dopo aver chiarito il rifiuto di una scrittura autobiografica in senso diaristico, esprime la propria poetica:

> L'intenzione di questo mio breve libro, che preferirei chiamare quaderno, non è tediarvi con il diario della mia quarantena [...]. Non voglio parlare del coronavirus alla luce di un certo tipo di disagio: ma voglio parlare di un certo tipo di disagio alla luce del coronavirus. E per farlo devo passare inevitabilmente per i fatti e per le storie delle persone che mi hanno ispirata. (Gamberale 2020, 18-19)

Nel corso del romanzo, diventa chiaro come il disagio in questione nasca dal paradosso per cui la 'nostra' vita rischia continuamente di diventare una vita per gli altri, ovvero una vita il cui scopo principale è soddisfare le aspettative:

> La rapacità di cui è capace la vita, appena si fa la *nostra* vita, con le *sue* stanze, i *suoi* impegni da rispettare, le *sue* scadenze, perfino le *sue* persone – da rispettare, amare, fare sentire importanti perché rispettino, amino, facciano sentire importanti noi, da tenere lontane, tenere vicine. (ibid., 47)

Anche Silvia Truzzi evidenzia i rischi di un'*agency* che, pur essendo continuamente impegnata nella proiezione progettuale, sfocia nell'alienazione, nell'essere per gli 'altri', e vede nella pandemia un evento a questo proposito rivelatore: «Ho capito che lungo tutta la mia vita adulta ho esercitato pochissimo la mia volontà, pur essendo un tipo apparentemente volitivo. Mi sono fatta dettare i tempi da altro e da altri» (Truzzi 2020, 288).

Antonella Frontani, in modo simile a Chiara Gamberale, dichiara, in apertura del suo racconto *Il vaso di Pandora*, il rifiuto consapevole di una scrittura diaristica: «*Avrei potuto scrivere il diario di questo periodo tragico e surreale. Invece, ho provato a immaginare un piccolo miracolo [...]*» (Frontani 2020, 177). Distaccandosi dalla scrittura autobiografica, Frontani sviluppa due personaggi, un'imprenditrice in carriera e una scrittrice, che durante la pandemia entrano in confidenza. Anche in questo caso, l'interruzione di un approccio alla vita basato sull'*agency* progettuale porta Emma, l'imprenditrice, a riflettere su una vita attiva che si trasforma facilmente in alienazione nella volontà altrui: «Ho creduto di dover assecondare le aspettative riposte in me [...]. Come ho fatto a diventare una persona dura, incapace di essere veramente felice?» (ibid., 199). Colpisce il fatto che, nel racconto di Frontani, il rifiuto della scrittura autobiografica sia

---

spiazzamento che produce, assecondandolo e utilizzandolo come risorsa e come strumento interpretativo».

esplicitamente tematizzato, come se costituisse un'infrazione alle aspettative del lettore. Al tempo stesso il titolo – *Il vaso di Pandora* –, dal sapore distopico, non è sviluppato nei suoi esiti fantastici o fantascientifici ma in quelli psicologici, che sottolineano il valore epifanico della distopia. Se l'autobiografia tende alla rappresentazione degli altri, la distopia diventa così intima rivelazione.

METAFORE DI UN'*AGENCY* COLLETTIVA

La rappresentazione dell'unità simbolica di fronte alla crisi avviene anche attraverso un variegato spettro di metafore della totalità, che si applicano all'umanità o al virus stesso, nel tentativo di rendere tangibile un fenomeno ancora sconosciuto e di proporzioni troppo ampie per essere compreso.

Trasversale a molte narrazioni, la personificazione del virus come «nemico invisibile» (Auci 2020, 27; Bosco 2020, 97; Lahiri 2020, 256). Si tratta di una personificazione che ha l'ovvio scopo di concretizzare, seppure ossimoricamente, una minaccia altrimenti troppo generalizzata per essere affrontata.[15] Una simile immagine è tuttavia talvolta oggetto di critica. Così ad esempio Antonella Frontani:

> Il mondo non parla d'altro, a qualunque ora, attraverso tutti i palinsesti internazionali: siamo in guerra contro un nemico invisibile. Quella sensazione, ormai, si è impossessata anche di me ma una differenza mi consola. La guerra, infatti, è una tragedia alimentata dall'odio [...]. Non l'ho vissuta, ma posso immaginarla e mi consola, invece, l'idea che questa guerra si fondi sulla solidarietà, sulla *pietas*. Il pianeta, colpito, si coalizza e, finalmente, in difesa dei più deboli...». (Frontani 2020, 198)

Il brano di Frontani sottolinea come l'immagine del «nemico invisibile» porti spesso con sé quella della guerra, e il pericolo di un'aggressività non razionale, che resta sul piano pulsionale.[16] A questa aggressività l'autrice oppone la

---

15 Questa oggettualizzazione costituisce un meccanismo di difesa attraverso cui l'individuo, come mette in evidenza Giungato (2020, 110), tenta di gestire l'ansia: «[I]l soggetto ansioso desidera oggettualizzare la propria condizione poiché ciò gli consente – come già accennato – per naturali processi di difesa, di trovare delle vie di scarico e di decongestionare la condizione ansiosa».

16 In relazione alla metafora bellica utilizzata per descrivere l'evento pandemico, scrive Salvadori (2021, 154): «Segue la coppia invisibilità-esclusione (Boni 2020, p. 5), con

personificazione del «pianeta» finalmente unito, a causa della crisi, nella solidarietà. Anche Gianni Biondillo evidenzia come la retorica della guerra evochi un facile patriottismo, che non aiuta a elaborare razionalmente il problema.[17]

Tra le immagini che rappresentano, più che lo scenario bellico, la solidarietà, spicca la personificazione dell'Italia: «L'Italia dà prova di un'unità e un'abnegazione senza precedenti […]. Proviamo un senso di appartenenza che non abbiamo mai condiviso prima» (Bosco 2020, 114-115; cf. anche Bellomo 2020, 59). A fare da contrappeso a queste immagini di solidarietà, si possono forse ricordare i già citati ammonimenti di altri autori a non lasciarsi andare a un facile patriottismo.

Nel romanzo di Chiara Gamberale, la personificazione del virus assume le sembianze non di un nemico invisibile, ma di un mostro infantile – «un gigantosauro cieco» (Gamberale 2020, 19) – che si sottrae ad ogni dialogo. La protagonista autobiografica ha la sensazione di non avere possibilità di *agency* all'interno del «film» in cui tuttavia, per il coinvolgimento emotivo, è protagonista: «Arrivo a casa, il resto del pomeriggio scivola così, pigramente, come se tutti fossimo in attesa delle indicazioni di un regista che ci ordini che cosa fare nella prossima scena di questo film di cui ci ritroviamo protagonisti senza avere letto prima la sceneggiatura» (ibid., 30). Il desiderio di orientamento si proietta così nel personaggio del «Grande Peppe» – il Presidente del Consiglio Giuseppe Conte –, «regista» che, con le sue direttive, solleva la protagonista da ogni responsabilità: «Finché il Grande Peppe ci dice che cosa fare e non fare, persone come noi sono tutto sommato salve» (ibid., 64). La personificazione dell'istanza salvifica gioca così un ruolo ambiguo, dando orientamento, ma anche lasciando regredire l'individuo ad una condizione di dipendenza e irresponsabilità dalla quale, tutto sommato, ha paura di distaccarsi: «Ho paura che, quando guarirà il mondo, tornerò ad ammalarmi io» (ibid., 93).

Un'interessante elaborazione metaforica è infine al centro del romanzo-saggio di Paolo Giordano, *Nel contagio*. Qui le immagini non ruotano attorno ad un processo di antropomorfizzazione, ma si concentrano sull'inorganico, o sul genericamente biologico. Tali immagini consentono un distacco emotivo dall'ansia e da

---

un chiaro rimando all'*altrove* da cui il virus proviene e – in chiave squisitamente imagologica – alla retorica della purezza culturale dell'Occidente. Nello specifico, l'invisibilità dell'agente xenobiotico legittima la metafora della guerra e rende il virus nemico, facendo ricorso a quel bellicismo linguistico della scienza medica su cui già si era soffermata Susan Sontag nel suo *Illness as a Metaphor* (1978)».

17 «Non reggo i dibattiti dove si parla di guerra, eroi, combattenti. Tutto un armamentario retorico, gonfio di patriottismo di seconda mano. Non è una guerra, è una pandemia» (Biondillo 2020, 73).

eventuali reazioni aggressive, veicolando l'analisi oggettiva, scientifica, del problema e delle possibili soluzioni: «Facciamo che siamo sette miliardi e mezzo di biglie [...]. Quella biglia infetta è il paziente zero e fa in tempo a colpire altre due biglie prima di fermarsi. Quelle schizzano via e ne colpiscono altre due a testa» (Giordano 2020, 11). L'immagine viene sviluppata nel corso del testo, nel tentativo di convincere il lettore che «Bisogna allontanare le biglie una dall'altra» (ibid., 19), e che, come il contagio, anche l'azione individuale può avere effetti esponenziali (cf. ibid., 29).[18] La sfera del non-umano non è tuttavia il punto di arrivo della dimensione retorica del testo, ma una fase preliminare che consente di neutralizzare l'egoismo e l'aggressività, conducendo progressivamente a recuperare la dimensione emotiva, empatica. Nel contagio siamo infatti «un organismo unico» (ibid., 27), e non biglie: «Non siamo biglie. Siamo esseri umani, pieni di desideri e di nevrosi» (ibid., 34); «Basterebbe ricordarsene, per ricordarsi anche di usare un po' più di cautela del solito, un po' più di compassione» (ibid., 41).

CONCLUSIONI

Attraverso il concetto di *agency*, l'articolo ha analizzato tre opere uscite in Italia agli inizi del 2020 che hanno al centro le ricadute psicologiche e sociali della pandemia di Covid-19 – *Come il mare in un bicchiere* di Chiara Gamberale, l'antologia *Andrà tutto bene*, e *Nel contagio* di Paolo Giordano – evidenziando le strategie attraverso cui i protagonisti cercano, nonostante la crisi, di mantenere una narrazione coerente di sé.

Un primo elemento che è emerso, ben visibile anche a livello formale, soprattutto nella raccolta *Andrà tutto bene*, è la necessità di creare strutture temporali comprensibili. Queste strutture variano, secondo gli autori, da un'autodisciplina che tenta di rimuovere il futuro per concentrarsi sul presente, a una proiezione nel futuro che cerca, invece, di dare un senso alla quotidianità in vista di uno scopo condiviso, a un'oscillazione continua tra presente futuro che non riesce a stabilizzarsi e sfocia nell'ansia.

A livello dei generi, si nota una dialettica tra narrazioni a matrice autobiografica e riferimenti alla distopia. Da una parte la matrice autobiografica, talvolta dichiarata, cerca di ricreare, nonostante l'isolamento causato dal *lockdown*, un piano simbolico condiviso che consenta l'elaborazione collettiva della crisi e combatta

---

18 Nota Gianfranco Bruschi (2020, 557), a proposito di *Nel contagio*: «L'effetto delle nostre azioni individuali insieme ha uno sviluppo moltiplicato, esponenziale, si afferma nel testo. Più della somma di quello che può ogni persona».

la fuga in un immaginario sommariamente catastrofico o salvifico. In questa prospettiva lo sviluppo della narrazione porta a una rinegoziazione dell'*agency* dei protagonisti che, proprio relativizzando la propria capacità di azione, senza tuttavia cedere alla disperazione, possono ricreare un orizzonte di senso. Dall'altra la distopia viene ad avere un valore epifanico, che rivela, nel quadro di una crisi da cui nessuno può dirsi escluso, le diverse tipologie umane in base alle reazioni psicologiche e le diverse ricadute della pandemia in base alle condizioni socio-economiche.

Il problema di una quotidianità povera di eventi è superato attraverso il recupero degli 'altri', che talvolta, come nel romanzo di Chiara Gamberale, passa per un'indagine intima dei protagonisti, tesa a distinguere i rapporti emotivamente rilevanti da quelli meramente strumentali. Questa dimensione intima si oppone al ricordo della vita di prima, caratterizzata da un'*agency* paradossale che, dietro l'aspetto della progettualità, nasconde un'alienazione nell''essere per gli altri' e nel soddisfare le aspettative.

Si sono infine rintracciate le metafore che, nelle opere prese in esame, cercano di esprimere un'*agency* collettiva: accanto alle personificazioni del virus come «nemico invisibile» su cui canalizzare un'aggressività non sempre meditata, e alle personificazioni dell'Italia, che intendono veicolare una solidarietà condivisa, si è analizzato l'uso di metafore che si concentrano sull'inorganico o sul genericamente biologico, al centro di *Nel contagio* di Paolo Giordano, che neutralizzano l'egoismo e l'aggressività per condurre poi progressivamente al recupero dell'empatia.

In questo quadro complesso, i protagonisti cercano di rimanere tali non rinunciando alla creazione di senso, rinegoziando la propria *agency* che si caratterizza come proiezione in una struttura temporale che comprenda gli 'altri' a livello simbolico – colpisce il recupero della domanda 'come stai' (cf. Bosco 2020, 116; Carrisi 2020, 143; Galiano 2020, 203), al di là di una formalità vuota.

Come ulteriore orizzonte di ricerca, resta da indagare in che misura l'evoluzione del quadro pandemico incida sia sulle modalità letterarie in cui l'*agency* dei protagonisti viene rappresentata che sulla dialettica tra autobiografia e *fiction*.

BIBLIOGRAFIA

Corpus analizzato

Armeni, Ritanna (2020) "Un'ora dopo l'altra", AA. VV. *Andrà tutto bene*, Milano, Garzanti, 13-24.

Auci, Ştefania (2020) "Se ci fosse luce, sarebbe bellissimo", AA. VV. *Andrà tutto bene*, Milano, Garzanti, 27-34.

Basso, Alice (2020) "La quarantena di Vanni Sarca", AA. VV. *Andrà tutto bene*, Milano, Garzanti, 37-49.

Bellomo, Barbara (2020) "Tra smart school e affetti lontani", AA. VV. *Andrà tutto bene*, Milano, Garzanti, 53-62.

Biondillo, Gianni (2020) "Attraversare il buio", AA. VV. *Andrà tutto bene*, Milano, Garzanti, 65-82.

Bosco, Federica (2020) "Che fretta c'era, maledetta quarantena…", AA. VV. *Andrà tutto bene*, Milano, Garzanti, 95-118.

Buticchi, Marco (2020) "Andrà tutto bene, piccoline", AA. VV. *Andrà tutto bene*, Milano, Garzanti, 121-127.

Carrisi, Donato (2020) "Lettera sul futuro a due bambini", AA. VV. *Andrà tutto bene*, Milano, Garzanti, 143-146.

Dalton, Anna (2020) "Ore 18.00", AA. VV. *Andrà tutto bene*, Milano, Garzanti, 149-162.

Frontani, Antonella (2020) "Il vaso di Pandora", AA. VV. *Andrà tutto bene*, Milano, Garzanti, 177-200.

Galiano, Enrico (2020) "Serendipità", AA. VV. *Andrà tutto bene*, Milano, Garzanti, 203-214.

Gamberale, Chiara (2020) *Come il mare in un bicchiere*, Milano, Feltrinelli.

Gazzola, Alessia (2020) "My Sweet Quarantine", AA. VV. *Andrà tutto bene*, Milano, Garzanti, 217-229.

Giordano, Paolo (2020) *Nel contagio*, Torino, Einaudi.

Gramellini, Massimo (2020) "L'amore ai tempi del Coronavirus", AA. VV. *Andrà tutto bene*, Milano, Garzanti, 249-252.

Lahiri, Jhumpa (2020) "Lettera all'Italia", AA. VV. *Andrà tutto bene*, Milano, Garzanti, 255-258.

Sánchez, Clara (2020) "Il termometro", AA. VV. *Andrà tutto bene*, Milano, Garzanti, 261-268.

Truzzi, Silvia (2020) "Caro microbo, ti scrivo (così mi proteggo un po')", AA. VV. *Andrà tutto bene*, Milano, Garzanti, 283-291.

Tuzzi, Hans (2020) "Eredità di affetti", AA. VV. *Andrà tutto bene*, Milano, Garzanti, 305-309.

Opere citate

Boni, Federico (2020) "Frammenti di un discorso virale. Le cornici del coronavirus", *Mediascapes journal* 15, 3-12.

Bruschi, Gianfranco (2020) "Nel contagio: Paolo Giordano, Einaudi, Torino, 2020", *Ricerca Psicoanalitica* 31/3, 555-558. DOI: 10.4081/rp.2020.304.

Emirbayer, Mustafa/Mische, Ann (1998) "What Is Agency?", *American Journal of Sociology* 103/4, 962-1023. DOI: 10.1086/231294.

Giungato, Luigi (2020) "Niente sarà più come prima. Il Covid-19 come narrazione apocalittica di successo", *H-ermes. Journal of Communication* 16, 99-122. DOI: 10.1285/i22840753n16p99.

Laakso, Maria (2020) "Social Dreaming and Uses of Narrativity, Tellability and Experientiality in Literary Dystopia", Teppo Eskelinen (ed.) *The Revival of Political Imagination*, London, Zed Books, 78-96. DOI: 10.5040/9781350225633.ch.005.

Lejeune, Philippe (1996) [1975]) *Le pacte autobiographique*, Paris, Seuil.

McAdams, Dan P. (2019) "'First We Invented Stories, Then They Changed Us': The Evolution of Narrative Identity", *Evolutionary Studies in Imaginative Culture* 3/1, 1-18. DOI: 10.26613/esic/3.1.110.

Meozzi, Tommaso (2017) *Visioni dell'alienazione*, Ospedaletto (Pisa), Pacini.

Obermayr, Julia/Völkl, Yvonne (2022) "Corona Fictions as Cultural Indicators of Social Cohesion and Resilience in the Wake of the Covid-19 Pandemic", *Momentum Quarterly* 11/2, 129-142. DOI: 10.15203/momentumquarterly.vol11.no1.p129-142.

Research Group *Pandemic Fictions* (2020) "From Pandemic to Corona Fictions: Narratives in Times of Crises", *PhiN-Beiheft* 24, 321-344, http://web.fu-berlin.de/phin/beiheft24/b24t21.pdf, 2022-09-19.

Ronchi, Rocco (2020) "Metafisica del populismo VI / Teologia del virus", *Doppiozero*, 2020-04-06, https://www.doppiozero.com/teologia-del-virus, 2022-09-19.

Salvadori, Diego (2021) "Narrare il contagio", *Medical Humanities & Medicina Narrativa* 2/1, 151-160.

Corona Fictions Agents: Cinematic Representations of Hopeful Pandemic Protagonists in Early Corona Fictions[1]

Julia Obermayr (Graz University of Technology)

Abstract

During the Covid-19 pandemic numerous early Corona Fictions (including films) emerged, creating a multitude of pandemic protagonists across media.

The aim of this article is to examine these protagonists of two European Corona Fictions comedies: *8 Rue de l'Humanité* (2021) and *¡Ni te me acerques!* (2020). Applying Stuart Hall's (1997) circuit of culture lens (encoding/decoding model), as well as various concepts of hope (e.g. Snyder 2002, Grodal 2006 and 2017, Van den Heuvel 2020), essential aspects of the comedy genre and film analysis (e.g. Eder 2008, Krützen 2006, Grodal 2005), the results of this study support the idea that reclaiming agency is an essential factor for fictional pandemic protagonists when coping with lockdowns and other pandemic restrictions.

Both films, thus, demonstrate that comedy is particularly appropriate for the portrayal of transformational processes of initially fearful or anxiety-driven protagonists becoming hopeful Corona Fictions agents in the end.

---

1   This research was funded by the Austrian Science Fund (FWF): P 34571-G; Project team: Julia Obermayr, Elisabeth Hobisch and Yvonne Völkl.

INTRODUCTION

Early audiovisual Corona Fictions[2] embrace a great variety[3] of formats and genres to capture and express the essence of the Covid-19 pandemic. While the challenges of lockdowns and containment measures forced many individuals into an unknown physical isolation, many Europeans also experienced the strains of social isolation provoking anxiety, depression and loneliness (cf. Singer et al. 2021, 10, 58ff.), proving once more that virtual connection may be helpful but cannot replace the value physical presence or even touch holds for humans. Hinderk M. Emrich (2011, 2f.) hereby not only discusses the loneliness arising due to isolation of the individual but – more importantly – he points out loneliness due to lack of touch and the "virtualization of our relationship to the world through technical media".

Pandemic protagonists comprise both, fictional protagonists from pandemic fictions[4] as well as Corona Fictions. The following article hereby focuses on the format of Corona Fictions feature films, particularly on two comedies. The chosen audiovisual Romance language focused Corona Fictions corpus for this article – *8 Rue de l'Humanité*[5] and *¡Ni te me acerques!*[6] – constitutes primarily of initial scenes and endings. Michaela Krützen (cf. 2006, 89; cf. Branigan 1992, 4f.) and

---

2   "Corona Fictions [...] emerge during the COVID-19 pandemic and negotiate the latter in their stories, continuing in parts the tradition of creating pandemic fiction. We argue that Corona Fictions reactivate certain structures and elements in the form of metanarratives. The pandemic produced collective experiences which can be understood as transnational and transcultural phenomena translating into the crisis while simultaneously tapping into existing pandemic narratives" (Obermayr/Völkl 2022b, 161). Early Corona Fictions emerged between 2020-2022.

3   Dennis Henkel (cf. 2022, 1622f.) believes to have detected a grand lack thereof. Contrary to his beliefs, the Corona Fictions research team friendly suggests a peek into the online Corona Fictions Database (cf. Hobisch et al. 2021-), offering comedies beyond the corpus of this article.

4   "Pandemic fiction[s] includ[e] works such as the antique description of the Athenian plague by Thucydides, the *Decameron* (1349-1353) by Boccaccio or *A Journal of the Plague Year* (1722) by Daniel Defoe. Also, more recent cultural productions such as the movie *Outbreak* (1995) or a Canadian series called *Épidémie* (2020 [...]) and novels like, for example, *Los días de la peste* (2017) by Edmundo Paz Soldán all fall under the category of pandemic fiction[s] [...]" (Obermayr/Völkl 2022b, 161).

5   English film title: *Stuck Together*. Throughout this article the abbreviation *8RH* is used.

6   English film title: *Stay Away!* Throughout this article the abbreviation *NTMA* is used.

Jens Eder (cf. 2008, 717) both argue that the transformational process of a theme closely connected to or even embodied by the protagonist and its surroundings may best be demonstrated by juxtaposing the initial state with the end state as they hold important information on its characterization. This theme may e.g. be an emotional message or morale embodied by the protagonist or narrative means of filmic storytelling (cf. Stutterheim/Kaiser 2011, 368). As Edward Branigan (1992, 4) suggests, "narrative can be seen as an organization of experience which draws together many aspects of our spatial, temporal, and causal perception". This seems of main interest regarding the Covid-19 pandemic, since the creation of Corona Fictions narratives, therefore, is an organization of pandemic experiences that will later on determine which stories enter (and remain in) the collective memory (cf. Halbwachs 1950 [1935]; Assmann/Hölscher 1988; Assmann 2005 [1992]). Furthermore, this also ties into Eder's (cf. 2008, 720) claim that the interface of action and characters is their motivation. In particular, whatever drives the protagonist also drives the overall storyline. Hence, a hopeful protagonist makes for a determined, goal-oriented, agency holding central character, as we will examine in the analysis part of this article.

While both, France and Spain, decided upon comedy as a suitable genre for telling their Corona Fictions, a 'pinch' of romance was added as well. In comparison to tragedy, comedy was often treated as "philosophically and artistically inferior" (Knight 2009, 536). Tragedy, seen not only as a genre but simultaneously as a world view and a way to live, claims moral questions for itself, while ignoring the important role of comedy. Deborah Knight (2009, 542) critiques this point of view by stating that "[i]t is simply false to suggest that the other master genres are silent on the question of how one should live. The master genre of comedy's answer is as follows: as a member of a welcoming community". When looking at different concepts of hope (also see the following theory part 'Encoding Hope') it becomes clear, however, that Knight's position on the function of comedy is right. Particularly in times of high anxiety levels, depression, and loneliness within 'pandemicized' societies, a genre provoking frequent moments of laughter while honoring the seriousness of the situation seems a relief and coping strategy for the spectators.

Thus, the proposed hypothesis and research question arising are the following:

a)   The genre of comedy regarding Corona Fictions feature films is particularly appropriate for the portrayal of the transformational process of a fearful or anxiety-driven pandemic protagonist becoming a hopeful one and the representation of hope as a theme throughout the movies investigated in general.

b)   How do Corona Fictions create and encode this message of hope?

In the following, we will take a closer look at the concept of hope from an inter-disciplinary cultural studies perspective and what role agency plays for both, hope and the protagonist who drives the story forward, before investigating the chosen Corona Fictions corpus.

ENCODING HOPE

Using Stuart Hall's (cf. 1997, 1) circuit of culture (encoding/decoding model) lens considering numerous aspects of cultural analysis interacting (identity, produc-tion, consumption, regulation, and representation), this article examines the con-cept of hope encoded as a theme (a linking element; cf. Stutterheim/Kaiser 2011, 368) and hope represented via pandemic protagonists in the chosen Corona Fic-tions corpus mentioned above.

Fear, in contrast to hope, is an involuntary autonomic response, an emotion,[7] as "[t]he first experience, common in elements of comedy, melodrama, and horror, is an involuntary autonomic response such as laughing, crying, or fear" (Grodal 2006, 6f.). Although Rick Snyder (cf. 2002, 254) does not consider hope to be solely an emotion, emotions do play an important role regarding his concept of hope as a whole (see below).

Jens Eder (cf. 2008, 509) demonstrates how characters in film may provoke certain emotions in the viewers and describes the protagonist as a character hold-ing significance for something positive. This includes a process of goal-oriented pursuit defined as hope, as mentioned below. The audience tends to adopt the pro-tagonist's perspective when identification[8] takes place since their portrayal com-monly evokes positive emotions or is positively associated with a set of own socio-culturally relevant values. The Spanish dictionary Real Academia Española

---

7   Thomas Schick (cf. 2018, 36) elaborates on the difference between emotions and moods. Emotions, e.g. fear, require an object to fear, to be afraid of. Moods, on the other hand, have a lower intensity than emotions but are of longer duration and do not neces-sarily have to be related to a concrete object. "[T]he proposed definition of emotion, namely, as *any mental experience with high intensity and high hedonic content* (pleas-ure/displeasure) [italics in orig.]" (Cabanac 2002, 80). For a more in-depth analysis of emotions and film, see Schick (2018, 31-109).

8   This process of identification may also be interpreted as an invisible contract between film/filmmakers and audiences. Upholding a basic emotional tension, the so-called 'hu-man factor' (cf. Zag 2010[2], 14), keeps the viewers engaged and may mainly be created by taking artistic/filmic measures to consciously provoke it.

(2022), furthermore, briefly defines the 'protagonista' as a "personaje principcal de la acción" but also as "[p]ersona o cosa que en un suceso cualquiera desempeña la parte principal".[9] The protagonist in film commonly holds the main agency,[10] hence, drives the storyline forward. To represent their endeavour on-screen, they receive the most screen-time and are created in an empathy stirring as a way to engage the audience and ease the process of identification. Although the protagonist does not necessarily have to be the (only) main character,[11] this character is broadly considered as such in the filmic landscape.

The protagonist, visible or invisible as a character (but visible through a certain theme throughout the movie), dominates the storyline, receives more on-screen time than secondary characters and holds essential agency. When invisible, the protagonist comes to life through the filmic storytelling itself and may be what Eder (cf. 2008, 507) calls a 'Thementräger' in German, meaning the one carrying a consistent theme (e.g. hope) including the matching symbolism to represent it. Encoded in objects, spaces, actions, etc. the protagonist comes to life even when invisible as a character. Thus, the virus itself, invisible on-screen may be decoded while observing the chain of contagion. The spreading, or an outbreak of a certain illness connected to this virus, may show itself e.g. in colour choices and music used to distinguish between clean and hygienic surroundings (e.g. in medical settings in *Épidémie* (Qub 2020, a TV-series from Québec) versus contaminated areas or infected people by depicting e.g. red objects, clothes or changing the camera filter/colour coding for entire scenes dedicated to the invisible danger of the virus. Animals may also function as carriers of the virus, as seen in *Épidémie* (Qub 2020). Their movements as carriers indicate the possible spread and outbreak. In this case, the virus itself holds agency as we, the viewers, follow its chain of contagion.

In the analyzed corpus *8 Rue de l'Humanité* (2021) and *Ni te me acerques* (2020), however, the virus rather functions as a generator for the Covid-19 pandemic framework and its visual protagonists. Invisible, or rather not exclusively

---

9   "the main character of action" ... "[p]erson or thing that in any event plays the main part" (author's translation).

10   "A model of agency typically implies that a body is pervaded by an agency that possesses the ability to perceive, to be conscious, to have thoughts and emotions, to have specific traits, and to have the ability to intend and to act. It is therefore not surprising that a major mode of explaining film focuses on agency" (Grodal 2005, 15).

11   Due to the scope of this article, however, we will not pursue further the possibilities of multi-protagonist films (cf. Del Mar Azcona 2010) and antagonists (cf. Eder 2008, 493, 509) as a main character option.

personified via main characters but simultaneously represented through a theme, is the concept of hope. Before analyzing the audiovisual Corona Fictions mentioned, we therefore briefly have to consider this complex matter of hope from an interdisciplinary perspective, as it holds essential agency throughout both of the movies.

Hope: The Protagonist's Pursuit of Goals and Agency

> i am trusting the uncertainty
> and believing i will
> end up somewhere
> right and good
> *Rupi Kaur in Home Body*

Rupi Kaur's (2020, 27) poem above sums up essential aspects of hope, particularly the aspect of trust in the human good and a good outcome or positive future in general. While there exist vast concepts of hope across time (as can bee seen e.g. in Steven C. Van den Heuvel's edited volume *Historical and Multidiciplinary Perspectives on Hope*, 2020), according to G. Scott Gravelee (2020, 21) in ancient Greek philosophy it was already considered as something sustaining and motivating, "serving as a foundation for human agency". In early Christian thinking, where hope is "a *theological* virtue alongside faith and love [italics in orig.]" (Milona 2020, 113), a reflection towards a more communal focus of hope was taking place (cf. Webber/Kok 2020, 42). In the Middle Ages hope was mostly accepted as a "supernatural virtue of desire for the happiness of heaven" (Pinsent 2020, 58). During the Enlightenment and in the context of theories of affect, "hope consists of a desire and a belief in the possibility, but not the certainty, of the desired outcome" (Blöser 2020, 75). Ronald T. Michener (2020, 92) sums up the postmodern definition of hope under a Christian lens, suggesting a hope "that provides consolation for the past, motivation for the present, and joyful expectancy for the future". As this motivational value for present and future, "[h]ope can [furthermore] have instrumental value because hoping for something can make it more likely that it will happen [...]. The instrumental value of hope here is rooted in its motivational power" (Milona 2020, 110). In short, hope fuels our agency. However, this is not a new idea, since the US-American psychologist (Charles Richard) Rick Snyder (2002, 249), known for his pioneering work in the field of positive psychology and the theory of hope, defines hope as "*the perceived capability to derive pathways to desired goals, and motivate oneself via agency thinking to use those pathways* [italics in orig.]". As his own views about hope theory evolved over time, Snyder identified further details for his own definition, e.g. that "the only appropriate goals are those that fill a profound void in a person's life" (Snyder 2002, 250). In his elaborated hope model (cf. fig. 1) he further explains how pathways and agency thinking originate in what we learn throughout our childhood and beyond (cf. ibid., 253). Hence, the hopeful thinking we have learned in the past "is accompanied by trait-like emotional sets or moods" (ibid.), influencing the motivational process of pursuing the set goal.

We then analyze the importance of the goal pursuit in the pre-event phase or at the latest by starting our pursuit process. Hereby, "the pathways and agency thoughts are activated" (Snyder 2002, 254) and emotional reactions may occur. In this context, "[e]motions [...] are not task avoidant and harmful; rather, they contribute to, and are a natural part of, an active, productive, goal-directed type of thought" (ibid.). However, hope itself is not (just) an emotion but "was primarily a way of thinking, with feelings playing an important, albeit contributory role" (ibid., 249). As can be seen in Snyder's model (cf. fig. 1), the hopeful pursuing of one's goals can be disturbed by stressors impactful enough to jeopardize the process. Ultimately, the goal (non-)attainment reinforms pathways and agency, depending on the outcome that has been achieved.

Recalling Snyder's aforementioned goal-oriented definition of hope, his theory is supported by memory research, as Krützen (cf. 2006, 94) points out: a goal stated at the beginning of a narrative is easier to follow. This is a well-known strategy in e.g. classical Hollywood cinema which has been used until today when driving forward a plot by a character trying to achieve their goal. This goal, however, may often be redefined or even discarded (cf. Krützen 2006, 93f.). Interestingly, the location of cinema culture hereby plays an important role as well (ibid.): Hollywood cinema[12] focuses on the wants, needs and desires of the main characters, whereas European cinema protagonists often do not know if they want something or what they want exactly, which is harder to follow for the audience.

What protagonists desire or how their emotions and/or hopeful states affect the audience's perception when watching a film, may illustrate the following model by Torben Grodal, a Danish film and media studies professor emeritus. He worked intensely on film experience and film aesthetics. His central model surrounding perception, emotion, cognition, and motor action – referred to in short as PECMA flow[13] –

---

12 Classical Hollywood cinema narrates how a protagonist reaches their goal in a spiral (not a circle) (cf. Krützen 2006, 96).

13 "The basic assumption of semiotic film theory – and even the implicit assumption in some strands of cognitive and philosophical film theory – is that viewers are looking at

described the flow from perception, through emotional activation and cognitive processing, to motor action. [...] An additional feature of the PECMA flow model is the evaluation of reality status, based on combining a radical constructivism with evolutionary realism. (Grodal 2006, 1)

He further claims that "[t]he model also helps film historians in the sense that it provides a better understanding of what aspects of films should be described historically and what aspects should be described psychologically" (ibid., 3). To elaborate on his interdisciplinary approach, Grodal (cf. 2006, 3f.) mentions the importance of understanding the design of the brain, as sensory organs such as eyes and/or ears receive an input and transform this information, sending it to specific parts of the brain where associations take place before acting out bodily internal states via e.g. laughing or crying, while simultaneously the limbic system interacts with PECMA, the above-mentioned mental processes. Hence, "film not only provides propositional meanings but also a range of perceptual, cognitive, and emotional experiences cued by the playful activation of our embodied brains" (Grodal 2006, 5). This view on experiencing a film is particularly essential when it comes to e.g. fear affecting the bodies of spectators watching a certain fear inducing sequence.

---

moving film images, and that those images are seen initially as representations and then matched to a referent (a pro-filmic event, a meaning, etc.). In contrast, the PECMA flow model takes what I sometimes call a 'direct drive' approach. PECMA flow starts when light information enters the eyes. Whether this information is derived from the real world or from moving images does not make a fundamental difference for most of the brain systems connected to film viewing, although part of the brain is very much occupied with assessing the reality-status of what we see. When watching a film, we do not primarily see representations of people and landscapes; we simply see people and landscapes, although we know that this seeing is induced by artificial means. Our knowledge that our seeing is artificially induced creates a conscious feeling that the objects are not real. This feeling can vary in strength depending on the film and the viewer. When speaking of films and other aspects of reality, it is easy to forget that although the world outside our heads has an objective existence, we only have access to films or reality through our brains. Therefore, our experience of film exists side by side with our experience of real events; the film experience runs on the same brain circuits as those used for real world experience, and only mental 'reality-status markers' indicate the difference between visual fiction and online fact" (Grodal 2006, 3).

From Fear to Hope

Emotions change how we view the world, how our body feels, how we interact with each other, thus, also how our social fabric functions. During the Covid-19 pandemic and its first lockdowns and containment measures, fear dominated public discourse (daily TV news, newspapers, speeches held by politicians) in the Western world. When we talk about fear, we understand that apart from fear as an emotional dimension, there also exist "political, social, and cultural dimensions of fear" (Linke/Smith 2009, 4).

Almost simultaneously, however in contrast to the dominating mass media discourse, many artistic expressions focused on elevating the spirits of their audiences, e.g. through uplifting music (cf. Obermayr/Hobisch 2023) or the production of films within the comedy genre to strengthen resilience and support social cohesion (cf. Obermayr/Völkl 2022a).

Fear has not suddenly emerged during the pandemic but has been a constantly reactivated emotion through certain impactful events such as 9/11 in the US, and moreover repeated in media and political discourse and socio-cultural practices. Since then, it again is accompanying Western cultures to a higher degree, also steering the diverse societies of Europe towards concepts such as 'security', 'safety', 'protection' or 'defense' mentioned by Uli Linke and Danielle Taana Smith (2009, 3):

> These are among the terms circulated as part of a global public discourse of fear which encourages proactive military action, legitimates war as a surgical intervention, and authorizes faraway acts of violence as a means of national border fortification. The securocratic language of the contemporary western state is war talk: it not only empowers a state's military reach across national borders, but diminishes civil society, abandons human rights, diplomacy, and visions of peace. (ibid.)

This war talk' indeed reappears at the beginning of the Covid-19 pandemic as, for example, the French president Emmanuel Macron (cf. Schmelzer 2020)[14]

---

14 "Dagmar Schmelzer (2020) draws a discursive performance comparison between German, French, and Spanish speeches addressed to each nation at the very beginning of the pandemic in Europe. [Their] rhetoric had the same goal: to foster social cohesion in a time of crises to obtain a behavioral shift within the population in order to contain the spreading virus. Constructing the virus as the collective enemy, declaring war, and building on a collective 'we,' as Marcon did, aims to (re)establish a sense of social

mentions the virus as an enemy and declares the French nation at war against it. Thus, when watching a fear inducing movie sequence, the audience may experience a reactivation of 'cultures of fear',[15] which may be useful as a 'modus of population management' (cf. Linke/Smith 2009, 4f.). However, the population does have the ability to regulate and influence their emotional state by avoiding or enforcing certain habits of exposure to cultures of fear or of cultivating hope, as Matthew Price and colleagues (cf. 2022) elaborate on in their article "Doomscrolling During COVID-19: The Negative Association Between Daily Social and Traditional Media Consumption and Mental Health Symptoms During the COVID-19 Pandemic". Doomscrolling, therefore, destroys hope and optimism as their study has shown:

> [R]egular social media exposure, or doomscrolling, is associated with an increase in depression and PTSD, even when accounting for prepandemic mental health. This effect was magnified for those with histories of maltreatment. This result highlights a major challenge imposed by the COVID-19 pandemic – remaining informed is associated with a mental cost. Strategies to limit doomscrolling and engage in positive activities may offset the detrimental effect of engaging in these behaviors. (Price et al. 2022, 1345)

To sum up, not only the mood spread by media discourse but also a Corona Fictions' protagonists' mood and emotions are highly contagious, even through the screen. Carl Plantinga (cf. 2009a, 91) asks about the degree of identical emotions shown by both the spectators and the protagonists, underlining the fact that Torben Gordal's (also see PECMA model) view on this matter is that the audience and the protagonists have largely identical emotions (cf. Plantinga 2009a, 91; Grodal 2006). "Emotional response is typically rooted in the spectator's appraisal of the narrative in conjunction with character goals and desires" (Plantinga 2009a, 91).

---

cohesion necessary to introduce harsh containment measures such as a lockdown [...]" (Obermayr/Völkl 2022a, 135).

15 "Cultures of fear have a political grounding: negative emotions like fear or terror are produced and sustained to govern populations within the carceral spaces of militarized societies. In this sense, an emergent cultural system of fear cannot be understood solely as a byproduct of violence or as an inevitable symptom of war. Forms of terror are artifacts of history, society, and global politics. Cultures of fear and states of terror are affective tools of government that come into being as a modus of population management deployed by military, political, and administrative actors [...]" (Linke/Smith 2009, 4f.).

Hence, a hopeful protagonist is likely to inspire, at the very least, a hopeful mood in spectators.

It must be taken into account that models of identification and empathy of the spectator/reader do not apply to the multiple structural levels (Ger. 'Mehrebenen-struktur') of narratives (cf. Hiergeist 2014, 65). As Teresa Hiergeist (cf. 2014, 62) suggests, the reader – or in the case of audiovisual formats the spectator – develops own ideas and wishes on how a protagonist should act within the storyline narratives. Similarly, Roland Zag (cf. 2010[2], 65) argues that the so-called 'human factor' in a contract between audience and filmmaker/film plays an essential role in a protagonist's potential to offer aspects of identification for an audience. In this sense, conventional character constellations[16] ease the identification process for the audience, particularly with a protagonist's rich inner life and emotional state, whereas more non-conventional character creations with higher levels of 'difference qualities' (Ger. 'Differenzqualitäten') are harder to affectively experience (cf. Schick 2018, 99).

Applying this logic to Corona Fictions, particularly the two chosen examples, the artistic agency of relatable characters may foresee a certain potential for provoked reactions from their audiences. Hence, the choice of the comedy genre allows for the thematizing of e.g. Covid-19 deaths or negative effects of lockdown restrictions by adding enough comic relief for spectators to be able to laugh about the hardships and challenges rather than to cry in sadness and despair. The moral reminder thus, does not finally have to be how serious an illness can be but how much value your life and well-being have despite the pandemic chaos. Corona Fictions are able to enter the dystopian pandemic world of their audiences by creating a certain familiarity/possibility of identification with the characters, before transforming and at best dissolving potential fears to offer a hopeful future. In any case, "[h]ope and fear both depend on our sense that the future is open [...]" (Gravlee 2020, 19).

In the next chapter we will examine the process of the pandemic protagonists to reclaim their agency and as a consequence to go through a transformational process towards a more hopeful character.

---

16 Character constellations on the level of 'histoire' hereby refer to the relations amongst the characters, not the character configuration (how often they interact in a scene) on the level of 'discours' (cf. Gräf et al. 2011, 174, 173).

CORONA FICTIONS AGENTS AND COMEDY: ENCODING HOPE AND THE POWER OF AGENCY

The focus of this article lies not primarily on affective effects of feature films on their audiences but more so on artistic productions and representation of Covid-19 pandemic related aspects in audiovisual media – namely Corona Fictions and the role of their protagonists. Although the selected franco- and hispanophone corpus – the two comedies *8 Rue de l'Humanité* (2021) and *¡Ni te me acerques!* (2020) situated during the pandemic in Europe – are not by any means representative for the diversity of all early audiovisual Corona Fictions, they do demonstrate a clear pattern of how pandemic protagonists may operate, particularly within the comedy genre. This narrative pattern deviates from the pandemic fictions' related norm – rather than the Corona Fictions' related norm – of outbreak narratives[17] which mainly concentrate on the spread and/or containment of a virus or other contagious illnesses.

This selective corpus, as with many other Corona Fictions (cf. Obermayr/ Völkl 2022a/b; Obermayr/Hobisch 2023), enters the audiences'[18] minds by references to the beginning of the Covid-19 pandemic (e.g. the empty streets of Paris in *8 Rue de l'Humanité* while hearing Macron's speech "Nous sommes en guerre", cf. *8RH* [00:00:25 min.]; or the lonely drive of a 'madrileño' called Juan in a Spanish natural scenery, cf. *NTMA* [00:00:27 min.], before entering a local bar in a small village as the only one with mask and gloves on in *¡Ni te me acerques!*, cf. *NTMA* [00:04:14-00:04:28 min.]). These scenes paint the initial image of both the current state of the situation and the film protagonists as rather negative, fearing others or at least feeling anxious and experiencing the first acute lockdown shock effect (cf. Singer et al. 2021). Juan's editor also mentions the extremely worried Spanish president on the phone ("El presidente está preocupadísimo", *NTMA* [00:15:38 min.]).[19] Interestingly, the mental state of the audiences in general, often coincide with those of the numerous protagonists, as certain actions, objects, ideas, emotions etc. may provoke affective reactions (cf. Eder 2005, 115f.). Remarkably, the Corona Fictions investigated result in the transforming of a hopeless and disoriented state of their protagonists and/or their surroundings by introducing a hope

---

17 For more details on outbreak narratives/pandemic films see Priscilla Wald (2008) and Denis Newiak (2020).

18 "Film spectatorship [...] is the experience of viewing and hearing fictional feature films, together with the psychological and social contexts in which such viewing/hearing occurs" (Plantinga 2009b, 249).

19 "The president is very preoccupied" (author's translation).

narrative inscribed in both the theme and the protagonists. Unlike most Zombie movies, where hopelessness constitutes a central element (cf. Jones 2020/2022), in Corona Fictions creating hope either for the protagonist and their world or their audiences is essential. This not only applies to the corpus chosen for this article but also e.g. in regards to uplifting music videos (cf. Obermayr/Hobisch 2023).

Pandemic Protagonists and Agency

As has been discussed previously, the concept of hope applied to a filmic protagonist uses the character's agency to determine a pathway to their set goal. "Agency is enabled by narrative understanding when we are able to put our current situation into a larger narrative context, whereby some possible actions, but not others, make sense" (Hardt 2018, 535). In the case of Corona Fictions, this larger context points towards reactivated narratives originating in pandemic fictions such as isolation ('aislamiento social') or anxiety ('la ansiedad') (cf. Hobisch et al. 2022, 200f.).

These reactivated themes, however, merely function as a starting point for the initial scenes of the corpus, introducing the audiences to the pandemic, its challenges (e.g. containment measures etc.) and ultimately the anxious feeling at the beginning of a lockdown. The directors' – Norberto Ramos del Val's (*NTMA*) and Dany Boon's (*8RH*) – artistic choices in regard to comedy may also be interpreted through the lens of 'artistic agency'.[20] In this sense, agency not only plays an essential role in the realm of hope but also in the creation and production of cultural artefacts. Thus, artistic agency

> provides us with an understanding of how a biological entity, an auteur, processes a range of different biological and cultural determinants and causalities into art by a process that is located in a specific time, place, and agency, thus producing a specific work of art and a specific *oeuvre* [italics in orig.]. (Tybjerg 2005, 28)

The Covid-19 pandemic functions as a very specific timeframe for anchoring films which is essential to categorizing them as Corona Fictions. The chosen movies are moreover located in Paris (*8RH*) and a Spanish village called Ariño (*NTMA*). Both mainly take place in one edifice. While in France the audience follows protagonist

---

20 "Agency is an empirical fact and it is the cornerstone of social life. The production of artefacts and meaning is performed by biological entities, and the makeup of each individual agency influences the product. [...] The individual agent is a unique configuration of an infinite number of general forces and influences" (Tybjerg 2005, 27).

Martin and a group of characters living in the same building, the Spanish protagonist Juan arrives in the countryside to live in an empty hotel (the real Hotel Balneario de Ariño). The character agency does not solely fall on each of the protagonists, but some agency is rather socially distributed among these groups of secondary characters. The Parisian tenants introduced bond during lockdown, as they each find themselves (couple/family/single) confined to their apartments, the building's stairways (cf. *8RH* [00:22:00 min.]) and courtyard (cf. *8RH* [00:23:11 min.]). The 'ariñeros' in Spain, on the other hand, are initially shown as even further separated from Madrid's protagonist Juan, as they inhabit the village whereas Juan watches over the hotel referred to, which is located on a hill away from the village centre, where he plans on writing his novel. During lockdown, however, the Spanish characters (Alicia, Evaristo and Antonio) also start to build a relationship with him in a manner similar to the Parisian tenants – the only difference being that their challenges result from being confined to the same building and not because of loneliness in a secluded hotel. Another parallel can be drawn regarding a similar timeframe: both films start at or around the beginning of the obligatory lockdown and end simultaneously by the end of it. While in Paris, the tenants form a close-knit group with lots of emotional closeness and physical proximity (cf. Obermayr/Völkl 2022a) in the end, the Spanish characters also demonstrate a development towards both factors (more details see in Obermayr/Völkl 2022b) before Juan leaves the village to return to Madrid. Hence, the evolution from isolation towards an ultimate strong social cohesion plays an important role in both feature films as their characters – despite all kinds of pandemic restrictions – focus on the collective. The outlook at the end of both films is full of hope as the creators both opted for an open ending. Social cohesion and hope seem strangely connected, enhancing the feeling of a) community and b) change towards more agency:

a)   Hope encoded in community (social cohesion):

All the Parisian tenants, for example, support Diego who lost his wife due to Covid-19 (cf. *8RH* [01:55:49 min.]), while Juan receives a big piece of regional 'jamón' (Engl. 'ham') from Evaristo and a long hug before leaving the village (cf. *NTMA* [01:31:56 min.]). Both films hereby demonstrate a development towards a stronger social cohesion.

b)   Hope encoded in change towards individual agency:

Martin, the hypochondriac constantly disinfecting everything, almost completely loses all his agency when the scientist of the building experiments on him to find a vaccine against Covid-19. Justice prevails in the end as the police take the mad scientist away (cf. *8RH* [01:50:58 min.]) and Martin leaves forced quarantine, regaining his individual agency. Shortly thereafter he participates in a courtyard party with the other tenants, seen standing close to different people, touching them, laughing and enjoying himself (cf. *8RH* [01:53:18-01:53:48 min.]). In the end, he stops panicking and succeeds in abandoning his role of the hysterical man.[21]

The Spanish protagonist Juan breaks the rules of physical distancing by sharing a joint with Evaristo in the hotel pool indoors (cf. *NTMA* [01:05:07 min.]) and later on making out with Alicia (cf. *NTMA* [01:21:20-01:24:00 min.]). Furthermore, he finally starts writing his novel back in Madrid, using the same sentence as we see him write in the beginning, thus, functioning as a framework for the movie. (cf. *NTMA* [01:33:27 min.]). This goal allowed him to experience the lockdown from a writer's perspective, observing (and later on documenting) certain aspects in a testimonial manner (see the countdown of seemingly random days in *NTMA* [01:08:15 min.]). Even though Juan is portrayed both without and far away from the 'ariñeros' at the end of the film, he seems more connected and grounded as he finally starts writing his novel, bringing the transformational power of the lockdown experience with him to Madrid.

Social cohesion functions in a sense as a goal within the hope model for the pandemic protagonists, especially when contrasting it with isolation and loneliness in the initial scenes at the beginning of the lockdown. The filmmakers hereby created characters aspiring to human connection and positive change after a time of fear, anxiety, uncertainty, personal turmoil and the lack of physical touch.

Mixing film genres – as shown in *¡Ni te me acerques!* by integrating dreamlike sequences and fantastic elements (cf. *NTMA* [00:16:27 min.]) – has an affective effect and consciously applies mood-cues, evoking expectations regarding certain emotional, narrative and stylistic patterns (cf. Schick 2018, 156). To portray hope, agency, as discussed earlier, is an essential factor for (pandemic) protagonists. At the beginning of the Covid-19 lockdowns, in both films, the protagonists Juan and Martin are both heavily restricted in their agency in terms of moving freely or

---

21   For an analysis of the hysterical man as a typical protagonist within Corona Fictions, see the contribution of Elisabeth Hobisch in this volume.

having to practice physical (and to some extent also social) distancing and are represented as rather cautious (or in the case of Martin even hysterical and hyper-vigilant) characters. Agency, however, is essential to life satisfaction as "[it] reflects efficacy expectations, and a perception of satisfaction-promoting control, even if external conditions do not permit the activation of problem-solving skills (e.g., as in chronic illness)" (Bailey et al. 2007, 173). As the Covid-19 pandemic progresses, both pandemic protagonists, thus, reclaim their agency and transform into agents of Corona Fictions.

Corona Fictions Comedies

The functioning of genres seems to depend on 'historically developed psycholog-ical dispositions of the spectator' (cf. Wuss 2020, 331). In their multidimension-ality, genres represent cultural constructions (cf. Grodal 2017, 7) and "a central group of genres is based on their ability to cue basic emotions: [r]omance, [c]omedy, [t]ragedy/sad melodrama, thrillers and horror films" (ibid.). Comedy, for example, develops when deviating from common behavioural patterns or ritu-alized actions while simultaneously questioning what we take as given or what we know (cf. Stutterheim/Kaiser 2011, 298). Thus, it is a suitable genre in Covid-19 related times when social behaviour has been more regulated and heavily re-stricted by containment measures. Simultaneously, we constantly question other-wise common behavioural patterns from pre-pandemic times. From this perspec-tive, allusions to war rhetoric also make sense when breaking patterns of a peace-ful societal state. Additionally, the task of comedy as a film genre is to question the moral values of society as it reflects the collective unconscious/subconscious, bringing to light society's suppressed but (re)surfacing emotions (cf. ibid., 300). When social conflicts arise, as observed in both of the films investigated, comedy reacts by offering the audiences a good laugh[22] where otherwise it would not be allowed to express e.g. anger (cf. ibid., 297). The protagonist's desires in a comedy embody a certain conflict in their community or society as a whole (cf. ibid., 304).

In *8 Rue de l'Humanité* Martin initially embodies the conflict between obedi-ence and autonomous adjustments regarding the lockdown rules. In *¡Ni te me acerques!* Juan adjusts these rules more quickly, seemingly due to his complete isolation without friends or family members. Family, however, is the central focus of every story's human factor (cf. Zag 2010², 65). This is how you gain empathy for the main characters, particularly the protagonist. As Juan pretends to lose the

---

22 Laughing helps to counteract those in power (state and church) and functions as a mech-anism against fear (cf. Stutterheim/Kaiser 2011, 297).

cell phone signal in the countryside while talking on the phone to his mother (cf. *NTMA* [00:11:48-00:12:12 min.]), he is not initially portrayed as the most likeable of characters. Similarly, he seems very annoyed by an audio message from his partner a little earlier, calling her back but keeping the call short (cf. *NTMA* [00:11:00 min.]).

Martin embodies the hysterical man, an exaggerated version of a hypochondriac, constantly disinfecting himself and his family – even when just returning from clapping for healthcare workers on the balcony of his apartment with masks on (cf. *8RH* [00:02:59 min.]). His anxiety levels are initially high, negatively affecting not only his wife and daughter but also stressing the rest of the tenants throughout the movie. Martin is painted as a purposefully exaggerated pandemic protagonist. The first scenes in particular introduce him as a pessimistic and fearful character following the new pandemic rules beyond reasonable measure. He constantly imposes his extreme behaviour on everyone who approaches him in some way as following examples illustrate: In conversation with his worried daughter, he explains how the virus enters the lungs and paints horrible scenarios of difficulties in breathing etc. until his wife stops him and hands him a paper bag to calm his own hyperventilating breath, reassuring him that they all respect all the health measures (cf. *8RH* [00:04:28-00:4:56 min.]). Moreover, when the concierge's husband Diego brings him the mail, Martin pulls back his wife as he learns that Diego's wife is in the hospital with Covid-19. The hypochondriac instantly measures everyone's temperature while his wife focuses on being friendly, compassionate and supportive towards Diego (cf. *8RH* [00:4:56-00:07:00 min.]).

Towards the end of the movie, however, when Martin appears in one of the last scenes (cf. *8RH* [01:55:14 min.]), he participates in group hugging of Diego with all the other tenants in the courtyard after learning that his wife Paola has passed away due to Covid-19. As a comedic protagonist, his function is to provoke laughter in the audience and not to laugh at himself.[23] In all of this seriousness, the last scene brings all the Parisian tenants including the hysterical protagonist Martin, one after another out onto the balcony (cf. *8RH* [01:55:56 min.]). Each character brings on signs of encouragement for Diego after the death of his wife. The collective as well as its function and importance of social cohesion are once again demonstrated, as Diego reads the collectively spelled sentence as he looks up from the courtyard towards the balconies while holding an urn with his deceased beloved wife Paola. It only makes sense as long as each tenant participates with the separate signs or e.g. by playing a (piano) keyboard as a contribution to the

---

23 According to Stutterheim and Kaiser (cf. 2011, 304) characters in comedies hardly ever laugh about themselves.

collective ritual as Martin's wife does: "Merci Paola. On vous [sic] oubliera pas. On prendra bien soin de Diego" (*8RH* [01:55:43 min.]).[24] When addressing death, this French comedy focuses on the tenants' social bonds formed during lockdown, lifting up Diego's spirit by caring and showing compassion, honoring his wife. This artistic choice coincides with the following findings on death and optimism in films:

> The results of this study ['How Movies Can Ease the Fear of Death'] support the idea that meaningful films shape our response to death-related thoughts, but only when they contain elements of life, hope, positivity, and optimism. This study therefore clarifies that it is not meaningful films per se that help people to deal with death-related thoughts but only those films that emphasize life instead of death. (Rieger/Hofer 2017, 726)

By emphasizing Diego's life in supporting him and by integrating a tenant's pregnancy in the movie, allowing for her baby to be born and then later to be held also in the arms of non-related tenants in one of the last collective scenes (cf. *8RH* [01:53:18 min.]), the audience may in the end – despite the sadness – feel positivity and hope where unity and a strong social cohesion prevail.

Both Corona Fictions comedies send a message of hope to their audiences in the end. In *8 Rue de l'Humanité* Paola's picture hangs in the corner of the courtyard, with flowers around her portrait and Diego sets Paola's birds free (cf. *8RH* [01:57:23 min.]). The film ends with a dedication to all those who have suffered and who stand in solidarity with humanity ("À celles et ceux qui ont souffert. À l'humanité solidaire", *8RH* [01:57:28 min.]).[25] Similarly, in the Spanish *¡Ni te me acerques!* Juan in the end (after the credits) is shown in the countryside again, clapping outside alone, screaming "¡Viva la sanidad pública!" (*NTMA* [01:35:41-01:36:10 min.]).[26] Additionally, during the credits a song with the title 'Deberías (hacer algo con tu vida)'[27] by Luis Prado is played at the end, singing about taking charge of your life (cf. *NTMA* [01:33:29-01:35:41 min.]). In this sense, this Spanish Corona Fictions film invites the viewers to reclaim their own agency in their lives.

---

24 "Thank you, Paola. We won't forget you. We will take good care of Diego" (author's translation).
25 "To those who have suffered. To human solidarity" (author's translation).
26 "Long live public healthcare!" (author's translation).
27 "'You should (do something with your life)'" (author's translation).

CONCLUSION

The applied interdisciplinary cultural studies approach of Stuart Hall's (cf. 1997, 1) encoding/decoding model 'circuit of culture' – in combination with theories of hope (mainly as suggested by the psychologist Rick Snyder, 2020), cinematic storytelling (according to Jens Eder 2005 and 2008) and examining mainly the initial and end scenes as encouraged by Michaela Krützen (cf. 2006, 89) – all allowed for the posed research question to be answered as follows:

The investigated franco- and hispanophone Corona Fictions films – the two comedies *8 Rue de l'Humanité* (2021) and *¡Ni te me acerques!* (2020) – each create and encode a twofold message of hope:

a) In the overall theme of both Corona Fictions films investigated due to e.g. the choice of genre (comedy and its mood-cues, e.g. to make the audiences laugh) as well as open endings. Both Corona Fictions films thereby confirm the proposed hypothesis that comedy was particularly appropriate for the portrayal of transformational processes of a fearful or anxiety-driven pandemic protagonist becoming a hopeful one. Reclaiming agency furthermore dissolves this anxiety.

b) In their pandemic protagonists – mainly in the protagonists' (individual) agency and community building. The characters are heavily restricted in their agency of movement and social interactions due to lockdowns imposed on them by the authorities. Juan starts out as an isolated writer in a secluded hotel in the Spanish countryside, while Martin embodies the hysterical man living in Paris with his wife and daughter. As the films progress, however, the Spanish protagonists Juan in *¡Ni te me acerques!* (2020) and the French protagonist Martin in *8 Rue de l'Humanité* (2021) both reclaim their agency. They both disobey various lockdown rules, physically coming close to other characters, strengthening social cohesion and to some extent normalizing common human behaviour regarding spacial proximity while becoming emotionally closer to others. Social cohesion hereby functions as a goal for the pandemic protagonists, especially when contrasting it with isolation and loneliness in the initial scenes at the beginning of the lockdown.

Let me conclude by quoting Snyder (2002, 268):

> People rhetorically ask, "Surely you would much prefer to have a nonrisk-taking pessimist flying your plane rather than a risk-taking optimist?" Ignoring the questionable assumption that the optimist is necessarily a risk taker, I would ask the

readers to think about this question when it is posed differently: Do we really want the pessimistic pilot – filled with anxiety, tension, worry, sadness, rejection, anger, self-criticalness, and profound uncertainty – to be at the controls when our jet is landing during a thunderstorm? Not me. I want a high-hope pilot in that cockpit.

When transferring this thought to the Covid-19 pandemic, we must ask ourselves what kind of pilots we want to become in the cockpits of our lives: the ones doom-scrolling (cf. Price et al. 2022) the apocalyptic news daily or the ones relaxing as they watch a hopeful comedy?

Ultimately, hope begins with setting a goal and reclaiming, and thus regaining your own agency as a pandemic protagonist (on and off screen), and thus also becoming a Corona Fictions agent – or in the words of Becky Piatt Davidson: "I'm no longer a hostage but an agent, with choices about how to proceed when fear sets in" (Piatt Davidson 2021/2022).

BIBLIOGRAPHY

Corpus Analyzed

Boon, Dany (dir.) (2021) *8 Rue de l'Humanité*, France, Netflix.
Ramos del Val, Norberto (dir.) (2020) *¡Ni te me acerques!*, Spain, Norberfilms.

Works Cited

Assmann, Jan (2005 [1992]) *Das kulturelle Gedächtnis. Schrift, Erinnerung und politische Identität in frühen Hochkulturen*, 5th edition, München, C. H. Beck.
Assmann, Jan/Hölscher, Tonio (eds.) (1988) *Kultur und Gedächtnis*, Frankfurt am Main, Suhrkamp.
Bailey, Thomas C./Eng, Winnie/Frisch, Michael B./Snyder, C. Richard (2007) "Hope and Optimism as Related to Life Satisfaction", *The Journal of Positive Psychology* 2/3, 168-175. DOI: 10.1080/17439760701409546.
Blöser, Claudia (2020) "Enlightenment Views of Hope", Steven C. Van den Heuvel (ed.) *Historical and Multidisciplinary Perspectives on Hope*, Cham, Springer. DOI: 10.1007/978-3-030-46489-9_4.
Branigan, Edward (1992) *Narrative and Comprehension of Film*, London/New York, NY, Routledge.
Cabanac, Michel (2002) "What Is Emotion?", *Behavioural Processes* 60/2, 69-83. DOI: 10.1016/S0376-6357(02)00078-5.

Del Mar Azcona, María (2010) *The Multi-Protagonist Film*, Chichester, Wiley-Blackwell.

Eder, Jens (2005) "Affektlenkung im Film. Das Beispiel *Triumph des Willens*", Oliver Grau/Andreas Keil (eds.) *Mediale Emotionen. Zur Lenkung von Gefühlen durch Bild und Sound*, Frankfurt am Main, S. Fischer, 107-132.

Eder, Jens (2008) *Die Figur im Film. Grundlagen der Figurenanalyse*, Marburg, Schüren.

Emrich, Hinderk M. (2011) "Liebe als Berührung: Zur Tiefenpsychologie von Nähe und Distanz (mit Filmbeispielen)", *Internationale Zeitschrift für Philosophie und Psychosomatik (IZPP)* 2/5, 1-6.

Gräf, Dennis/Großmann, Stephanie/Klimczak, Peter/Krah, Hans/Wagner, Marietheres (2011) *Filmsemiotik. Eine Einführung in die Analyse audiovisueller Formate*, Marburg, Schüren.

Gravlee, G. Scott (2020) "Hope in Ancient Greek Philosophy", Steven C. Van den Heuvel (ed.) *Historical and Multidisciplinary Perspectives on Hope*, Cham, Springer, 3-24. DOI: 10.1007/978-3-030-46489-9_1.

Grodal, Torben (2005) "Agency in Film, Filmmaking, and Reception", Torben Grodal/Bente Larsen/Iben Thorving Laursen (eds.) *Visual Authorship: Creativity and Intentionality in Media*, Copenhagen, Museum Tusculanum Press, 15-36.

Grodal, Torben (2006) "The PECMA Flow: A General Model of Visual Aesthetics", *Film* Studies 8/1, 1-11. DOI: 10.7227/FS.8.3.

Grodal, Torben (2017) "How Film Genres Are a Product of Biology, Evolution and Culture – An Embodied Approach", *Palgrave Communications* 3, 17079, 1-8. DOI: 10.1057/palcomms.2017.79.

Halbwachs, Maurice (1950 [1935]) *La mémoire collective*, Paris, Presses Universitaires de France.

Hall, Stuart (1997) "Introduction", Stuart Hall (ed.) *Representation. Cultural Representation and Signifying Practices*, London et al., Sage Publications, 1-11.

Hardt, Rosa (2018) "Storytelling Agents: Why Narrative Rather than Mental Time Travel Is Fundamental", *Phenomenology and the Cognitive Sciences* 17, 535-554. DOI: 10.1007/s11097-017-9530-2.

Henkel, Dennis (2022) "Der Kampf der Ansteckung im frühen Kino. Eine Retrospektive in Zeiten von Covid-19", *Deutsche Medizinische Wochenschrift* 147/24-25, 1617-1625. DOI: 10.1055/a-1933-1596.

Hiergeist, Teresa (2014) *Erlesene Erlebnisse: Formen der Partizipation an narrativen Texten*, Bielefeld, transcript.

Hobisch, Elisabeth/Völkl, Yvonne/Obermayr, Julia (2021-) "Corona Fictions Database", *Zotero Group Library*, https://www.zotero.org/groups/4814225/corona_fictions_database/library, 2023-01-02.

Hobisch, Elisabeth/Völkl, Yvonne/Obermayr, Julia (2022) "Narrar la pandemia. Una introducción a formas, temas y metanarrativas de las Corona Fictions", Ana Gallego Cuiñas/José Antonio Pérez Tapias (eds.) *Pensamiento, Pandemia y Big Data. El impacto sociocultural del coronavirus en el espacio iberoamericano*, Berlin, De Gruyter, 191-211. DOI: 10.1515/9783110693928-013.

Jones, Cian (2020/2022) "Hope and the Zombie Trope in the Time of Corona", *Varsity – Independent Student Newspaper for the University of Cambridge*, 2020-10-16, https://www.varsity.co.uk/film-and-tv/19949, 2022-12-09.

Kaur, Rupi (2020) *Home Body*, London, Simon & Schuster.

Knight, Deborah (2009) "Tragedy and Comedy", Paisley Livingstone/Carl Plantinga (eds.) *The Routledge Companion to Philosophy and Film*, London/New York, Routledge, 536-545.

Krützen, Michaela (2006 [2004]) *Dramaturgie des Films. Wie Hollywood erzählt*, 2nd edition, Frankfurt am Main, Fischer.

Linke, Uli/Smith, Danielle Taana (2009) "Fear: A Conceptual Framework", Uli Linke/Danielle Taana Smith (eds.) *Cultures of Fear. A Critical Reader*, London/New York, PlutoPress, 1-17.

Michener, Ronald T. (2020) "Post-Kantian to Postmodern Considerations of (Theological) Hope", Steven C. Van den Heuvel (ed.) *Historical and Multidisciplinary Perspectives on Hope*, Cham, Springer, 77-95. DOI: 10.1007/978-3-030-46489-9_5.

Milona, Michael (2020) "Philosophy of Hope", Steven C. Van den Heuvel (ed.) *Historical and Multidisciplinary Perspectives on Hope*, Cham, Springer, 99-116. DOI: 10.1007/978-3-030-46489-9_6.

Newiak, Denis (2020) *Alles schon mal dagewesen: Was wir aus Pandemie-Filmen für die Corona-Krise lernen können*, Marburg, Schüren.

Obermayr, Julia/Hobisch, Elisabeth (2023) "Uplifting Corona Fictions. *No tengas miedo, Ya pasará* and *Andrà tutto bene*", Martin Butler/Sina Farzin/Michael Fuchs/Florian Hempel (eds.) *Pandemic Meets Fiction* [forthcoming].

Obermayr, Julia/Völkl, Yvonne (2022a) "Corona Fictions as Cultural Indicators of Social Cohesion and Resilience in the Wake of the Covid-19 Pandemic", *Momentum Quarterly* 11/2, 129-142. DOI: 10.15203/momentumquarterly.vol11.no1.p129-142.

Obermayr, Julia/Völkl, Yvonne (2022b) "¡Ni te me acerques! (Stay Away!) Negotiating Physical Distancing in Hispanophone Corona Fictions", *Altre Modernità* 28, 158-174. DOI: 10.54103/2035-7680/19125.

Piatt Davidson, Becky (2021/2022) "How to Reframe Anxiety and Fear in a Pandemicized World. Because Pandemics Are Here to Stay", *Medium.com*, 2021-03-19, https://becky-davidson.medium.com/how-to-reframe-anxiety-and-fear-in-a-pandemicized-world-cf5e87dfc641, 2022-12-19.

Pinsent, Andrew (2020) "Hope as a Virtue in the Middle Ages", Steven C. Van den Heuvel (ed.) *Historical and Multidisciplinary Perspectives on Hope*, Cham, Springer, 47-60. DOI: 10.1007/978-3-030-46489-9_3.

Plantinga, Carl (2009a) "Spectatorship", Paisley Livingstone/Carl Plantinga (eds.) *The Routledge Companion to Philosophy and Film*, London/New York, Routledge, 86-96.

Plantinga, Carl (2009b) "Emotion and Affect", Paisley Livingstone/Carl Plantinga (eds.) *The Routledge Companion to Philosophy and Film*, London/New York, Routledge, 249-259.

Price, Matthew/Legrand, Alison C./Brier, Zoe M.F. et al. (2022) "Doomscrolling During COVID-19: The Negative Association Between Daily Social and Traditional Media Consumption and Mental Health Symptoms During the COVID-19 Pandemic", *Psychological Trauma: Theory, Research, Practice, and Policy* 14/8, 1338-1346. DOI: 10.1037/tra0001202.

Qub (2020) *Épidémie*, TVA Plus, https://www.qub.ca/tvaplus/tva/epidemie, 2022-12-15.

Real Academia Española (2022) "Protagonista", *Diccionario de la lengua española – Edición del Tricentenario*, https://dle.rae.es/protagonista, 2022-11-24.

Research Group *Pandemic Fictions* (2020) "From Pandemic to Corona Fictions: Narratives in Times of Crises", *PhiN-Beiheft* 24, 321-344, http://web.fu-berlin.de/phin/beiheft24/b24t21.pdf, 2023-01-21.

Rieger, Diana/Hofer, Matthias (2017) "How Movies Can Ease the Fear of Death: The Survival or Death of the Protagonists in Meaningful Movies", *Mass Communication and Society* 20/5, 710-733. DOI: 10.1080/15205436.2017.1300666.

Schick, Thomas (2018) *Filmstil, Differenzqualitäten, Emotionen. Zur affektiven Wirkung von Autorenfilmen am Beispiel der Berliner Schule*, Wiesbaden, Springer VS. DOI: 10.1007/978-3-658-19143-6.

Schmelzer, Dagmar (2020) *"New We*. Die diskursive Performanz gesellschaftlichen Zusammenhalts in Corona-Zeiten – ein deutsch-französisch-spanischer Vergleich", *PhiN-Beiheft* 24, 129-148, http://web.fu-berlin.de/phin/beiheft24/b24t8.pdf, 2023-01-21.

Singer, Tania/Koop, Sarah/Godara, Malvika (2021) "The CovSocial Project: How Did Berliners Feel and React during the COVID-19 Pandemic in 2020/21? Changes in Aspects of Mental Health, Resilience and Social Cohesion", *The*

CovSocial Project, Berlin, Max Planck Society, 1-107, https://www.covsocial. de/wp-content/uploads/2021/11/CovSocial_EN_WEB.pdf, 2021-11-28.

Snyder, C. Richard (2002) "Hope Theory: Rainbows in the Mind", *Psychological Inquiry* 13/4, 249-275. DOI: 10.1207/S15327965PLI1304_01.

Stutterheim, Kerstin/Kaiser, Silke (2011 [2009]) *Handbuch der Filmdramaturgie. Das Bauchgefühl und seine Ursachen*, 2nd edition, Frankfurt am Main et al., Peter Lang.

Tybjerg, Casper (2005) "The Makers of Movies: Authors, Subjects, Personalities, Agents?", Torben Grodal/Bente Larsen/Iben Thorving Laursen (eds.) *Visual Authorship: Creativity and Intentionality in Media*, Copenhagen, Museum Tusculanum Press, 37-66.

Wald, Priscilla (2008) *Contagious. Cultures, Carriers, and the Outbreak Narrative*, Durham, NC, Duke University Press.

Webber, Martin I./Kok, Jacobus (2020) "Early Christian Thinking on Hope", Steven C. Van den Heuvel (ed.) *Historical and Multidisciplinary Perspectives on Hope*, Cham, Springer, 25-46. DOI: 10.1007/978-3-030-46489-9_2.

Wuss, Peter (2020) *Künstlerische Verfahren des Films aus psychologischer Sicht. Zum Wirkungspotenzial des Spielfilms*, Wiesbaden, Springer VS. DOI: 10.10 07/978-3-658-32052-2.

Zag, Roland (2010 [2005]) *Der Publikumsvertrag. Drehbuch, Emotion und der »human factor«*, 2nd edition, Konstanz, UVK.

FIGURES

Figure 1: Snyder's (2002) Model of Hope

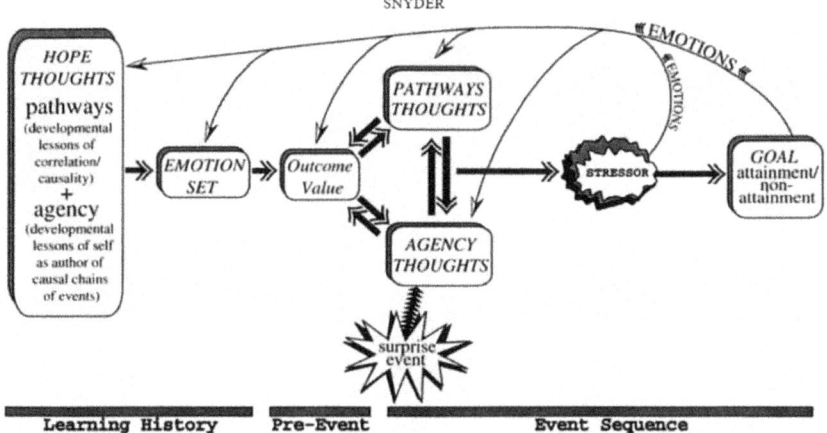

Figure 1. *Schematic of feed-forward and feedback functions involving agency and pathway goal-directed thoughts in hope theory.*

Source: Snyder 2002, 254.

Authors

Bermúdez, Luana, is a literary scholar in the field of Spanish Studies. She is currently a scientific collaborator and lecturer at the University of Geneva. Her research focuses on the reconstruction of traumatic historical events of the recent past both in Spanish graphic novels and in contemporary theatre, and contemporary Corona Fictions.

Demoulin, Claire, is a research associate at Yale university. She holds a PhD dissertation entitled *Hollywood Transatlantic.* Her research focuses on Classical Hollywood, transatlantic cultural transfers, migration networks, German Exile Cinema and politization of American films. As a 2017-2018 Fulbright grantee, she has been affiliated with Yale University's Film and Media Studies as well as its German Department. In 2020, she has been elected treasurer of the French Association of Film Historians (AFRHC), which edits the film journal *1895* to which she contributes regularly.

Guerios, Aureo Lustosa, is a literary scholar working within the field of the Medical Humanities. His PhD thesis investigates the representation of epidemic cholera in European literature in the 19th and early 20th centuries. He specializes in comparative literature, history of health and medical anthropology. His present research focuses on how contagious diseases and Tropical jungles are imagined in South American literatures.

Hobisch, Elisabeth, is a literary and cultural studies scholar in the field of Romance Studies. For her PhD thesis on the epistolary form in the Spanish Spectators, she received the *Award of Excellence 2016* of the Austrian Minister of Science, Investigation and Economy. Her main research interests concern 18th century moral press in France and Spain (Spectators, *Moralische Wochenschriften*), the digital humanities and Corona Fictions.

Hopkins-Loféron, Fleur, devotes her work to the study of the diffusion of science and weird sciences in popular culture, literary and visual, of the first half of the 20th century. Her thesis, winner of the SHS PSL 2020 award, focused on the exhumation of a little-known French literary genre, the *merveilleux-scientifique.* Her CNRS postdoctoral fellowship, which she is currently pursuing within the THALIM laboratory, explores the emergence and success of a form of neo-fakirism in the performing arts and French media culture in the 1880s-1930s.

Meozzi, Tommaso, is a Teaching Scientist for Italian at the Institute of Romance Studies, University of Graz. He received his trinational doctoral degree in comparative literatures (*Founding Myths of Europe*, Florence – Bonn – Paris IV Sorbonne) with a dissertation on the genre of literary and film dystopia, published with Pacini in 2017 (*Visioni dell'alienazione*). His main areas of research are, in addition to the genre of dystopia, the literary representation of language learning and the analogical dimension of political thought.

Mühlethaler, Louis, is a PhD student at EHESS (School for Advanced Studies in the Social Sciences) in Paris. His thesis – entitled *Literature and Immunity* – attempts to blend Comparative Literature and Medical humanities and to investigate the spectrum of the representations of immunity (and community) in modern and contemporary literature.

Obermayr, Julia, is a cultural studies and media scholar. In 2019 she received the 14th Scientific Award of the Austrian-Canadian Society for her research on female identities in Lesbian Web Series. She specializes in cultural studies, social change, lesbian/LGBT+ studies and diversity, minority identities and female representations in audiovisual media – currently in Corona Fictions – mainly in Romance speaking Europe and the Americas.

Pająk, Paulina, is a literary scholar and psychologist. In 2022, she received the Excellence Initiative – Research University Award for her publications, including *The Edinburgh Companion to Virginia Woolf and Contemporary Global Literature* (2021). Her research focuses on interwar culture and modernist literature, Virginia Woolf, the Bloomsbury Group, transnational publishing networks, and modernist legacies.

Stemberger, Martina, is a permanent lecturer at the University of Vienna (Habilitation in Romance Studies and Comparative Literature, 2017) and an associated member of the Centre de Recherche sur les Cultures et les Littératures Européennes (CERCLE) at the University of Lorraine; she has been Visiting Professor at Humboldt University Berlin (2018/2019), Research Fellow at Technical University Dresden (2019) and Alfried Krupp Wissenschaftskolleg Greifswald (2019/2020). Her main research areas are 17th-21st century French literature, Romance-Slavic comparative literary and cultural studies, travel literature, gender studies, popular culture (especially fanfiction), intertextuality/intermediality and metafiction.

Sugiera, Małgorzata, is a Full-time Professor at the Jagiellonian University in Cracow, Poland, and Head of the Department for Performativity Studies. Her research concentrates on performativity theories, environmental and decolonial studies, particularly in the context of the history of science. She published twelve single-authored books in Polish, and co-edited several books in English and German. She translates scholarly books from English, German and French. She carries out a three-year international research project "Epidemics and Communities in Critical Theories, Artistic Practices and Speculative Fabulations of the Last Decades" funded by the National Science Centre (NCN).

Torquato, Ana Carolina, is a literary and cultural studies scholar working with Animal Studies. Her doctoral research investigated how animals were portrayed in Brazilian literature, from the 16th to the mid-20th centuries. She specializes in comparative literature, Brazilian and English literatures, and animal studies in general. Her current postdoctoral investigation discusses animal captivity in zoos by combining expertise from literary criticism, anthropology and architecture.

Völkl, Yvonne, is a literary and cultural studies scholar in the field of Romance Studies. For her habilitation project which explored gendered ways of worldmaking in the French and Spanish Spectator press (transcript, 2022), she received the *Josef Krainer Würdigungspreis 2022* by the Steirisches Gedenkwerk. Her research focuses on 18th century literature and press, French-Canadian migrant literature and contemporary Corona Fictions.

Wörsdörfer, Anna Isabell, is a literary and cultural studies scholar in the field of Romance studies. Her habilitation project on the staging of magic in 17th century Spanish and French theatre has been funded by the German Research Foundation (DFG) since 2021. Her research focuses on theatricality in the early modern period, reception history (especially of the Middle Ages and the French Revolution) from the 18th to the 21st century and seriality (especially fantastic motifs and pandemic narratives).

Ziarkowska, Justyna, is a literary and cultural studies scholar in the field of Romance Studies. She has published five books and numerous articles. Her book on surrealism in Spanish literature as well as the critical edition of Federico García Lorca's poetry have been reviewed, commented and cited in several scientific publications. In recent years her research focuses on the ethical turn in current Spanish narrative and the agency of literature and its impact on shaping reality.

Cultural Studies

Gabriele Klein
Pina Bausch's Dance Theater
Company, Artistic Practices and Reception

2020, 440 p., pb., col. ill.
29,99 € (DE), 978-3-8376-5055-6
E-Book:
PDF: 29,99 € (DE), ISBN 978-3-8394-5055-0

Markus Gabriel, Christoph Horn, Anna Katsman, Wilhelm Krull,
Anna Luisa Lippold, Corine Pelluchon, Ingo Venzke
Towards a New Enlightenment –
The Case for Future-Oriented Humanities

October 2022, 80 p., pb.
18,00 € (DE), 978-3-8376-6570-3
E-Book: available as free open access publication
PDF: ISBN 978-3-8394-6570-7
ISBN 978-3-7328-6570-3

Sven Quadflieg, Klaus Neuburg, Simon Nestler (eds.)
(Dis)Obedience in Digital Societies
Perspectives on the Power of Algorithms and Data

March 2022, 380 p., pb., ill.
29,00 € (DE), 978-3-8376-5763-0
E-Book: available as free open access publication
PDF: ISBN 978-3-8394-5763-4
ISBN 978-3-7328-5763-0

All print, e-book and open access versions of the titles in our list
are available in our online shop www.transcript-publishing.com

Cultural Studies

Ingrid Hoelzl, Rémi Marie
Common Image
Towards a Larger Than Human Communism

2021, 156 p., pb., ill.
29,50 € (DE), 978-3-8376-5939-9
E-Book:
PDF: 26,99 € (DE), ISBN 978-3-8394-5939-3

Anna Maria Loffredo, Rainer Wenrich,
Charlotte Axelsson, Wanja Kröger (eds.)
Changing Time – Shaping World
Changemakers in Arts & Education

September 2022, 310 p., pb., col. ill.
45,00 € (DE), 978-3-8376-6135-4
E-Book: available as free open access publication
PDF: ISBN 978-3-8394-6135-8

Olga Moskatova, Anna Polze, Ramón Reichert (eds.)
Digital Culture & Society (DCS)
Vol. 7, Issue 2/2021 –
Networked Images in Surveillance Capitalism

August 2022, 336 p., pb., col. ill.
29,99 € (DE), 978-3-8376-5388-5
E-Book:
PDF: 27,99 € (DE), ISBN 978-3-8394-5388-9

**All print, e-book and open access versions of the titles in our list
are available in our online shop www.transcript-publishing.com**

GPSR Authorized Representative: Easy Access System Europe, Mustamäe tee 50, 10621 Tallinn, Estonia, gpsr.requests@easproject.com